INSANITY

a study of major psychiatric disorders

PSYCHIATRIC TOPICS for community workers
General Editor: Alistair Munro
Psychiatrist-in-Chief, University of Toronto

Left Behind: a study of mental handicap
Dr. Alan Heaton-Ward, Stoke Park Group Hospital, Bristol

Signs of Stress: the social problems of psychiatric illness
J. Wallace McCulloch, University of Bradford
Herschel A. Prins, University of Leicester

Alcoholism and Addiction
Dr. R. Swinson, Toronto General Hospital
Dr. Derek Eaves, Western Regional Medical Centre, British Columbia

Growing Pains: a study of teenage distress
Dr. Edna M. Irwin, Hollymoor Hospital, Birmingham

INSANITY
a study of major psychiatric disorders

Robert G. Priest

Professor of Psychiatry (University of London)
St. Mary's Hospital Medical School, St. Mary's Hospital

With a chapter by

Dr J. Steinert

Consultant Psychiatrist
St. Bernard's Hospital, Southall
King Edward Memorial Hospital, Ealing

MACDONALD AND EVANS

MACDONALD & EVANS LTD.
Estover, Plymouth PL6 7PZ

First published 1977

© Robert G. Priest 1977

ISBN: 0 7121 0941 2

Text set in 11/12 pt Photon Times, printed by photolithography,
and bound in Great Britain at The Pitman Press, Bath

While writing this book I have been greatly helped by the encouragement of Marilyn, by the patience of Ursula and by constructive advice from both of them.

I am grateful to my colleagues for allowing me to publish details of the histories of patients under their care. I am especially indebted to Dr. Thomas Pastor for all his work in preparing the index.

I gratefully acknowledge permission given by Pergamon Press Ltd. to reproduce Figure 20 from the *Journal of Chronic Diseases* 1964, Vol. 17.

R.G.P.

To Marilyn, Ian and Roderick

Contents

List of Illustrations

Editor's Foreword

The authors' aim has been to write about the so-called 'major' mental illnesses, the conditions we know as 'the psychoses'. Now, all psychiatric disorders are *potentially* serious, although in fact the great majority never reach a profound degree of pathology. The psychotic illnesses, by definition, are those which present with many of the most dramatic symptoms seen in psychiatry. Included in their manifestations may be seriously disturbed behaviour, loss of contact with reality, severe delusions and hallucinations, loss of memory and of other intellectual functions, and many others.

In other words, they are the illnesses which to most people represent the concepts of 'Madness' or 'Insanity'. Despite the undoubted advances in our thinking about these disorders, we still tend to cross our fingers and hope that they will not happen to us. The fear—and the stigma—of mental illness is not yet dead.

The authors of this book recognise that psychiatric illness still carries this aura of doom in many people's minds. Rather than be coy about this, they have chosen a frank and constructive approach to the problems posed by the psychotic disorders they describe and discuss. They have used the title *Insanity* to emphasise how close we are to the period when mental disorder was a scourge with little hope for recovery in many cases, but equally, to inform the reader how far we have moved in spirit and in skill from this hopeless position in a relatively short time.

We can disagree about the causes of mental illness, and some people would even argue that concepts of mental illness are a fabrication of the medical profession. When faced with abnormalities so definite as those seen in the psychoses, it becomes very difficult to deny that these illnesses exist or that their phenomena fall into recognisable patterns. Of course each patient is unique, because each human being is unique, but it is becoming increasingly possible to diagnose psychotic illnesses on firm criteria and to base rational therapy on one's diagnosis.

We are nowhere near perfect in this process, but we are improving all the time and it is this constructive, progressive approach that Professor Priest and Dr. Steinert emphasise.

When treatment is ineffectual and the outlook is fairly uniformly hopeless, any attempt at classification and diagnosis is bound to be rather academic. As treatment becomes more available and more efficient, there is every incentive to diagnose carefully, to separate those cases which will respond to active treatment from those whose condition can only, at best, be palliated, and to design a programme of case management which will deal with the patients' individual needs while attacking the characteristic illness pattern.

The psychotic illnesses are a very mixed group indeed: mixed as regards causation, symptomatology, outlook and response to treatment. But we have a paradox in association with them. Although they are the 'serious' psychiatric disorders with the most dramatic manifestations they are, in some ways, the illnesses which are coming to be diagnosed and treated most effectively. In some instances we are able to intervene long before the really serious mental disturbances appear, so that the patient never becomes truly 'psychotic'. Increasingly in practice the terms 'psychotic' and 'neurotic' are losing their diagnostic significance, but they remain convenient in designating two groups of illnesses whose assessment and management tend to have rather separate characteristics. In designing this series of books it seemed right to allocate separate volumes to the psychotic and to the neurotic disorders.

Insanity concentrates on the former group and a sister volume dealing with the neuroses will appear later. Let me stress that this division is one of convenience and does not imply any difference in philosophy in the psychiatrist's attitude to one or other type of illness.

Let me particularly stress that there is certainly no difference in the degree of hopefulness with which he approaches the treatment of the conditions in either category. It is right to be increasingly optimistic in present-day psychiatry. That we cannot yet afford to be euphoric will be gathered from the down-to-earth and reasoned approach of the authors of the present volume.

This book, with its companion works, has been written with a non-medical readership in mind. Psychiatric illness exists and psychiatry is the rapidly developing speciality which deals with it. Many people want to know about modern advances in the field and on *a priori* grounds it is good that ignorance should be dispelled.

But in addition there are many people in the community who, in the course of their professional or voluntary work, or even through personal experience, come in contact with mental illness and the problems it poses. For all of these groups this book gives a straightforward, factual but eminently readable account of one aspect of psychiatry. It concentrates on those features which the non-psychiatrist will find most useful, but I cannot help thinking that many medical students and even postgraduates would learn a great deal from it. Professor Priest and Dr. Steinert have managed to combine factuality, commonsense and humanity in what they have written.

As editor it was my duty to read this book but I found it a very pleasurable duty. I am sure that you, the reader, will find it as readable and as helpful as I did.

Alistair Munro
   Toronto, 1977

Preface

The purpose of this book is to enable the reader without a medical background to understand as much as possible about the serious disorders of the mind. The term 'serious disorders' might be taken the wrong way. I am using this expression to mean those disorders of the mind that give rise in the patient to feelings, thoughts and behaviour that are usually quite different from normal patterns. These disorders are technically called *psychoses* and often require in-patient treatment.

In the first chapter I discuss how they differ from the 'minor' illnesses of the mind, the *neuroses*, which are much more similar to the experiences that all of us are subject to when in distress in everyday life.

The word 'serious' is not a good one though. Many of us would rather have a brief-lived psychosis which happens to clear up completely than suffer from symptoms of a neurosis which may go on for years—for the truth is that because a mental illness is severe in form it does not necessarily go on for longer than one that is minor in form. This is just one of the facts that you will learn if you go on to read the rest of the book.

The fact that you have had a short episode of psychosis from which you recover completely is not necessarily serious unless you wish to emigrate or to run for high office, when of course you are at the mercy of public opinion rather than nature.

Some of you who are familiar with textbooks of psychiatry will be surprised at my choice of ingredients. Even though this book should be understood by those with no previous knowledge of the subject, it includes topics not usually considered as part of orthodox psychiatry. For instance, I have included a large section on the recent discoveries about the normal physiology of sleep. I have done this because I believe that they will form the basis of a further leap forward in the understanding of the workings of the human mind. In addition, I have included facts on what would normally be regarded as the territory of the neurologist rather than the psychiatrist where it seemed that this helped to complete one's understanding—as you flick through the book you may come face to face with the world as seen by someone with a brain tumour. Anyone seeing a number of persons with psychiatric symptoms may find that some of them suffer with actual disease of the brain. Although the neurological features of a patient with brain tumour should be familiar to medical students, for other audiences it seems a good idea to include them.

Like most authors, I suppose, I have the fancy that my book will be read by a lot of readers for whom it was not specifically designed. Whoever you are, I hope you enjoy it. Do feel free to write to me (care of the publishers) and tell me how the book could be improved.

Robert G. Priest
March, 1977

1 Diagnosis

In this chapter we look at the wide field of mental abnormalities in general. We see what the words 'hysteria', 'schizophrenia' and 'obsession' really mean to a psychiatrist. We disentangle delusions from illusions and hallucinations. We consider such varied topics as paralysed arms, handwashing rituals, obsessional doubts, vanity and suicidal feelings.

PSYCHIATRIC DISORDER

This first chapter is intended to give some idea of the different ways in which psychiatric disorder shows itself. Like other branches of medicine, psychiatry has its *diagnoses*, and these diagnoses have a logical relationship to one another, at least in theory. For the sake of clarity, I have set out the main diagnoses in the form of a diagram (*see* Fig. 1), and I shall now try to explain how it works.

Firstly, psychiatric disorder may affect either the mind or the body. Where it produces actual disease of the body it is known as a psychosomatic illness. Clearly, psychiatric disorder can affect the body without producing a disease. When we waited outside the headmaster's study, or outside the examination hall, we may have experienced intense anxiety, and this could have shown itself in a rapidly beating heart, or sweating hands, or shaking. We would have had no disease of the heart or hands, or whatever part was shaking, and the symptoms would have disappeared without trace.

PSYCHOSOMATIC DISEASE

On the other hand, suppose that long-continued worry produces an ulcer in the stomach, then we may be said to have a *psychosomatic disease*. The ulcer is there, and will take time to go away even if this

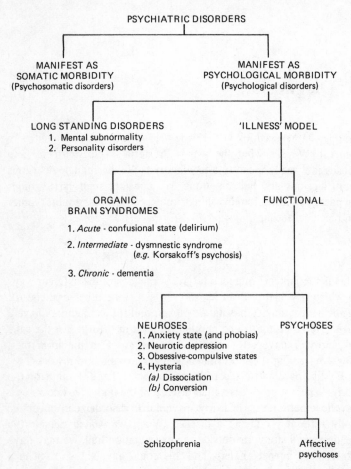

Fig. 1. Diagram of psychiatric descriptive diagnoses.

worry suddenly ceases. The ulcer itself may perforate or produce a haemorrhage. The ulcer is a disease in its own right. Other diseases that are thought to be caused by psychological stress (at least partly) include asthma, many skin rashes, ulcerative colitis, obesity, anorexia nervosa, hypertension and some forms of heart disease. Psychological factors have even been shown to be associated with the development of cancer. Within this group of diseases the importance of mental stress in the causation of the illness will vary from one person to another, and mental stress is not always the main cause of the illness.

PSYCHOLOGICAL DISORDER

Now let us come to the psychiatric disorders that show themselves by their effects on the mind itself. Here the psychiatrist distinguishes between those disorders that come upon a previously normal individual—the mental illnesses—and those that the patient is likely to have had for most of his life, including mental handicap and personality disorder.

Mental handicap and personality disorder

Mental handicap (mental deficiency, mental subnormality) is defined as the presence of impaired intellectual function from an early age (legally from before the age of 18 years). When character traits reach proportions that have to be regarded as pathological, the subject is referred to as suffering from a personality disorder.

One of the most severe forms of personality disorder is that known as psychopathic (or sociopathic) personality. This type of person is sometimes responsible for repeated senseless crimes, and is likely to be impulsive, antisocial, lacking in remorse and unable to form relationships based on affection and trust.

Psychiatric illness

Looking back at Fig. 1 we now come to consider the psychiatric *illnesses*. With a typical psychiatric illness a previously healthy person will develop distressing symptoms. In some cases the cause is to be found in disease of the brain itself, such as brain tumour, syphilis or tuberculosis of the brain tissue, death of parts of the brain because of arterial disease, or degeneration of the brain associated with senility. These are known as the organic illnesses. The majority of patients presenting with psychiatric illnesses will not have any demonstrable disease of the brain, however, and in contrast will be said to be suffering from functional illnesses.

ORGANIC AND FUNCTIONAL ILLNESS

Organic illness

It is probable that a great many readers of this book will have suffered from a psychiatric illness. Quite severe while it lasted, it may have involved loss of contact with reality and diminished awareness of one's surroundings. One may have failed to recognise relatives and friends, may not have known whether one was at home or in hospital, or what day it was. One may even have seen visions of frightening animals. If this clinical picture has not rung any bells yet, let me explain that what I have just described is an acute organic illness, known technically as a confusional state, but more easily recognisable by its lay name of *delirium*. The term 'acute' implies that it is of short duration. Since such psychiatric illnesses accompany the infectious diseases of childhood, it can be seen that when the measles or the scarlet fever (or the fever) clears up, then the psychiatric illness clears up too.

Other organic illnesses are not so predictable. A severe impairment of memory can result from deficiency of certain vitamins such as vitamin B_1 (thiamine) and vitamin B_{12} (cyanocobalamin). If treated promptly with replacement vitamins these illnesses respond; thus, the illness will then have lasted only a short time, and so will have been *acute*. If treated late or not at all, then irrevocable damage to the brain may have occurred, and the illness will become a long-standing one, that is to say *chronic*.

Some organic illnesses are not susceptible to any curative treatment known at present. This is the case with the two commonest types of organic brain disease of old age—arteriosclerotic dementia and senile dementia. Once the intellectual faculties of the patient are lost, the patient is bound to suffer permanently from such impairment. The word *dementia* implies such a permanent deterioration in brain function. At present research is going on into drugs that it is hoped may improve blood flow to the brain, but until a suitably effective drug is found to prevent death of the nerve cells, treatment has to concentrate on relieving distress and supporting what faculties remain.

Functional illness

We turn now to the functional psychiatric illnesses. If a patient with a functional psychiatric illness were to die suddenly, the autopsy would reveal no peculiarity in the appearance of the brain, and even examination under the microscope would fail to show any difference from normal. Since there is no demonstrable abnormality of *structure* of the brain, then what is important in these illnesses is abnormality of its *function*. The functional illnesses themselves are divided into two groups, neuroses and psychoses.

PSYCHOSES AND NEUROSES

Psychoses

The neuroses are the minor illnesses and psychoses are the major illnesses. The psychoses include those conditions where the patient is so divorced from reality that he suffers from *delusions*. A delusion is a demonstrably false belief (and one that is not customary in persons of the patient's cultural background). Thus a patient may believe that she is matron of the hospital, that her 'insides have all rotted away', that the staff are putting poison in her food, or that her feet are nailed to the floor. One is not justified in assuming that because a person is a member of one of the more extreme political parties, or a devotee of an obscure religious faith, that this of itself constitutes a delusional belief, no matter how much one may disagree with him. On the other hand, a belief that one has been put under an evil spell by the next door neighbour is clearly much more likely to be a delusional belief in this country than it is in parts of West Africa where such beliefs are part of the traditional culture and, therefore, as acceptable as political and religious beliefs are in this country.

Affective psychoses

Functional psychoses are of two main types, the affective and the schizophrenic. In the affective psychoses the patient is either excessively depressed and low in spirits, or on the other hand elated and high in spirits.

Together with these changes in mood (or *affect*, as the emotional state is called technically) are changes in the patient's thoughts and behaviour. In the cases of psychotic depression the patient tends to be preoccupied with unpleasant thoughts, concerning disease, poverty, unworthiness or guilt. He may suffer from delusions that he has an incurable illness, or that he has committed the unpardonable sin. He may believe he is bankrupt or a pauper, when in fact he has many thousands of pounds in the bank: in such cases any attempt to persuade him to the contrary (for instance, by showing him the current bank statements) will be dismissed, possibly as benign attempts to disguise from him what he knows to be the truth. The unpardonable sin that he is preoccupied with may be a trivial fault that occurred years ago.

Case 1 Miss M.D.
Miss M.D., an elderly spinster, was found wandering by the canal, thinking about finishing herself off. She said that 'evil thoughts' had been passing through her mind. She had lost her appetite, lost over 14 lb. in weight, was constipated and talked slowly.

She complained that she heard the Devil's voice talking to her saying, 'You won't be saved'. She believed that she was being given bad food since she had been admitted to hospital. 'God is influencing them to punish me', she said.

She attributed her dire straits to an episode some time previously when she had blasphemed.

In keeping with this mood and thought content are changes in the patient's behaviour. The movements are *retarded*, so that he will sit doing nothing at all for hours on end. He will reply to questions, if at all, only after a long delay, and the reply can be painfully slow. In extreme cases of retardation movements may be so rare that the patient lies as if in a stupor. By contrast, some patients with severe depression behave rather differently, and show signs of agitation. They pace up and down restlessly, wringing their hands in despair. The difference is not so marked as it might appear—the agitated patient certainly suffers a severe lack of any *useful* energy.

Elation of mood can be associated with *mania*. Mania is the polar opposite of depression. The patient is high in spirits, over-active and bursting with energy. The classical picture of such a patient rushing round in an uncontrollable frenzy of activity, breaking up the furniture and prone to violence, is not usually seen nowadays. As a rule the most that is seen is one stage short of this—hypomania, so that as a result we usually contrast depression with hypomania. Fortunately, mania is rare because hypomania usually responds to treatment and the patient does not progress to the more severe stage.

The thoughts of the hypomanic patient are usually on pleasant topics or wish-fulfilling fantasies. While the depressed patient has ideas of unworthiness, the patient with hypomania has ideas of grandeur. While ideas of poverty are typical of depression, in hypomania the patient is liable to spend lavishly and beyond his means. He is not likely to be worried about illness, and rather denies the fact that he is currently ill. He is not prone to ideas of guilt and is in fact likely to blame others, in a paranoid way, for any difficulties that he may experience.

At first sight it does seem a pity to treat such a state of apparent happiness, and sometimes it really is permissible to allow a patient to remain in a state of mild hypomania under good supervision. However, anything more than the mildest elation requires intervention. This is partly because the patient is out of touch with reality and may commit indiscretions that he will later regret—if he has spent thousands in the shops it is difficult to get his money back. He requires treatment, too, in order to avoid the clinical state escalating into that of mania, in which he is liable to become violent or to develop serious physical illness through exhaustion.

By now the reader will be able to make out the pattern of the typical affective illness (see Fig. 2). The depressed patient is low in his spirits, his thoughts are gloomy, and under these circumstances

	DEPRESSION	HYPOMANIA
Mood	low	high
Thought content	pessimistic	optimistic
Energy level	diminished	increased

Fig. 2. Features of affective illness.

it is not surprising that his energy is lacking. The hypomanic patient is elated, his mind dwells on cheerful subjects and his drive is correspondingly increased.

Schizophrenia

This understandable relationship between emotions, thoughts and behaviour tends to be lacking in schizophrenia. Like the affective psychoses, schizophrenia is a functional psychosis, but unlike them the patient's mental processes cannot be understood as being an extension of normal extremes of mood.

He may show *incongruity of affect*—the mood does not match the subject. He may tell how his dearest friend died recently as if it were a pleasant topic or even amusing. Alternatively the mood may show a conspicuous lack of response to events, a limitation of its range that is referred to as affective 'flattening' or 'blunting'.

The thought content is often strange and bizarre. The patient may have depressive or hypomanic delusions, but has in addition delusions that are not easily understood as reflecting either elation or depression. His behaviour can be unpredictable or he may stand in abnormal positions for long periods.

Commonly the schizophrenic patient experiences *hallucinations*. A hallucination is an experience in which the subject perceives a stimulation in any of the five senses that does not arise from external reality. Thus, if someone looking at what is really a blank wall can see spiders, rats or snakes, then he is seeing a vision or a visual hallucination. The essence of a hallucination is that there is no physical sensory input—if a dark shadow is misinterpreted as a human figure this is an illusion, not a hallucination.

The hallucinations that occur in schizophrenia are most typically auditory in type. The patient may hear a voice (or voices) talking about him. They may be saying nasty things about him, or nice things, or strange inexplicable things, but characteristically they talk about him in the third person: it is 'he' this or 'she' that—not 'you—'. Many of the patient's symptoms in schizophrenia are clearly far removed from the day-to-day feelings and thoughts that most of us have.

Neuroses

By contrast, the experiences encountered in the neuroses are commonplace, and it is often only their severity or disproportion that warrant them being regarded as illnesses. There are four main categories of neurotic illness—anxiety states, hysteria, obsessive–compulsive states and neurotic depression.

Anxiety states

Anxiety is the emotion that accompanies a fear of something unpleasant about to happen (as opposed to depression, which generally *follows* the unpleasant event). As a rule the subject only fears that the occurrence *may* happen. Anxiety, then, is the appropriate affect for future events and is to do with apprehension, dread or feeling one's security threatened. Often the subject cannot place exactly what it is he fears, and this state is known as *free-floating anxiety*. Indeed, the person may not even be complaining of the subjective feeling of anxiety; he may instead present with physical shakiness or tremor, with consciousness of his heart beat or unduly rapid beats (palpitations), or with excessive perspiration. The diagnosis of anxiety state may be missed in such patients, who tend to turn up at general medical clinics.

In a different type of anxiety state the fears may be associated with specific objects or situations. These conditions constitute the *phobias* or *phobic anxiety states*.

Hysteria

In hysteria the patient develops symptoms which enable him to resolve his anxiety. A soldier in the front line of battle may suddenly develop a psychological paralysis of his right arm. No matter how hard he tries consciously, he is unable to move it. The effect is that he is taken away from the front line, and therefore from the anxiety-provoking situation. In civilian life a paralysis of the legs may be the primitive unconscious psychological answer to the unbearable domestic or work situation, effectively removing the patient from the conflict. In a *fugue* (or flight) with amnesia a similar mechanism for reducing anxiety can be seen. The patient may turn up in a different part of the country (having made the flight or fugue) and be unable to remember anything of the past (amnesia). In some cases this may lead to the patient taking on a second personality and identity in the new district. Although the press sometimes refers to such patients as suffering from schizophrenia, the reader will now realise that such a split in the personality is a far cry from the psychiatric condition of schizophrenia. In the more serious state of schizophrenia itself the mind is not split into two so much as fragmented.

Those types of hysteria which present with apparently physical effects, such as paralysis, are grouped as *conversion hysteria*. The types that more obviously involve the mental state, including cases of fugue amnesia, stupor, faints or hysterical fits and convulsions, are referred to as *dissociation hysteria*.

Obsessive–compulsive states

In obsessive–compulsive states a typical symptom will have three main characteristics:

1. The patient regards it as abnormal.
2. He will try to resist it.
3. He finds that resistance leads to tension and anxiety.

The fact that this patient regards his symptom as abnormal is in contrast to some psychotic delusions that a psychotic patient appears to accept as real. An obsessive patient who cannot wash his hands unless he washes them three times will complain of this, saying that he knows it is not right. He will try to avoid carrying out this ritual, telling himself after washing his hands once that that will do. Doubts about whether his hands are really clean come back to his mind insistently, and he finds it difficult to think of anything else. He resolves the tension by washing them again. Need he really wash them a third time? Again, the tension rises and he finds peace of mind only when he has fulfilled the magic number of ablutions only to lose the entire cycle after a short respite.

There are four main types of obsessive–compulsive symptoms:

1. The *compulsive ritual* This is illustrated above by the handwashing symptom. Other patients may be disabled by having carefully to fold and refold their clothes until they get it just right, or maybe spend hours making sure they put their clothes on in the morning in exactly the right order and manner.

2. *Obsessional doubts (folie de doute)* Here the patient is unable to believe the evidence of his own mind. This may be in the realm of memory ('Did I really do that, or do I just think that I did?') and this may lead to the patient going downstairs at night to check that

he locked the front door not just once, but a whole series of times.

(Where thoughts alone are affected they are sometimes referred to as 'obsessions', whereas overt actions are called 'compulsions'. Unfortunately not everyone sticks to this division, and some use these terms differently.)

3. *Ruminations* The ruminating patient suffers from intrusive thoughts that either stop normal activity or severely impair it for the time being. He may cogitate endlessly over abstract problems or pointless thoughts. Distressing images, words or other thoughts, often to do with sex or religion or philosophy, repeatedly force themselves on his mind.

4. *Obsessional phobias* Here the ideas that intrude are, as in other phobias, of a fearful or anxiety-provoking kind. Like other obsessional symptoms, however, they also have the quality of temptations or impulses to do something against the normal nature of the patient or against his will. They may take the form of recurring fears that, despite himself, he may stab someone, or strangle his children, or perhaps behave as a Peeping Tom.

As in other psychiatric illnesses of neurotic degree, the symptoms of obsessive–compulsive states are found fairly frequently in the normal population.

Neurotic depressive illness

The final neurotic category that we come to is that of neurotic depressive illness. This can be seen as a state somewhere mid-way in severity between, on the one hand, those moods of depression to which we are all subject on occasion and, on the other hand, the melancholic state of depressive psychosis. As in depressive psychosis, the spirits are low, thought content is unpleasant and activity retarded. Delusional beliefs do not occur, though, and retardation is not so extreme, often being confined to a subjective sensation rather than being a conspicuous feature of the observed behaviour. Thus, the patient with a neurotic depression may feel slowed up in his movements, or may feel tired and lacking in energy. Even minor jobs seem a great effort. A central feature is loss of interest; an experience that most of us are familiar with is that when we lose interest in a particular topic it is difficult to conjure up the energy to deal with it. It is understandable, then, that when the patient loses interest in almost everything about him, that general loss of energy is a serious feature of his psychological state.

The loss of energy may not be confined to physical activity. The depressed person may lack energy for mental activity, and complain of a loss of concentration, of absent-mindedness, or of impaired memory. This last feature might call to mind the mental state of the patient with organic brain disease, but it is usually quite easy to distinguish the two types of memory difficulty. The patient with a depression complains of the fallibility of his memory but, in spite of the subjective experience of requiring much increased effort of concentration, objectively he is able to retain newly-learned material quite well. In the case of organic brain disease, where the patient may not even complain of his memory disorder, it is found on testing his memory that he obtains scores quite different from the normal population, showing obvious impairment.

The mind of the patient with neurotic depression dwells on the same subjects as those of the patient with psychotic depression. He may be preoccupied with disease, but he 'wonders if' he may have a serious disease, or fears that he may have, rather than having the unshakeable conviction of the psychotic depressive. Similarly, he may be self-reproachful, or worry how he is going to manage on his money, rather than have frank delusions of guilt, unworthiness or poverty.

The patient does not have to be psychotic to think of suicide. Many patients with neurotic degrees of depression have a pessimistic outlook, and feel that the future looks bleak. They see no end to their troubles and wonder if it is worthwhile trying to go on. Many admit to seriously contemplating ending their own lives. Some have already made attempts by the time they seek professional help. Others, for religious or cultural reasons, would not wish to admit such thoughts (even to themselves) because the idea of taking a positive step to end one's own life is regarded as morally wrong.

It is particularly difficult, when talking to these latter patients, to get an idea of how desperate they feel until perhaps it is too late. They may agree, though, that when they retire for the night they would not care if they did not wake up again. Such a thought does not carry with it the idea of a sinful desire to destroy oneself and instead transfers the responsibility to fate or one's Maker.

PERSONALITY DISORDERS

Having seen the range of diagnostic categories of mental illness on the one hand, we are now in a position to get a clearer view of those conditions referred to as 'personality disorders' on the other.

In general, the *symptoms of mental illness* are distressing, transient, and regarded by the patient as foreign to his normal self. In contrast *personality features* (which all of us have) tend to be long-continued and an integral part of the self, accepted by the subject (*see* Fig. 3). There are some notable exceptions to these

PERSONALITY FEATURES	SYMPTOMS
1. Not distressing (ego-syntonic)	1. Distressing
2. Long lasting or permanent	2. Transient or foreign
3. Universal (possessed by everyone)	3. Non-universal (not suffered by everyone)

Fig. 3. Contrast of symptoms of mental illness with personality features.

generalisations; in some chronic mental illnesses the symptoms are scarcely transient and not always obviously distressing, and there are few persons who by no means find all features of their personality acceptable. The notion of a contrast of personality features and symptoms is nevertheless a firmly entrenched one, and often useful as a medium for talking about psychological phenomena.

Hysterical personality

What is more of a problem is that of separating disorders of personality from normality. One recognises, for instance, that there are persons who might be described as having an hysterical personality. Such persons may show a tendency to exaggerate, to overact, to show lability of affect (in tears one minute and in laughter the next), to be vain (or, in psychiatric jargon, *narcissistic*), to be seductive in their behaviour towards the opposite sex, and yet to be shallow in their relationships or even, paradoxically, frigid. They tend unconsciously to manipulate others around them, and to derive secondary gain from their psychiatric symptoms. Such a disordered personality may leave the subject with a severe incapacity in interpersonal relationships, and there may be no doubt that he (or she) is pathologically disturbed. Many of these features are, however, found in persons well within the normal range of personality types, and we are in the difficult position that it is merely a matter of subjective judgment whether one regards someone as suffering from a personality disorder.

Depressive personality

For nearly every diagnostic group the relevant adjective can be used to designate a variety of personality disorder. Thus, if a person shows lifelong traits of pessimism, lack of energy, lack of interest—never, for instance, wanting to go to the party: 'It won't be any good, the one last year was awful'—or is preoccupied with dire forebodings— 'Just look at what's in the papers every day'—such a person might aptly be described as a depressive personality.

Hypomanic personality

The opposite type will be full of energy, always bustling round with new ideas, talkative and sociable—probably organising the party. Entertaining and witty, his company may pall after a while because of his tendency to be intrusive and to organise one. Such a person may be justifiably regarded as a hypomanic personality. The cyclothymic personality swings from a rather depressive behaviour to a somewhat hypomanic one and back again with excessive facility.

Obsessional personality

The obsessional (or anankastic) personality tends to be obstinate; over-conscientious and scrupulous; punctual; meticulous; showing great attention to detail, miserliness, stinginess or a tendency to hoard things.

Schizoid personality

The schizoid personality will be emotionally cold, relatively unaffected by fortune or disaster, callous and uninvolved in his personal relationships.

It will be seen that these personality types have a clinical basis, and are considered separately from other dimensions of personality. To take the familiar introversion–extraversion axis, features of the extrovert may be seen in the hypomanic and hysterical personality disorders, and features of the introvert may be found in the schizoid, the depressive and the obsessional personality disorders.

There are yet other epithets used to label unusual behaviour that prove to be even more unsatisfactory than the above, such as unstable and inadequate personalities. There is a danger that such terms are used in a judgmental and pejorative sense, so that anyone more extrovert than onself is called 'hysterical', or anyone less extrovert is called 'schizoid'.

THE DIAGNOSTIC LADDER

We now go back to reconsider the relationship of the diagnoses to one another. Earlier in the chapter they were depicted as set out in something like a family tree (*see* Fig. 1). This relationship has some truth in it, in that it expresses the idea that a patient has one illness *or* another, that the illness is either psychotic or neurotic and that it is associated with organic brain disease or not.

Relationship between the diagnoses

It does not mean that the symptoms of each illness are entirely distinct. Even apart from the problems of allocating borderline cases, two quite different diagnoses may show some symptoms in common. Anxiety symptoms may occur in organic brain disease, for instance, and are quite common in depressive illness (whether neurotic or psychotic in degree). It has been shown that patients with psychoses are likely to be suffering from many neurotic symptoms—just as many as the patients with the neuroses in fact. So a patient with schizophrenia may have delusions and hallucinations, but along with these psychotic symptoms he may have features of anxiety, hysteria, obsessive–compulsive states and depression.

Patients with organic brain disease may show features of any other psychiatric illness. It is well known that a patient presenting with hysteria for the first time in middle age may well turn out to have a disease of the brain. Any of the schizophrenic features may be produced by a dementing illness; one patient that I treated came up originally with a typical paranoid psychosis, and later turned out to be suffering from a brain tumour.

Anxiety symptoms may occur in *any* other psychiatric illness. This makes the diagnosis of anxiety state one of the 'softest' diagnoses in psychiatry, since further examination of the patient may at any time reveal that there are also features of a different underlying condition.

Use of the diagnostic ladder
This new aspect of the relationship between the diagnoses may be expressed by putting them in the form of a ladder (*see* Fig. 4). Any illness on the ladder will, of course, show its own specific diagnostic features. In addition, two things may be said about it. Firstly, the illness may, in addition, show any of the features of the illnesses placed above it. Secondly, the correctness of the diagnosis will be called into question if it is possible to demonstrate features of any of the illnesses placed below it. This second statement is relevant to the procedure known as making the *differential diagnosis*. Whenever (in any branch of medicine) a provisional diagnosis is reached, it behoves the clinician to go through the various alternative possibilities that might explain the symptoms and signs shown by his patient.

Anxiety state
Other neuroses (hysteria, obsessive states)
Depressive neurosis
Affective neurosis
Schizophrenia
Acute organic brain disease
Chronic organic brain disease

Fig. 4. The diagnostic ladder of illnesses.

It will be seen from Fig. 4 that the diagnosis of anxiety state has achieved little, since it leaves the field wide open. The diagnosis of organic brain disease clearly leaves little else to remain for conjecture, although of course it is then necessary to take the next step in the investigation of the patient—establishing the *cause* or the nature of the brain disease.

Having become familiar with this concept of arranging the diagnoses in a series, the point of it will become self-evident. It does not make sense to regard a patient as suffering from an anxiety state with a touch of schizophrenia, whereas schizophrenics may obviously have anxiety symptoms without calling the diagnosis into question. This does raise the question of the nature of affective flattening or blunting, which is a recognised feature of schizophrenia, because at first sight it seems a paradox that a patient may show affective flattening and at the same time have anxiety and depressive symptoms. This anomaly is more apparent than real. The term 'affective flattening' refers to a failure to show an appropriate response to a given *event*. It does not mean to say that, over and above what is happening from day-to-day, the patient cannot suffer long-continued distress or symptoms of affective disturbance. This is in fact a well-recognised picture in chronic schizophrenia, where the patient may be preoccupied with his symptoms (including his affective symptoms) and may weather all sorts of bad news and disasters without turning a hair.

The reader should be warned that the use of the term 'diagnostic ladder' is to some extent an idiosyncrasy of the author's—do not be surprised if others do not know what you mean by the expression. The concepts expressed in it are more widespread though. Foulds (1965) drew attention to the frequency of neurotic symptoms in psychiatric illnesses, and tried to explain the fact that it was not always appreciated that this occurred. He thought that the explanation might lie in what he referred to as the 'King Lear principle', that 'Where the greater malady is fixed, the lesser is scarce felt'.

CLASSIFICATION OF DIAGNOSES

Shortcomings of classification table

In this chapter I have tried to give a picture of the different psychiatric diagnoses, and their relationship to each other, by setting them out in the structure of a classification table. In the scheme given (*see* Fig. 1) the categories are divided serially into two, and the two resulting subdivisions (*a*) are mutually exclusive and (*b*) together make up the whole of the original category.

The reader may be sceptical about a scheme for classifying abnormal human experiences that appears to depend upon principles of the traditional formal logic, and he would be right to have reservations.

To achieve clarity, the scheme oversimplifies what is found in real life. For instance, a patient may have more than one diagnosis simultaneously, *e.g.* someone with a long-standing personality disorder may present with a depressive illness. Secondly, not all psychiatrists are agreed about the theoretical position; if a patient has a complex system of delusions of persecution, should this be classified with schizophrenia, or with affective psychoses, or by itself?

Allocation of diagnoses to categories is not always possible in practice. We defined organic brain syndromes as those conditions associated with demonstrable physical brain disease, but where do we put the psychiatric conditions associated with epilepsy, where sometimes organic pathology can be found but where in other subjects the brain appears normal at autopsy?

Phenomenological diagnosis
The classification given here is largely phenomenological. That is to say, it is based on those features of the diagnosis that can be *elicited* on examination of the patient. When we make phenomenological diagnoses, we include as grist for the mill the phenomena of symptoms and signs. Symptoms are those abnormalities of which the patient complains; signs are those abnormalities which the examiner observes. If a patient complains that he hears voices that no one else seems to hear, that is a symptom. If the observer notices that a patient lies mute and motionless, that is a sign.

Aetiological diagnosis
After taking a history from a patient, perhaps hearing an independent version from a friend or relative, and then examining and observing the patient, one is in a position to make a phenomenological diagnosis. The main alternative is to make an aetiological diagnosis. 'Aetiology' is the study of the causes of disease, and ideally one would like to classify diseases by their causes. However, in many diseases the cause is not known; in others there may have been several causes, all contributing to the development of the disease; and even where causes are known it is not always

possible to identify them at an early stage of contact with the patient.

One particular type of aetiological diagnosis is the *dynamic* diagnosis. On the assumption that the present psychiatric state is the result of previous experiences in interpersonal relationships, the dynamic diagnosis tries to tie up the complex interplay of forces relevant for that patient into a neat bundle. It would certainly be premature to try to do this after only a brief period of contact with the patient.

Theoretical difficulties

So one advantage of making a phenomenological diagnosis is that it can often be done in a short space of time. This advantage also carries with it a problem: suppose that the phenomena change from day to day? The patient who has had no schizophrenic features during his illness over the last few weeks suddenly develops symptoms or signs diagnostic of a schizophrenic illness: does this mean that his type of illness has changed, or was he 'really' suffering from schizophrenia all along?

In practice, when caught in such a theoretical difficulty, the clinician considers what the alternative therapeutic implications are for the patient before coming to a decision. There is then often an obvious choice of action (*e.g.* giving the safer treatment of the two, or the one that gives the answer sooner).

The theoretical difficulties are still with us, but it is doubtful if the situation will ever be otherwise. It will be a sad day when we are all neatly pigeonholed, allocated to a number, and with no attention paid to our individual persons.

SUMMARY

In this chapter we have learned the meaning of the terms 'psychosomatic disorder', 'personality disorder', 'mental subnormality' or 'handicap', and 'mental illness'. The neuroses have been separated off, to leave clear the position of the psychoses in this classification.

We have discovered that delusions are false beliefs, hallucinations are perceptions without any external stimulus, and illusions are distorted or misinterpreted perceptions. Psychotic illnesses may be associated with brain disease (organic psychoses) or may occur in the absence of a demonstrable physical cause (functional psychoses). The principal features of each of the mental illnesses are outlined.

Finally, it has been pointed out that organic brain disease may cause *any* psychiatric symptom, and a psychosis may produce (in addition to its essential features) a distracting crop of neurotic symptoms.

2 The acute organic brain syndrome

In the following pages we shall look at a form of insanity that does occur in young adults, but that is more typically associated with children and the aged, where the patient does not know what is going on around him. The relationship between visions and night-mares leads us to look at modern advances that have been made in our knowledge of sleep processes. As a result, we come intriguingly close to understanding the *delirium tremens* that occur as a well-known feature of alcoholism. We see that it occurs in other forms of addiction too.

DEFINITION OF TERMS

Many of the readers of this book will have suffered a period of acute psychosis—a temporary form of insanity. Most will have forgotten the details, and probably the fact that it ever occurred. At the time, though, they will have been out of touch with reality, failing to recognise people around them, and maybe seeing visions or having other hallucinatory experiences.

Put in such a way, this may seem to be a rather sweeping state-ment. Many of us wonder about our own sanity from time to time, but to have had such an overtly psychotic illness is another matter. In fact, describing it like this is a bit of a tease, because described another way the event is instantly recognisable. What I am referring to is what is called by the lay person an episode of *delirium*. You will recall that this is a common complication of childhood fevers. Yet there is no doubt that, phenomenologically, it counts as a psychosis. Because it is caused by a physical disturbance of brain function, it is classified as an *organic* psychosis. Those readers who have been assiduously following the classification outlined in the previous chapter may be puzzled that organic conditions did not come under 'psychoses' but were listed separately.

An alternative way of depicting this relationship would have been to divide mental illnesses into neuroses and psychoses, and then split psychoses into organic and functional (*see* Fig. 5). This would be quite acceptable, and is an equally valid way of looking at it. The approach in the first chapter merely seemed clearer as an initial exposition.

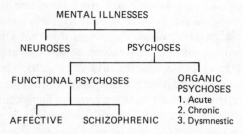

Fig. 5. An alternative classification of mental illnesses.

So delirium may be called an organic illness or psychosis. It is called *acute* because it is typically of short duration (in medicine the terms 'acute' and 'chronic' merely refer to short and long illnesses respectively—they carry none of the lay connotations of severity or seriousness).

In the chapter heading delirium is also referred to as a *syndrome*. This word is an alternative to words such as 'illness' or 'disease', and is used to indicate that what is being described is merely a collection of symptoms and signs in a certain pattern: it is an attempt to avoid any implications that might be read into terms like 'illness' (such as the idea that there is a specific or known cause of the condition). It is clear that many different causes can give rise to a delirious state—for example, there are many different reasons for becoming feverish.

FEATURES OF DELIRIUM

Most readers will have some idea of the clinical picture that is conjured up by the word 'delirium'. To be specific, they are as follows:

Diminution in consciousness
The degree of diminution in consciousness will vary widely, but obviously the completely unconscious patient can hardly be said to be delirious. Many of the disease processes that give rise to delirium can also produce *coma* or *stupor*—states of unconsciousness from which the patient is unrousable or rousable respectively.)

In delirium the patient may be drowsy, but otherwise the diminution in consciousness shows itself as an *incomplete awareness* of what is going on in the environment.

Disorientation in time, place or person
The delirious patient rapidly loses his knowledge of what time of day it is, and then of what day of the week or what date it is. When his meals are brought to him he does not know whether he is eating breakfast, lunch, tea or dinner. He is said to be disoriented (or disorientated) in time.

Disorientation literally refers to a loss of sense of direction, and this can also occur. The patient may be unable to find his way back to his bed, especially in unfamiliar surroundings. He may not know whether he is at home, at hospital, or where he is at all. He is then disoriented in place or space.

Disorientation in person may also occur. The delirious subject then fails to recognise friends and relatives. In severe degrees he may not recognise the intimate members of his family. When the door of his room opens and someone walks in he will have little idea who that person is or why they have come. The term 'disorientation in person' might theoretically be taken also to mean the loss of sense of personal identity, so that the patient would no longer know who he himself is; it is likely that this is rare, but clearly such things are difficult to judge. Although disorientation in other respects may be assessed by the patient's behaviour, the quality of personal identity is a subjective experience which it may be difficult to elicit from a patient in such a state as this.

The two features of diminution of consciousness and disorientation are cardinal signs of the acute organic brain syndrome, and they enable the diagnosis to be made. Other features may occur, however, and add colour to the clinical picture.

Hallucinations

The delirious patient frequently has *hallucinations*. These, it will be recalled, are apparent sensations in the realm of sight, hearing, touch, taste or smell that arise without any corresponding sensory input from reality. It might be readily understood if the delirious patient were to misinterpret sensory information as *illusions, e.g.* to think that the dressing gown hanging on the door was a strange man might happen in a state of diminution of consciousness (as it might happen in a setting of diminution of light intensity in normal mental states). However, the delirious subject can also conjure up experiences out of nothing. In visual hallucinations he may look at a blank wall and yet see the form of a human being as clearly as if there were one really there. Children may scream at hallucinatory spiders on the wall, grown men may cower in fear at the products of their imagination. Delirious visions are not always frightening, and the patient may be amused at the antics of Lilliputian figures on the bedclothes, or be intrigued to find the tools of his trade to hand.

The most characteristic type of hallucinations in acute organic states are *visual*. It will be seen later that in functional psychoses *auditory* hallucinations are more typical, but auditory hallucinations can certainly occur in the acute organic brain syndrome. They may take the form of voices talking to the patient, voices that no one else seems to hear. The patient cannot always tell where they seem to come from, but may be able to identify them as male or female, or even to say to which particular person they belong. The words they say may be clear or indistinct, the meaning obvious or obscure.

They may just consist of the patient's name being called. This is in any case a frequent experience in everyday life, but then is usually found to be an illusion, *i.e.* a misinterpretation of another sound. The hallucinations of the delirious subject may be less organised than human speech and consist of ringing noises, buzzing sounds, or other elementary sensations.

The occurrence of hallucinations will not of itself be sufficient for a diagnosis of acute organic brain syndrome. They may occur in functional psychoses, as has been implied. They may also occur in normal subjects at times; one particular time at which they may be experienced by an otherwise healthy person is on falling off to sleep at night. These are called *hypnagogic* hallucinations. The diagnosis rests on establishing the fundamental features of diminished consciousness and disorientation.

Other symptoms of delirium

Apart from hallucinations, almost any other psychiatric symptom *can* occur in the acute organic brain syndrome. Symptoms of anxiety, depression or hysteria are common, and patients may exhibit features of the functional psychoses, such as paranoid beliefs or delusions.

Confusional states

A frequent synonym to be found for the acute organic brain syndrome is 'confusional state'. I find this a particularly unhelpful term. There is no doubt that patients with an acute organic brain syndrome are entitled to be called confused if anyone is, as I think will now be clear. But the word 'confused' is also applied to many other persons, and so indiscriminately that it has come to have little specific meaning. If it were restricted to refer to disorientation, then the term 'confusional state' would be a fair description of the acute organic brain syndrome. In fact, patients who are bewildered by the effects of their functional psychosis are also described as confused at times, as indeed are normal subjects (for instance, when acutely embarrassed).

The adjective 'confused' is one which complicates a description as often as it clarifies one, and I prefer to see it either abandoned or, at least, if it is to be brought in, qualified by an indication of the sense in which it is being used at the time.

THE PHYSIOLOGY OF SLEEP

Sleep is the closest thing in daily life to the delirious state. When we are drowsy we are in a state of diminished awareness or diminished consciousness and when we are dreaming we may be said to be having 'visual hallucinations'. Even though this analogy may seem forced, the reader will find that a knowledge of the modern discoveries about the physiology of normal sleep will help in understanding the occurrence of certain clinical states of delirium.

Orthodox sleep

One way of studying sleep is through the use of all-night electroencephalograph (E.E.G.) recordings. Electrodes applied to the scalp pick up the 'brain waves' which are then amplified and fed to the recording pens. When the subject is awake, but with his eyes closed, the pens record a rounded (sinusoidal) wave form at a frequency of about 10 cycles per second, known as the 'alpha' rhythm.

As the subject becomes drowsy the E.E.G. becomes irregular and what rhythmic activity there is slows down. Then characteristic bursts of 14 cycle-per-second activity occur. Each burst tends to build to a climax and then die away again. The resulting shape gives rise to the description of this phenomenon as a *sleep spindle* (*see* Fig. 6)—presumably an allusion to the shape of yarn being wound on to a spool.

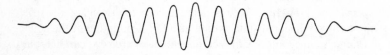

Fig. 6. A sleep spindle.

When these spindles occur, we can be sure that the subject is asleep. As sleep becomes deeper the background rhythm (between the spindles) becomes slower and slower, eventually reaching from 1 to 4 cycles per second in really deep sleep. Often the sleep spindles are superimposed on the slow waves (*see* Fig. 7). By inspecting the E.E.G. as it is running, one can tell fairly well how deeply asleep the subject is at any point in time. In a normal night our sleep will become progressively deeper during the first hour,

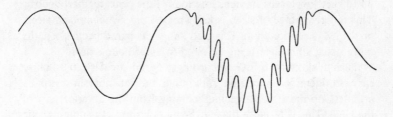

Fig. 7. A sleep spindle superimposed on slow waves.

and then become lighter again. This cycle will repeat itself several times during the night (*see* Fig. 8).

So far, then, there is little new, and the last diagram bears a close resemblance to some advertisements for bed-time beverages.

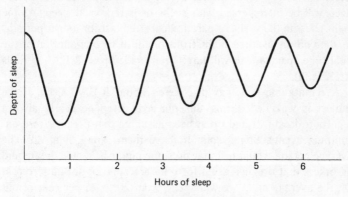

Fig. 8. Cyclic variations in depth of sleep.

R.E.M. (paradoxical) sleep

But a different type of sleep has been discovered. As a rule the eyes of a sleeping person are still, or they make only slow, rolling movements. At certain times during the night, though, the eyes make rapid flickering movements. At the same time as these rapid eye movements other physiological changes take place. The blood pressure, pulse rate and respiration become irregular. The state of slight tension (the 'tone') in which muscles are normally held falls off to very low levels. In men, erections of the penis regularly occur. This different stage of sleep is known as *rapid eye movement* sleep, or R.E.M. sleep for short. It is also known as paradoxical sleep, the more usual state then being referred to as orthodox sleep.

During all-night E.E.G. recordings, paradoxical sleep is fairly easy to identify, since the rapid eye movements show up as artefacts on the E.E.G. tracings coming from the anterior part of the head. This is because the eye, being polarised, sets up magnetic waves which produce currents that are quite large by E.E.G. standards and which are superimposed on the normal records.

During a typical night's sleep, the subject will go into the first cycle of orthodox sleep, and it will not be until he is coming out of the deeper stage of this about an hour and a half later that he enters his first period of R.E.M. sleep. This episode of R.E.M. activity will last for only a few minutes, and then he will revert to orthodox sleep. The pattern will continue during the night: cycles of orthodox sleep will be interspersed with spells of paradoxical sleep. As the night goes on the spells of paradoxical sleep last for longer periods, so that on an average night from one-fifth to one-quarter of the total time spent asleep will have been made up of R.E.M. periods (*see* Fig. 9).

A remarkable fact was discovered about R.E.M. sleep. If the subject is wakened during this phase of sleep he nearly always reports a dream. It had often been assumed that dreams were uncommon events. Some claim to have them rarely, if at all. The average person would feel that on some nights he would dream and on others that dreams lasted for only a second or so. Far from it. On the average night we will spend from 20 to 25 per cent of our time dreaming.

Nightmares, nocturnal emissions, etc.
The pattern of sleep that we can now describe, illustrated in Fig. 9, gives us landmarks for placing various events that take place during sleep. Nightmares, for instance, take place during R.E.M. sleep, as might be expected. The *night terrors* that occur in children are rather different: in these attacks the child wakens, often with a scream, but remains inaccessible—he appears to take no notice or not to hear when he is reassured, but goes back to sleep in his own

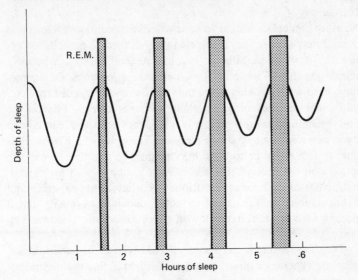

Fig. 9. Alternating pattern of orthodox sleep and R.E.M. (rapid eye movement) sleep.

time. In the morning he does not recall the episode. These night terrors are found to take place in orthodox sleep.

Nocturnal emissions occur during R.E.M. sleep, and sleep-walking or *somnambulism* takes place during orthodox sleep. *Enuresis* (bedwetting) takes place during orthodox sleep, generally during the first cycle, after the child has passed through the deepest trough of sleep.

These observations raise interesting speculations, and may force us to reconsider treasured beliefs. For instance, many have considered that enuresis is of psychological origin, and represents the acting out of a conflict (*e.g.* dependence on, and hostility towards, the parents) in a symbolic way. It now looks as if this explanation is less likely, at least if the mechanism were thought to be the same as that of the dream, the nightmare or the nocturnal emission. Now the episode of bedwetting is seen to be more linked in timing with sleep-walking and night terrors. Further information on these events will be awaited with interest.

Narcolepsy

Another clinical condition to which sleep physiology is relevant is that of *narcolepsy*. This is a state in which the subject falls asleep, not like most of us after he has had a good meal, but actually during the meal—while he is eating his soup perhaps. Or he may fall asleep while walking along the road. It has been noted that certain other features often go along with narcolepsy. First is the phenomenon of *cataplexy*: this is a tendency to collapse in a heap upon experiencing any strong emotion. The unfortunate person has only to feel angry or to burst into laughter to find that he ends up weakly on the ground. The second association is with *hypnagogic* hallucinations. It was mentioned earlier that experiencing hallucinations on falling asleep could occur in normality but it occurs with greater frequency in those who suffer from narcolepsy.

The third feature is *sleep paralysis*. Many of us have had the unpleasant experience of waking up in the night to find that we cannot move a limb. We may also have the impression (fortunately a false one) that we are not breathing. This is likely to be an episode that lasts only a few seconds before we are 'asleep' and blissfully unaware again (it is a matter of opinion whether we should be regarded as asleep *during* the episode). A striking example of this is what is called 'night nurses' paralysis'. The nurse is sitting at her desk in the poorly lit ward in the middle of the night. With open eyes she sees the night sister entering the ward in the course of her rounds. The night nurse feels she has been asleep and has woken up, but is unable to move a muscle. She is fixed to her seat like a hypnotised rabbit. Again, night paralysis, although occurring in normal states, is much more prevalent in narcolepsy.

On investigating the sleep physiology of narcoleptics, it was found that they were most unusual in one respect. The normal person, on falling asleep, goes straight into orthodox sleep. He does not go into R.E.M. sleep, even if he has just woken from a dream. In fact, at the beginning of the night it would be most unexpected if he were to have his first R.E.M. period before 30 or 40 minutes had elapsed. It is found in narcolepsy that the subject will *begin* the night with an episode of R.E.M. sleep. This is more likely to be true if he has somehow managed to avoid falling asleep during the day. It looks as if it might be possible that the narcoleptic attack during the day is an attack, not of orthodox sleep, but of R.E.M. sleep.

What of the associated features? Well, if the subject were going straight into R.E.M. sleep at the beginning of the night, he would be taking the unique step of going straight from consciousness to dreams. It might well seem to him as if he were suffering from hallucinations. A tendency to experience the features of R.E.M. sleep might include the experience of the profound loss of muscle tone that is one of the central features of this state. Such a loss of tone might easily be interpreted as paralysis or manifest itself as cataplexy.

It may turn out that this explanation is oversimplified, but clearly we are on the threshold of many more new discoveries about abnormal sleep.

Effect of hypnotics on R.E.M. sleep

Experiments have now been carried out on the effect of various sedatives on R.E.M. sleep. Volunteers acting as experimental subjects had all-night E.E.G. investigations. For a few nights, to act as a base line, they received no drugs, and the *proportion* of the night spent in R.E.M. sleep was plotted. For each subject this would be fairly constant at a level of 20 per cent or 25 per cent of the whole night's sleep.

Then the drug under investigation would be administered. The drugs investigated so far have often been those casually referred to as 'sleeping pills' and known medically as *hypnotics*. The best known of these are probably the barbiturates.

In the experiment the effect of a barbiturate was to cause the proportion of R.E.M. sleep to drop. The hypnotic was continued each night and for a few nights the R.E.M. proportion stayed low. Gradually it recovered, so that after about ten nights on the drug the proportion was back to its original base line level. What happens if you then increase the dose of the barbiturate? Sure enough the proportion of R.E.M. sleep plummets again and recovers once more in about ten days.

So here we have the subject, by now taking quite a large dose of barbiturate each night, with his sleep E.E.G. back to normal. What happens when he stops taking the drug? The answer is that a 'rebound' occurs, and the proportion of R.E.M. sleep in the night shows a sharp increase (*see* Fig. 10). This increase will itself tail off in time, but it may be some weeks before the physiology of his sleep recovers from *drug withdrawal*.

During the few days immediately after withdrawal, when the increase of R.E.M. sleep is at its height, it might be expected that the amount of dreaming during the night would increase. What was not entirely anticipated, though, was that it was found that the *quality* of the dreams changed. When the increase in R.E.M. sleep is at its height, the dreams associated with the R.E.M. sleep are intense, vivid and tend to wake the subject from his sleep. They are often frightening and, in other words, at this stage we have a tendency to nightmares. Various other changes in sleep physiology, of a related kind, also occur at this time; for instance, the subject tends to go into his first episode of R.E.M. sleep much earlier in the night than is customary (Oswald and Priest, 1965).

We have now, then, the interesting situation of changes in the body's functioning taking place as a result of *not* having a drug. These changes last for some weeks, gradually petering away, long after the drug has gone from the tissues.

Effects of other drugs on R.E.M. sleep

Much work is now being done investigating the effects of other drugs on the proportion of R.E.M. sleep in the night. Other hypnotic and tranquilliser drugs have been found to have a similar action to the barbiturates. The drugs used for the treatment of depressive illness are found to depress R.E.M. sleep even more. This is true of the most commonly used group—known as the *tricyclic* antidepressants. It is even more true of a rather controversial group of drugs, the mono-amine oxidase inhibitors, or M.A.O.I.s for short. The M.A.O.I.s have an inhibitory action on certain biochemical processes in the body, and have been used for the treatment of a number of diseases in man. One effect is to clear up or improve certain types of depressive illness, but doctors tend to be cautious about prescribing them because they have dangerous interactions with some other drugs and they are notorious for producing severe symptoms when some foodstuffs, such as cheese, are taken at the same time.

The M.A.O.I.s are found, then, to reduce the proportion of R.E.M. sleep. At least one of them has the remarkable action of

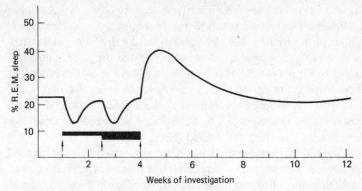

Fig. 10. Effect of sodium amylobarbitone on the proportion of R.E.M.
sleep (after Oswald and Priest, 1965).

abolishing R.E.M. sleep entirely. This can be done with doses of the
drug that are only moderately large, and can occur within a few
weeks of starting on the drug.

When used for depressive illness, it is known that there is a latent
period before M.A.O.I.s can be expected to produce any appreciable benefit. This latent period is unlikely to be less than ten
days and may take a month or more. Sleep studies on such patients
have now demonstrated that the improvement in the patient's
depressive state often coincides with the day that R.E.M. sleep
touches zero.

It had previously been suggested by some that R.E.M. sleep was
essential to. our mental well-being, and that deprivation of R.E.M.
sleep could do a person serious harm, perhaps even producing a
psychotic state. This is now seen to be not the case, at least when
the abolition of R.E.M. sleep is achieved by the use of M.A.O.I.s.
Some of these patients have gone for months without experiencing
untoward effects, and certainly without becoming psychotic.

We will now leave the subject of sleep and return to delirium.

DELIRIUM TREMENS AND DRUG WITHDRAWAL

Alcohol and delirium tremens

The condition known as *delirium tremens*, or just as D.T.s, is
notorious for being associated with alcoholism. In recent years we

have been able to see more clearly the nature of this association.

When we talk of *addiction* to a drug we usually mean that in addition to a *psychological* dependence on the drug the subject has also developed a *physical* dependence on the drug. This physical dependence may be shown as *tolerance, i.e.* the addict is able to take large doses of the drug without, for instance, becoming unconscious. A morphine addict may take a dose that would kill an ordinary man. The subject finds, in fact, that increasing doses are necessary to produce the desired effect.

Physical dependence may also be demonstrated by a *withdrawal syndrome*. This withdrawal syndrome is different for each class of addicting drug. For morphine addicts, withdrawal causes cramp in the limb muscles, nausea, vomiting, diarrhoea, abdominal pains, sweating and yawning.

In addiction to alcohol the withdrawal syndrome may take one of two forms. In one the patient suffers from convulsions or fits, identical with those found in major epilepsy. The other form is *delirium tremens*. Although the association between D.T.s and alcoholism is notorious, it was not widely appreciated until recently that D.T.s is a feature of the withdrawal stage of alcohol addiction. (It had been supposed that an alcoholic might develop D.T.s at any time if he had been addicted for long enough.)

Like other forms of delirium, in D.T.s there is:

1. *Diminished consciousness* or awareness; and
2. *Disorientation* in time, place or person.

There are also two other features which are characteristic of *delirium tremens*:

3. *Tremor* This is a pronounced shaking of the muscles of the body that is practically continuous. It can easily be demonstrated by asking the patient to stretch his hands out, when the regular tremor will not be missed, but it seems to affect most of the voluntary muscles of the body.

The alcoholic is likely to suffer from such a tremor even in states of withdrawal that fall short of full-blown D.T.s. For instance, he may notice (and complain of) the 'shakes' each morning, having been abstinent only during the hours of sleep.

4. *An affective state of fear* Another name for D.T.s among alcoholics is the 'horrors', and extreme fear is frequently an obvious feature. The patient may cry out in terror for no obvious reason.

The fear may be associated with terrifying hallucinations: one can understand someone trying to get away from the snakes manifested in his visual hallucinations, or the ship's captain cowering in the corner terrified of the rats he can see approaching him (because he has run out of alcohol half-way across the ocean). Certainly, small frightening animals seem to be commoner hallucinatory objects than the vast pink elephants that roamed the imagination of gin-dependent expatriates in remote outposts of the Empire!

It is not clear to what extent, if any, the tremor is analogous to the shaking that normally accompanies fear. The thought that these two features do go together in more familiar frightening situations is at least an easy way to remember the two special characteristics of D.T.s.

Hypnotics and delirium tremens

Alcohol is not the only drug whose withdrawal may be signalled by *delirium tremens*. The barbiturates can cause physical dependence and, like alcohol, withdrawal may precipitate either convulsions or *delirium tremens*. The barbiturates share a number of other actions with alcohol. Both can cause sleep in large enough doses. In higher doses they will both cause progressively deeper sleep, then un-rousable coma, and finally death. On a moderately large dose, and if the subject can be prevented from falling asleep, he will show three disturbances of movement that are related to each other—ataxia (staggering), diplopia (double vision) and dysarthria (slurred speech).

There are a number of drugs, used medically either as hypnotics (sleeping tablets) or sedatives, that can produce the type of physical dependence associated with *delirium tremens* as a withdrawal syndrome. These include chloral hydrate (a bitter-tasting sleeping draught), paraldehyde (a strong-smelling chemical given by injection or as a draught), methyprylone (Noludar), ethchlorvynol (Arvynol), and glutethimide (Doriden). Many of the above have been advocated as 'non-barbiturate sedatives', as if the fact that they were not barbiturates conferred on them immunity from the tendency to produce either addiction or the other side-effects for which the barbiturates are notorious.

One of the latest hypnotics to be brought onto the market is methaqualone. This is sold by Boots as Melsed (or Melsedin, depending on the dosage in the tablet). It is also sold, in combination with the antihistamine compound diphenhydramine, as Mandrax. Mandrax has proved to be a potent source of drug abuse, very popular in illicit drug-taking circles, and it has been shown that the addiction associated with methaqualone can include *delirium tremens* as a withdrawal syndrome.

The drug meprobamate (sold as Miltown or Equanil) used to be classified as a tranquilliser, but the discovery that withdrawal sometimes led to the onset of D.T.s gave rise to a re-examination of its action and it too is now regarded as a sedative or hypnotic. Presumably it had been generally used in a dosage too low to make the other actions obvious at first.

In fact it is not only D.T.s that links all these drugs together. Withdrawal of the drug from the dependent individual may be followed in many cases by convulsions. Also, many of these drugs have been shown to be similar to barbiturates in their tendency to produce coma (or even death), ataxia, dysarthria, diplopia, etc. It might be thought by the reader that alcohol is the odd man out, since this is not generally regarded in exactly the same light as the barbiturates. However, it certainly shares all the features catalogued, and on Saturday nights one can find many volunteer subjects who demonstrate staggering, slurred speech and double vision!

The main difference between alcohol and the barbiturates is that alcohol may produce a few extra effects of its own, such as flushing (due to an action on the blood vessels), vitamin deficiency, cirrhosis of the liver, gastritis and other physical diseases, as well as the characteristic odours associated with indulgence in alcoholic beverages.

Delirium tremens and R.E.M. sleep

You will recall that barbiturates produce a temporary reduction in R.E.M. sleep, and that their withdrawal produced a rebound excess of it. Furthermore, during the rebound, dreams were not only presumably excessive in quantity but they had a more intense quality, sometimes producing a frank nightmare.

This was noticed on sudden withdrawal of drugs administered in a dosage similar to that in normal clinical usage. We might expect, then, that when an addict, taking much larger doses than normal, is withdrawn suddenly from his drug, the rebound increase of R.E.M. sleep would be even greater. Where this has been investigated it has been found to be true, some subjects spending virtually 100 per cent of the withdrawal night in R.E.M. sleep.

Under such circumstances the patient is frequently woken from his sleep by terrifying dreams. One more thing, too, takes place that does not occur in normal sleep. If the proportion of R.E.M. sleep is about 100 per cent, this means that the subject in the withdrawal phase goes straight from the waking state into R.E.M. sleep on many occasions when he drops off again. You may remember that this happens in narcolepsy, but not usually otherwise.

To put it another way, the patient is going backwards and forwards from the waking state into a state in which he experiences nightmares, which are after all frightening visual hallucinations. It can now be seen that we are very close to describing *delirium tremens*. Normally, when we have a nightmare, once we have woken up completely we can understand what has happened because we realise that we have been asleep. But to go from consciousness into a nightmare, and back into consciousness, may confuse both the patients and the staff alike.

This interpretation will not necessarily explain all the features of D.T.s. For instance, why does the patient have diminished consciousness or awareness even when not hallucinated? Possibly because he is still drowsy, having been deprived of his *orthodox* sleep. However, these attempts at explanation remain conjectural until the recent understanding has been assimilated and further research has been done to consolidate the tantalising glimpses of underlying mechanisms that we have so far.

What certainly remains unexplained at present is why some drugs are addicting, and have D.T.s as their withdrawal syndrome, while other drugs that are just as potent in suppressing R.E.M. sleep are not addicting at all.

OTHER CAUSES OF DELIRIUM

We have seen that *delirium tremens* is a specific state associated with drug withdrawal. Delirium in general is anything but specific, and can occur after many different sorts of physical insult to the brain.

Illness
In the mind's eye it is probably most commonly thought of in connection with fever. The fever need have no specific cause, and
delirium can occur with most of the infectious illnesses of
childhood. It can occur in adult life, either with fever or with heart
failure, renal failure, or liver failure. In these situations there is interference with the brain's functioning caused by conditions outside
the cranium.

Delirium can also be caused by intracranial lesions such as brain
tumour, encephalitis or infarction. In infarction a piece of the brain
dies off: the commonest reason for this is arteriosclerosis impairing
the blood supply to that part of the brain to such an extent that
eventually the artery is no longer able to support the life processes.
The affected brain tissue becomes soft, and is largely absorbed,
leaving a scar. The patient develops an acute organic brain syndrome at the time of the infarction, which gradually clears to leave
him in clear consciousness but without the use of that part of the
brain. The neurones in the brain are incapable of multiplying, so
that regeneration of the tissue involved is never possible, but with
small areas of damage other parts of the brain can take over the
function of the diseased part or at least disguise the defect. So if the
part of the brain involved is that governing movement of, say, the
left arm, then the paralysis or paresis (partial paralysis) that ensues
immediately after the infarct may show considerable recovery or
even clear up entirely.

Alkaloids
The acute organic brain syndrome may be caused by various
drugs. Perhaps the best-known drugs responsible are the naturally
occurring alkaloids found in certain plants, such as the deadly
nightshade. Poisoning with the berries of these *solanaceous* plants
impairs the action of the parasympathetic nervous system, causing
dry skin, dilated pupils, dry mouth and difficulties with evacuating
bowel and bladder. One of the drugs that can be isolated from such
plants is called *atropine*, and such effects are called parasympathetic blockage or (when caused by other drugs) just 'atropine-
like' effects. In larger doses these alkaloids cause delirium and in
still larger doses death.

Synthetic chemicals and drugs
It is not only naturally occurring alkaloids that produce 'atropine-like' effects. A similar result can ensue from contact with synthetic chemicals, such as certain commercially available insecticides. They may also be produced by some synthetic drugs used in medicine. The most notorious group in this respect are the drugs used for the treatment of *parkinsonism*. In Parkinson's disease, the 'shaking palsy' described by Dr. Parkinson in 1817, the patient develops abnormalities of posture and movement. These include a stiffening or rigidity of the muscles, slowness or weakness of movements, a mask-like facial appearance, and a gait that is robot-like or progresses by small shuffling steps. There is an absence of the associated movements that usually accompany our actions (such as swinging the arms when we walk) and there may be abnormal movements added, for instance the tremor that affects the hands to give the disease its alternative name.

The clinical picture thus described results from defective action of nerve cells in certain parts of the brain that have to do with control of movement and posture. This control, therefore, becomes unbalanced. The solanaceous alkaloids in some way seem to help to correct this balance and have been used to treat Parkinson's disease. There are other synthetic drugs now available that are rather more satisfactory than the alkaloids in this respect. Many of them still share a lot of the actions on the parasympathetic nervous system, so that the patient may complain of dry mouth, blurred vision, constipation and the rest, and in large doses *these drugs can also cause delirium*.

The story now takes a curious turn. A condition very similar to Parkinson's disease may occur as a side-effect of certain psychotropic drugs. Schizophrenia, for instance, is commonly treated with one of a number of drugs known as the phenothiazine group. The drugs of this group may cause, at least while the patient is taking the drug, a condition that closely mimics Parkinson's disease and is therefore called 'parkinsonism'. If this happens, and it is felt that it is important for the patient to continue taking the phenothiazines, then the clinician has a choice of two steps. One is to reduce the dose to levels that do not cause parkinsonism, or at any rate only produce it to a tolerable degree. The other is to give the patient the phenothiazine in the same dose and also prescribe at

the same time an anti-parkinsonian drug. The latter choice is
frequently taken.

What now if the patient develops some new psychiatric symptoms? Are these a development of his original illness, or a sign of
the acute organic brain syndrome that can accompany intoxication
by the anti-parkinsonian drugs? There is clearly a danger of
producing one serious psychiatric condition while trying to treat
another.

If the patient becomes frankly delirious, then it should be possible
to distinguish that state from schizophrenia without too much
trouble. Phenothiazines, however, are also used in the treatment
of organic brain disease. Although it is impossible to restore nerve
cells that have been destroyed by disease, patients with various
forms of dementia can be helped to some extent with phenothiazine
drugs—at least they become more peaceful and their behaviour
becomes less disturbed. If they require anti-parkinsonian drugs as
well, then it is clearly much more difficult to assess the significance
of any symptoms of acute organic brain syndrome that they may
develop. If this happens it may be necessary to stop all drugs to see
if the delirium is improved that way.

TREATMENT OF THE ACUTE ORGANIC
BRAIN SYNDROME

Prophylaxis
Although there are ways of relieving the symptoms of delirium, a
better treatment is obviously to find the cause and treat that
specifically. If the patient's delirium results from his acute heart
failure, then obviously that is where the main therapeutic interest
will come. Even better 'treatment' would be to prevent the underlying condition occurring at all—what is known as *prophylaxis*.
The immunisation of young children against the common
childhood fevers is a good example of prophylactic action.

Major tranquillisers
The incidence of delirium has been reduced a great deal in recent
years, partly as a result of immunisation and partly as a result of
improved general medical treatments, including the availability of

powerful antibiotics with which to treat bacterial infections. The other event that has made delirium less conspicuous is the availability of effective drugs to treat the delirious state itself when it arises, so that the symptoms rapidly subside. The drugs used for this are referred to as the *major tranquillisers*. The best-known of these is chlorpromazine (Largactil, Thorazine). When the delirious patient is given this his hallucinations tend to disappear, he is less worried about those that remain, he is able to sleep peacefully again and he is more rational when he is awake.

In the days before the introduction of this drug there was, in one large well-known hospital, a ward set aside especially to deal with patients who developed delirium in the course of their illnesses, or after their operations. It soon became clear that, with chlor-promazine, it was no longer necessary to transfer such patients. A doctor ringing up from another ward would be met with the message, 'Is our chlorpromazine any better than your chlor-promazine?' This particular ward is now used instead for treating a somewhat different problem, the numbers of which have been swelling in recent years—attempted suicide.

Chlorpromazine has the effect of reducing the blood pressure below its normal level, so that if the patient gets out of bed he may feel dizzy or fall down. There are now a variety of major tranquillisers to choose from as alternatives to chlorpromazine. At present the major tranquillisers are the preferred treatment in the management of delirium. As a rule more traditional sedatives, such as barbiturates, are avoided, since by diminishing consciousness still further they can make the patient even more confused.

There is at least one notable exception in which sedatives may be prescribed—this is where the delirium itself has been *caused* by the dose of sedative being reduced or abolished in an addict. It is reasonable in *delirium tremens*, therefore, to include large doses of a suitable sedative in the treatment regimen, reducing the dose gradually over the course of the following ten days or so. It will be recalled that a patient in the drug withdrawal state is liable to con-vulsions, so a suitable sedative to prescribe during the withdrawal phase is one that is itself used for treating epilepsy—phenobarbi-tone. This is all the more appropriate since one of the side effects of the major tranquillisers is a tendency to increase the risk of fits by a slight extent.

There is no reason why the patient with *delirium tremens* should not receive both major tranquillisers and phenobarbitone at the same time, but there have been recent claims that there is one group of drugs which can be used in place of the combination. This is the *benzodiazepine* group of drugs which includes chlordiazepoxide (Librium) and diazepam (Valium). These are normally used as minor tranquillisers in the treatment of neuroses, so it will be interesting to see if they do prove to be of value in this quite different condition.

Psychological management

We come now to the *psychological* management of delirium. It may or may not strike the reader as curious that there *is* a psychological management for such an organic condition as delirium, but there is. Indeed, before the advent of the major tranquillisers it was all that we had, but it remains important as an adjunct to treatment, especially while one is waiting for drug treatment to take effect, or if for some reason drug treatment is contraindicated.

It can be very frightening to realise, even dimly, that one has lost the powers of the mind, to think that others around do not understand how one is feeling, or to find it difficult to follow what is happening. A friend of mine had an attack of encephalitis, a brain infection caused by a virus, and after she recovered she was able to tell of the horror of not knowing what was going on. Disoriented in person, she would not know who it was coming through the door. Was it a friend, or a nurse, or even a relative? Someone would bring her a meal, and she would have no idea whether it was breakfast, lunch or supper.

What she found most reassuring was when the unknown person would identify himself, *e.g.* 'I am Dr. Smith' or 'I am Uncle John'. She was grateful to nurses who told her what meal it was that she was having. The principle, then, is that those around the delirious patient should try to imagine how it feels to be deprived of elementary brain function and to treat the patient accordingly. In part this means *supporting* the patient psychologically, providing crutches for the limping mental functions by giving information liberally and gratuitously. Information does not have to be limited to the word of mouth. A calendar and a clock should be prominently displayed. A small light should be left on during the hours of darkness. Although they may not be able to recognise where they are, at least they will be able to see what is around them.

Old persons are sometimes moved to a hospital or a different house when they are suffering from a 'confusional state'. This is often a necessary step, but it is a pity in a way because at home they at least have the familiarity of their surroundings to help them with their disability. It is doubly disturbing to be in a delirious state and in unfamiliar surroundings. It may be of some comfort to them to have, in addition to aids to orientation, some of their own belongings around them. The nightmarish quality of the experience may be reduced if they can see at least some things that they recognise.

Other psychological measures include sympathy, reassurance, encouragement, understanding and advice. The extent to which one uses these clearly depends on the circumstances and on the individual patient. What appears as welcome sympathy to one sick person may seem like cloying condescension to another. Here the art of interpersonal relations takes over from science. If the patient thinks that those around him understand how he feels, and are friendly towards him, then treatment has been effective.

SUMMARY

The acute organic brain syndrome is characterised by impaired consciousness and disorientation in time, place or person. In addition other florid psychiatric phenomena may occur, such as hallucinations (often visual), paranoid delusions or fear. *Delirium tremens* (or D.T.s) is one withdrawal syndrome that may follow addiction to alcohol or sleeping tablets. Modern findings of sleep research are marshalled to show how the features of D.T.s may be understood as a fluctuation between semi-consciousness and nightmares (excessive 'rapid eye movement' sleep). Other causes of delirium of quite different origin include atropine (a poisonous alkaloid found in deadly nightshade) and similar drugs, cerebral infarction and fever. Nowadays there are potent forms of treatment for delirium.

3 The dysmnestic syndrome

In common speech, the 'first sign' of failing intellectual faculties is memory impairment. In this chapter we take the absent-mindedness of everyday life and the common difficulty in remembering things (found by depressed patients) and we distinguish these features from the true signs of organic brain disease. We look at what is meant by 'registration', 'retention', 'recall', 'confabulation', 'beri-beri', 'pernicious anaemia' and the 'hippocampus'. We see more of the damage that chronic alcoholism can produce.

DEMONSTRABLE OBJECTIVE MEMORY LOSS

The *dysmnestic syndrome* is a condition in which the most important clinical factor is *demonstrable objective memory loss*.

Registration, retention and recall

As an isolated finding objective memory loss is uncommon. A *subjective* impression of difficulty with memory is quite common in patients with functional psychiatric illnesses. Foulds and Hope (1968) found a complaint of increasing 'absent-mindedness' among two-thirds of their patients with depressive illness. Nearly 10 per cent of their normal subjects also described this symptom. If such persons are given formal tests of their memory it will be found to be intact. The difficulty is similar to the complaint of physical tiredness which is found so often among depressed patients; they feel that it is a great effort to do anything. The problem with either physical or mental activity in depressive illness is that the patient has difficulty in getting going. Everything seems a great effort and too much trouble and there is no motivation or interest behind the activity. If subjects with the memory difficulties of depression can be persuaded to concentrate for the occasion (and usually they can), it is found that having taken in the information and learned it, it then sticks and they can repeat it again later if asked.

The usual terms for these processes are registration, retention and recall. Provided the concentration and attention can be summoned to *register* the data to be remembered, then the information is *retained* well and can be *recalled* on request.

Any or all of these stages can be impaired with organic brain disease, but in the particular case of the dysmnestic syndrome there is usually evidence of decreased retention of learned material. Some patients are so impaired in this way that nothing is retained longer than a minute.

Memory tests

It is not too difficult to design a simple test to assess a person's memory. There are a few important points to be kept in mind when doing so. A potential source of error is to ask the subject something that must then be verified through a third party. A doctor may ask an ageing patient, 'What did you have for breakfast this morning?' After what seems like an appropriate degree of hesitation the patient will reply, say, 'scrambled eggs'. The doctor then goes to the ward sister and asks her what in fact the patient had. The ward sister may tell him that the patient had kippered herrings. This could then be entered in the patient's notes as evidence of impaired memory. Possibly, special investigations are set in motion to look for evidence of brain disease in that patient—and such investigations are often expensive and not always without danger to the patient.

A few days later, in our imaginary situation, the ward sister will say, 'By the way—you were asking about what Mrs. Jones had for breakfast the other day. I realise now that she would not have had the usual breakfast because she is on a special diet. She had scrambled eggs that day'.

The way to avoid such mistakes is to base one's judgment of memory on a shared experience. If you and the patient were both there at the time then you know what the facts were. It is even better if you write them down, thus avoiding the distortions of your own memory process. A relatively simple way of doing this is to make up a fictitious name and address for the subject to memorise. Tell him that you are going to give him a name and address to remember, and to repeat each one after you. It is permissible to make the name and address quite a full one—it is surprising how much the individual with an intact memory can register when he tries under these circumstances.

When you have been through the whole address make sure he has registered it by asking him to repeat it immediately. If he is not absolutely correct, repeat the whole procedure (with the same address) up to three times, say, to ensure that registration has been carried out as thoroughly as possible. Make a note of the time.

Then talk about something else for 10 minutes or longer, and at a suitable time in the conversation go back to the memory test and ask him to recall it (making a note of the time again).

A record of the testing might look like this:

REGISTRATION	1st trial	2nd trial	3rd trial
Mr. D. E. French	French	Mr. D. French	Mr. D. E. French
39 Green Street	Green Street	Green Street	39 Green Street
East Finchley	East—	East Finchley	East Finchley
London N20 32W	London N20	London N20 32W	London N20 32W

Completed 11.08 a.m.

RECALL (11.21 a.m.)
Mr. D. French
39 Green Street
East Finchley
London N20 32W

If you practise this test on enough persons you will get an idea of what sort of results you can expect under different circumstances. There are no absolute 'normal values'—the results depend on the intelligence of the subject, his emotional state at the time, his motivation to cooperate and the degree to which he attended and concentrated. If there is any doubt that the memory is impaired after doing the test, the record as set out above is a permanent reminder of how he performed on that occasion, and can be used as a base line against which to compare future test results.

In severe memory disorder the name and address is not remembered at all. In moderately severe dysmnesia only one or two fragments of the address are recalled. In transient emotional states the impairment may be present on one occasion and absent on the next.

Disorientation in time
Those who suffer from demonstrable objective memory loss also tend to have one other obvious disability. They are disoriented in time. If asked, they have difficulty in telling the time of day without reference to a clock or watch. Unless they have a newspaper or calendar in their range of vision they find it difficult to state the date or the day of the week. It is understandable that this should be the case. It is probable that we normally orient ourselves in time by identifying a recent event and estimating the time that has since elapsed.

'I had lunch', you might say to yourself, 'and then I had to listen to so-and-so for what seemed an age, but for what was probably only an hour. Then I picked up this book and started reading it, and possibly another hour has gone by. The time now must be about 3.30 p.m.' It is clear that by this technique it will be impossible for you to have any idea of the time if you cannot remember anything that happened as little as 10 minutes ago.

The features of (a) memory loss and (b) disorientation in time are central to the dysmnestic syndrome. They were described by the Russian physician Korsakov, and this syndrome is often referred to as 'Korsakov's psychosis'. In the full-blown state this also shows the two other features that Korsakov described, that is to say confabulation and peripheral neuropathy.

Confabulation
The confabulation is compensatory. It is the making up of tales to fill in the blank spots in the memory. If the patient is asked what happened earlier that day, or the day before, he may launch into a

fictitious account rather than confess that he cannot remember. The tale that he produces may or may not be plausible. Sometimes it is rather dull and prosaic, at other times it is colourful and imaginative or it may be wild and clearly impossible.

When students see a dysmnestic patient it is often the confabulation that most clearly sticks in their minds afterwards. In a sense, however, it is one of the least important clinical findings. It is of little diagnostic importance, since you do not get confabulation unless there is a clear-cut memory impairment to start with, and it seems to carry no implications for treatment or management.

The reason why some patients confabulate and others do not probably lies with their previous personality. It is a matter of common observation that normal persons will not always say 'I don't know' when asked a question to which they do not have the answer. To take the man in the street (quite literally), one finds this when asking directions. Go to an urban centre and ask the way to a large public building. If we assume that the majority of the milling crowd have heard of it, but that few will be absolutely sure of its exact situation, then the answers will be of two sorts if we ask how to get there. Some respondents will answer frankly, and possibly apologetically, that they do not know. Others will happily volunteer directions which are, taken overall, fairly random, so that after a time one ends up having been advised to go towards a large variety of points of the compass. Why do they do it? One can only guess, but two reasons suggest themselves. To put a generous interpretation on it, the respondent giving the random directions thinks, 'Now, where is it? I'm sure I have an idea. What a shame if I gave him no help at all. I'm sure I at least know the general direction. I'll tell him where I *think* it is', and replies confidently with the feeling that he is doing his best to help. The less generous interpretation is that the respondent does not want to look foolish and stupid by saying he does not know at all, and so gives a fictitious reply to save face.

So, to return to our case of Korsakov's psychosis, the fact that a patient shows confabulation does not tell us much about the nature of his *illness*, although it may indicate something about his underlying *personality*.

Peripheral neuropathy

We come now to the fourth feature that Korsakov described—the *peripheral neuropathy*. This, if present, does tell us something about the nature of the illness. The term 'peripheral neuropathy' means that there is damage to the peripheral nerves of the body, in contrast to the brain and spinal cord (which in turn are referred to as the 'central nervous system'). One cause of Korsakov's psychosis is deficiency of a vitamin of the B group, vitamin B_1 (also known as 'thiamine' or 'aneurine'). This is essential for the health of neurones in the peripheral nervous system as well as the cells in the brain. If there is a deficiency of this vitamin, then both types of nerve cell may become affected.

By contrast, if the disease is limited to one part of the nervous system the clinical picture will be different. It is possible for the dysmnestic syndrome to be caused by a lesion that is confined to the brain. For instance, a primary tumour of the brain may be responsible. In this type of disease one will *not* find the peripheral nerves affected.

CAUSES OF THE DYSMNESTIC SYNDROME

Thiamine deficiency

We have just considered vitamin deficiency as a cause of the dysmnestic syndrome, and in particular deficiency of thiamine (vitamin B_1). Alcoholism is one of the most prominent reasons for developing thiamine deficiency, partly because alcoholism is a common disease, and partly because alcoholism can contribute towards thiamine deficiency in various ways. For a start, alcoholics often neglect their diet, and there is not much thiamine in whisky or gin. Secondly, alcoholic beverages may damage the lining of the stomach, and the chronic gastritis that ensues is not likely to improve their digestion.

However much these two factors contribute, there seems little doubt that the alcoholic is more likely to show evidence of thiamine deficiency than a person on a starvation diet. This is probably because of the third factor, the effect of alcohol on the metabolism. Thiamine is required for the chemical processes in the body in which carbohydrates are 'burned up' to provide energy. The person on a starvation diet is not taking in carbohydrate, and so needs less thiamine. It appears that alcohol is treated by the body like a carbohydrate and consumes what thiamine stores there are in the body as it is burned up itself. In this way thiamine deficiency is precipitated much sooner in alcoholism than in starvation.

Alcoholism is not the only cause of thiamine deficiency, and in this country starvation is rare. Other possible causes of thiamine deficiency are cancer of the stomach, and prolonged vomiting. Both of these were present among the cases that Korsakov described. The prolonged vomiting was associated with pregnancy in his original case, but nowadays this is more easily brought under control with the use of anti-emetic drugs.

In countries where gross malnutrition occurs more frequently, thiamine deficiency is the the cause of the disease known as *beri beri*. This takes one of two forms, wet and dry. The dry form is the one in which the neurones are affected. In the wet form the heart is affected first, and the distension of the tissues of the body with fluid as a result is the reason why it is called 'wet'. It is known that alcoholics can develop heart disease but it is not clear what part thiamine deficiency plays in this. Any alcohol we take makes our hearts pump less efficiently for a while, but most of us have a reserve of sufficient working that protects us from overt ill effect.

Cyanocobalamin deficiency

The dysmnestic syndrome may be caused by deficiency of another well-known member of the B group, vitamin B_{12} (cyanocobalamin). The most well-known medical condition that is caused by lack of this vitamin is *pernicious anaemia*. In this condition the stomach and intestine fail to absorb in adequate quantities the vitamin B_{12} that occurs naturally in the diet. The deficiency of the vitamin in the tissues of the body usually makes its mark most obviously on the blood-forming bone marrow, with the consequence that anaemia results. It is a very special type of anaemia in that under the microscope many of the red blood cells can be seen to be *larger* than normal. There are just too few of them to carry the haemoglobin round the body in adequate quantities.

It has been known for many years that patients with inadequately treated pernicious anaemia might develop a disease of the central nervous system known as 'subacute degeneration of the cord' in which there would be evidence of patches of disease in parts of the spinal cord. Until recent years it was fairly common to come across patients who had been inadequately treated. At present the treatment is to have an injection of vitamin B_{12} every two weeks or so, and most patients are able to steel themselves to this. In the past the treatment was to give enormous quantities of vitamin B_{12} by mouth, from natural sources. One of the few natural sources to have large quantities of B_{12} is animal liver. Vitamin B_{12} is destroyed by cooking. The result was that the health of the patient with pernicious anaemia would be maintained only if they were willing to eat large quantities of raw liver per day. Inadequate treatment was often the predictable result.

Deficiency of B_{12} may also cause impaired action of the peripheral nerves. This may show itself in tinglings, numbness and loss of sensation if the sensory nerves are affected, or as weakness and even paralysis if the motor nerves are involved. In either case the reflexes may be found to be diminished when the patient is examined. Thus, deficiency of vitamin B_{12}, like deficiency of vitamin B_1, can cause peripheral neuropathy.

In general, if a patient suffers from deficiency of vitamin B_{12} the anaemia is the first effect of this to come to notice, and it is usually not until later in the course of the untreated disease that we find developing the neurological complications of subacute combined degeneration of the cord or of peripheral neuropathy. It appears that in most people the blood-forming (haematopoietic) tissues are more dependent on vitamin B_{12} than the nervous tissues, but occasionally one does see a patient in whom the neurological effects are present without anaemia.

It is now known that the neurological effects are not limited to the spinal cord and the peripheral nerves. Disease of the brain itself may also result from deficiency of this vitamin, and the dysmnestic syndrome is one form that it takes.

Since one also frequently finds peripheral neuropathy, the clinical picture can be similar to that described by Korsakov in cases of vitamin B_1 deficiency. The typical anaemia will usually be present as well, but whether it is or not, it is now possible to measure the level of vitamin B_{12} in the blood to confirm the cause of the clinical features.

This is an important diagnosis to make for at least two reasons.

Firstly, the treatment is simple and safe—giving vitamin B_{12}. The vitamin itself does not appear to be dangerous, even in large quantities. At present it is usually recommended that it should be given by injection, but it is possible that an acceptable oral form will be developed in the future. Here we have a treatment which is not likely to prove worse than the disease as far as the patient is concerned. (By contrast, discovering a brain tumour is not necessarily going to prove a therapeutic triumph. It may prove necessary to take away parts of the normal brain, leaving a further disability, in order to remove the tumour.)

Secondly it is important to make the diagnosis because early treatment counts. If the diagnosis is not made until the neurones have died off, then full recovery is not possible since neurones in the central nervous system are not replaceable. If the diagnosis is made earlier in the disease while the vitamin-deprived neurones are merely sick and ailing, then clearly they can recover. The picture just painted is perhaps a little too black and white, since although neurone regeneration does not occur after cell death, the brain can sometimes in time learn to compensate (presumably by other neurones taking over a different function). However, there are limits to this sort of adaptation and the principle remains that early diagnosis is of great importance.

A third reason why it is important to think of the diagnosis is that the investigation of the patient is relatively safe and simple. Although this is perhaps not as crucial as the other two reasons given above, it should be borne in mind that some investigations themselves carry a risk of complications, whereas here the main requirement is merely a sample of blood for the estimation of the vitamin B_{12} level.

Infection

So far we have considered two types of vitamin deficiency as causes of the dysmnestic syndrome. Quite a different type of cause is found in *infection*. If the brain is permanently damaged as a result of encephalitis, perhaps itself caused by a virus infection, then the dysmnestic syndrome may result. Why should memory be picked out to suffer, rather than any of the other intellectual functions? The answer to this lies in the anatomy of the human brain.

The reader will recall that the brain is split symmetrically into a right and a left hemisphere, and that, looking from the side, each hemisphere has the appearance shown in Fig. 11. The anatomy of the brain is quite complex and difficult to visualise, but each hemisphere may be thought of simply as a sausage-shaped structure bent in half. Try looking at Fig. 11 again from this point of view.

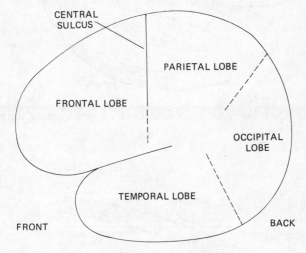

Fig. 11. Lobes of the brain, left side.

The sausage has a rather thick skin—the grey matter or *cortex* (containing the cell bodies of the neurones). The bulk of the sausage is composed of the white matter or *medulla* (containing the connecting strands that link the neurones—the *axons* and *dendrons*). The sausage is of rather poor quality because it has a central cavity (the *ventricle*) filled with fluid (*cerebrospinal fluid*). The result is shown diagrammatically in Fig. 12.

Sometimes it is necessary to remove the temporal lobe, or part of it, in the course of treatment of a patient who has disease there. If this is done it is found that, as a rule, a patient who has had such an operation on one side can still remember things satisfactorily afterwards—because he is still 'ticking over on one cylinder', so to speak. Removal of both temporal lobes is more serious, and is

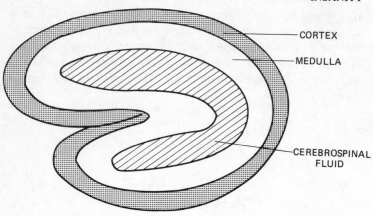

Fig. 12. Diagrammatic section through one hemisphere of the brain.

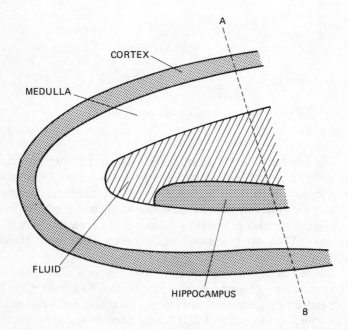

Fig. 13. Diagram of anterior part of temporal lobe shown from the side (in section).

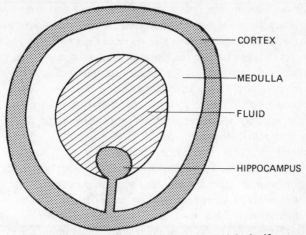

Fig. 14. Diagrammatic cross-section through temporal lobe (as if cut across A–B in Fig. 13).

likely to cause severe and permanent impairment of memory function because the mass of grey matter known as the hippocampus is an essential part of the 'limbic system', that part of the brain concerned with memory (*see* Figs. 13 and 14).

When a patient has encephalitis the brain becomes swollen with the inflammation, but since it is encased in the rigid bony box of the cranium there is little room for expansion. Under these circumstances it tends to squeeze out its own blood supply. The temporal lobes are thought to have a more marginal blood supply than other parts of the brain, and whether for this reason or some other, when permanent damage occurs to the brain in encephalitis it is often the temporal lobes that suffer. If this happens to both temporal lobes, then the dysmnestic syndrome is the outcome.

The clinical picture that results will include the memory defect itself, disorientation in time, and possibly confabulation. It will not include peripheral neuropathy, in contrast to the typical dysmnestic syndrome produced by deficiency of vitamins B_1 or B_{12}.

Other diseases causing the dysmnestic syndrome
Objective difficulty with memory function may result from almost any disease of the brain that affects the *hippocampi* or other parts of the limbic system. A tumour that impinges on the central con-

nections of the limbic system may do it. The tumour may be one that arises from the brain tissue itself (a primary tumour). Alternatively, a cancerous growth elsewhere in the body may allow tiny particles to break off into the blood stream and resume their growth in other parts of the body (secondary tumours). Such secondaries are often multiple and, although memory disorder is likely to be conspicuous if the limbic system is affected, further investigation of the patient may show impaired action of other parts of the brain from secondaries lodged there.

Infections other than virus encephalitis may interfere with memory processes. Tuberculosis and syphilis can both end up by causing brain disease, but both are becoming rarer with the advent of more effective treatment in their early stages of each disease. Psychiatric in-patients are still often tested routinely for syphilis; although positive results from the test are uncommon, for the price of a simple blood test one may discover a readily treatable cause for the patient's illness.

Other diseases of the brain that cause *widespread* damage may first show themselves by producing objective memory disorder. Senile brain disease and arteriosclerotic brain disease, both usually occurring only in old age, are notable examples. Persons who have repeated trauma to the head include both the 'punch-drunk' boxer and some poorly-controlled epileptics who have on many occasions injured themselves during a fit. Again, the subject will often have his memory conspicuously impaired, although special forms of testing may reveal more widespread cerebral injury.

EFFECTS ON THE INDIVIDUAL OF THE DYSMNESTIC SYNDROME

Memory disorders

In minor degrees of organic memory impairment the effects on the individual concerned can be quite similar to the memory difficulties subjectively experienced by patients with functional psychiatric states such as depressive illness. In fact, they are similar to the memory difficulties that many normal persons have from time to time. They will forget where they put things and have to spend a lot of time searching for them. They will forget the names of acquaintances, or of objects that are slightly out of the ordinary. They will go into a room and forget why they went there. I think it can be seen that these experiences are not uncommon in the general population, and the individual with a mild dysmnestic state may demonstrate his memory disorder merely in the excessive degree to which he gets these problems. Where the normal individual may have such lapses occasionally, the dysmnestic patient will get them frequently. Moreover, he may get them with *increasing* frequency, and at a rate which is much higher than he has ever had in the past.

Even at this stage the person whose memory difficulties are caused by organic brain disease is likely to be demonstrably impaired on objective tests of memory. Exceptions may occur when the person previously had much above average ability intellectually. Most tests of intellectual function rely on comparing the results with expected norms from the population—on the results of the *average* person. If the patient was a good deal above average to start with, then his disease may merely have brought him into the normal range.

There are ways around this limitation of tests. The most reliable is probably re-testing the individual at intervals. With progressive brain disease his performances will be seen to fall; here the subject is being used as his own norm or 'control'.

At an early stage of the dysmnestic syndrome, then, the patient will have sporadic difficulties with recalling names and recent actions very similar to the effects of failing to attend to or register the event or name in the first place. Later these lapses of memory become more frequent, so that the afflicted patient has to write down anything he wishes to be sure of remembering. Shopping lists become essential, even for two or three articles. The patient carries a notebook for noting down anything he may have to recall later.

In the most severe cases life becomes very difficult unaided. The patient will have difficulty in recalling if he has had lunch or tea, and may go into the same restaurant twice or even three times for the same meal.

At this stage especially, the patient will have trouble with disorientation in time. If he has forgotten everything that has happened more than 10 minutes ago he will not be aware of the time of day unless he looks at his watch every few minutes or unless by chance some key event has taken place within his short time span for memory. For the same sort of reason he will find it difficult to remain aware of the date and the day of the week.

Emotional effects
So far we have considered the effects on the individual in a logical way as if he were some cold, calculating robot. We have argued that if he shows a certain degree of defect, he will be able to do certain things but unable to do others. What we have not yet taken into account is the emotional effect of the disability on the patient. How does it feel to have a memory defect?

Anxiety
It is likely to be very worrying. Some readers of this book may be afflicted themselves, and I was conscious of this when talking about such experiences as forgetting where one had put things, or having difficulty in recalling names. How many readers will now start to feel concerned that they may have early brain disease? I did not enjoy putting you in this anxious position. Such worrying thoughts are part of the process of concerning onself with disease process and illness, and difficult to avoid. Although this may not be exactly what Alexander Pope was thinking of, we would probably agree that 'a little learning is a dangerous thing'. If it is any consolation it is probably true that a prolonged contact with the facts of illness will not make one even more worried. It enables one to deal with one's own ill-health (or fears of it) in a more appropriate way on the whole, and may even help to prevent groundless preoccupation with possibilities of ill-health.

The point of this aside was to draw attention to the anxiety that many people experience when they wonder if their memory is impaired. For many, if not most, human beings one of the worst fates to contemplate is losing one's mental faculties, and loss of memory is commonly regarded as one of the 'first signs' that this is occurring. What horror, then, must strike the heart of the person who feels this is really happening to him.

Denial
Some will react stoically to memory impairment, others develop an anxiety state, hysteria, or a depressive illness. Others put the whole

affair out of their mind or deny that it is a possibility. We are all prone to use methods of protecting our self-esteem when reality becomes threatening, and one of these *ego defence mechanisms* is the one known as *denial*. Although primitive, this works. So long as no one is unkind enough to break down one's defence, one can remain happy and go about one's daily activities in the usual way. In the case in point, the patient cheerfully refuses to acknowledge any memory difficulty that may be obvious to all around him, and if anybody points out the consequent errors or omissions to him the afflicted person will metaphorically look the other way and still avoid seeing them.

This method of preserving equanimity is obviously threatened when a psychiatrist or psychologist tries to perform searching tests of memory function on the patient. The patient may then become defensive and unco-operative, and refuse to have any truck with such tests. If he can be persuaded to co-operate, then as his deficiencies are revealed unequivocally he may break down into tears or panic. The clinician is obviously put in an unpleasant quandary in this situation. Should the tester respect the patient's vulnerability and proceed on the unproved assumption that he has objective memory disorder? Often there is no easy answer to this question. Clearly, if one decides to proceed and test the memory thoroughly then this should be done in an as expeditious way as is possible, allowing the patient to restore his defence again as soon as he can.

While the protective value of such massive denial is obvious, this particular defence mechanism is not very adaptable. For instance, it is likely to be incompatible with taking such action as using shopping lists and notebooks to record items that may be forgotten. The result is that the patient becomes unreliable at a much earlier stage of the memory disorder than is necessary. He may, by denying his disorder, lose his job when a tolerant employer would have kept him on if he had been prepared to guard against lapses of memory by writing things down (or dictating them onto a tape recorder).

Rationalisation
There are other ways of protecting oneself from the full brunt of the significance of the disease. In *rationalisation* the patient may tell himself that he is having difficulty with his memory because he has

been tired and run down recently, and his concentration is not very good. This mechanism has the advantage that the subject does not have to go to such lengths to avoid reality, and he can even take steps to support his mental function by various aids 'until he is over this bad patch'.

Attempts to remove defence mechanisms

There is obviously a great temptation to try to persuade a patient to give up a crude mechanism like denial, at least in favour of a slightly more realistic one such as rationalisation. However, such attempts are fraught with danger, and often the patient's choice of defence mechanism depends on fundamental features of his personality or environment which are not always easy to appreciate and may anyway be impossible to change.

The dangers of such attempts to remove or change defence mechanisms are not just that anxiety or depression may be engendered. They may result in the patient becoming delusional and developing other features of functional psychosis.

In many cases there is little advantage to be accrued from enabling the patient to achieve insight into his disability, and it is reasonable to leave his defences intact. If such insight seems to be of important potential value to him, then it is permissible for the therapist to see what happens when gentle efforts are made in that direction.

To set about this, it may be unnecessary to challenge the patient directly by suggesting to him that he has a memory defect. Clearly, the patient already feels vulnerable on this score, or he would not need a defence. A more subtle, and certainly safer, method of approach is to get him to talk about his work, for instance. At this stage comments from the therapist would be confined to remarks designed to encourage a further flow of talk by the patient if he was in danger of drying up. In this way the patient is given the opportunity of talking about his problems when he feels ready to do so, without being forced to do so, and therefore without being forced to deny them. Early references to his defect are likely to be oblique and tentative, and should be met with reassurance, advice and sympathy (equally tentative and suitably phrased so that they do not focus down on memory faster than the patient would wish). If the aim is eventually to encourage rationalisation as a method of defence, then rationalisations may be offered by the therapist at intervals to see which (if any) ring any bells with the patient. In general, one should avoid catastrophic premature confrontation, the aim being to enable the patient to set his own pace, and to achieve change in his own time and his own manner, if at all.

REACTION OF FRIENDS AND RELATIVES

The emotional effects of the early evidence of memory disorder on those around the patient may at first be very similar to those on the patient himself. They may be horrified at the idea that their nearest and dearest, their breadwinner or their trusty colleague, is suffering from a progressive deterioration in his mental faculties.

Spouses with loving feelings

Friends and relatives may react with anxiety, depression or denial. On the whole, their reaction will be milder and shorter-lived than that of the patient, but this is not necessarily true, especially in the case of the spouse for whom the realisation may be disastrous. The precise feelings of the husband or wife will depend on his or her own personality, and on their precise relationship with the patient. If their relationship has been good, and particularly if they lean heavily on one another for emotional and material support, then the reaction of the partner will be one of grief, sadness and a sense of great loss. It will be similar to the feelings in bereavement by death, on the one hand mitigated by the fact that their partner is not actually dead, but on the other hand worse because of the continual reminder of the cause of the sorrow.

Spouses with ambivalent feelings

If their relationship has been very ambivalent, a mixture of love and hate in nearly equal proportions, then depression may also ensue. This type of depression is rather special. There is a tendency for the husband or wife to grieve, as in the previous case, and there is a tendency for the hostility towards the patient to be bottled up, and turned inwards towards the spouse himself. How can you hate someone who has become weak and vulnerable, without losing your own self-esteem? The marriage partner who has simply suffered the loss of a loved one can weep and allow his thoughts to dwell on the memory of the deceased, and thus work through his feelings in an appropriate way, eventually bringing the mourning process to a conclusion over time. This process is, to some extent at least, available to the first case. In the second case, the spouse with ambivalent feelings finds it difficult to weep over the loss and let his feelings rise up to the surface, because this means giving free vent to the hostile feelings as well as the positive ones. If we take into account the difficulty that we have in our culture with acknowledging our hostile feelings, we can see that this may be turned back in on the spouse himself, producing guilt, self-criticism and further depression.

Spouses with negative feelings

This description is a necessarily over-simplified account of a general case and the reality is clearly a complicated story. To complete the picture with the third and last case—that of the spouse who has entirely negative feelings towards the patient—the tale is much more simple. Let us take the case where the feelings of the husband towards his wife, before she developed her dysmnestic syndrome, were those of hate, despite and disdain. When she develops her illness, his reaction is less complicated—she becomes an irritation and a nuisance, and is now worthless to him. His impulse is thus to get rid of her, to send her to a mental hospital perhaps, and to have as little as possible to do with her.

Social implications

I have been at some pains to describe the emotional reaction of the relative of the patient before coming down to practical details, because the reaction governs to a great extent the social implications of the patient's defect.

Consider what happens when a woman, suffering from memory failure, is having difficulty coping with her work as a housewife. She will have problems in remembering which articles she has to buy in the shop, she will forget to turn the gas off under the kettle, parts of the house will go neglected and there will be meals that she forgets to prepare. Whether this proves insurmountable will depend upon what support she can get from her family. If her husband is tolerant and patient, he will help her prepare a shopping list, avoid destructive criticism for chores that she neglects, accept the occasional empty meal table philosophically, and perhaps buy an automatic kettle that switches itself off. He may even allow his mother-in-law or another relative to live with them after resisting such a move for years—then at least there will be someone around to turn off the gas when the food is in danger of burning. A variety of other ways of coping with the situation will occur to the reader.

The hostile husband will act in a rejecting and intolerant way, and the dispirited wife will not have the motivation to do even those things that she should be capable of doing.

Case 2

At the time of her illness the patient was in her late 30s. After leaving school she had worked as a cashier, and she married at about the age of 30. Her parents had both died before her illness began.

She was admitted to a general hospital with fever, headache, convulsions and later unconsciousness, and encephalitis was diagnosed. Ten days later psychological examination showed a severe memory defect—she was able to retain information for less than a minute. She was confused and unable to deal with any intelligence test that demanded immediate intellectual effort. There were gross abnormalities on the electro-encephalogram (E.E.G.).

A week after this she was transferred to a mental hospital. After two months the E.E.G. had improved, and she was able to perform such arithmetical tasks as substracting seven from one hundred accurately, but was unable to give the name for a watch correctly.

After a year had elapsed her main problem was with memory for recent events, and she was disoriented in time. From then on the picture did not change very much. If she was given a name and address to remember, she had great difficulty in registering the name and address to start with, and recalled only fragments of it 10 minutes later. In spite of her severe memory impairment, she was still able to double the number 96 correctly, and sometimes even to double the number 192. (This is part of a test in which the patient is asked to double three, then to double six, and so on until he fails with two consecutive errors.) Her success in this test might be related to her previous occupation as a cashier.

When asked something that she could not remember she would usually say that she did not know, but would sometimes make up the answer. Even 5 years later she would still give her age as the age when she first became ill.

She remained in the mental hospital over these 5 years and was rarely visited by her husband. He never took her out for the day. On a few occasions (at the suggestion of the hospital staff) he took her home for the weekend, but he then complained that she could not cope.

At the end of the 5 years he appeared at the hospital to ask for a medical report on his wife in connection with a divorce. At that time (before the present legislation was in force) a divorce was likely to be granted if the patient had been a hospital in-patient continuously for 5 years, and a 'cure' was not envisaged. He had not been to the hospital for $2\frac{1}{2}$ years. When asked what the problem was about having her home, he said that when she was there she was restless, she turned the gas on without lighting it, and he was afraid that she might wander from the house.

In due course he obtained his divorce, and the patient remains in hospital to this day. Whether he was right or wrong in the course he took is not the point at issue here—there are clearly two sides to such a question. The point is that with a different attitude on his part quite a different practical outcome might have resulted.

Another factor that was loaded against this particular patient's discharge was the sudden onset of her illness. Many patients, often later in life, with a gradual onset of memory impairment are able to cope as long as they remain in their own familiar surroundings, where they are supported by familiarity and years of habit in their daily routine, and can rely on many subtle cues to tell them what otherwise they would have forgotten. The habitual and rigid patterns of behaviour act as a crutch to the patient as long as a disruption of the living pattern can be avoided. This is the sort of patient one should avoid hospitalising as far as possible, even for a short time, since it may destroy an ability to cope that is based on a precarious level of current mental functioning.

Fortunately, it is rare for a person to develop a severe memory disorder at a young age. Objective memory loss is much more often seen as an accompaniment of the brain diseases of later life that will be considered in the next chapter—in other words the dysmnestic syndrome is not so often seen in the pure state as it is when forming part of a larger picture.

SUMMARY

Subjective difficulty with memory is found with functional conditions such as depression. If the material can be adequately registered then objective impairment of retention is indicative of organic brain disease. The other major feature of the dysmnestic syndrome is disorientation in time. This may be produced by vitamin deficiency (as in alcoholism) or by physical trauma (*e.g.* being 'punch-drunk').

The *psychological* effect of losing one's memory is considered as it affects the feelings of the patient himself and his relatives. If the patient can be supported in his familiar environment then he may continue to live in the community even with a profound memory loss. This job is made harder when the patient denies his disability.

4 The chronic organic brain syndrome

Many new technical terms are now introduced and at the end of this chapter you will find a miniature index listing these terms. You can glance at it now to see some of the subjects that will be covered and the list may save time if you wish to refresh your memory as you work through the chapter. For instance, the déjà vu phenomenon is covered in the first half of the chapter on pp. 73–4; if by the time you are reading the second half of the chapter you have forgotten what déjà vu is, you can turn to the chapter index quickly to remind yourself where it is defined. This may be quicker than going through the full index at the back of the book.

DEMENTIA

The *chronic organic brain syndrome* is a term used to describe the clinical picture that results when there is a disease causing general impairment of intellectual abilities, an impairment that is by definition of a long standing nature and that is often progressive and irreversible.

Generalised and permant impairment of intellect has now tended to become synonymous with the term *dementia*. This term used to be used for even a temporary loss of use of mental function—in lay speech people are still said to be 'demented' with worry. Certainly patients with depressive illness will complain of problems with attention, concentration and memory. These complaints are not only complaints of subjective *difficulty* rather than of complete objective *inability* on these tasks, they are also features that clear up as the depressive illness improves.

The term 'dementia' does still linger on in one non-organic area, and that is schizophrenia. Patients with severe and chronic unremitting schizophrenic illness who are completely unable to live an independent life are still sometimes referred to as suffering from 'schizophrenic dementia'. This is despite the fact that one assumes that their faculties are lying dormant rather than destroyed, for one can see some such cases cured or substantially relieved after years like this, with a prompt return of their mental abilities. When a schizophrenic patient comes out of his inaccessible state it may be obvious that he had been mentally alert during that time, and can remember clearly what happened to him.

The particular term 'schizophrenic dementia' does not, then, imply that the intellectual faculties are lost forever, but in general if a psychiatrist uses the term 'dementia' without any qualification this is a brief term implying that the patient has a chronic organic brain syndrome.

It has been estimated that possibly as many as one in ten of the population over the age of sixty-five suffer from some degree of organic brain disease. This may be caused either by a condition known as *senile dementia* (with its own characteristic microscopic appearance in the brain) or by arteriosclerotic brain disease. If arteriosclerosis affects the blood vessels supplying the brain, then the patient may on the one hand develop a paralysis or stroke, or on the other hand it may be the mind that is affected (or possibly both). The two diseases of senile dementia and arteriosclerotic dementia are in practice difficult to distinguish from one another in life, and between them they account for the majority of the demented elderly to be found in mental hospitals.

In the final stages of dementia the patient loses every intellectual function. He is unable to wash himself or even feed himself. He is unable to walk and may be bedfast. He is incontinent of both urine and faeces. It can be seen that he is virtually back to the earlier stage of infancy, before he has learned to walk or talk or to control his bladder and bowel.

CLINICAL FEATURES OF DEMENTIA

The clinical features of a person with chronic organic brain disease
may include:

Impaired intellectual function

This may be at any stage from the most advanced that has just
been described, to the mildest change that will be noticed only by
the patient's closest relatives or by the patient himself. Impaired intellectual function may take the form of difficulty in understanding
what is said to him, difficulty in making logical use of the information when he has understood it, or difficulty in expressing himself.
The affected person may find it a problem to give the correct
change, or to perform other financial transactions or arithmetical
calculations. He may have lost his sense of direction and be unable
to find his way around, or he may be *disoriented in place* and not
know whether he is in hospital or at home. He may not be able to
distinguish right from left, or to give the right name for common
objects when they are shown to him.

The evidence of impaired intellectual function may be more
subtle than this and take the form of a change in *personality*. He may
start to do things that are quite out of character (although not particularly abnormal in themselves). He may become more violent. In
one patient, a woman, one of the earliest signs of her dementing
process was that in bed at night she would start beating her husband on
his back with her fists for no obvious reason (but clearly it was not
possible to make the diagnosis of organic brain disease from this
feature alone).

Often the out-of-character behaviour would be considered inappropriate in any case, as with the chauffeur who deliberately drives
the wrong way down a one-way street, or the company chairman
who starts to make obscene remarks during the board meeting.
Such behaviour is often uninhibited and the norms of polite society
are flouted in a way that suggests a loss of the highest critical
faculties. One patient with organic brain disease tried to make his
wife have sexual intercourse with him in front of their children.
Another may become callous and indifferent. Sometimes the
changes may be rather negative and less spectacular—the patient
losing his drive and initiative and becoming content with a
vegetable-like existence.

Memory impairment

In addition to the feature of impaired intellectual function described above, the patient may develop memory impairment. He does not necessarily do so, particularly in the early stages, so that the presence of an intact memory does not exclude the possibility of widespread organic brain disease. Nevertheless, memory impairment is a very common accompaniment of dementia, so much so that the stereotype of the patient with senile changes in the brain is probably that of an old lady who can no longer remember things.

The patient will be suffering from the features of the dysmnestic syndrome described in the previous chapter. If the central defect of memory is at all severe then it is likely to be accompanied by disorientation in time. If the patient is asked something, and he has forgotten the answer, then he will either say 'I don't know' or he will make up a fictitious answer (confabulation). Whether he does one or the other probably depends on his underlying personality. Thus the patient may show three of the features that are common in dysmnestic states—objective memory impairment, disorientation in time and confabulation. Whether he shows the fourth feature described by Korsakov—peripheral neuropathy—depends on the cause of the dementia. If it is one that threatens the health of the peripheral nerves as well as that of the brain, then peripheral neuropathy may be found too. In the commoner conditions of senile dementia and arteriosclerotic dementia peripheral neuropathy is not an expected accompaniment.

Diminution of awareness and disorientation

The third group of features that are likely to be associated with the chronic organic brain syndrome are those of the acute organic brain syndrome. These are:

1. Diminution of awareness; and
2. disorientation in time, place and person.

To suggest that the features of dementia include those of delirium may sound paradoxical at first, but it can easily be seen that it is true. A patient with dementia may lose his grasp on what is taking place and fail to appreciate the significance of what is going on in his immediate environment. Just as he may be unable to understand the meaning of what is said to him, so too he may be unable to perceive the implications of what he sees.

However, dementia does not necessarily include delirious features in the early stages: orientation and grasp may remain intact for a while even though the other features described above may be developing. Certainly the reverse is not true—by definition the acute organic brain syndrome does not involve a progressive and permanent loss of intellectual function.

Symptoms found in functional psychiatric states

By now I expect that the reader will have been able to predict one other group of features of the chronic organic brain syndrome—the patient may develop any symptom found in the *functional* psychiatric states.

Case 3

A middle-aged woman developed a paranoid psychosis, for which she was admitted to hospital. Routine investigations revealed an abnormal chest X-ray and she was found to have lung cancer. (She had smoked fifty cigarettes a day for many years.) The psychiatric picture was caused by multiple secondary deposits of growth in the brain.

Case 4

An elderly man was admitted with a classical history of depressive illness. He was found to have been living in squalor: his wife may have been schizophrenic, though this was never proved (he said that she walked round the house talking to herself). In these circumstances the only wonder when he was admitted was that he had not become depressed years earlier. Treatment failed to clear up his depression, and gradually it became obvious that he was finding difficulty in making himself understood. Slowly, further signs of organic impairment developed and it was not long before he died. Autopsy showed a large tumour on the left side of his brain.

It would be wrong to give the impression that all, or even most, patients with organic brain disease are as difficult to diagnose as those in the above two cases. The majority are fairly straightforward, at least by the time they come to the attention of the psychiatrist.

Case 5

Mrs. O. B. presented to the psychiatric clinic complaining of a memory deficit for recent events which she said had been going on for about 5 years (although her mother had noticed it only in the last 2 years). She also complained of 'dithering and stuttering' when trying to get words out. She was an intelligent woman and was able to cover up most aspects of her memory loss except on formal testing. When given a name and address to remember she had almost completely forgotten it after an interval of 12 minutes.

LOCALISATION OF BRAIN
FUNCTION

The effects of disease of the brain depend on which part of the brain is principally affected. Disease may impair the function of either the *cortex* (surface layers) of the brain or of the *deeper structure.*

It is convenient to consider the effects of damage to the cortex under the headings of the four different lobes of the brain—the frontal, parietal, occipital and temporal lobes (*see* Fig. 15).

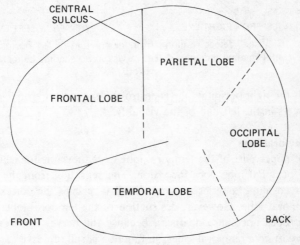

Fig. 15. Lobes of the brain: (left) side.

Occipital lobe

The occipital lobe is the most straightforward. This lobe—at the back of the brain—serves the function of vision, and destruction of the lobe on one side (for instance, in a severe brain wound) will result in blindness on the opposite side. That is to say, destruction of the left side of the brain in the occipital area will result in inability to see anything to the right in the visual fields.

This is because the nerve connections from the left side of both eyeballs end up in the left side of the brain, in the occipital lobe. Since, with the simple lens system of the eye, the retina of the left side of the eye receives the light rays from the *right* side of the visual field, it is this side that is no longer perceived after such a brain injury (*see* Fig. 16).

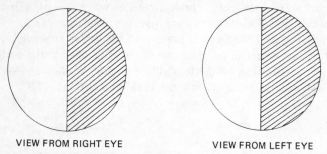

VIEW FROM RIGHT EYE   VIEW FROM LEFT EYE

Fig. 16. Visual defect resulting from destruction of left occipital lobe. Horizontal shading indicates defective vision; no shading indicates intact vision.

If the right occipital lobe is destroyed, the patient is unable to see objects in the left half of the visual field.

Temporal lobe

The upper part of the temporal lobe does the same for hearing as the occipital lobe does for vision. The sensation from the ears is relayed along a series of nerves until it reaches the cortex of the temporal lobe. However, destruction of the temporal lobe on one side does not cause deafness, because the nerves from each ear relay to *both* temporal lobes, so function is still preserved after unilateral brain damage.

However, the auditory function of that part of the brain may be shown in a different way. If disease affects the upper part of the temporal lobe without completely destroying it the patient may experience *auditory hallucinations*. In the absence of any auditory stimulus in the outside world, he may hear humming or buzzing noises, bells ringing, or even voices talking.

Interestingly enough, if destruction of the temporal lobe occurs,

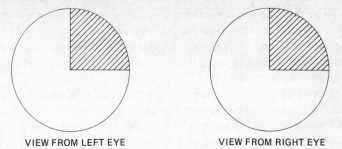

VIEW FROM LEFT EYE   VIEW FROM RIGHT EYE

Fig. 17. Visual defect resulting from destruction of left temporal lobe. Horizontal shading indicates defective vision; no shading indicates intact vision.

the sensory defect that results is one of *vision*. This is because some of the nerve fibres passing from the corresponding side of both eyes on their way to the occipital lobe on that side go through this area. The nerve relays from the *lower* part of the eyes loop their way through the temporal lobe (whereas those from the *upper* part of the eyes pass deep in the parietal lobe) to get to the occipital region.

The lower part of the eye sees the upper part of the visual field. The result, then, of destruction of the left temporal lobe is to produce absence of vision in the *upper* and *right* part of the visual field in both eyes (*see* Fig. 17).

It will be recalled that the hippocampus lies deep in the temporal lobe (*see* Figs. 13, 14); damage to it may cause difficulty with memory. This is unlikely to be serious unless the damage occurs on both sides.

There are a number of other miscellaneous effects of damage to the temporal lobe. The patient may experience *olfactory hallucinations*—that is, he may smell smells that are not there. Alternatively, he may have the sensation of curious tastes and flavours—*gustatory hallucinations*. This may give rise to the observable behaviour of the patient smacking his lips. It looks as if the areas of the brain concerned with the perception of smell and taste are to be found in the temporal lobe—they may overlap with the parts of the brain that serve the function of memory.

One particular quirk of memory function is associated with temporal lobe disease—that of déjà vu. Here one has the sudden conviction that what one has just seen is very familiar. Maybe passing along an apparently unknown street there is a flash of recognition, a sense that one has been there before, even though that is impossible. This occurs in normal people from time to time, and may be an experience that the reader has had, but it is much more common in temporal lobe disease, and presumably results from irritation of the memory pathways.

Not so easy to explain are the features of macropsia and micropsia. In *macropsia* objects appear much larger than normal, and in *micropsia* everything seems to be smaller than normal. Why this should be caused by disease of the temporal lobe is not clear.

Frontal lobe

The frontal lobe is known as one of the *silent areas* of the brain—disease there may develop for a long time without producing any symptoms or signs at all. Nevertheless we can describe the effects of loss of function of the frontal lobe with some certainty as a result of the operation known as prefrontal leucotomy or lobotomy. This is an operation which was in vogue mainly before the actions of modern forms of psychotropic drugs became well known, but which is still used occasionally to treat psychiatric patients who remain intolerably distressed despite all other appropriate methods of treatment. The theory is that the frontal lobes exercise some form of higher control over the behaviour resulting from actions of other parts of the brain, exercising such powers as self-criticism, conscientiousness, drive, self-control, social judgment and so forth. If a patient becomes so tormented by guilt, anxiety and tension that life is not worth living, then even a brain operation may be worthwhile. Generally nowadays such patients respond to other forms of treatment (whose effects are reversible) so that the drastic measure of surgery is much less often required.

It remains useful for that small proportion of patients, with a variety of diagnoses, whose severe state of tension remains after perhaps years of other forms of treatment have failed to help. When done at the present time a much smaller amount of brain tissue is divided than in the past, so that the unfortunate sequels of large operations are not usually produced.

If a high proportion of the nerve connections to both frontal lobes are severed, the patient develops what is called the *frontal lobe syndrome*. He loses his drive, initiative and energy, and may be quite content to live a cabbage-like existence, letting the world go by. Since he is unlikely to experience tension and anxiety, he is not bothered by the effects of his lethargy. He may also remain unconcerned by the presence of severe physical discomfort, and intractable pain (caused, for instance, by cancer) is one of the reasons why the operation is sometimes performed for non-psychiatric conditions. He remains cheerfully free from anxiety, even when a measure of anxiety would be appropriate—a state described as *euphoria*. (One such patient was quite unruffled when told he had a dangerously high blood pressure. He remained smiling, and even appeared amused.) He loses the ability or inclination to behave in a manner that is socially desirable as self-criticism is impaired. This may result in obscene or insulting language that is not in character, carelessness about dress or dangerous driving. He may be unable to refrain from impulsive actions.

Case 6
A young man sustained severe damage to his frontal lobes in a motor-cycle accident. He was subsequently handicapped not only by the lack of sufficient drive and energy to get back to work, but also by the fact that his impulsive behaviour would repeatedly get him into trouble. This behaviour often took the form of shoplifting, but also on occasion led him to make improper suggestions to schoolgirls he met in the street.

The frontal lobe is divided from the parietal lobe by a groove known as the *central sulcus*. Just in front of this sulcus, and therefore at the extreme posterior end of the frontal lobe, is the area of the brain concerned with bodily movements. Stimulation of this part of the brain experimentally by an electric current will cause a movement of a part of the opposite side of the body. Either experimentally or in some forms of epilepsy the result may be twitching of the thumb, hand, arm, foot, leg, etc. Destruction of this part of the brain, or the nerve fibres running from it, will result in the paralysis of part of the opposite side of the body that is known as a stroke or as *hemiplegia*. This is frequently the result of a cerebral haemorrhage.

Parietal lobe
The very front portion of the parietal lobe, lying just behind the central sulcus, has to do with *sensation* from the opposite side of

the body. If it is damaged, sensations from the opposite side of the body may still remain accessible in a crude way, but the finer points will not be registered. For instance, a touch will still be felt, but it will be difficult for the patient to say when touched by two objects how far distant they are from each other, or even whether it is a stimulus by one object or two objects. Similarly the patient may know that an article has been put in his hand, but may find it difficult to estimate its weight.

The functions of that part of the parietal lobe that lies further back than this are different on the two sides of the brain. In a right-handed person the left hemisphere of the brain (which controls the right side of the body) is referred to as the *dominant* hemisphere, and the right side of the brain is the *non-dominant* hemisphere.

Dominant posterior parietal lobe
This area has a number of very important functions. If the patient has a lesion in this area he may develop one of the following disabilities:

1. *Disorientation in space* The affected individual has difficulty in keeping his bearings, and may easily become lost. Eventually, even districts that he has known well become difficult to negotiate and it is impossible to learn new directions. One of the last things to go is the ability to find his way round his own house, and it is here that he is likely to be most at ease.

2. *Difficulty with calculation* Difficulty in carrying out arithmetical operations (*dyscalculia*) is likely to show itself in trying to give the right amount of coinage when shopping. This can often be disguised by handling over an excess, in the hope that the right change will be honestly returned. It will clearly be a serious matter if the patient himself serves in a shop.

Case 7
A woman in her late '30s (described in Case 2, Chapter 3) had brain damage following acute encephalitis. Although she had a severe memory impairment, and was at the time unable to remember anything that happened more than a few minutes previously (unless it had happened before the encephalitis), she was able to carry out an arithmetical task. She was asked to double three; when she gave the correct answer she was asked to double six. When she answered 'twelve' she was asked to double that, and so on. Even though she was not allowed to use a pencil and paper, she was able to get as far

as 192 before making an error. The posterior parietal lobe on the dominant side was considered to be intact.

Case 8

A woman, aged about 60, had noticed increasing memory impairment, and moderately severe objective memory loss was demonstrable. She realised that she was suffering from a progressive lesion but the knowledge had not destroyed her spirit, and she was intent on carrying on the part-time job she had. This was one of selling tickets from a kiosk which she was still able to do apparently to everyone's satisfaction. Again, the brain disease did not seem to have spread to the dominant parietal lobe.

By contrast, many patients with chronic organic brain disease are unable to give their age correctly. If a person is asked his date of birth, the current date and his age, then there should obviously be a straightforward relationship between the three items. Some patients with early dementia are able, in the absence of current disorientation, to give the current date accurately and, in addition, can give (as a matter of habit) their date of birth correctly as well. Often they will, however, then proceed (when asked) to give an age that does not correspond to the difference between the two. If confronted with this they remain unable to correct their mistake if they suffer from dyscalculia. It is an interesting fact that, even in dementia, the incorrect age is usually *less* than the true age of the subject. This is not necessarily due to vanity, of course; the patient may search through his mind for an age that seems correct and familiar—he is then likely to light upon an age which at one time *has* been correct, rather than an age which he has not yet reached or come to call his own.

One curious feature that is found with impaired action of the dominant posterior parietal lobe is that of difficulty in naming fingers. Severely affected patients are unable to indicate which is, say, the ring finger on their left hand, or the index finger on their right hand. Less severely affected subjects will be able to do this for their own hand, but not for someone sitting opposite them. The explanation of this difficulty is obscure. Partly, it may be explained as a result of a combination of dyscalculia and disorientation in space. It is tempting to speculate that it is connected with the link between the use of the term 'digit' literally as a finger, and the use of the same term applied to a unit of calculation.

3. *Dysphasia* Dysphasia is difficulty in handling structured speech or thoughts. Thus in *receptive dysphasia* the subject finds it hard to understand what is said to him, and in *expressive dysphasia* the patient finds it difficult to make himself understood.

In receptive dysphasia the patient will hear what is said to him, and may be able to repeat it. The individual words have obviously penetrated, but he is unable to make sense of them. This can be very distressing since not knowing what others are saying implies that, even if he can in fact speak to them intelligibly, he may not *know* whether they have understood him, since he cannot make out their answers.

In pure expressive dysphasia the patient is not so cut off from those around him, since he can understand what they are saying. His frustration comes from his own awareness that he is not making *himself* intelligible. He will search for the right phrase in vain, and resort to mime and gestures, or pointing to something appropriate in a book or magazine.

It is convenient to bring up the topic of dysphasia when discussing lesions of the parietal lobe, but it may also be produced by disease of other parts of the brain. On the whole, receptive dysphasia may be produced by damage to the posterior half of the brain (therefore including also the occipital lobe and the posterior part of the temporal lobe), whereas expressive dysphasia results from damage to the anterior half of the brain (including the frontal lobe and the anterior part of the temporal lobe).

To put it another way, dysphasia may be a feature of, but is not diagnostic of, disease of the parietal lobes.

Non-dominant posterior parietal lobe
Like the frontal areas of the brain, this area is relatively 'silent'—disease can occur here without the deficit being very obvious, especially in the early stages. With gross damage, three rather strange features can be detected. To illustrate these features let us take the case of a patient who has had a stroke, perhaps as a result of cerebral haemorrhage, and who develops a paralysis down the left-hand side of the body (due to haemorrhage into the right cerebral hemisphere).

The first feature that one may notice on interview is that the patient fails to acknowledge that the left side of the body is in any way disabled. This denial of illness of the affected side of the body is known as *anosognosia*. The second feature is that the patient may even fail to recognise the affected limbs as his own —*autotopagnosia*. The third feature depends on a comparison of sensation from the affected limbs with the unaffected side of the body. It may be possible to demonstrate that sensation is detected when the affected side is stimulated, just as it is when the normal side is stimulated. Ask the patient to tell you when you touch him (with his eyes closed) and he will detect contact and call out when either side is stimulated alone, calling out 'right side' or 'left side' as instructed. If you then touch him on both sides at once he will call out 'right side', suggesting that when stimuli are competing for his attention the touch on the affected side is ignored. This is known as *sensory extinction* or *sensory inattention*.

Both the autotopagnosia and the sensory extinction are illustrations of a general lack of attention to the left half of space that may be found in such a patient. This may impair various day-to-day activities. The patient may put his shoe on the good foot only. A woman may put make-up on only one side of her face. Serious difficulty may arise when the patient tries to put on his clothes.

The deeper structures
Some of the deeper-lying structures that may be impaired by disease are (*a*) the limbic system (serving memory function), (*b*) the connecting fibres for conveying nerve impulses for sight or for body movement, and (*c*) groups of nerve cells governing sensation of pain on the one hand or co-ordination of movement on the other.

One of these has already been considered in detail. The *limbic system* is a complicated array of nerve cells and fibres on which memory depends. The effects of damage to it were gone into in the last chapter.

Nerve fibres governing vision and movement
The nerve fibres carrying the impulses on which vision depends have been dealt with only partially. The reader will recall that a lesion in the temporal lobe may destroy sight in one quarter of the opposite visual field (the upper and opposite quarter), because the fibres from the lower part of the retina loop round the ventricle in that part of the brain. To complete the story we must now reveal

that fibres from the *upper* part of the retina pass deep in the *parietal* lobe to get to the visual cortex in the occipital lobe. A disease occurring in the substance of the parietal lobe, then, may produce loss of sight in one quarter of the visual field—the *lower* and opposite quarter as seen from both eyes (*see* Fig. 18).

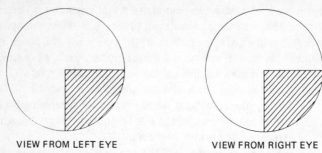

VIEW FROM LEFT EYE   VIEW FROM RIGHT EYE

Fig. 18. Visual defect resulting from lesion deep in left parietal lobe.

The fibres that conduct the nerve impulses producing movement (in the opposite side of the body) stream down from the cortex to the brain stem. They come mainly from a strip of cortex in the hindmost part of the frontal lobe, lying just in front of the central sulcus, and the fibres themselves form a thick band in each half of the brain known as the *internal capsule*. Damage to this band of fibres (as may be caused by cerebral haemorrhage) will produce the paralysis of the opposite side of the body known commonly as a 'stroke', or in Scotland as a 'shock', and technically as a *hemiplegia* or as *hemiparesis* (if incomplete).

These bands of fibres that run through the deep, inner, parts of the brain are made up of the long *axons* that run out from the nerve cells to connect up with the next nerve cell in the chain of command. Together the fibres make up the *white matter* of the brain. The *grey matter* is composed of the *bodies* of the nerve cells where they occur in abundance. The grey matter is found characteristically in the cortex of the brain (in layers) but is also found in large masses in other areas. One such mass is the *hippocampus* found in the temporal lobe, considered earlier.

Nerve cells governing sensation and co-ordination
To one side of the internal capsule lies another such mass known as the *thalamus*. This is a group of nerve cells concerned with sen-

sation—and particularly with sensation of pain. Damage to the thalamus can produce a condition where mild stimulation of the opposite side of the body is relatively pain-free, and where a gradually increasing stimulus suddenly produces intense agonising pain when it exceeds some apparent threshold.

Other collections of grey matter in the deep substance of the brain are concerned with movement. They are known as the *basal ganglia* or (more recently) as the *basal nuclei*. Their action can be illustrated if we imagine that someone starts walking. The decision to put a leg forward is communicated to the motor cortex in the frontal lobe, and the impulses in the chain of command in the nervous system stream down the internal capsule to the spinal cord and eventually to the legs.

However, walking does not just consist of putting one leg in front of the other. The walker does not usually progress with both arms hanging down limply at his side and his head staring ahead in a fixed way. In addition to the movements in the legs there are at least three other types of muscle action. Firstly, when the left leg is swinging forward so is the right arm, with the left arm swinging back; one movement is not made in isolation, it is usually accompanied by, or *associated* with, other movements for ease of function, smoothness of action and balance. Secondly, each other muscle of the body is maintained in a state of partial contraction, however slight, known as the muscle *tone*: this keeps the body in a life-like and suitable posture (in this present case an upright one). Thirdly, the person walking along will make other movements which vary from person to person and minute to minute: these *spontaneous* movements include looking from object to object, gestures, scratching or rubbing actions, and facial expressions.

In disease of the basal nuclei the patient keeps the power to put one leg in front of the other, but shows abnormalities of tone and of associated and spontaneous movements. There are two main directions that such abnormalities may take. In *chorea* (St. Vitus' Dance) the patient has a low muscle *tone* so that the limbs are floppy. Actions are accompanied by exaggerated associated movements—the patient may put up his hand to touch his head and the increased associated movements of trunk and shoulder may send his hand flying past the mark. Spontaneous movements come thick and fast, at a higher rate than normal, so that the patient seems to be in a perpetual state of activity.

The other direction that may be taken in disease of the basal nuclei leads the patient to a state of parkinsonism ('shaking palsy'). Here the patient has a high muscle tone so that his limbs are relatively rigid. Associated movements are diminished: when he walks along his arms *do* hang by his side without swinging naturally. Spontaneous movements are fewer, so that in walking he may stare fixedly ahead, and in other situations his face has a mask-like expressionless quality. When his expression does change as a result of emotion the grimace gives only a brief fleeting glimpse of his underlying mental state before the mask descends again.

The abnormalities in movement described above are differences in *degree* from the normal state. Both chorea and parkinsonism may be accompanied by movements that are different in *kind* from the normal state. In chorea the pathological movements take the form of involuntary jerks, affecting first this part of the body and then that, so that neither the patient nor the observer can tell where the next jerk is going to be seen. Together with the increase in spontaneous movements, this can result in a state where the body appears to be in constant motion—giving rise to the traditional name of St. Vitus' Dance.

In parkinsonism the involuntary pathological movement is quite different. It is a shaking action, but the shake or tremor is regular and repeated several times a second. Among the chief areas to be affected are the hands, where the opposition of the thumb to the nearby fingers gives rise to the description of 'pill-rolling' movements, and the traditional name for the complete picture as the 'shaking palsy' is seen to be appropriate.

The word 'palsy' really means a paralysis, and patients with parkinsonism may experience some difficulty with voluntary control over their actions. Yet the nerve tracks serving voluntary actions are intact. The fibres that start in the posterior part of the frontal lobe and, after a variety of connections, end in the muscles, are not diseased and are able to function. These fibres collect together as they pass through one area of the brain and the bundle projects as a triangular mass on the surface, known as the 'pyramid' in the anatomy books. The whole series of connections from the frontal lobe to the muscle has come to be known as the *pyramidal tract*. It is this tract that is interrupted when a patient suffers from a stroke.

The effects of parkinsonism and chorea are due to influences arising outside the pyramidal tracts, and those parts of the nervous system (such as the basal nuclei) that are involved are known as the *extrapyramidal system.* The two conditions of chorea and parkinsonism (together with some other states such as those found in spastic children) are known collectively as the *extrapyramidal disorders.* The contrast between chorea and parkinsonism is shown as a table in Fig. 19.

MANIFESTATION	CHOREA	PARKINSONISM
Tone	Low	High
Associated movement	Increased	Decreased
Spontaneous movement	More	Less
Pathological movement	Involuntary jerks	Rhythmic tremor

Fig. 19. Manifestations of extrapyramidal disease.

REACTION OF THE PATIENT TO ORGANIC BRAIN DISEASE

Pyschological reaction to the realisation of disease

The description of the effects of organic brain disease would not be complete without an account of the psychological effect on the subject of the knowledge that his intellectual faculties are impaired, or at least the suspicion that this is the case.

Some ways of reacting to this realisation were described in the previous chapter on the dysmnestic syndrome. As in that case, the reaction will depend a lot on the habitual personality patterns of the person affected. In addition, in the case of more generalised brain disease, the psychological reaction will depend heavily on the areas of the brain that are principally affected. When the frontal lobe is involved the patient may be fatuous, euphoric and unconcerned about his predicament. It is fortunate in many ways that with widespread brain disease the frontal lobe syndrome usually makes its appearance sooner or later.

When this does not happen the patient may be severely distressed by the fact that his brain is beginning to show signs of impaired action. To many people this is a dreaded fate, far worse than the prospect of cancer or some illness that brings early death, physical disability or severe pain. The reactions then follow the same pattern as with the dysmnestic syndrome with denial, rationalisation or other ego defence mechanisms invoked. The patient may experience anxiety and depression, and a frank depressive illness may ensue.

We have already seen that in organic brain disease any symptom or collection of symptoms of functional psychiatric illness may occur. It is sometimes difficult to tell whether the depressive illness, anxiety state or whatever functional state materialises is a direct biological result precipitated by action of the disease on the appropriate areas of the brain; or whether the functional state is a psychological reaction to the realisation by the patient that he has disordered brain function. This distinction may be important in the management of the patient. If, however, the management is going to depend largely on the administration of physical methods of treatment (such as anti-depressant drugs), then the distinction becomes of academic importance only.

Psychological reaction to the effects of disease

In addition to the effect of the realisation of the *fact* that he has organic brain disease, we have to consider too the reaction of the patient to the *effect* of the organic brain disease.

Case 9

A young woman, Mrs. O., subject to attacks of migraine, was distressed one day to find that she could not understand what her family were saying to her. She was terrified to think that, not only was something serious happening to her, but that it was something that was depriving her of the power to communicate with others. Although in fact she was speaking quite coherently, and was explaining very clearly what she was experiencing, she did not know that she was even achieving this, since she could not understand the replies of those around her.

What she was suffering from was an acute form of receptive dysphasia. Migraine affects the blood supply to the back of the brain—commonly the impaired action of the occipital lobe results in hallucinations of bright lights or zigzag patches, or areas of temporary blindness. In this case the impaired blood supply had affected other posterior parts of the brain, causing the receptive dysphasia. The difficulty in comprehension cleared up with the passing of the migraine attack. This was an isolated experience, and did not recur with subsequent attacks of migraine. The patient was able to describe clearly the shock and terror that she experienced with this sensation, and the incident gives us some understanding of the distress that those persons with a chronic disability of this sort must endure.

Short of frank distress of this sort the effect of organic brain disease on the subject is so often one of *frustration*. This is readily understood in the case of expressive dysphasia, with the patient struggling to find words to say what he means, and all the time perceiving with more or less clarity that he is failing to achieve this.

Even with other features of organic brain disease frustration is the theme. Patients with depressive illness tend to lose interest in things around them and to abandon attempts to overcome the obstacles that they see looming blackly over them. Schizophrenic patients, at least in the chronic stage, tend to lose their drive and initiative, so that they too are no longer striving. The patient with organic brain disease, by way of contrast, tends to show large chunks of his normal previous personality shining through intact, with all the drives and desires still pressing for fulfilment. This, together with his severe and often intractable impaired function, gives rise to the overwhelming sense of frustration.

I have at times looked after large numbers of long-stay patients in mental hospitals. The most frequent diagnoses that these patients have are either organic brain disease or chronic schizophrenia. One noticeable feature of the organic patients, in contrast to the schizophrenics, is that the libido of the former remains more intact. Sometimes one is greeted by a small act of affection—they may even try to kiss one. The chances are that a patient doing this suffers from organic brain disease. This sort of patient, even short of overt physical acts of this nature, will maintain an active interest in things going on around him. The schizophrenic patient, on the other hand, typically withdraws into himself and cuts himself off from interpersonal relationships. Often the sexual drive is diminished, but what is left may be resolved by masturbation. It can be understood that the patient with organic brain disease (with intact drive, energy and libido) is the one most likely to encounter frustration. If the patient is elderly he may be frustrated too by his physical handicaps, to add to his troubles.

REACTION OF FRIENDS AND RELATIVES

The results of the organic brain disease may cause problems for friends, relatives and those that feel responsible for the patient. On the one hand, the patient's drive and will-power may still be strong, and on the other many of the things that he wishes to do will be inappropriate or even dangerous.

Where the patient is at home
If the patient is living alone the relatives may worry that he will leave the gas taps turned on accidentally after preparing his meal, or that (apart from any physical debility) he may not have the coping ability to deal with any emergency. If the patient lives with the relatives they may feel that looking after him is a full-time and onerous task. In some ways this responsibility is similar to that of looking after a child, but there are difficulties that the average parent does not usually encounter. For instance, most young children will spend a good deal of the night asleep (although some over-wrought parents will greet that statement with a hollow laugh). One may have to wake up and deal with them if they cry, but otherwise they do not need looking after when the parent is trying to sleep. The patient with organic brain disease, on the other hand, may suffer from restlessness and insomnia. He (or she) will turn night into day, and spend much of the hours of darkness pottering around the house, taking snatches of sleep in the armchair during the day to compensate. This may prove to be a source of great anxiety to the relatives, who fear that an accident may happen during those unguarded hours or that granny may wander off into the streets and lose herself.

Institutional care

These relatives often become preoccupied with the question of whether the patient should be sent away to some form of institutional care. Their dilemma is that if the patient stays at home she (the elderly organic patient is more often female) worries them (as described above), but if she goes away they feel guilty because they have rejected her. For the professional person advising them there is a further dilemma. True enough, if such organic patients are admitted to a hospital or other residential form of care they may be more closely and expertly supervised, but on the other hand one knows that the best recipe for preserving their remaining intellectual function most efficiently is to leave them in their familiar surroundings for as long as possible. Bringing them into hospital will only increase their disorientation, and disrupt their familiar habit patterns. Even if the hospitalisation is only brief, the disruption may prove enough to break their behaviour patterns to a degree from which they do not fully recover. Otherwise the dilemma of the professional adviser might be solved by bringing the patient into hospital for a short spell and seeing in fact how it worked out—is what this particular patient gains on the swings worth more than what she loses on the roundabouts?

The issue is often decided on quite other factors. In some areas the provision of accommodation for geriatric patients is so inadequate that admission can in any case only be considered as a last resort, when patient, relatives, family doctor, social workers and other agencies are all at the end of their tether. The family doctor, worried by the fact that his elderly demented patient living alone is leaving unlit gas taps turned on, may be told that this in itself is not an indication for that patient to be admitted, since many other elderly persons in that area are in the same position.

The reader may wonder how such inadequacies of provision of institutional care arise. The usual answer is that the responsibility for providing this care is divided. In the United Kingdom, for instance, until recently the provision of hospital beds has been the responsibility of the central government, while provision of non-medical residential accommodation for the elderly has been the job of the local authority. If challenged about inadequate provision, those responsible for hospitals could point out that more beds might be made available if some of the patients at present occupying them could be transferred to other residential accommodation. The local authorities, who have the duty for providing this accommodation, could talk about competing demands on their budget and the pressing need for, for instance, better schools in their area as well. It remains to be seen whether the unification of health services, which happened in 1974, will eventually provide a more vigorous response to this problem.

MANAGEMENT OF DEMENTIA

General discussion

It is easy to maintain an attitude of insensitivity to the fate of someone who appears to lead a vegetable-like existence and for whom there is no radical curative treatment. A member of the helping professions (whether nurse, doctor, social worker or one of the many others) may feel uncomfortable in the presence of such a patient (or client) and will wish to turn his head away. After all, he has come into this profession to try to help those in need, and it seems that here is someone who is beyond help. The same situation can be seen where a patient has cancer and the doctors hurry past the end of the bed with a perfunctory smile and as little conversation as possible.

This reaction is understandable. It arises because the professional persons concerned think that there is nothing to do to help the patient, and they *feel* themselves to be in an impossible position, *i.e.* thrown into contact with the patient but impotent to relieve his distress.

This need not happen, however, and the fact that the situation arises is often because the professional wants to do too much. He wants to be a knight in shining armour riding in on his white charger to slay dragons and rescue damsels in distress. He experiences chagrin when he finds that the disease is incurable or the personal situation of the subject is beyond redemption. Under such circumstances he needs to take great care that he does not appear to reject the person concerned.

In fact, although he may have to abandon his rescue fantasies, the situation is not usually so hopeless as it first appears. The woman with a malignant condition can be very appreciative of the opportunity to talk about her feelings, and the man with a severe intractable personality disorder is not necessarily asking to be transformed into a superman—a slight decrease in the extent of his maladaptive attitudes may be of great significance to him although it may seem little to the professional who is awed by the total extent of his deviance.

After this aside, let us now return to consider what can be done to help the person with chronic organic brain disease, even where the disease itself is incurable.

Medication

The principles of drug treatment are similar to those that apply to the acute organic brain syndrome. One wishes to use drugs that will help the emotional and behavioural problems of the patient without further hindering the already impaired intellectual faculties.

It is widely known that the barbiturates are unsuitable for this purpose. Although they are useful for relieving anxiety, they are likely to produce stupor, intellectual impairment and ataxia. In other words, they make the patient sleepy, dopey and drunk.

Most of the drugs that were available before the Second World War were tarred with the same brush—including chloral, paraldehyde and, of course, alcohol.

Phenothiazines

Since the Second World War the concept of the *tranquilliser* has developed as a drug which will relieve anxiety without producing excessive drowsiness. The *benzodiazepine* groups of drugs are useful for this purpose including, for instance, chlordiazepoxide (Librium) and diazepam (Valium). If anxiety is the main emotional problem of a demented patient then these may be prescribed with advantage.

Other tranquillisers (referred to as the *major* tranquillisers or the *neuroleptics*) will have more profound actions. They will affect not only *minor* psychiatric symptoms (such as anxiety) but also *major* psychiatric symptoms (such as delusions and hallucinations). Typical of this class of drug are the *phenothiazines*. Other groups within this class are the *Rauwolfia* alkaloids and the butyrophenones: their characteristics are basically similar to that of the phenothiazines.

Phenothiazine drugs in common use include chlorpromazine (Largactil, Thorazine), trifluoperazine (Stelazine) and thioridazine (Melleril or Mellaril). As implied above, these drugs are particularly useful in ameliorating psychotic features of the sort that, had the patient not got organic brain disease, would normally be associated with the functional psychoses. They are particularly useful for clearing up schizophrenia and hypomanic types of symptoms, and not always so helpful with depressive symptoms (which they sometimes even exacerbate).

So the patient who has paranoid delusions and believes that she is being followed, or the patient who has unpleasant hallucinations (often visual in the case of organic brain disease) will find relief on this type of medication.

The phenothiazines do rather more than clear up this type of overt psychotic symptom. They also have a normalising effect on disturbed behaviour. So the old lady who has been turning night into day, and who not only has been pottering around at night-time, to everyone's concern, but who also has been irritable and unco-operative with it, reverts on her regular phenothiazine (perhaps ad-ministered in the form of a syrup) to a normal sleep pattern and becomes her previous placid self again.

This effect on behaviour has led to the major tranquillisers being stigmatised as 'chemical straightjackets'. I think that this is an un-fair gibe. It implies that somewhere inside the calm exterior of the patient there is a disturbed patient trying to get out, but he can't because of the pharmaceutical manacles. I know of no evidence to support this, and clinical observations of patients treated in this way suggest that they have merely lost interest in the abnormal patterns of behaviour. Nevertheless, for some critics the very idea of chemical 'control' of behaviour is a nauseating thought, and one can understand their fears. What I think is a more cogent criticism is that patients treated with large doses of these drugs may lose in-terest in fighting to overcome their difficulties, but this is more of a problem with the younger patient and will be dealt with when we consider the use of neuroleptic drugs in schizophrenia.

The effect of these drugs is long lasting and a once-daily dose régime may be sufficient. They have a number of potential side effects which tend to be more marked within an hour or two of taking the drug. One common side effect is drowsiness (more so with chlorpromazine and thioridazine than with trifluoperazine). For this reason, it is sometimes convenient to give the total dose (or the lion's share of it) at night-time before the patient goes to bed. This has two added advantages. Firstly, the other side effects (such as dry mouth or blurred vision) are operating when the patient is unaware of them and therefore not bothered by them. Secondly, the cantankerous patient may be reluctant to take a 'tranquilliser' during the day but may be quite agreeable to having something at night to help get her off to sleep.

This brings us to one disadvantage of drug treatment with the demented patient. If the patient is living alone, how do we know that she is in fact taking the medication prescribed for her? Well, it is everyone's right to pour their medicine down the sink if they want to, but usually if a doctor suspects that the lack of effect of a course of treatment might be due to this, then there is a chance that the patient will admit to it if confronted with the possibility. Under these circumstances, then, the doctor can re-examine whether he should make further efforts to persuade the patient to persevere or, on the other hand, just abandon that line of treatment. With the case of organic brain disease, however, the patient may just not remember whether she has taken the medicine or not.

This makes the process of finding the right dose for the patient a very difficult one. With these drugs, as with many others, there is no fixed dosage system which is suitable for every patient. It is the usual practice, therefore, to start the patient on a low dose and gradually increase the number of tablets, either until a satisfactory response is achieved or until side effects of the medication begin to make their appearance. The trouble is, if the patient is unreliable in taking the drug, the physician, in ignorance of this, may go on recommending higher and higher doses because he does not see any response. If at one point in time the patient decides to start taking the medication, and takes the dose currently being written on the bottle (from the latest prescription), she may suddenly suffer from the full blast of side effects.

Side effects of phenothiazines

1. *Extrapyramidal effects* The patient may develop features of Parkinsonism. These will usually respond to a reduction in dose, or

anti-parkinsonian drugs may be given in addition to the phenothiazines. Other less common extrapyramidal effects are *akathisia*, a restless inability to sit still, *oculogyric crises*, in which the eyes turn forcefully (usually upwards) with a painful spasm, *dystonia*, where curious postures and facial expressions are adopted, and *dyskinesia*. A troublesome form of dyskinesia, or abnormal movement, is one that causes chewing movements and protrusion of the tongue—*oro-facial dyskinesia*.

2. *Autonomic effects* The autonomic nervous system includes the *sympathetic*, with secretion of adrenalin in response to sudden stress, and the *parasympathetic*, which is concerned with nutrition and affects heart rate and internal muscles of the eye. Many psychotropic drugs dampen the action of the parasympathetic, resulting in a dry mouth (inhibition of salivation) and constipation. Blurred vision may also occur. Some drugs, including the phenothiazines, also inhibit the sympathetic. The effects of this are lowering of blood pressure (leading to dizziness and fainting) and sometimes the isolated symptom of failure of ejaculation in men.

3. *Other side effects* Sometimes patients taking tranquillisers complain of drowsiness. This is not the same as the effect of sedatives like barbiturates, which with increasing doses give rise to deeper sleep followed by coma or even death. The tranquillisers seem more to *allow* the patient to go to sleep rather than *force* him asleep—he can almost always be roused even after very large doses.

Some patients on phenothiazines put on weight, and rarely patients may develop anaemia or rare disorders of the blood. Patients taking chlorpromazine are especially liable to jaundice and sunburn, and patients on very large doses of thioridazine develop opacities in the eye.

After this formidable list of side effects it should be said that the most common side-effects (those affecting the autonomic and extrapyramidal nervous system) usually clear up promptly on stopping the drug or even reducing the dose, and many patients never experience anything in the way of side-effects at all. As in most therapeutic decisions, a judgment has to be made as to where to draw the line, so that the treatment does not become worse than the disease.

Psychological management

Conversing with the patient

Talking to the patient with chronic organic brain disease is made easier if certain principles are kept in mind. To start with the patient may suspect, but not admit, the full extent of his disease. The idea of having a disease of the brain is a horrible one—it is remarkable that some patients are able to endure it phlegmatically. The average patient will find painful anything that focuses attention on his intellectual ability. If he thinks that you are calling into question his memory or orientation he will become irritable, cantankerous, querulous or tearful.

If this happens then it may be necessary to turn to a different subject. For instance, he is likely to be able to talk about his own occupation (or past occupation) from strength, and will feel on safer ground. So the first principle is to assume that the patient will be defensive about any real or imagined threat to expose his intellectual deficiencies, and if he suddenly becomes unco-operative or resents a question for no obvious reason, try to see if the line of conversation might have been construed in this way.

The next point to realise is that the *mood* of the patient with organic brain disease is often subject to wide fluctuations. He may be euphoric one minute and in tears the next. This is rather different from having a depressive illness or hypomania, since these diagnoses are not usually invoked unless the patient has a sustained deviation of mood (say, elation) for days and weeks rather than hours. In organic brain disease the affect swings in seconds and may be sustained for only minutes. This tendency to unstable mood state is known as *affective lability*. If a patient shows this phenomenon then a slight misjudgment in what is said to him may result in a torrent of tears. If you realise that it is a case of affective lability then you will know that this does not necessarily indicate a sustained mood state, that the patient will probably be feeling all right again in a few minutes, and that the situation can probably be dealt with adequately with a little sympathy and reassurance. Although the emotional reaction in affective lability may be exaggerated and uninhibited, the fact that a particular event or comment triggered it off may give you a window into the patient's more permanent values and attitudes.

Informing the patient of this dementing illness

Given these first two principles, should the patient be told that he has a dementing illness? The situation is similar to the one where a doctor must decide whether to tell a patient that he has cancer. The latter is probably easier. In my opinion the basic rule is to be guided by the patient. One should not gratuitously blurt out to the patient that he has cancer: on the other hand, it is equally unfair to him to rush past the end of the bed without giving him a chance to ask any questions. Clearly the right approach is to sit with him and allow him plenty of time to bring up the subject if he wishes to do so. If he avoids every opportunity to ask for information about his condition it can be taken as a sign that he does not want to be told in so many words (even though he may well have an idea of the truth at the back of his mind).

Suppose that he does ask directly what the matter is, he can be told that he does have a serious illness. Again, this gives him the choice of pressing on with this line of talk or of preserving his state of ignorance.

Even if we go a little further with our information than he was prepared for, the damage is not necessarily lasting provided the conversation was in sufficiently vague and general terms. Most of us are able to forget what we are told—or even that the conversation took place—to preserve our self-esteem and happiness. We can at least forget the significance and details of the conversation *provided that the words used were not a shock in themselves*. If at this stage the patient has had as much as he can take the subject need not be pursued. If necessary he may be left in ignorance for good (with the same proviso as above, that he does get the *opportunity* to raise the topic if he wishes).

If, however, he indicates that 'serious illness' is not a sufficiently specific term for him the enlightenment can be taken a stage further. This procedure can be continued until, if his reactions indicate that it is appropriate, he should be told the complete truth.

This is obviously a short and simplified account of what is a very delicate procedure. A number of points are important:

1. *Should you use his terms or yours?* Again, taking the analogy of malignant tumours, if he uses the word 'cancer' should you? There is a basic principle in psychotherapy that you use the terms used by the patient himself. If the patient talks about anger towards

someone then you should refer to it yourself as anger, and not for instance as hate—a word which may mean something quite different to the patient.

The relevance of this lies in the exploration of the topic of the illness with the patient. If he uses the term 'cancer', then explain that the word has different meanings to different people and ask him what he understands by it. This can be an opportunity if the time seems right to go on to ask him what his feelings are about it, so that he has the opportunity, if he wishes to take it, of pouring out his fears and fantasies.

During this process it is right, clearly, that one should employ the very words the patient used. These are the words that have the precise meaning and the precise emotional significance for him.

When it comes to explaining your views to the patient, *then* it is permissible to use your own terminology, bearing in mind that you may have to define the terms as you use them—in case they carry a different significance for the patient.

2. *How fast should you go?* How rapidly should you carry out the process of imparting information to the patient? I have already indicated that you should use his reactions to give you a guide. Accepting this, one should still proceed with caution, and go *slower* than you think is necessary. This is because some patients cover their feelings and may bottle them up until suddenly they break down and burst into tears. Especially at risk is the patient who breezily claims, 'It's all right—you can tell me everything'. Such a patient may just be whistling to keep up his courage.

It is often a good idea to break off the interview early and arrange to talk about the subject again a few days later. After the lapse of time you can get a fresh idea of how fast the patient really wants to go towards understanding his illness. It is better that the patient should think that you are ultraconservative or even evasive, rather than that you should wound him by taking the easy way of accepting his words at their face value.

If you do go much too slowly, then it is an interesting fact that he will probably find the right words for you. We often tend to assume, in a rather superior way, that this process of telling the patient about himself is a fairly one-sided affair of *us* telling *him*. We are sometimes surprised to find that if we give him the helm, and he feels safe from wounding remarks by us, then he will make his own voyage of discovery with the minimum of help on our part.

3. *Your tone of voice is important* Use a natural, comfortable manner. Obviously this may be difficult advice to follow. Equally obviously it is not going to make it easier for the patient if you are talking about his future in hollow tones of portent and doom. Even if you are telling someone he has cancer, or disease of the brain he will be able to take the news better if you can be undramatic about it.

I've said that this may be difficult advice to follow. If you ask yourself why, you come across one of the key problems in this whole area, and that is the problem of *handling your own emotional reactions* while talking to the patient. One thinks of the trite adage, 'This hurts me more than it hurts you'—a feeling claimed by innumerable adults about to punish children. In this context it is not necessarily true either, but certainly it can be a painful experience to have to go through the process of informing the patient. This is all the more so because it is a threat to the professional person that is doing the telling. We go into such caring professions to help other people, and we are forced to tell someone now that, in some ways at least, they are beyond help. So this is a poignant event in our lives, too, and we should avoid the error of indulging our sense of tragedy when we can make things easier for the patient by being as matter-of-fact as possible. The rule in these situations is to *recognise* our own emotions but to avoid *acting* on them.

4. *Who should you tell?* It is self-evident that if you have told the patient the nature of his illness, or on the other hand have decided that he cannot tolerate knowing, then you should tell the other persons that have responsibility for caring for him about your progress. This should certainly include any other professionals that are involved, and at least one has the advantage in telling them that one can be frank.

Whether you should also tell the relatives is a complex matter, depending partly on whether *they* can tolerate being told the news (or whether they indicate they would rather not be told for certain that their suspicions are well founded).

A deciding factor may be the size of the estate of the patient. If it is necessary for his affairs to be put in order as soon as possible, then it will be necessary to clarify with someone (*e.g.* a relative, friend, solicitor or manager) the prognosis.

This business of talking to a third party in the absence of the patient is repulsive to many psychiatrists. Much psychological treatment is carried out on the basis that the transaction is between the patient and the therapist alone. It can certainly make the rapport with the patient much better if all contact with relatives, employers and other interested parties is done with the patient present (even if he is only present in the sense of sitting in at your end of your call while you speak with them on the telephone).

Where important legal matters are involved the interests of the patient (or his dependants) may best be served, for once, by going behind his back and telling the person responsible for his affairs what the position is.

The patient with organic brain disease does pose special problems in management that one does not see in the patient with cancer or even in the person with a functional psychosis. Having carefully come to a judicious conclusion about how much he can be told, and having gone through the delicate process of telling him, you may find that his objective memory impairment is such that he remembers nothing of it the next time that you see him. Alternatively, his cognitive impairment may be of a nature that makes it very difficult for him to understand anything that you do say to him. The management of this type of problem was considered in the chapter on the acute organic brain syndrome.

Supportive psychotherapy
Under the above circumstances one may decide to abandon all attempts to give him insight into his condition, opting to be purely supportive and concentrating on relieving his distress. The contrast between supportive and insight-oriented psychotherapy will be gone into more fully later in the book, but a particular illustration of it may be given here.

Rationalisation
For instance, the patient may be concerned over his loss of memory. He may bring up this subject himself. How do you deal with this supportively? The easiest way is probably to supply a *rationalisation* (or, if the patient is already using a rationalisation, buttress that one). You can say to him, 'You know that you have

been feeling depressed'—that's likely to be true—'well, when people get into a depressed mood they often have difficulty with their memory and concentration' (and that's undoubtedly true).

The type of rationalisation or reassurance that any particular patient will accept varies, and usually clues can be found in his attitude towards, and statements about, his illness, which can lead you to find a face-saving 'explanation' that is satisfying to him.

The example above is particularly apposite—the story of impaired memory resulting from depression. Many times it *is* worth while treating the depression in its own right and you may be surprised at the improvement in intellectual function that results. In fact, some patients have been completely misdiagnosed—what was labelled an organic brain syndrome, because of the severity of intellectual impairment, later proved to be solely a depressive illness. Admittedly it would be a severe depression, but it would be one that responded well to treatment.

Community care

It is recognised by geriatricians that if an old lady is taken off to hospital, away from all that she knows and loves, and is put in bed and left there, then her condition may deteriorate out of all proportion to the extent of her intellectual deficit. The bedridden patient, incontinent and in danger of getting pressure sores, may improve dramatically if she is allowed up to go to the toilet at frequent intervals. The 'incontinence' may be a combination of a small degree of loss of control and a large degree of loss of spirit and self-respect. She will improve still further if she is allowed to remain active during the day. Most do best if ways can be found of keeping them out of hospital in the first place.

In practice, there are innumerable ways in which the partially demented patient can be kept in the community despite her deficits. A common problem is that she may forget to turn the gas off after using the cooker. In fact there are special safety gas taps that can be provided. 'Meals-on-wheels' and other similar services may give her physical and emotional assistance. But now I am going beyond the scope of special psychiatric knowledge, and am in danger of teaching my grandmother to suck eggs.

The management of the geriatric patient is a complicated one, the main reason for this being that so often they have *multiple* deficits or problems. A patient with minimal intellectual deterioration may be kept out of hospital if some way can be found of assisting her with her physical debilities. Providing her with a handrail along the wall (if she has difficulty in walking) is one way. Another is to give her cutlery and water taps with especially large handles if her dexterity is impaired.

Support for relatives

If the person with organic brain disease is looked after by relatives, then often they can continue to look after her longer, and with a better spirit, if they are given support themselves. Providing the services of a district nurse and home help is one way. Another is to take the patient into hospital, not on a permanent basis, but just for a week or two every so often to allow the relatives a break and a rest from their arduous responsibilities. One method that is used is to agree with the relatives to have the patient 'half in, half out'. That is to say, that half of the year she will reside in hospital and half of the year at home. Besides making economical use of scarce hospital facilities, this also avoids the guilt felt by relatives when the patient is 'put away' permanently, and keeps their interest in the progress of the patient alive. It is, however, a potential source of disorientation and distress to the patient. It works for some, but not others.

If the patient has not yet got to this stage, then use can be made of day hospitals. For anything from 1 to 5 days a week the patient can come up to the day hospital (or day centre, if not attached to medical services) and a professional eye can be kept on her. Again, it gives the relatives some respite, and occupational therapy can be designed to suit the patient. Progressing problems can be nipped in the bud when spotted early by the regular supervision, relatives feel that they have the support of professionals readily available, and at night the patient returns to her comfortable familiar surroundings.

The dependent patient

The demented patients that are found in psychiatric hospitals are of degrees of severity that vary from the patient being totally bedfast and unable to carry out the most elementary services for herself, to the person who has only minimal intellectual loss and has been admitted for social reasons, *e.g.* no relatives, not acceptable to local authority homes, or perhaps just that no-one cares.

In some ways the completely dependent patient, remaining quietly in bed, is the one that fits in most neatly with the way hospitals are organised, and the staff may become impatient with the ambulant patient who is still curious and a 'wanderer'. There is a danger of keeping such a patient in bed (or even fixed in a chair as is sometimes done) unnecessarily during the day. The staff are afraid that the patient may wander off and perhaps get lost or fall down the stairs. When the winds of change swept through the mental hospitals bringing in more liberal policies, symbolic of which was the unlocked door, some hospitals unlocked the door of the geriatric ward but arranged that there was always a member of staff available to make sure that no-one left the ward. There is an ingenious alternative. It is possible to fit two handles, of different design, and at different levels, to the same door. One can be opened by the right hand and the other by the left simultaneously. The reasoning behind it is simple. If a patient is demented enough not to be allowed to leave the ward unsupervised, then she is unlikely to be able to work out the formula for opening the door. The door is thus unlocked to the knowing, but locked to the dement.

This does not help deal with the problem of patients who roam around within the ward and who are in danger of falling, If an elderly patient does fall, a frequent result is fracture of the neck of the femur. This may prove lethal. If a frail elderly patient is unable to get out of bed for some weeks or months as a result of the fracture, it is found that they become very vulnerable and often for apparently trivial reasons develop pneumonia (or other infections) and die. If they die after sustaining a fracture, then the death has to be reported to the coroner. Even if they only become bruised as a result of the fall the relatives will become upset and tempted to wonder if they have heard the correct version of the 'accident'.

The net result is that the hospital staff responsible for caring for the elderly dement may be tempted, understandably, to err on the side of caution and to be rather restrictive in what they will allow the geriatric patient to do. This is presumably the reason for sometimes being greeted with the sorry sight of the old ladies tied to their chairs—ever so gently, and just round the waist—but nevertheless tied. Many of these problems could be avoided if enough nurses could be provided to give closer personal supervision to the patient.

The care of the patient with irreversible and progressive organic brain disease is a delicate task and often a thankless one. It calls for dedicated staff. Difficulties will always be present, but there are at present more obstacles than there need be in the way of adequate care. This is likely to remain so until society can be more wholehearted in voting funds to supply proper levels of staffing and adequate facilities for the job.

SUMMARY

In this chapter further effects of organic brain disease are described. If the disease is widespread, then the generalised deterioration of intellect known as *dementia* results. The field of vision is impaired with lesions in the occipital, and sometimes the temporal, lobes. The *frontal lobe syndrome* may occur with extensive damage but small foci of disease in the frontal lobes may remain 'silent' for long periods. Disorientation in space is a frequent result of parietal lobe damage. Damage to anterior parts of the brain gives *expressive* dysphasia, and that to the posterior parts *receptive* dysphasia.

Delirium, delusions and many other symptoms can add to the clinical picture. Treatment with neuroleptic drugs will not restore the intellectual faculties but may give great symptomatic relief.

The psychological management of the patient has also been dealt with. Do you tell him he has brain disease? Does it make any difference what you say to him? In fact a case is made out for paying great attention to what information is given *to* the patient, both about his illness and about day-to-day affairs. The effect of hospitalisation, and its consequent pros and cons, is described. Admission of the patient to hospital provides support for the caring relatives but proves disorienting for the patient.

In this chapter we have looked also at the psychological *reaction* to organic brain disease both in the patient and in the friends and relations of the patient, and what can be done about it.

INDEX TO CHAPTER 4

5 Aetiology of organic brain disease

CLASSIFICATION OF CAUSES

Aetiology is the study of causes, and if you look in classical medical text-books you will often see a list of headings of different types of cause that has become hallowed by long use. It reads something like this—infective; trauma; toxic; deficiency; neoplastic; degenerative; endocrine; hereditary.

This is not a logical system—it is a hotch-potch of different concepts and levels of causation. A disease might come under more than one heading. This list is merely a number of convenient pegs on which to hang one's ideas when talking about aetiology.

The different items, then, are not necessarily mutually exclusive. The total list only makes pretence at being totally inclusive because 'toxic' can be construed as meaning excess of anything and 'deficiency' as lack of anything. There could perhaps be a ninth category—Of unknown cause.

For the lack of a more watertight classification we shall use this list in considering the different types of organic brain disease.

INFECTIVE

Syphilis

Syphilis, particularly in its later stages, may cause disease of the brain. At the time of writing this is fairly rarely seen. It has been more common in the past, but with the current trends towards what one may call 'permissiveness' (if one is in favour) or 'promiscuity' (if one is against), we may see more of it again in the future. There is certainly already a resurgence of syphilitic infection in Western society. This is, in theory, curable with antibiotics, especially if treated in the early stages. Time will tell whether all who contract the infection are treated adequately.

General paralysis of the insane

When mental illness is caused by syphilis of the brain, the classical form taken is called *general paralysis of the insane*, or G.P.I. for short. In the nineteenth century there were large numbers of cases with G.P.I. in mental hospitals, and it has the distinction of being one of the first mental illnesses to become susceptible to physical methods of treatment.

At that time it was probably not always distinguished from other forms of mental illness. With hindsight we can now characterise it as presenting a fairly typical picture of the chronic organic brain syndrome. As the disease process could be spread widely throughout the brain, there would be a general deterioration of intellectual ability. There was also interference with muscular power, similar to that seen in a stroke, but potentially affecting both sides of the body (general paralysis). This was not necessarily conspicuous, and nor always was the dementia. The clinical picture was often dominated by euphoria or by such 'functional' symptoms as delusions of grandeur. A combination of ideas of grandeur, euphoria and a certain lack of insight might lead the patient to present you with a cheque for a million pounds written out on a dirty scrap of paper he had picked up.

Cause of G.P.I.

G.P.I. led to several landmarks in the understanding and treatment of mental illness. It was one of the first psychoses for which a specific *brain pathology* was found: a pathologist looking at the brain could first of all say that it was diseased, and secondly state the specific nature of the disease. The cause of the disease was found—the corkscrew-shaped bacterium referred to as a 'spirochaete' (nowadays called 'treponema pallidum').

Later a curious blood reaction was found to occur when the

body was infected by this organism—the Wassermann reaction. In this test with blood from the affected patient, serum curdles when in contact with a particular liver extract. (In G.P.I. the cerebro-spinal fluid will often curdle as well as the serum.) To this day no-one knows why the reaction takes place—it was discovered by chance; but it proved to be a fairly reliable way of diagnosing the disease without having to wait for the post-mortem examination of the brain.

It is paradoxical that it was G.P.I. that was one of the first psychiatric illnesses whose cause was to be discovered. One of the big problems with research in psychiatry is that one so often depends on what the patient chooses to tell one about his past history. Can you think of anything less reliable than making a diagnosis based on eliciting a history of an incident of furtive sexual behaviour?

Treatment of G.P.I.

The greatest advance came when a method of treating the disease was discovered. It was found that the spirochaete could not survive in temperatures a little above body heat; if the patient could artificially be made feverish, then the infection would often disappear. This was done either by giving the patient malaria (which would itself be treated later with quinine) or by putting the patient in a special container in which his body heat could be raised. When the treatment was successful the infection was eliminated, and progress of the disease was halted. Clearly, brain tissue that had been destroyed by the results of infection could not be restored, but clinical results were not always limited to stopping further deterioration. Improvement in the patient's state could also occur to a degree; one presumes this was partly because of re-learning by other parts of the brain and partly because of improvement in function of sick cells and of cells previously affected by surrounding inflammation.

G.P.I. was therefore the first of a long line of medical discoveries (carcinoma of the lung is one of the most recent) where it was found what causes the disease, but where it still proved difficult to persuade people not to expose themselves to the chance of getting it. The right to risk becoming ill is one of the basic human freedoms.

The discoveries made with G.P.I. brought about significant

changes in attitude. There was a less nihilistic and more hopeful attitude towards the treatment of the mentally ill (a change of attitude which had its parallel for neurotic illness in the teachings of Freud, which were starting at about the same time). There was also the chance of distinguishing between the various mental illnesses to be found in the hospital, and in particular between organic brain disease on the one hand and functional psychosis on the other.

Penicillin

A further advance came after the Second World War when it was found that effective treatment was possible with one of the most harmless of therapeutic agents—*penicillin.* One difficulty in medicine is that of ensuring that the treatment is not a worse hazard than the disease—so many types of treatment themselves damage a high proportion of the patients treated. For instance, it is of tantalising consequence to find that the patient's illness is caused by a 'benign' brain tumour, if to cure it means removing a large portion of brain to get at the tumour. In the case of drug therapy it is well known that the patient's original illness may be cured only for him to have to suffer from toxic effects of the drug—which may themselves have no curative treatment.

Penicillin itself is not entirely in the clear. It may produce a drastic allergic response in some patients. However, this is rare, and the vast majority of patients on penicillin suffer no serious side effects at all.

Conclusion

So, in one sense syphilitic infection is a gratifying diagnosis to make, because one knows there is an effective and safe treatment available. The only drawback is that in the advanced case of G.P.I. full restoration to normal will not occur. This is a strong argument in favour of keeping an ever-watchful eye on the possibility that:

1. The patient's illness may be organic in origin; and
2. the cause may be treatable.

Other infections of the brain

Other infections of the brain are not so good an example of psychiatric illness treatable on general medical lines. *Encephalitis* may occur in a variety of virus infections (*e.g.* mumps), but treatment of virus encephalitis is neither so safe nor so predictable as using penicillin in G.P.I. So far we do not have the same success in using antibiotics for virus infections as we do with their use in bacterial infections.

Tuberculosis of the brain is a bacterial infection that is treatable, but does not usually present as a psychiatric condition. Other forms of bacterial inflammation of the brain, or brain abscess, may give rise to delirium, but from the psychiatric point of view do not often cause diagnostic difficulty. Such patients usually find themselves fairly promptly in the hands of the general physician and surgeon, and need not be discussed here further.

TRAUMA

Epilepsy

Even a small, localised cerebral injury may produce a disturbance in brain function. After a penetrating wound either a splinter of bone, or even the scar remaining from the injury, may serve as a focus for abnormal electrical discharges in the brain producing one form or another of *epilepsy*. The patient's seizures sometimes only involve that part of the body served by the section of the brain affected, but in many cases the electrical discharge spreads to the remainder of the brain to produce a generalised convulsion identical to what is seen in *grand mal* or major epilepsy. This does not usually bring him to the psychiatrist unless the local part of the brain affected produces abnormal feelings, thoughts or behaviour.

The prime site for such abnormal phenomena is the *temporal lobe*. In temporal lobe epilepsy the patient may turn up with auditory hallucinations, olfactory and gustatory hallucinations, peculiar tricks of memory and sight, elated or depressed moods, and disturbance of behaviour. Small wonder that such afflicted subjects attract psychiatric diagnoses.

Patients who experience the grand mal type of major epileptic seizure are occasionally referred for a psychiatric opinion because of *post-ictal automatism*. 'Post-ictal' means 'after the convulsion'; the 'automatism' refers to a period of disturbed behaviour that sometimes occurs in which the patient wanders round as if conscious, but in a dazed and dissociated state, like a robot or automaton. In this state the patient does not know what he is doing, or at least has impaired recollection of it subsequently. This may be of great importance in law. Sometimes serious crimes of violence, even homicide, may be committed by an epileptic, and the possibility has to be entertained that the crime was committed in such a state of mind. Obviously such a plea cannot always be accepted at its face value, or else a person who suffered from fits might scarcely ever be found guilty of a serious crime.

So far we have been considering how even a tiny lesion in the brain may cause psychological disturbance through epileptic discharges. In larger traumatic lesions the loss of function of the affected parts will be more conspicuous. The 'punch-drunk' boxer may be found to have a severe memory impairment, for example. Some parts of the brain are more vulnerable than others. The cerebral hemispheres are supported by membranes or curtains of tough fibre that are strung across the inside of the skull. If the trauma causes displacement of the brain, then tears or damage may occur where the brain scrapes past the edge of the membrane. One such place is the temporal lobe, and the scars from damage may later trigger off temporal lobe epileptic attacks.

Trauma may itself be *caused* by epilepsy. During a convulsion, not only is the patient liable to suffer from impaired oxygen supplies to the brain while breathing ceases in the seizure, but also the fall to the ground at the beginning of the attack may cause a head injury. If a patient has major convulsions arising from a focus in the temporal lobe, it may be difficult to tell whether the temporal lobe abnormality was the cause or the effect of his tendency to fits.

Subdural haematoma

One other type of lesion produced by trauma is a notorious cause of psychiatric symptoms, and that is the *subdural haematoma*. Usually seen in the elderly, it can result from a blow so light that the patient may not even remember it occurring. The *dura* is a particularly tough sheet of tissue that surrounds the brain, and the *haematoma* is a collection of blood, like a bruise, that forms underneath it as a result of the trauma. Instead of being absorbed in a few days like a bruise elsewhere, it may become walled off by scar tissue and behave like a cyst, causing symptoms from pressure on the underlying brain. It can produce a confusional state (delirium) or fluctuating consciousness. varying from day to day. The patient often complains of headache, and may suffer from an unsteady gait or profound apathy.

It is important to diagnose this condition, because the treatment is simple and the prospects (when treated) are good. At operation the collection of fluid is removed, and the patient can be expected to show a complete remission of his symptoms in the majority of cases.

TOXIC

Symptoms of poisoning

Psychiatric syndromes are not often caused by deliberate attempts to poison the patient. Plants of the deadly nightshade family (solanaceae) contain chemicals, referred to as the solanaceous alkaloids, that produce delirium. The deadly nightshade itself, *atropa belladonna*, contains a compound (atropine) which is lethal if taken in large doses, but very useful medically in small, accurate doses. The family includes the henbane plant (but also the potato, tomato, tobacco, paprika and petunia plants).

The symptoms of poisoning with atropine, belladonna or deadly nightshade include dry skin, dry mouth, and dilated pupils, as well as the delirium. These symptoms will be seen if children accidently eat the forbidden berries of the deadly nightshade plant, and are the delight of the detective fiction writer (with the would-be murderer slipping the atropine eye-drops into the victim's food).

The dry mouth and dilated pupils are caused by inhibition of the parasympathetic nervous system, and you will recall that this sort of effect was produced, too, by certain drugs used in psychiatry (*see* Chapter 4). These same drugs may also, occasionally, produce symptoms of delirium—especially the anti-parkinsonian agents. So again we have the predicament of drugs being given to psychiatric patients which may themselves produce a psychiatric syndrome. This is not usually too difficult to disentangle provided that:

1. One remembers that the drugs may be the cause of the delirium;

2. the patient is not actually being treated for organic brain disease.

Withdrawal of drugs

Delirium can also be caused by *withdrawal* of drugs, and you will remember that *delirium tremens* may be precipitated by withdrawal, or even relative withdrawal, of high doses of barbiturates, alcohol and other sedatives.

Alcohol may also cause the other two main organic syndromes, the dysmnestic state and dementia. Here the action is probably not direct, but is mediated through vitamin deficiency, and it is considered under that heading.

Body chemicals

The remaining type of toxin to be considered is that produced by the body itself. If, through impaired action of the liver or the kidneys, the body is unable to rid itself of the products of its own chemical processes, then these dammed-up compounds circulating in the bloodstream may cause impaired consciousness and delirium or coma.

The same applies to the chemical that is excreted by the lungs—carbon dioxide. Normally, high concentrations of carbon dioxide in the blood stimulate respiration, and the faster and deeper breathing automatically clears the excessive amounts that were in the blood. This automatic feed-back process can break down in certain lung conditions or when the blood supply to the brain is impaired. Paradoxically, giving the patient oxygen may make matters worse—since having the oxygen needs satisfied can still further depress respiration, so allowing the carbon dioxide to accumulate even more. The carbon dioxide intoxication may produce delirium or even unconsciousness and death.

DEFICIENCY

Diet

Essential foodstuffs include things like *protein, fats* and *carbohydrates* that, together with water and vegetable fibre, make up the main bulk of our diet. Deficiency of any of these items does not usually present as a psychiatric problem. Lethargy, lassitude and weakness may be associated with deficiency of common salt and other elements used in the body such as *potassium* and *calcium*. A large trade is still done in correcting alleged weakness in the nervous system caused by a supposed deficiency of *phosphates* in the diet. This is derided by many orthodox physicians, and is undertaken to a large degree by do-it-yourself cures and proprietary medicines sold over the counter, but some doctors will still prescribe phosphate mixtures as 'tonics'.

Vitamin deficiency

More acceptable to the academic physician are the diseases caused by deficiencies of *vitamins*. Vitamins are organic chemicals found in natural foodstuffs which are essential to health, even though they are required in only tiny quantities. Psychiatric disturbance is not especially likely when vitamins A, C, or D are lacking, but can occur when there is deficiency of various members of the B group.

Probably the best-documented example of vitamin deficiency is the development of organic cerebral disease with an impaired supply of vitamin B_1 (aneurine or thiamine) to the brain. The story of vitamin B_1 deficiency centres round one of the types of the dysmnestic syndrome—Korsakov's psychosis (*see* Chapter 3). Korsakov described cases where impairment of memory was associated with disorientation in time, confabulation of stories to fill in gaps in the memory, and degeneration of the peripheral nerves of the body. Some of his patients had severely impaired intake of foodstuffs, either through protracted vomiting or through disease of the stomach. Presumably vitamin B deficiency was one of the first results because vitamin B (like vitamin C, but unlike vitamins A and D) is water soluble. Vitamins A and D are fat soluble and supplies of these substances may gradually seep out of the body's fat stores over a period of time.

Alcoholism and thiamine deficiency

Other cases described by Korsakov were patients with alcoholism. Alcoholics are especially prone to deficiency of vitamin B_1. Several factors may contribute to this. Firstly, alcoholics themselves may suffer from impaired food intake. For the normal person a small quantity of an alcoholic drink can act as an appetite stimulant, but the alcoholic may be interested in the intake of alcohol to the exclusion of other components of his diet. When he does eat he often does so sporadically and in an unbalanced way.

A second factor in the poor nutrition of the alcoholic is the effect of some alcohol-containing beverages, especially spirits, on the lining of the gastro-intestinal tract. He may develop gastritis, and whatever effect this has on digestion it is certainly likely to produce a loss of appetite which will make matters still worse. Many spirit drinkers find that the idea of breakfast, for instance, is particularly repulsive.

The third factor is the effect of alcohol after it has been absorbed into the body. There it is treated as a food in its own right. The channels of metabolism in the tissues are therefore flooded with this unusual chemical. The vitamins play an important role in the metabolic chemistry of the body and thiamine in particular is used in the processing of carbohydrates. It is thought that alcohol requires the same processing channels as dietary carbohydrate and so promptly uses up what thiamine there is remaining in the body. This result is similar to the observation that men who are starved of all food in equal proportions take longer to develop clinical thiamine deficiency (usually known as 'beri-beri') than men who continue to receive thiamine-free carbohydrate (e.g. polished rice).

The alcoholic, then, is at risk of developing disease due to thiamine deficiency for various reasons. There are two forms of beri-beri—a 'wet' form and a 'dry' form. The wet form is so called because the body becomes swollen with fluid as a result of the effects of the deficiency on the heart. In the dry form the patients develop disease of the nervous system instead. Alcoholics can get a form of heart disease, but more relevant to the psychiatric sphere are the effects on the nerve tissue.

The dymnestic syndrome (Korsakov's psychosis in this case) is the most typical way in which the thiamine deficiency of alcoholism affects the brain. In some cases of alcoholism a more generalised organic brain disease is produced, giving rise to dementia. To complete the picture, the reader will remember that we saw that *withdrawal* of addicting doses of alcohol will sometimes lead to an acute organic brain syndrome (*delirium tremens*). Thus, apart from the direct befuddlement of thought that can be caused by a large dose of alcohol, in one way or another alcoholics can develop all three of the major organic brain syndromes—delirium, dysmnesia and dementia.

Vitamin B_6 deficiency

The role of the other B vitamins in the aetiology of organic brain disease is not so clear as that of thiamine (B_1). There is inconclusive evidence about the part played by both folic acid and pyridoxine (B_6) in maintaining the integrity of the nervous system. Pellagra is caused by lack of nicotinic acid (on maize diets, for instance) and its features are said to include dermatitis, diarrhoea and 'dementia'. This disease is now scarcely seen outside underprivileged areas, and it is likely, when it does occur, to be diagnosed and rectified before it has got past the stage of delirium, so that dementia should not develop.

Vitamin B_{12} deficiency

Vitamin B_{12} is in a rather different position from that of the other B vitamins. Deficiency in the body can occur despite normal supplies in the diet. This possibility arises because vitamin B_{12} (cyanocobalamin) is not taken up into the body unaided. It needs the presence of a secretion from the healthy stomach lining, called the *intrinsic factor*, to ensure its absorption. In those patients who have had a complete surgical removal of the stomach vitamin B_{12} deficiency is almost bound to ensue.

Anaemia

The most likely serious result of this deprivation is anaemia. The anaemia is of a special type in which the red blood corpuscles are actually larger than normal, although there are many fewer of them. In a proportion of cases damage to the nervous system also occurs.

This clinical picture can be found even with a superficially intact stomach. In the disease known as *pernicious anaemia* the B_{12} deficiency is associated with an abnormality of the stomach lining which results in a lack of secretion of the intrinsic factor. At present it is not known for sure what causes the peculiarity in the stomach lining. In untreated patients the typical anaemia develops. In those cases which also develop effects in the nervous system it is commonly the spinal cord that suffers the brunt. In others it is the peripheral nerves that show the disease, and in others it is the brain that is afflicted. It is the last group that concerns us here.

B_{12} deficiency may produce a similar picture to Korsakov's psychosis, or it may produce a chronic organic brain syndrome. The reader will recall that the latter condition can present with any of the symptoms of functional psychiatric disorders, which accounts for a wide variety of descriptions in the past of the psychological features that may appear with pernicious anaemia.

In some vulnerable individuals disease of the nervous system may occur in the absence of the blood change, so that the fact that the patient does not have anaemia does not exclude the possibility that his psychiatric symptoms may be caused by B_{12} deficiency.

Diagnosis
Fortunately, even apart from identifying the anaemia, there is a fairly simple way of diagnosing the condition—the level of B_{12} in the blood can now be determined in the laboratory. The treatment is very safe and straightforward—injection of the vitamin at two- or four-weekly intervals—so it is worth looking for the condition in any likely case.

Vitamin B_{12} deficiency is clearly different from the other forms of vitamin deficiency in that it usually has little to do with the levels of the vitamin in the diet, but results from the loss of the intrinsic factor from the stomach so that the normal dietary intake cannot be absorbed into the body.

Psychological causes of deficiency
For the remainder of the vitamin deficiencies that were dealt with in earlier pages, there is another link with psychiatric disorder: a psychiatric disorder may *result* in vitamin deficiency.

To make this clear let us take the case of the deficiency of another water soluble vitamin, *vitamin C*. Deficiency of vitamin C produces scurvy, in which the patient presents with swollen and bleeding gums, bruising, and a proneness to infection. There is not typically any psychiatric morbidity that results from this disease. However, how does the person *get* scurvy in the first place? The average person resident in, say, the United Kingdom or North America will obtain plenty of vitamin C in the diet. Even if he cannot afford citrus fruits, there is vitamin C to be found in other foodstuffs—even potatoes. The conclusion is that a person has to eat a highly unusual diet in order to develop scurvy. This can be done if the person exists entirely, say, on tea and biscuits, but who does that? The answer is that it may be a person forced to do so by exceptional circumstances, or it may be a person who does so *because* of his psychiatric morbidity. So we can see that if we come across a person with evidence of vitamin C deficiency, we should not be surprised to find a psychological abnormality as well which itself led to the lack of appropriate diet.

If we now return to deficiency of vitamins in the B group, we can see that even if we demonstrate a psychological disturbance, we do not necessarily know which caused which. We are faced with the old riddle, 'which came first, the chicken or the egg?' If one can get a good history, then one may be able to tease out the various strands of causation. Often, however, the patient will be a solitary person, living alone, and with few friends, and an accurate account of his previous behaviour may be lacking. Fortunately, if one has got as far as diagnosing the vitamin deficiency, at least *that* can be corrected while one is delving deeper into the underlying psychological or social causes of the deficiency.

NEOPLASTIC

Benign and malignant tumours

Tumours may be benign or malignant. In the benign group complete removal of the growth is curative, and as a rule the extent of the tumour can be defined clearly at operation, so that it is relatively easy to ensure that the whole mass has been cut away. Malignant tumours, on the other hand, are prone to recur after attempts at removal. This is partly because they infiltrate the surrounding tissues, so that it is difficult to define exactly how far the tumour extends. It is also because the cells of the malignant tumour detach themselves and float in the bloodstream to a distant site, setting up what are known as *secondary deposits* or *metastases* elsewhere in the body (the original tumour being known as the *primary* growth). In addition, the cancer can spread along lymphatic ducts and set up secondary growths in the lymph glands.

Secondary tumours

When psychiatric symptoms are due to tumours of the brain, it is often found that they are secondary deposits that have metatasised from a primary growth elsewhere in the body. In this situation there is rarely a surgical remedy. Heroic operations to remove the secondary growths as well as the primary are likely to be ill-fated: it is almost always found that, later on, other secondary deposits show themselves, which were too small to be detected at the time of the operation. The tumour that produces only one metatasis is a medical curiosity.

Primary tumours
If psychiatric symptoms are found to be due to a primary tumour the outlook is a little brighter, but still not rosy. Even if it can be cut away before it has metastasised it may be so difficult to identify that part of it may be left behind in error, only to recur. Obviously to remove a large part of the surrounding brain to be on the safe side will probably leave the patient with a severe and permanent disability.

Meningioma
There is one type of intracranial growth that has a relatively good prognosis, and this is the *meningioma*. A benign tumour of the membranes covering the brain (the *meninges*) can usually be removed intact, and will not be expected to recur. Unless it has damaged the underlying brain from prolonged pressure, the patient's symptoms can be expected to resolve with a satisfactory outcome.

DEGENERATIVE

The degenerative group of diseases generally show themselves in the second half of life and are of obscure aetiology. It is a category which is hard to justify logically, and the diseases placed in this category are likely to be reallocated to other causes when we improve our understanding.

Senile and arteriosclerotic dementia
The main two claimants for a position in this group are senile dementia and arteriosclerotic dementia. Senile dementia gives its own characteristic picture under the microscope, and results in general wasting of the brain with large troughs between the gyri (the folds of the cortex). The alternation of shrunken gyri and open troughs give the whole brain a shrivelled walnut appearance.

Arteriosclerotic dementia produces areas of softening in the brain which are later absorbed to leave scars. Despite the fact that senile dementia affects the brain generally and diffusely, while arteriosclerotic dementia hits the brain first here and then there, they are very difficult to tell apart in life. The continuous process of gradual deterioration expected in senile dementia may be produced by arteriosclerotic dementia, and the episodic course 'typical' of the latter may be witnessed in the former. If the onset of the illness is really sudden, and leaves the patient with a hemiparesis, then it is probably arteriosclerotic—but even this is not an absolute rule.

Senile dementia shows some tendency to run in families. It also affects women more often than men. Otherwise, little is known about possible predisposing factors. Even these two items can be argued away by the sceptic: a family that has had one case of senile dementia may be more aware of such a progress in another member; women tend to survive to a later age than men, so naturally there will be more of them with senile dementia.

A little more is known about arteriosclerotic dementia. After all, we know that it is associated with disease of the arteries. The commonest disease to be found in association with the areas of softening is *atheroma*, a deposit of porridge-like material in the lining of the large blood vessels. But this, too, is not straightforward: at autopsy the affected artery may appear to be *wider* in internal diameter than normal, presumably because of weakening of its wall. Although this does not look healthy, it is difficult to see how it interferes with the *flow* of blood to the brain.

Cholesterol
The 'porridge' material has been found to contain large amounts of cholesterol—a fatty chemical. Deposits of this chemical are to be found in a high proportion of the population somewhere or other in their arteries, even in young men, but their prevalence increases markedly with advancing years. It has been suggested that it is more common with a high fat diet, a high carbohydrate diet, a high cholesterol diet, obesity and hypertension. It is seen more often among diabetics and in men. In some patients with atheroma a high level of cholesterol in the circulating blood can be demonstrated, which itself may affect several members of a family.

Various drugs and diets have been shown to be capable of reducing the blood level of cholesterol, but it is not yet clear for whom the long-term advantages of taking these drugs and diets outweigh the disadvantages. By the time that symptoms of cerebral arteriosclerosis have made their appearance, it may be too late to clear up the atheromatous deposits by administering drugs at that stage.

Other drugs act to widen the small blood vessels by relaxing the smooth muscle that is present in their walls. *Vasodilators* that act in the rest of the body, for instance, produce flushing or a sense of warmth in the skin. Some drugs are supposed to produce their effect especially on the cerebral vessels.

The diameter of the larger blood vessels is relatively fixed, and it is mainly the small vessels whose bore can be varied by the action of smooth muscle, and which therefore are affected by the vasodilator drugs. Of course, if the main trunk of the artery is largely blocked by atheroma, it is unlikely that a vasodilator acting on the smaller twigs will have more than a marginal effect.

On the other hand, we have already seen that the mechanism of the effect of the atheromatous deposit is sometimes obscure, and furthermore in someone with a borderline blood supply to the brain even a marginal improvement in flow may produce a welcome benefit. So, at present, the value of these drugs is conjectural. Some experiments have shown measurable improvement in performance with their use, others have been disappointing.

Presenile dementia
For the sake of completeness in this section on degenerative diseases I should mention the *presenile dementias*. These include Pick's disease, Alzheimer's disease and Jakob-Creutzfeldt's disease. They have been described elsewhere in this book and their precise aetiology is unknown, although, like senile dementia, they tend to occur more often in women and to run in families. They are rare, and will not be considered further here. Huntington's chorea also produces a chronic organic brain syndrome, and the onset is usually below the age of 60; it is therefore sometimes included in the presenile dementias but will be considered a little later in this chapter in the section on hereditary diseases.

ENDOCRINE

Endocrine glands

The endocrine glands are the *ductless* glands. This contrasts them with such organs as the salivary glands, sweat glands, the mucous glands of the bronchial tubes or the digestive glands of the stomach, all of which produce a secretion or juice which runs down a duct into a cavity where it performs its function. The endocrine glands have no duct—the chemicals that result from their labours diffuse into the bloodstream in which they are carried round the body. They can thus exert their effects at distant sites (at 'target organs') or systematically throughout the body.

The endocrine glands include such well-known structures as the thyroid, the adrenal glands, and the testis or ovary. True, the testis does have a duct. In fact it has a double function: for the production of sperm it requires a duct, but for the production of male sex hormone it does not and is part of the endocrine system.

Pancreas

Another organ with a double function is the *pancreas*, which lies in the upper abdomen behind the stomach. The pancreas does secrete a juice, which is used in the digestive process, and a duct leads this juice along into the duodenum. The pancreas also secretes a chemical into the bloodstream—insulin—which controls the level of blood sugar, so that part of the pancreatic activity is endocrine. The name for a chemical that is let loose in the blood like this is a *hormone*. Somehow this seems a familiar and well-known term when applied, as above, to the male sex hormone, but it is not always realised that insulin is a hormone. Yet it is not only a genuine member of the group, it is the original one—the first that was identified.

It is well known that deficiency of insulin leads to excessive levels of blood sugar, or *diabetes mellitus*. The opposite can also happen. The pancreas sometimes produces excessive quantities of insulin, leading to pathologically low levels of blood sugar. If this happens the brain is particularly affected since it is peculiar in that, of all the organs of the body, it is the one that relies exclusively on the sugar in the blood to keep it going. If the sugar level is low, other organs can use up some of the alternative nutrients in the blood, but the brain's function inevitably becomes impaired. As the blood sugar sags, the patient suffers from an episode of irritability, confusion, or even unconsciousness. With repeated episodes permanent brain damage can occur.

This condition of *spontaneous hypoglycaemia* can be diagnosed by recording blood sugar levels while the patient fasts. An exploratory abdominal operation may reveal a small, benign tumour of the pancreas, and removal of this is likely to produce a satisfactory result (provided that the patient has not yet got to the stage of brain damage).

Thyroid hormone
Deficiency of *thyroid* hormone results in the slowing down of the actions of the body, and the resulting state is known as *hypothyroidism* or *myxoedema*. The patient becomes much more vulnerable to cold temperatures, the voice becomes husky, the skin becomes dry, the hair gets dry and thin—even on the eyebrows, and since the general slowing down affects involuntary muscles as well the patient becomes constipated. Fluid accumulates under the skin, giving a puffy appearance to the face and thickening of the tissues of, say, the legs. It is this accumulation of fluid that is technically known as myxoedema, but this term is often used to refer to the entire hypothyroid state. Along with the rest of the functions of the body, the activity of the brain slows up. The patient will have difficulty in carrying out tasks involving intellectual activity, and his condition may mimic dementia. Certainly, any of the features of functional psychosis can appear, when it has been called 'myxoedema madness'. In advanced cases the patient may become semi-conscious, and the temperature of the body may fall well below the normal range (*hypothermia*).

In theory the treatment is simple. Thyroid extract has been available for decades, and nowadays the pure chemical version of the thyroid hormone is available. The patient can take a dose of this each day, as a tablet, to replace the missing hormone in his body. In the mild case this will be sufficient for a complete return to normal. In the severe case, with hypothermia, a sudden restitution of full levels of thyroid hormone may be dangerous. If one organ or system of the body starts firing at full pace while another system is still in cold storage, serious mischief can occur, and sudden death under these circumstances has been known.

In practice, therefore, the patient is given tiny doses of the hormone which are built up to normal levels over a period of weeks or months. In many cases, again, the patient returns to a completely normal state. In some, however, the patient is revealed to suffer from defects when the full dose of hormone is once again being taken. Partly this is because patients who develop myxoedema are often elderly to start with, and cannot be expected to be in perfect health. Partly it is because the prolonged state of myxoedema predisposes to certain pathological conditions—such as atheroma of the arteries. The extent to which the long period of 'cold storage' itself produces permanent damage is difficult to assess.

To take the case of the patient who has been treated for hypothyroidism, but who still has features of the chronic organic brain syndrome, there are at least three possibilities to account for this. Firstly, the patient may have had some dementia before developing myxoedema. Secondly, the atheroma of the arteries produced by the hypothyroidism may have given rise to arteriosclerotic dementia. Thirdly, the neurones may have become irreversibly damaged by the condition of low circulating levels of thyroid hormone.

It is difficult to say, as a rule, to what extent the third reason operates, if at all. In fact, in our present state of knowledge it would be possible to believe that this last alternative is never the explanation—that if there is no concurrent disease process then restitution of normal hormone levels will produce a normally functioning brain.

The opposite condition—*hyperthyroidism*—gives rise to many symptoms that are identical with those of anxiety states, but there is no problem of distinguishing these from organic brain disease.

Adrenal hormone
Deficiency of the adrenal hormones produces a state of apathy and inertia that might be confused with depression, but not dementia. Similarly, the syndromes produced by the over- or underproduction of other hormones may also produce symptoms of psychological importance, but none that are of direct relevance to the chronic organic brain syndrome.

HEREDITARY

Often, as in senile dementia and arteriosclerotic dementia, it is difficult to tease out the influence of heredity in organic brain syndromes from the other possible factors in their causation (*see* the section on degenerative diseases above).

Huntington's chorea

There are, however, a few diseases affecting the brain that have a clear-cut pattern of inheritance. The most striking of these is Huntington's chorea. In the fully-developed case the patient has a combination of dementia and chorea. The features of chorea have been noted previously (*see* Chapter 4). The patient seems to be permanently on the move with first one part of the body jerking, then another. They are quick short-lived movements, which the patient may disguise as changes of position, gestures or grimaces. As a result of the movements, the changes in tone, and the other neurological features of chorea, the patient becomes progressively disabled and has trouble with walking or talking. The age of onset is on average about 40 years, but this varies widely, and it is not unknown to have the first signs develop either at 20 or 60 years of age.

In the early case either the dementia or the movements may be missed. The chronic organic brain syndrome is likely to be misdiagnosed when it presents as personality change rather than intellectual deterioration. Frequently the first indication of the disease, the significance of which is seen in retrospect, is an episode of antisocial behaviour. The abnormal movements, too, may have been present for a long time before they are recognised. The patient may be thought to be fidgety, restless or agitated for a long time before suddenly the realisation occurs that the movements are those of chorea.

The inheritance of Huntington's chorea is by a dominant gene. With one affected parent there will be a 50:50 chance that a child will himself develop the disease in time. With this high proportion of affected family members the hereditary nature of the disease is likely to be well-known to the family, who will be aware that a grandparent and great-grandparent were affected too, together with half of their descendants. Many of the family will live through much of their adult life in fear of eventually developing the condition themselves.

Treatment of Huntington's chorea

At present there is no curative treatment. The chorea, and to some extent the behaviour disorder, can be alleviated by phenothiazines or, possibly, other major tranquillisers. These will not, however, halt the progress of the dementia.

The fact that it is inherited as a dominant condition does not necessarily mean that a cure will never be found. It may be that at some future date a means will be found of altering the gene itself that is responsible for the disease. Apart from that, though, it may be that one could find a way of ensuring that inheriting the gene did not mean that developing the disease was inevitable. If you ask geneticists how this could be, they will point to the fact that although the average onset of the disease is about the age of 40 years, the considerable variation in the actual age of onset indicates that other factors must be at work in deciding when exactly the disease shows itself. If we understood more about these other factors then we might be able to prevent the disease from showing itself until much later in life, or even at all.

Phenylketonuria

The idea of a disease with a clear pattern of inheritance being treated successfully is not unknown in medicine. The condition called *phenylketonuria* is inherited as a recessive. Two parents, both carrying the gene but unaffected by it, will have a 25 per cent chance that any child born to them will show the disease. The child will have inherited an affected gene from both parents and will therefore have no chance of escaping from *the inherited tendency to develop that disease*—which is a form of mental handicap or subnormality. Nevertheless he can escape the disease if a certain chemical in the diet (phenylalanine) is avoided. If one eats natural foods this is virtually impossible, but nowadays a synthetic diet can be prepared which is phenylanine-free, and the child can grow up with a normal intelligence. The tendency to phenylketonuria can be detected early in life by a single urine test, and this test is now a standard practice with young babies.

SUMMARY

General paralysis of the insane (G.P.I.) is a diagnosable illness of specific cause (syphilis), which can be halted with treatment (*e.g.* penicillin). Vitamin deficiency (*e.g.* vitamin B_{12} deficiency) can be identified accurately and the treatment is also simple and safe. Brain tumour can be diagnosed but treatment is sometimes un-rewarding. Some effects of trauma (*e.g.* seizures, subdural haematoma) can be ameliorated. Poisoning of the brain is caused by disease (renal failure), by the patient (alcoholism), or by the physician (toxic effects of medical drugs).

It may be that in the future further knowledge will make diseases of such apparently hopeless aetiology as heredity and degeneration amenable to preventive treatment (as already has happened with phenylketonuria).

6 The detection of organic brain disease

In this chapter we see the hints that are given on first seeing the patient that brain disease may be present. We see how intelligence tests may be used to clarify the issue, and how we may test the ability of the patient to learn new material—a task that patients with diffuse brain disease find most difficult.

We look at the use of X-rays, brain waves (electro-encephalogram), blood tests and ultrasound in helping to make this diagnosis, and see that some of these tests bring with them their own dangers. Some patients even have a piece of the brain removed (*brain biopsy*) to help with the diagnosis. Luckily this is rare.

INITIAL INVESTIGATIONS

We have already seen that a patient with organic brain disease may present with *any psychiatric symptoms*. What appears to be a case of schizophrenia, or depressive psychosis, or even a neurotic illness, may turn out in time to be an organic condition. The first problem we shall face in this chapter, then, is sifting those patients with brain pathology from the larger numbers of patients with psychiatric symptoms of functional origin.

If the patient does have organic brain disease we wish to know what is its cause or nature. In some circumstances investigations to

elucidate this aspect do not even have to wait until we have definitely established that brain disease is present. Sometimes we suspect
that a patient has an organic condition in the early stages, but we
cannot prove it. The tests are all equivocal or on the borderline, and
considerable doubt remains. Under these circumstances we may
decide to proceed with investigations into the cause of the disease,
even though we have not proved that it is there. Why wait for
definite proof? If we can treat a disease in its early stages so much
the better. So, sometimes even before the investigations on the first
question are complete, we start investigating the patient to see if,
for instance, he is suffering from an easily remediable condition
such as deficiency of vitamin B_{12}.

For the sake of clarity, though, let us consider the investigations
separately under two different headings.

DOES THE PATIENT HAVE ORGANIC
BRAIN DISEASE?

In the more obvious cases the patient may be referred for a
professional opinion precisely because relatives or friends fear that
brain disease is present. The patient may have shown obvious signs
of intellectual deterioration. Sometimes the patient himself may
have perceived this.

Verbal and non-verbal intelligence tests
At an early stage of intellectual deterioration it may be difficult for
an outsider to confirm it objectively. How can you tell a person
with average intelligence, say, from a person with previously above-
average intelligence who is now slightly demented? This is not a
purely rhetorical question, because there are some ways in which
the two states differ. For instance, the previously highly-intelligent
person whose powers are now failing will have a different
vocabulary range from the person who has never exceeded a
modest intelligence. It is found that the understanding of the
meaning of words does not deteriorate as fast as other aspects of
intelligence when a patient suffers from diffuse organic brain disease. (Of course there will be exceptions in the case of dysphasia.)
If there is a large discrepancy, therefore, between a patient's ability
to perform on vocabulary tests and his poorer performance on, say,

visuomotor tasks, then this would be consonant with a dementing process.

A more general case can be stated. On the whole *verbal* components of the battery of intelligence tests are preserved better than *non-verbal* components. Suppose that the I.Q. given by the verbal tests is 100. Then, if the I.Q. given by the non-verbal tests is 98 or 102, this degree of discrepancy is of no particular significance. Now take a case where the verbal I.Q. is 120. If the non-verbal I.Q. is 80, clearly there is a serious anomaly, one explanation of which could be organic brain disease.

Memory tests

There are other peculiarities of the intellectual performance of the patient with dementia. As is well known, a frequent accompaniment is memory disorder. A simple test for this, using a name and address, was spelled out earlier (*see* Chapter 3).

Case 10 Miss J.

Miss J. was 70 years old. She looked well-groomed, and she conversed alertly and with spirit. An unmarried lady, she responded indignantly but politely when a new doctor inadvertently asked her how many children she had. She gave her own name and home address promptly and accurately. She recalled her date of birth correctly, but gave her age as sixty-five. Surprisingly, she could not say how many siblings there were in her family of origin (in reply to the question, 'How many children did your parents have?'). She was vague about the day of the week, and gave the current year as 1892 (the year of her birth, in fact). She evaded questions about current events.

On formally presenting her with a name and address to remember, she failed to register any of the elements of the address at the first attempt. The process was repeated three times, and it was not until the fourth time that she remembered one fragment on immediate recall—the town. Continuing the process of registration did not seem warranted in view of the incipient distress. After 11 minutes recall was again attempted, but she could remember nothing of the address at all—indeed, it was not entirely certain that she remembered being given the name and address.

With certain assumptions, a failure on memory testing as severe as this is likely to represent intellectual deterioration. The first assumption is that the patient's memory had been better in the past.

There is a certain amount of correlation between powers of memory and other intellectual abilities, but for her usual memory to have been as poor as this the patient would have had to have suffered from a life-long gross subnormality of intelligence. Another assumption is that the patient was *trying* to co-operate in the testing. In this particular case there seemed to be no wilful lack of co-operation. Other assumptions are that the patient is able to give attention and concentrate during the registration phase. Often, anxiety or depression will distract or dishearten the patient, but this in itself will not produce the degree of impairment shown above.

Provided that the patient is of previously normal intelligence, is in a co-operative frame of mind, and is not too disabled by functional psychiatric disorder, then the failure in memory testing will be evidence of organic brain disease. *Subjective* impairment of memory is a common symptom of depressive illness (together with difficulty in concentration and absent-mindedness), but such patients do surprisingly well as a rule on memory testing.

Learning tests

If demonstrable memory impairment is present, then one suspects brain damage. On the other hand, brain damage can be present *without* severely impaired memory function.

Is there any way of testing for early dementia other than the two considered so far—verbal and non-verbal comparison, and memory testing? This question may be answered in the following way. We know that if a person has generalised brain disease at a very early stage, they still have much information and skill available to them. They are able to use, in fact, all the knowledge that they acquired before getting the disease (or certainly a great deal of it). What they become increasingly unable to do is to acquire fresh knowledge. Their capacity for *new learning* falls.

Paired-associate test

Various tests have been devised to assess a person's ability to learn new material. Some involve learning definitions of words that the patient has not been familiar with before; others involve making new associations between words. One of the latter kind is called the *paired-associate test*. In the full version of the paired-associate test, devised by Inglis, the subject is led through three stages. In the first stage he is given a few pairs of words to associate that are already commonly encountered together—such as knife and fork, east and west. He is then presented with the first of each pair, and asked to give the second. The whole process is repeated several times, in random order. At each stage the correct answer is given if he failed to produce it himself. The time intervals are short so that memory, as considered above, is not such an important factor (unless he forgets things in less than a minute all told).

In the second stage the process is repeated with words that are connected, but which are not the most common of associates—pairs of words such as cup and plate, gold and lead, being given.

In the final stage words are presented that are not commonly associated at all, such as bottle and comb, or sponge and trumpet. In Inglis' original test this stage is continued for much longer than the other two (unless the patient gets the answers right to start with). The idea of this is to get a measure of exactly how long it *does* take for the subject to learn the completely new association. Unfortunately, until he has learned them, his errors are exposed to him again and again, and this can become distressing for him.

Brief paired-associate test

A briefer form of the test was tried out by Isaacs and Walkey, and they found that giving just the first two stages was a fairly good way of discriminating between those with organic brain disease and those without. This 'brief paired-associate test' (B.P.A.T.) is found towards the end of this book in Appendix I.

On this occasion, it probably *is* worthwhile making the digression to look up the cross-reference. Have a look at Appendix I now.

Having looked at the Appendix, I suggest you now read the last few paragraphs once again, for they will be easier to understand after seeing the example of the brief paired-associate test that was given in the Appendix.

You will have seen in the B.P.A.T. that there are eighteen possible answers, and therefore eighteen possible mistakes that the subject can make. Isaacs and Walkey recommended *two mistakes* as the cut-off point. That is to say, they found that their subjects with organic brain disease usually made three or more errors, but their normal subjects made two, one or even no errors. There was a small amount of overlap in scores, but this cut-off point was valid even for subjects over the age of 60 years.

My colleagues and I have used this test to try to distinguish patients known to have organic brain disease from long-stay patients with functional psychoses in a mental hospital. Obviously the separation of severe mental disorder from organic brain disease is a more stringent criterion than the separation of those with organic brain disease from *normals*. So it is satisfying to record that the B.P.A.T. *is* a valid method of doing this job, at least as a screening test. Again there was some overlap in the scores, but a cut-off point of two errors proved to be an efficient stage at which to split the populations (Priest *et al.*, 1969).

So, using the B.P.A.T. as a screening test, one *suspects* organic brain disease when more than two errors are made. Like memory, learning ability is likely to be correlated with intelligence, so that one would like to know that the patient was not previously mentally handicapped. This still leaves us with the problem of the over- lap—those patients with organic brain disease who get normal scores, and those patients without it who get abnormal scores.

If we suspect organic brain disease on other grounds, then we would not let a normal score on the B.P.A.T. convince us it was ab- sent. This situation can happen especially where the disease is focal or patchy, rather than diffuse and even. If the remainder of the in- vestigations do not help, it is worth repeating the B.P.A.T. at inter- vals to see if deterioration occurs.

What about the case of the patient without brain disease who scores more than two errors? Clearly, if the patient is psychotic and very disturbed, he may not do well on the test. More com- monly, perhaps, the problem is encountered of the patient who is depressed. In the majority of cases we can distinguish the two groups. On the one hand, we have patients with a depressive illness who are functioning badly because of it; on the other hand we have patients with organic brain disease whose depressive features are merely features of the organic brain syndrome or a reaction to the realisation that something is wrong. As a rule it is possible to separate these two sets. There remains, though, a number of patients on the borderline who cannot easily be allocated. In these cases it is usually worthwhile treating them for the depressive symptoms and repeating the tests. It is sometimes necessary to go as far as a course of electro-convulsive therapy (E.C.T.). After E.C.T. patients with organic brain disease will be no better, but those with depressive illness will typically have improved their scores on intellectual testing. Anti-depressant drugs may do the trick in milder cases.

Case 11 Mrs. M.

Mrs. M. was a 66-year-old housewife with three grown-up children. She had worked in domestic service until her marriage at the age of 26. She attended the psychiatric out-patient clinic with the complaint: 'I have a terrible shiver right down the back of the neck and it wakes me up'. Together with this mysterious symptom she also complained of depression over the previous two weeks, loss of energy and insomnia. The general practitioner who referred her said in his letter she was also suffering from headache, confusion and lack of concentration.

On mental examination the patient confirmed the depressive symptoms and the loss of concentration. She also admitted being absent-minded recently, and sometimes feeling that the future was hopeless.

So far, then, the symptoms were ambiguous. They raised the question of depressive illness (loss of energy, hopelessness, insomnia) or of organic brain disease (confusion, possibly headache) and some of the symptoms would be common to both possibilities (loss of concentration, absent-mindedness).

The mental examination continued. She was correctly orientated in time, place and person; to be specific she correctly identified the date, who I was, and where we were at the time of interview. I tried to test her memory using a fictitious name and address. She repeated each line after me quite co-operatively, but by the time we got to the end she was quite unable to remember the beginning—or to repeat any of the address back to me. We repeated the process. Again, she could not get the person's name, or the street and number, but this time she did get the town. The registration was poor and jumbled, even at the fourth attempt. On recall after 10 minutes, she was able to remember only the town again.

On the brief paired associate test she did the first half well. In the second half she made four errors. The total of four errors in eighteen chances put her in the pathological range, but only to a slight degree.

At this stage the results on the tests confirmed the initial impression that there could be more here than just the effects of a depressive illness. In addition we had discovered that 5 years previously she had been admitted to a mental hospital for an episode of 'confusion'. It was decided to investigate her further for possible organic brain disease.

She was admitted to hospital, and more extensive psychological tests produced results along the same lines—a suspicion of organic brain disease while not being unequivocally definite. Further investigations were set in train, but meanwhile she was also started on a course of anti-depressant tablets.

While we were waiting for the results of the other tests she showed a dramatic improvement on the medication and lost her depressive symptoms. At the same time her attention and concentration improved, and she did better on the tests of intellectual function. Her performance on the brief paired-associate test, for instance, now fell within the normal range (only one error out of eighteen possible). It was not surprising to find that the further tests for organic brain disease, when they came back, were all normal.

The electro-encephalogram

What other tests can be done to establish the presence of organic brain disease? If we leave behind paper and pencil tests now, we come to the instrumental techniques, of which the first is the electro-encephalogram (E.E.G.). This was discussed more fully earlier in the book (see Chapter 2). Briefly, the normal 'brain-wave' is a 10 cycle-per-second smooth rounded wave. Brain pathology is suggested by very slow waves (less than 4 cycles per second) or by the sharp waves or spikes that accompany a tendency to seizures. The E.E.G. is a harmless procedure, it is painless and not too expensive. Clearly it is not possible for every psychiatric patient to have it done as a screening test, but in cases where there is a strong clinical suspicion of organic brain disease, and where the machine is freely available, it can be used as a further source of evidence.

So far the tests that we have considered do not carry any risk of physical damage to the patient, and the question of whether or not to use them depends on the degree of certainty with which one wants to exclude brain disease. There are no reasons for not doing them apart from considerations such as the best deployment of one's time and resources. There are more controversial tests that could be regarded as testing for the presence of organic brain pathology, but they might also be looked at as providing evidence of the nature of the disease. So let us now consider the process of making a specific diagnosis.

WHAT IS THE SPECIFIC DIAGNOSIS?

The patient's history

If brain disease is expected, it is not necessary to wait until the presence of pathology is unequivocally demonstrated before looking for specific causes. If we take the different diagnoses in the order in which they are likely to crop up, then some will have been revealed early on—in the history-taking. The story given either by the patient or his relatives, if it is accurate, will reveal the picture of *chronic alcoholism* or *brain injury* (resulting from boxing or a motor-cycle accident, for instance). The family history will provide clues in *Huntington's chorea*. Examination of the patient will show the partial stroke that may be present in *cerebral arteriosclerosis*.

Blood tests

You may feel that these procedures are hardly what you think of when talking about 'investigations', so what about laboratory tests? It is possible to measure the amounts of vitamin B_{12} that are normally present in the blood. Vitamin B_{12} deficiency can be picked up by testing the blood in this way (although the test is still fairly time-consuming and expensive). Blood tests can also provide evidence of abnormal function of the thyroid gland (as in *myxoedema*). When the patient suffers from brain disease as a result of *syphilis* the serum will produce specific reactions for this disease in the majority of (but not all) cases.

Skull and chest X-rays

X-rays of the skull are not as fruitful in diagnosis as one might think. All sorts of brain disease can be present in a patient who has a normal skull X-ray. If a tumour is growing right next to the skull it might affect the bone shadow, or if the pressure inside the skull is raised changes in the skull (thinning of certain bones) can sometimes be detected on X-ray. Otherwise the evidence is usually indirect. There is a mysterious gland in the brain known as the *pineal body*. Although its function is obscure, it has a certain value in that it sometimes becomes calcified, and then it shows up on the X-ray film. It should be in the centre of the brain—in the mid-line. If there is a tumour or a blood clot in the left side of the brain and occupying a fair amount of space there, then it will shift the mid-line structures of the brain over to the right. The deviation of a calcified pineal body shown on X-ray can provide evidence of this shift. Sometimes the value of the skull X-ray is the gloomy one of demonstrating that there are multiple secondary deposits or metastases of a malignant tumour in the brain, coming from a cancerous growth elsewhere in the body. The organic brain disease may then be the result of secondaries in the brain.

A chest X-ray may give the same sinister evidence (with deposits showing in the ribs and spinal column). Sometimes secondary deposits in the brain come from a primary tumour to be seen in the lung fields, such as carcinoma of the bronchus.

The problem with X-ray examination is that it does not normally give a picture of the brain tumour itself. This is a serious limitation of its value. It is brought about by the fact that although the photographic film can pick up the contrast between bone and soft brain tissue, it is unable to show the much slighter contrast between the brain tissue and the tumour.

Brain scanning

There is another technique that has been developed to obtain a contrast known as *brain scanning*. A tiny dose of a radioactive compound is injected into the patient, and then the scan—a superior form of Geiger counter—is directed over the patient's head. Although the injection of a radioactive substance sounds awe-inspiring, this seems to be a relatively safe procedure. With some tumours the radioactive material is taken up into the growth, which then appears as an area of high activity (a 'hot spot') on the brain scan. This has proved to be a very sensitive technique, but is rather an expensive one.

Echo-encephalography

Another development of modern technology is the use of *ultrasound*. Very high-pitched vibrations, above the range of the human ear, can be bounced back from the structure inside the brain to build up a picture of the position of the cranial contents. Unfortunately, like X-rays, it is relatively insensitive to the more subtle distinctions between the tissues, but it can detect the tough mem-

branes that lie in the mid-line between the two cerebral hemispheres. It will show up, then, where there has been mid-line shift
(like X-rays of the pineal body) due to a space-occupying lesion
in one hemisphere. This technique is known as *echo-encephalography*.

Lumbar puncture

Evidence of disease in the central nervous system can be obtained
by putting a hollow needle into the fluid that surrounds the brain
and spinal cord. There is no break in continuity in this layer of fluid
(the cerebro-spinal fluid) from the top of the brain to the base of the
cord, so that inserting a needle between the vertebrae in the small of
the back (*lumbar puncture*) can reveal events taking place a long
way off. For instance, if disease in the brain alters the constitution
of the fluid surrounding the brain, then sooner or later the fluid surrounding the spinal cord will become abnormal as well. A small
specimen of this fluid can be removed and sent to the laboratóry for
a variety of tests. In a patient with syphilis of the brain (*e.g.* general
paralysis of the insane) the cerebro-spinal fluid will give the same
positive test as does the serum. Although in a substantial minority
of cases the blood test will be falsely negative, the test on the
cerebrospinal fluid is practically always positive in the untreated
case of G.P.I.

The procedure of lumbar puncture is not without danger,
however. The risk arises when there is a brain tumour, or some
other disease that raises the pressure of the contents of the skull. As
the fluid is removed from the spinal canal, the high intracranial
pressure forces the brain downwards, jamming part of it in the
funnel-shaped junction of the skull and spinal column. The con-
striction causes damage to the brain, sometimes with fatal results.
As a rule it is possible to detect those cases with raised intracranial
pressure: they will be suffering from headaches and vomiting, and
have a special appearance of the retina when the eyes are examined
with an illuminated instrument (the *opthalmoscope*).

All the same, you can see that we are now dealing with a
different category of investigation. If we are considering whether a
patient should have a lumbar puncture, it is no longer largely a
question of time and expense as it has been when talking about
blood tests and simple X-rays. We now have to take into considera-

tion the possibility of harm resulting directly from the investigational procedure itself.

Contrast studies

The above thought must give still more concern when we come to the topic of *contrast studies.*

Since the X-rays discriminate so poorly between the soft structures within the skull, ways have been devised of improving the contrast before taking the X-ray picture—these are the methods grouped together as contrast studies to which we have just referred. The two main procedures are air encephalography and cerebral angiography.

Air encephalography

In air encephalography some of the cerebro-spinal fluid is removed and replaced by air. Although X-rays do not differentiate between cerebro-spinal fluid and brain tissue, a very nice contrast can be obtained between air and brain tissue. The surfaces of the cortex can be outlined in this way, as can the ventricles. This provides a means of delineating the margin of a tumour projecting from the surface of the brain or into one of the ventricular cavities. In addition, if the brain is shrivelled or shrunken as a result of a dementing process (*e.g.* senile dementia or pre-senile dementia), then this will be given away by the appearance of widely-gaping sulci and dilated ventricles. This investigation is often uncomfortable for the patient, if only because he can be left with a fierce headache, and it can even be dangerous in some circumstances.

Cerebral angiography

A different way of providing contrast is used in cerebral angiography. Here the investigator employs a substance that casts a shadow on the X-ray, in the same way as a barium meal is used in investigating disease of the stomach. To get the radio-opaque dye into the brain, it is injected into an artery in the neck. A succession of X-rays is then taken, charting the progress of the dye into the cerebral arteries, then the capillaries, and finally the veins. If there is a tumour with a high blood supply this will show up as a 'blush' on the film taken at the appropriate time. This, then, will provide much the same information as is obtained by showing a 'hot spot' on a brain scan. In addition the *cerebral angiogram* (the picture of the blood vessels of the brain) can show up distortion in the route taken by the cerebral arteries. If there is a large tumour or blood clot in one part of the brain, then the arteries normally passing through that area may be pushed out of the way into an unusual position. This can be compared either with the normal anatomy of the brain, or with the path that the arteries take in the (usually symmetrical) other hemisphere. Even where there is no space-occupying lesion, this method may show up abnormalities of the arteries themselves.

This investigation, too, has its dangers. The wall of an artery may be weakened by passing a needle through it, and the blood supply of the brain is temporarily impaired when radio-opaque dye is taking the place of the blood that should be passing through it. Whether or not this is the full explanation, it has been known for patients to have a stroke just after they have been subjected to cerebral angiography. Again, we are considering a procedure where the possible dangers have to be put in the balance against the hoped for benefits.

Brain biopsy

If these methods of investigation are fruitless, then *brain biopsy* can be considered. Biopsy is the removal of a piece of living tissue for examination by a pathologist. If there is a generalised disease process throughout the brain, then the pathologist may be able to make the diagnosis from the specimen that has been removed. Such a dramatic step is not often undertaken in the average psychiatric practice. Sometimes a brain biopsy is carried out where a tumour has been identified and it is necessary to know the precise nature of the tumour before deciding on treatment: for example, whether to give a course of radiotherapy for a malignant growth.

Simple investigations

The majority of psychiatric patients, in fact, do not require the (from the point of view of the medical profession) heroic procedures that we have just been discussing of brain biopsy, air studies, or angiography. The simpler and safer investigations outlined earlier are generally enough to provide sufficient information on which to base the management of the patient. If they do not provide certainty in the diagnosis, then it is often permissible to wait for a while and then repeat the simple investigation again. In this way one can try to avoid the situation where the investigation seems worse than the disease.

Computer-assisted tomography

Before ending this chapter we will consider one more method of investigation. Very recently introduced, this technique is known as *computer-assisted tomography*. By taking successive X-rays of 'slices' at different levels on the head, and using the computer to build the series of pictures up into one whole view, it is possible to obtain a contrast between the brain and its surrounding fluids without any unusual danger to the patient. (Even the amount of radiation is no more than with other techniques.) The limitation of this investigation is that it is so far available in only a few experimental centres.

SUMMARY

The *presence* of organic brain disease may be suggested by the history of intellectual deterioration. Examination of the patient will show impairment on non-verbal intelligence tests, on memory tasks, and on *new learning* (as in the paired-associate test). In doubtful cases a trial of treatment for depressive illness may produce a prompt return to normal of poor intellectual function.

The special tests for brain disease are the electro-encephalogram (E.E.G.), X-ray examination (including computer-assisted tomography), contrast X-rays (air studies, angiograms), echo-encephalography and the brain scan. These, together with blood tests of various sorts, may indicate not only the presence but also the *type* of brain disease.

7 The functional psychoses

In this chapter we explore the borderline territory between neurosis and psychosis, sanity and insanity. We see how to define a 'functional psychosis'; having got our theoretical definition we find what problems we have in practice in being sure that a given patient *is* psychotic. On the one hand we learn about the hallucinations that normal people have, and on the other we look at the patients who have no delusions or hallucinations but who are psychotic. We distinguish between *symptoms* and *signs*.

FUNCTIONAL PSYCHOSES AND ANATOMICAL CHANGE

We come now to the psychoses in which there is no visible change in the brain. They include schizophrenia, depressive psychosis and hypomania. They are certainly not associated with gross physical brain disease, and at the present time there is no unequivocal evidence that is accepted by all psychiatrists that they are associated with microscopic changes in the brain. On the whole most psychiatrists agree that there is no detectable change in the anatomy of the brain with these illnesses. If there is no change in the brain's *structure*, then we must postulate a change only in the *function* of the brain—hence the term 'functional psychoses'.

The wary reader will have become suspicious of the length of my disclaimer. Why such an elaborate paragraph to define 'functional'? Maybe I am working hard to quieten my own doubts. I suppose I suspect that any day now there will be newspaper headlines with the news that a biochemical cause for schizophrenia or hypomania has been found, or that the electron microscope can enable scientists to distinguish between the brains of depressive psychotics and the brains of normals. Well, I certainly feel that such things are possible. Already, plenty of papers have been published that demonstrate differences in the body chemistry between patients with depressive illness and normals. What remains in doubt is whether these changes are part of the chain of causation, or whether they are brought about as a *result* of the illness.

Let us accept, then, that in the present state of our knowledge the structure:function dichotomy is at best provisional theory that may be disproved any day, and at worst just a convenient way of splitting up the psychoses for purposes of classification. Even if new discoveries are made it may remain more convenient to talk about the 'functional' psychoses than those psychoses that were not accompanied by changes in the brain that are visible macroscopically nor changes that were visible microscopically until the latter part of the twentieth century.

It is notorious that psychiatrists disagree about diagnoses. Not only may they disagree about the precise category—whether the patient is suffering from an anxiety state or from a neurotic depression, for instance—but they will even disagree about the broader divisions. One psychiatrist may diagnose a patient as suffering from a personality disorder, whereas a second may diagnose a mental illness. The symptoms that one will accept as neurotic will smack to his colleague as those of psychosis.

The area in which psychiatrists agree best, though, is in the distinction between organic and functional disorders. If one says the patient's disorder is organic, the chances are very high that another will agree. The reason for this unwonted unity may be that with this particular dispute we have an independent arbiter. In at least a proportion of cases it will eventually have been possible to carry out an autopsy, to see if there was organic brain disease. The autopsy would not help in distinguishing schizophrenia from an anxiety state, but it certainly tells you if you were wrong in your argument about whether it was organic brain disease or not. It is possible that over the years psychiatrists have learned from their mistakes.

In addition there is often a great deal of circumstantial evidence even before the stage of autopsy is reached.

Case 12 Mr. McB.

Mr. McB. was a 62-year-old retired plumber. He had been depressed since lung cancer had been diagnosed five months previously, and for the last three days had been described as 'confused'. His talk was irrelevant and lacked understanding. He was unable to give his home address or the correct date.

With a pen and paper he was unable to enter the numbers on a drawing of a clock face, and his memory had been very bad for the previous three weeks. He was unable to name the buckle on a watch strap—'I've never seen one of those before'. Even after several interviews he did not recognise the (female) ward doctor, and when asked who the woman was he suggested that she was 'a dispatch rider from H.Q.'

In addition to these difficulties with intellectual tasks he had a number of other psychiatric symptoms and signs. Apart from the understandable depression he had paranoid beliefs—he was convinced that another doctor on the ward was a policeman, and he would try to rush out of the ward in an overactive and suspicious way.

In spite of these other symptoms there was little doubt at this stage that he suffered from organic brain disease, and it was obviously possible that this was connected with the lung cancer. The electro-encephalogram was found to be grossly abnormal (confirming the presence of organic brain disease) and a brain scan showed the presence of multiple metastases.

There was not much doubt from the start that this was an organic illness, and by the time that the investigations were complete we did not need an autopsy or brain biopsy to confirm the fact. To make a positive diagnosis of functional psychosis we have no such independent technological criteria. To be able to state that certain patients suffer from functional psychosis we need to agree upon definitions, to make observations of the patient's behaviour and talk, and to take into account his own account of his feelings and thoughts. Let us assume by now that if organic brain disease is present we shall detect it. What we are left with is the problem of distinguishing the functional psychosis from other functional disorders or from normality.

WHAT IS PSYCHOTIC BEHAVIOUR?

What do we mean when we say the patient is 'psychotic'? The word has something to do with being removed from reality, but how far do you have to be removed before you are psychotic? Is the person who brings his work home from the office in his brief-case, and works all evening and all weekend without relaxation or diversion, psychotic? Is the person who, outside office hours, lies on his back, writes no letters, does no chores, but just relaxes all the time, psychotic? We may profoundly disagree with those courses of action, disapprove of the value systems they represent, and con-sider them to a degree unrealistic—but most of us would probably not go so far as to label such behaviour as psychotic.

Delusions

We are on firmer ground if the patient has frank delusions. If the patient has firm beliefs, that have been demonstrated to him to be false, and that he retains against all reason, then we say he is 'deluded'. There is one proviso, and that is that the belief is not held by others from the same cultural background. Clearly there are political and religious issues where there is considerable room for difference of opinion and where discretion has to be exercised in judging whether certain beliefs have been demonstrated to be false. In practice, there is not much difficulty in deciding whether a belief is delusional or not.

In the case of the patient whose sole abnormal belief was that he was a descendant of Queen Victoria, it might be thought that his was a difficult belief to disprove. In the event it was not necessary to disprove it—his whole attitude to his statement was quite different from anyone who really was of royal descent. Never-theless, this will be unconvincing to the sceptical reader. To take another example, when dealing with the patient who claimed that a transistorised radio device had been implanted behind his knee by a doctor in the past, in order to spy upon him and influence his behaviour, one knew that the belief was delusional without having to confirm the fact by (for instance) showing that there was not even a scar behind the knee.

If a patient has florid delusions, then we will accept that he is psychotic. However, it is not alway always possible to tell whether a patient's statements are delusional or not. One patient, Miss

D. B., was preoccupied with the fact that life had lost its savour. The colour had gone out of it—she no longer was moved by what she heard and saw; it was as if sensations had lost their impact. Now, when she said 'there is no connection between the front and back of my brain', did she have a delusion that she had an anatomical flaw, or was she metaphorically describing the loss of impact of what entered in at her eyes? When she said 'my head is empty inside' did she mean it literally, or was this a figure of speech? She made a number of statements of this sort over a period of time, and it was very difficult to tell exactly what she did mean by them. The above statements, taken on their own, could easily be metaphors. When she said 'my eyes are sliding about. . . . sometimes they come right forward, and at other times they slide back into my head', it is difficult to see what the figure of speech represents.

Another patient, Miss G.V., who had lived for a long time in a mental hospital, said that 'the nurses give patients a dream each morning which cures them' and that 'the King uses tutors to teach the country spiritualism' (at a time when there was in fact a queen on the throne). Such statements are a challenge to some to find interpretations of their symbolic meaning, but are brought in here to show how some beliefs appear to dwell on the borderline between everyday metaphor and psychotic delusion.

Hallucinations

Another feature that is characteristic of the psychoses is the hallucination. Again, in many cases there is no doubt that what the patient is describing is a psychotic phenomenon. Mrs. C.R. repeatedly complained, in broad daylight, that she could hear her mother's voice coming from the wall. In other cases the situation is not so clear. Patients will say that there is 'something inside' them that tells them not to do things, in a way that could refer to a hallucination, or could refer merely to the 'voice' of conscience. Other patients will say that it is *as if* a voice were talking to them, or that their experience was *like* a vision. It is customary to deny these similes the status of hallucinations. Some psychiatrists will even demand that to be categorised as a hallucination the voice, for instance, must be experienced as quite separate from the patient himself—which will exclude many voices that seem to arise in the patient's own head.

The experience of hallucinations is not necessarily sufficient in itself to justify a diagnosis of psychosis. They can occur in normal subjects—a common time is when dropping off to sleep at night, when they are known as *hypnagogic hallucinations*, or on waking in the morning, when they are then called *hypnopompic hallucinations*.

Formal thought disorder

A third feature of psychosis is *formal thought disorder*. Rephrased, this becomes disorder of the *form* of thought (rather than, for instance, the disorder of the *content* of thought that occurs in delusions). Formal thought disorder means that the logical connections normally present in thought are lost. There is no obvious link between successive sentences, perhaps, or in severe cases the sentence structure itself is lost.

Miss V.R. was asked by the doctor to tell him about the 'sounds in the head' that she had earlier mentioned. Her reply went as follows: 'Down in the pub the man who makes the beer accused me of drinking the beer. This is silly because I'd paid for it. A man treated me to two stouts and two cups of tea, but he used lemonade because the water was too cold. I bought two goldfish yesterday and they had big bulging eyes and no teeth. Charlie Chaplin is dead because Kit Dawson told me.'

There is obviously some connection between many of the ideas in this extract, but it it is difficult to follow the logic, either within the paragraph itself, or connecting it with the original question. However, psychotic patients are not the only persons to show a lack of logical connection in their successive statements. Politicians and poets do it, and many of us do it when we are using rhetoric rather than reason, although the switches may not be quite so obscure as with Miss V.R. When formal thought disorder is present in its more subtle forms the observer may fail to realise the looseness of the connections between the statements. It may only be at the end of a long interview that he realises he has failed to elicit even the most basic history from the patient, for instance, and then appreciates that something is wrong somewhere.

DEPRESSION

To summarise the position, although major psychotic phenomena such as delusions, hallucinations and formal thought disorder are at times conspicuous and unequivocal, at other times they are difficult to separate from the experience of normal persons, and the distinction remains a matter of judgment. This being the case, you can imagine that it is even more difficult to separate the psychoses from the neuroses. This difficulty is probably most conspicuous when dealing with depression. If we are considering how 'depressed' a person is, we can allocate him to one of at least four categories:

1. *Not depressed*

2. *Depressed but not psychologically ill* This will include fleeting moods of depression, sustained moods of depression that are not serious in degree, and sustained moods of depression that are serious in degree but which are not only understandable and appropriate (*e.g.* grief at the loss of a loved one), but are also expected to resolve spontaneously.

3. *Depressive neurosis* A sustained mood of depression which is inappropriate to environmental circumstances either in the depth of the depression or in the length of time that it has lasted (or both), but which is not accompanied by psychotic phenomena.

4. *Depressive psychosis* A sustained mood of depression which is accompanied by those psychotic phenomena characteristic of depressive illness (but not by features of other psychoses, nor by features of organic brain disease).

These categories form part of the conceptual framework which underlies the diagnosis of depressive illness. How do we allocate a particular person at a certain point in time to his proper category? This allocation itself is made on a basis of *judgment*. For instance, if we are choosing between categories 2 and 3, we may have to ask for how long a mood can be regarded as 'fleeting', and when does it become 'sustained'? If I feel depressed today, and I cannot account for it, I might agree that it was 'inappropriate to environmental circumstances', but I would not rush off to have it treated unless it lasted a bit longer. (I would regard it clearly as category 2 rather than category 3.) But how much longer should I wait? After a week I might be concerned, and start raking my mind for possible causes other than the usual disappointments and losses that one considers under 'environmental circumstances'. Had I had influenza before the depression started? Was I taking some medication which is known to produce depression? If not, then I would probably be prepared to continue to put up with it.

Family doctors do refer cases to psychiatrists in which the depression has lasted for less than a month. At the other extreme they also refer cases where the depression has apparently lasted for many years. The majority of referrals will give a history of the symptoms lasting for times ranging from a few weeks to a few years. This obviously gives plenty of scope for judgment as to what constitutes a 'sustained' mood.

The reader will readily see that the judgment becomes even more subjective when we have to consider whether or not the depression is understandable and appropriate to the environmental circumstances. As a rule the decision is made for us. If the depression is one for which the patient wants treatment, then usually we will accept his opinion that it is outside normal bounds (*i.e.* category 3 rather than category 2), and give him the benefit of any doubt.

Conversely, not many of us have the time and energy to go round canvassing for cases and thrusting persons falsely into category 3 when they should be in category 2.

Let us now explore the difficulties in the boundary between categories 3 and 4. The critical factor is the presence of features of psychotic depression. Probably the most convincing would be the presence of delusions. Patients with depressive psychosis may be preoccupied with beliefs about poverty, unworthiness, guilt and disease. We would be satisfied with delusions on these subjects as evidence of depressive psychosis. Of course, we run into the same problem of deciding when a belief becomes a delusion, as we discussed earlier, but there are other problems too. For instance, what other aspects of behaviour or feeling may be taken as evidence of psychotic depression? Apart from delusions, it is difficult to find anything that convincingly demonstrates that the depression is psychotic rather than neurotic. *Stupor* might be evidence—if a patient sits or lies unresponsive, doing nothing, saying little, and requiring assistance with eating and dressing, then we might agree that this was the sort of behaviour we thought of as psychotic rather than neurotic. Exactly *how* stuporous you have to be to attract a label of psychosis is a very subjective matter. Patients with even minor degrees of depressive illness *feel* slowed down in their actions, and it is common for 'retardation' of behaviour that is discernible by others to be present in depressive illnesses of moderate severity. There is no clear cut-off point between commonplace retardation and stupor—the one imperceptibly grades into the other. In any case, even among patients who require admission to hospital for depressive illness, frank stupor is rare, so it is of little value in picking out those who are psychotic.

We do not expect patients with depressive psychosis to behave in a bizarre way and hallucinations are uncommon. I think that by now you will have seen that, in the absence of clear-cut delusions, to differentiate between categories 3 and 4 is a difficult and subjective affair. 'Psychosis' is not something that in real life stands apart from the rest of psychiatric illness. One can describe it in theory, but in practice patients present with all grades of severity. You should be warned that when you think of 'a psychotic patient' you have a stereotype—a mould into which you may be tempted to force someone, and which may not fit very well.

The four categories of depression that we considered do not exhaust all of the possibilities. Another grade, that we might have called category 5, is the patient who has some other psychosis, such as schizophrenia or an organic brain syndrome, and who has depressive symptoms as well. Yet another grade (probably best considered in a quite different dimension to the 4-point scale above) is the person with *depressive personality features*. There are some individuals who have permanent character traits of pessimism, lack of energy, hypochondriasis and other features that we tend to associate with depression. They are the wet blankets or those who are permanently down-at-mouth. But we cannot call them sick or ill. They are not complaining about their personality. They accept themselves for what they are—although they may be puzzled at times by the fact that so many people seem to be (to them) irritatingly full of energy and enthusiasm, forever on the go, organising and pushing them, and fearfully jovial. We do not say that such a person is suffering from an illness, because in his case the features are character traits rather than symptoms.

CHARACTER TRAITS AND SYMPTOMS

Let us clarify the distinction between these two types of feature —character traits and symptoms. Character traits are long-lasting, symptoms are brief: the first one has all one's life, the second just since the onset of the illness. Character traits are 'universal' features—we all have them. Symptoms are not: we all show greater or lesser degrees of conscientiousness, sociability, drive, and stubborness; we do not usually have suicidal ruminations, delusions, paralysis, or loss of weight. Character traits are regarded as part of our personality, and accepted as such: symptoms are regarded as foreign intrusions and resented.

Again the distinction is a matter of convenience rather than an absolute system. The reader will be able to think of persons who have had symptoms most of their life. He will think of symptoms that are universal (most of us have *degrees* of energy fluctuation, occasional sleeplessness, moods of depression). Many readers will have character traits of their own that they resent or wish they could lose. All the same, the distinctions between character traits and symptoms, and between personality and illness, are of great practical value, both in describing patients and in getting goals for treatment.

SIGNS

There is one more term that we should define, and that is the word *sign*. This is a term borrowed from general medicine, where it is common to the talk of 'symptoms and signs'. A symptom is something about which the patient complains, such as a pain, a cough, a swelling or a weakness. A sign is something that the doctor detects on physical examination, such as noises through the stethoscope, dullness on percussing the chest (which normally sounds hollow), abnormal movement of a limb, or absent knee jerks. In the psychological sense the distinction is not quite so clear—one patient may complain of feeling pessimistic (when pessimism is the symptom) but another may show pessimism without complaining of it (when it is a sign). Certain features are usually presented by the patient, such as loss of energy, loss of confidence or fears of certain situations—and these are then easily thought of as symptoms. Other manifestations are more easily thought of as signs because they are readily detectable to the trained observer, but rarely complained of by the patient. A good example is formal thought disorder; patients showing this rarely complain about it, even when they have retained sufficient facility of communication to describe it if they so wished.

By now I think we have considered enough of the factors that have to be borne in mind when talking about the theoretical features of psychosis. We can get on and look at what we see in each of the functional psychoses in real life.

SUMMARY

In the functional psychoses we find delusions, hallucinations, or other severe breaks with reality, but no evidence of disease affecting the observable structure of the brain. Some beliefs may be quite clearly mistaken to everyone but the patient; some ideas *could* be delusional beliefs but could perhaps as easily be metaphorical turns of speech—here an element of judgment enters when one has to categorise the idea. Similarly, patients may complain of hearing 'voices' that must be hallucinations, but in other cases the experience will be 'as if' someone were talking to them.

To arrive at the correct diagnosis the psychoses need to be distinguished from neuroses, personality disorders and even from normality.

8 Schizophrenia and paranoid psychoses—the symptoms and signs

'You are talking to yourself—that's the first sign of insanity!'

'People who are *really* mad don't realise it themselves.'

'They (psychotics) are happy in their own way.'

'If you are afraid of going mad then you are safe—those who are afraid of it never do.'

In this chapter we look at the truth, if any, contained in these commonly heard lay statements. We also examine questions that arise in more professional circles. If someone hears voices, does that mean he is schizophrenic? Does a patient with schizophrenia ever really recover? Can you tell that a patient is psychotic just by looking at him? Do psychiatrists diagnose mental illness in persons who are merely eccentric? Can you make a diagnosis in a patient who does not talk? Are schizophrenic delusions understandable? The answers are illustrated freely with examples of speech and writing by patients in whom the diagnosis of schizophrenia was suspected.

BREAK WITH REALITY

Schizophrenia is the most serious of the functional psychoses. This is true in more than one way. When we say that a mental illness is 'serious' or severe we could mean either that it represents a gross break with reality at the time or that it carries a poor prognosis. Both are true of schizophrenia.

To illustrate this let us compare it with the other major groups of functional psychoses. If we consider the patient when he is at the height of his illness, then the schizophrenic is more disturbed. Compared with the patient with hypomania or depressive psychosis, the schizophrenic is futher removed from reality in being more bizarre in his actions or more inappropriate in mood and talk. Given the mood state of the hypomanic then the grandiose ideas and the overactive behaviour fit in. One can to some extent understand the patient with depressive psychosis being preoccupied (even deluded) with ideas of guilt, poverty, disease or unworthiness. The schizophrenic illness is not intelligible in such a pattern. Some psychiatrists use this very *non-understandability* of the schizophrenic illness as the criterion for diagnosis. This challenge to one's comprehension may show itself in the formal thought disorder, in the incongruity of affect, in the unpredictable behaviour, or in the lack of rapport with the patient. Even if we just look at the patient at a single point in time, then, we see that schizophrenia is at one further remove from reality compared with affective psychoses.

PROGNOSIS

Let us turn now to the other way in which schizophrenia is more serious—the prognosis. Characteristically depressive psychosis and hypomania are diseases that remit spontaneously to leave a relatively undamaged personality. At worst the patient is expected to have recurring attacks of his illness: one anticipates that between attacks he will return to his pre-morbid personality. This was true even before modern methods of physical treatment, which when given in the acute phase might be regarded as merely speeding up the return to normality which would have happened in time anyway. By contrast, schizophrenia is notorious for carrying with it the risk of chronicity. It may reduce the patient to a state of such permanent apathy and loss of contact with reality that the term 'dementia' has been applied to it.

This inexorable progress to the chronic state does not happen in all cases. Even before present-day methods of treatment were available a proportion of cases would recover completely from their schizophrenic illness. Now recovery is anticipated in the majority. One proviso must be made: some psychiatrists are so wedded to the idea of schizophrenia as a deteriorating illness that if the patient *does* recover they revise their diagnosis. This is to say that they consider the *prognosis* in the making of the diagnosis. There is nothing illogical in this, but it does mean that you cannot then go on to 'discover' the prognosis from the diagnosis.

My own point of view, equally tenable and shared by many other psychiatrists, is that one can make the diagnosis of schizophrenia on the symptoms and signs—that is the *phenomena*—of the illness in the acute stage. If the patient subsequently shows a full remission of his schizophrenic phenomena, then it was a case of schizophrenia with good prognosis.

DIAGNOSIS

I believe that it helps to understand the differing views that are propagated on the subject of schizophrenia if one appreciates that there are these two different ways of arriving at the diagnosis. The student is sometimes baffled by the extremes of attitude towards schizophrenic illnesses that he encounters. Some psychiatrists (let us call them group A) adopt a gloomy, nihilistic approach in which they regard the diagnosis of schizophrenia as a life sentence, in which recovery is impossible and for which treatment offers no more than symptomatic relief, if that. Others (let's say group B) cheerfully diagnose schizophrenia, looking at it as an acute illness from which they expect the patient to recover, and after which he should return to a normal life, all in the space of a few weeks.

The first group of psychiatrists tend to regard group B as being poor diagnosticians, who are capable of including atypical cases of depression and hypomania, together with various 'schizophreniform psychoses', in with the real cases of schizophrenia. They object to this loose use of the term on the grounds that they (group B) are gratuitously labelling a patient with the hopeless term of 'schizophrenia', which will stick to him for the rest of his life, and deter anyone from really trying to help him—apart from putting off potential employers or immigration authorities.

The second group of psychiatrists regard group A as falling into a logical trap. 'Look at what group A says', they might suggest.

'You take a group of patients, defined by the fact that they have not recovered on treatment, and then "discover" that this group has a bad prognosis. No wonder that you are so biased in your views!'

We shall come back to this argument later, but for the moment let me emphasise that I use the viewpoint of group B, and that for the rest of this chapter I shall talk about the diagnosis of schizophrenia as if it is made on the phenomena that present themselves purely at one point in time.

THE PHENOMENA OF SCHIZOPHRENIA

When the psychiatrist writes up the results of his examination of the patient in the case notes there are certain headings that it is customary for him to use. These vary from country to country and school to school, but one group of headings might be as follows—appearance; behaviour; affect; thought; perception; intellectual ability; insight and judgment; formulation (including interpretation).

This gives us a convenient scheme for looking systematically at the different features of schizophrenia—although not necessarily in order of their importance to the diagnosis.

Appearance

Under *appearance*, it would be difficult to think of an appearance which would definitely tell you that a patient had schizophrenia. The figure beloved of cartoonists is the lunatic asylum 'inmate' with straw in his hair and a vacuous expression on his face, leaning over the wall. I think it is true to say that most patients with schizophrenia do not look like that, and also that most persons with vacuous expressions are not schizophrenic.

The old idea that you can tell a 'lunatic' by his facial appearance has gone. In fact with progressive introduction of an informal approach and the use of everyday clothes by staff (instead of uniforms and white coats) there is now a new twist. The gibe is that it is impossible to tell the staff from the patients—except possibly by one method: over a period of time you notice it is the patients that leave.

There is possibly one condition which is an exception—that is the state known as *catatonic schizophrenia*. Here the patient may adopt bizarre postures for no obvious reason, and furthermore he may keep them up for long periods of time. Apparently catatonic postures used to be more common among schizophrenic patients in the past, and nowadays one rarely sees them.

There are some features of appearance that, while not being diagnostic of schizophrenia, are more common in schizophrenics. There is the stooped, cowed, hang-dog look of the chronic institutionalised patient. There is the zombie-like appearance of the patient on large doses of drugs (with parkinsonism). Many chronic schizophrenics are careless of their appearance, and this combined with their often straitened financial circumstances gives rise to a characteristic appearance. You may have seen, in the centre of a large city, a man shuffling along in a shabby raincoat of unfashionable length, down-at-heel and unkempt, and in need of a shave. He may be grubbing in the refuse bins, talking to himself or even shouting at no one in particular. Most of you will recognise what is known in the U.S.A. as a 'bum', in the U.K. as a 'tramp', in France as *le clochard*, and in Germany as *der Landstreicher*. In fact he will not necessarily be as vagrant as these names suggest, and will probably live in a common lodging-house or 'Skid Row' hotel. I have made a close study of men living in such hostels, and the majority of them suffered from psychiatric morbidity that was clear after only one psychiatric interview. Schizophrenia was the commonest diagnosis in the U.K., with alcoholism following close behind. In the U.S.A. I found alcoholism to be rather more common, but there are still many schizophrenics (Priest, 1971, 1976).

In giving the above description of our down-and-out I strayed a little from the strict terms of reference of considering *appearance*—you may have noticed that I threw in a few items of *behaviour* as well. It is sometimes possible to guess that a particular homeless man is schizophrenic purely by his appearance, providing that it is sufficiently bizarre.

Case 13

One subject was a familiar figure in the city. He would trudge along in rubber boots which gaped at the heels, and ancient raincoat and curious headgear. He carried an umbrella which had only a few inches of material left on it, and he had a pack of his belongings done up in a bag which he carried slung over his shoulder. I found out that he lived in one of the common lodging-houses in the centre of the city, but would tramp out each day for miles into the surrounding countryside, returning in the evening.

I asked to speak to him at his lodging-house, and he made no objection. At interview he removed his unique headgear, which turned out to be a British military steel helmet covered in plastic sheeting. In taking it off he revealed a close cropped head, with one earring, and cotton-wool stuffed in his ears.

Later in the interview he revealed his delusions and hallucinations which established his psychosis beyond reasonable doubt. Amongst other features he had *tactile* hallucinations, which he described as 'missiles and kicks', and one of his delusions was that he had cancer in seventeen different sites in his body (and was born with it).

Having given this illustration, I must emphasise that such persons are rare, and it is most unusual, even in a clinical situation, for it to be possible to make a diagnosis of schizophrenia on appearance alone.

Behaviour

What about behaviour? Under this heading it is customary to include bodily movements and actions, but to exclude speech and thought (which are considered separately at a later stage). Again it would be difficult for behaviour, considered in an isolated way, to enable one to make a firm diagnosis of schizophrenia, but it could certainly give one a clue, especially if it were bizarre or unintelligible.

Case 14 Miss V.R.

Miss V.R. was being interviewed by a student. In addition to schizophrenia, she also suffered from total alopecia so that her head was quite bald. This was normally disguised by a wig. Her manner was odd and stilted and it was certainly not possible to obtain any *rapport*. She seemed to look through him or often just to ignore him. The student was amazed when, soon after the interview had started, she asked a strange obscene question about the state of his back passage and then suddenly removed her wig to reveal her total baldness. The act of taking off her wig might in some circumstances have been understandable—if she were demonstrating her alopecia in a medical examination for instance—but at this interview there was no such context and the behaviour was quite unintelligible.

The patient went on to display a gross degree of formal thought disorder later in the interview.

Often it is a matter of judgment whether behaviour of individual schizophrenic patients should be regarded as bizarre and non-understandable or not. Frequently it is easier to agree that what they do is *inappropriate*. Some readers may prefer to use this more conservative term for Miss V.R.'s behaviour—depending possibly upon what you conjecture was in her mind at the time. Certainly the student concerned thought it was bizarre. Other examples are more equivocal.

Examples

A woman was admitted to hospital because people were worried about her behaviour. After being visited at her house by itinerant evangelists, she got up in the middle of the night and started planting daffodil bulbs. On admission she was rather thought-disordered, but even when she was talking clearly a few days later, the explanations she offered for her behaviour did not make sense.

A medical student was admitted to hospital because those around him were worried about his eating habits. He was on a self-imposed regime of such fierce dietary restriction that they were worried that his physical health might suffer. After admission he took his wallet out of his pocket and practised drop-kicks with it in the corridor, as if he were playing Rugby football.

A middle-aged woman (the wife of a doctor) was admitted to a psychiatric ward in a general hospital. As her schizophrenia improved she was allowed to go on shopping expeditions with other patients from the same ward. As they were completing their purchases they were embarrassed to find this woman sitting on one of the shop counters, dangling her legs.

The behaviour of schizophrenics, we can accept, is often *inappropriate*. Such a general adjective is unsatisfactory for diagnostic purposes in that you can say that a particular schizophrenic's behaviour is inappropriate, but you cannot say that anyone who behaves inappropriately is schizophrenic. Behaviour may be inappropriate in degrees ranging from the exquisitely bizarre down to the mistakes and oddities that characterise the behaviour of most normal persons, and ranging through the eccentricities of those characters whom we think of as most individual in their personality. Strange, inexplicable acts may make us think of schizophrenia, but they do not usually enable us to make a definite diagnosis in the absence of other features.

Affect
The next feature on the mental state listing is even more subjective in its assessment—the description of affect. When we talk about the affect, also known as the *mood* or emotional state, we customarily think about that feeling state which shows itself as depression or sadness at one pole and as elation or joy at the other. Logically it is possible to think of many other dimensions which might be considered as emotions (we shall come across a few during the course of the chapter) but it is the depression–elation polarity that we mean unless otherwise specified when we refer to the *affective* state. Although it sounds a rather antiquated expression, most patients seem to understand when you ask them, 'How are you in your spirits?', and they respond appropriately. On the whole the doctor with a strictly scientific approach tries to avoid questions that put words into the patient's mouth, but it is probably acceptable, if the patient does not comprehend this first question, to make it clear by asking the universally understood, 'Are you *low* in your spirits?'

Flattening of affect
One abnormality of mood that is found in schizophrenics is that of flattening. The highs and lows that most of the rest of us experience from day-to-day are absent in the schizophrenics, who respond to adversity and pleasure with equal lack of reaction. They seem unmoved by the death of those close to them, they pay scant attention to threats of divorce (or the statement that it has taken place) and they are apparently equally indifferent to sudden news of an improvement in their financial situation. This lack of response to what would otherwise be construed as good or bad news is also known as *blunting* of affect.

Flattening is not incompatible with the presence of affective symptoms. At first this may seem a contradiction in terms, but it is not really. A patient may suffer from long-continued depressive symptoms, for instance, and still be conspicuously unmoved by external events. The point is that his affective state does not *change* in response to these events.

Flattening of affect is something that is more easily diagnosed in chronic states rather than acute illnesses. If the patient in his acute psychosis is perplexed, incoherent and distressed, then it may be difficult to judge whether his affect responds appropriately from day-to-day.

Research report

If chronic schizophrenics have flattening of affect, are they really in distress as a result of their illness? Or does the blunting of the emotional state protect them from being worried? I carried out a study with Dr. Tarighati and Dr. Shariatmadari on schizophrenics in long-stay wards of a mental hospital, giving them the Personal Illness questionnaire (Foulds, 1965). This is a set of those questions which have been found to separate normal persons from acute psychiatric patients, and in fact consist mainly of questions about *anxiety and depressive symptoms.*

By giving this questionnaire to a population you can see what proportion gives answers in the normal range, and what proportion gives answers in the anxious and depressed range characteristic of acutely distressed psychiatric patients.

We found that between a quarter and a third of the long-stay patients had enough symptoms to place them in the 'distressed' category. So the idea of the patient with long-standing mental illness but 'happy in his own way' may have a certain amount of truth in it, but there are many exceptions.

Among schizophrenic patients who remain living with their families in the community, flattening of affect may be associated with a lack of manifest affection, or even a degree of cruel or callous behaviour.

Incongruity of affect

We have been considering one particular aspect of the affect in schizophrenia, but in a way the flattening or blunting may be thought of as just one particular example of a more general case—that of incongruity of affect. The affect is said to be incongruous when it does not match the thoughts or behaviour of the subject. A patient may be talking of disease and death, but behave as if he were laughing at a secret joke. Being cheerful in the face of adversity may be an admirable virtue, but when taken to extremes can appear to be grotesque.

Although in its derivation the term *schizophrenia* may mean 'split-mind' or 'split-soul', in its medical context it does not mean the same thing as the novelist's concept of 'split personality'. The reader will be familiar with the notion of the man who lives one style of life until a certain point in time, when a sudden break occurs, associated with a journey and a loss of memory. From this time onwards he lives in a different way, with no knowledge of his previous life. This is the popular idea of 'split personality', and in fact corresponds to one form of the medical concept of *dissociation hysteria*. This story, of two apparently normal personalities separated from each other by a point in time, is not the sort of split-mind that we mean by the medical diagnosis of schizophrenia.

The 'split' in schizophrenia, if it means anything at all, means a shattering or *fragmenting* of the mind. While the person has the illness the various parts of the mind are fissured and divided from each other.

This is reflected in the affect when it is incongruous. It has become parted from the thoughts, the drive and the behaviour of the patient, so that it no longer matches them. You can see now that flattening of affect is just a particular type of incongruity—the affect fails to match the thoughts of the subject in that it is unresponsive to them.

As a rule, in the affective psychoses ideas of guilt, disease, poverty and unworthiness go along with depressed mood, and grandiose ideas or delusions of omnipotence accompany elated mood. In the following patients there was a mismatch.

Case 15 Miss S.G.

The patient, Miss S.G., was an intelligent young woman, working in a professional career. In her own words: 'I felt most peculiar. If I stopped at traffic lights I was quite convinced that somehow because of me they would change from red to green. I felt when watching television that if I didn't know the next words in the play or film there wouldn't be any more words.'

She went on to make it clear that these feelings of miraculous power were not associated with delight or pleasure; she was depressed and anxious rather than hypomanic at the time.

It should be made quite clear that although such incongruity of affect occurs in schizophrenia, it is not *diagnostic* of it. We shall see, in the affective psychoses, that we do not always have cases of pure depression or pure hypomania and that what are called 'mixed affective states' are well recognised. If we observe that a patient's affect is incongruous, it may make us think about the possibility of schizophrenia, but it will not by itself establish the diagnosis.

Thoughts

The psychiatrist depends for the more subtle gradations of his diagnosis on his observations about the *thoughts* of his patient, and as a rule his judgments will be based on the patient's *talk*.

It is possible to make a diagnosis in the case of a mute patient, but it is more difficult to be sure that it is the correct one.

Case 16 Mrs. C.O.

Mrs. C.O. was an immigrant who spoke English with a heavy accent. On admission to hospital, however, she spoke very little at all. She would sit during interview mute for long periods. Some questions she answered in monosyllables, others she did not answer at all.

At this stage a diagnosis of (catatonic) schizophrenia was made. It was impossible to prove that this was the diagnosis, and she showed none of the other features of catatonic schizophrenia (described later in this chapter). She was treated appropriately for this diagnosis and within four weeks had shown an almost complete recovery.

When she was talking freely once more she was able to describe her thoughts during her mute period. She said that she had believed she was being watched and spied upon. She had also suspected her food was being poisoned. She realised, when she described them, that these ideas were not true.

She had a history of two previous episodes of schizophrenic illness, although this was not known at the time when the diagnosis of catatonic schizophrenia was made.

I have the impression that such a diagnosis is made on ill-defined criteria in a way that is difficult to explain. It is rather like recognising the bark of a dog—it is difficult to say how one knows one is right. It goes against the grain for a teacher to say so, though, so I shall try to spell out those pieces of evidence for the diagnosis of which I am aware.

Firstly, let us consider the alternatives for being silent. The patient may have a physical defect in speech mechanism or an organic brain lesion. Suffice it to say that there was no evidence of either. Of psychological reasons for failing to talk we may consider:

1. depression;
2. hysteria;
3. antagonism to the interviewer.

The mute state in depression would characteristically be associated with a general slowing up of activity, known as retardation, that might render the patient into a state close to stupor. To make a positive diagnosis of hysteria one would need to show that by being unable to talk the patient had unconsciously achieved a psychological *gain*, such as being removed from the possibility of an anxiety-provoking situation: for instance, if the situation at work had been getting unbearable, and not being able to talk meant not being able to work, then the patient would have to remain off work and therefore less anxious. Antagonism towards the interviewer is an attitude that might lead to silence or near-silence in an understandable way if the patient is angry or resentful for some reason and has taken umbrage.

In the case of Mrs. C.O. there was no suggestion of any of these three alternatives, and the near-silence was inexplicable. It was impossible to predict which questions she would answer, and often she gave no recognisable sign of having heard the question at the time it was asked. It was possibly the oddness and non-understandability of the situation that most suggested schizophrenia as the diagnosis.

There was no sense of hostility, and her attitude did not seem to be surly or sulky, although when she was better she did say that she had been afraid that in some way we were trying to read her mind. In a way, of course, we were, but clearly the idea had contained a sinister element for her.

Here, then, was a case in which the initial diagnosis was based (however intuitively) on *behaviour*, and confirmed later by the content of the patient's *thoughts* as reflected in what she told us. More often a diagnosis is based right from the start on the patient's thought and talk.

Four aspects of a person's thought or talk may be separately described:

1. Stream.
2. Form.
3. Possession.
4. Content.

Stream of thought

The *stream* of talk may be slowed down and hesitant. This occurs in schizophrenia, as we have just seen, but severe slowing can also occur in depressive illness and near-mutism may result under the other circumstances that we have just considered above. The disorder of stream that is most typical of schizophrenia is known as 'thought-blocking'. Here the patient may be talking quite normally to start with, break off for no obvious reason in mid-sentence, and then start up again on a different sentence a moment later. To call this 'thought-blocking' is an inference—what one has seen is 'talk-blocking'—but it does seem to be a reasonable conclusion quite often.

Form of thought

Under the heading of *form* we come across one of the prime features of schizophrenia. Disorder of the form of thought is more often known as 'formal thought disorder' or most frequently as just 'thought disorder'. In thought disorder the usual logical sequence of sentences is lost. In the mildest forms the connections are loosened between one sentence and the next. More severely, the sentences have lost any connection with each other. In the most severe forms of thought disorder there is loss of connection between words and phrases even within the sentence. When speech gets to the stage of a meaningless jumble of words, this is known as 'word salad'.

Sometimes in schizophrenia a patient who is able to talk coherently face-to-face degenerates into thought disorder when writing things on paper. The following is a letter that I received from a patient:

'Dear Doctor Priest,
It is a glorious night here and the lights are orange and line the way to morning side (M'side to me). I want to write to tell you

about what has happened. It distresses me to say I have received my second even less merited certificate. A strange series of events lead to it all. Perhaps I shall write a book about it all—not a best seller, but revealing of corruption in mankind. I once began a correspondence to Arsenic. Do you known him? An ex-colleague of yours. He pretended not to notice until I finally closed it with a book 'The Identity of Man' by Dr. Bronowski. It seemed so appropriate for nothing is by accident and everything by arrangement. Predestination exists if you wish to be predestinated. I do and am. It is not to be poo-pooed. These words indirectly learned by me at school by a learned comparatively unrecognised Scot. I do hope you learned something in Scotland. About its awareness of genius, about its total lack of appreciation of genius. Its unwanting of such qualities. About my lack of appreciation of the English of a white handkerchief freely given and a choice and I admit essential certificate. I do hope the printing was ...: Dear not gold nor guilt neither. I feel guilt as I write this guilt for that dry little note which did not come from the heart as this does. If it helps to feel that you were appreciated here. I can only repeated the remarks I had heard on M. le Canard qui a present et le depart—Dep. Doc. I guess: There is a rarified atmosphere eluding but nevertheless totally absinthe! Absent of all that is without and everything that is within a self-supporting community as this should be. An outcrop of hair, a green suit—not jodphurs but almost a blessed babe en route to join the Canardines—a brotherhood of noble men and women. Not like us, twice blessed and not to take the Bible too seriously. It seems strange to write so freely. Not as a friend nor yet as a body, a spirit in need of society not understands what life is. Not total experience but service to a much greater spiritual unity within the Christian faith. You might say—His Grace is present. I can teach <u>now</u> I say this boldly. 3 arduous years have lead me to the stars. Not to the moon for lunatics. I did strike land there at one time by pitching well to the left on the Axis at noon.

I regret the burning desire of youth. But these are youthful faults. Strange not Magic, wonderful and realing with a sense of purpose and yet no purpose. One day I woke up and thought I was dying—8 years ago almost and a $\frac{1}{2}$. How can I feel such pain and live. But I did, I have and I will for some time. Dogged determination. Now I am on the Dog star, very pointed with a long tail which swings around the sky telling all dogs to assemble. It is saying 'Don't race just don't race'. And you are <u>just</u> a doctor and I am just a patient and this is just a letter to a superior breed of Dog. What would you like to be? I am a Dalmation. If any of this is of use to you use it freely. I will attempt to write along any ideas you suggest. Time is precious of course. Ideas should not be wasted if man is given them. It is one strand of ECTOPLASM stretching to another strand of PROTOPLASM across the Atlantic I am told.

I have again been moved to write this. If you are in the U.S.A. stay British be a dollar earner only. It is worth it for M.B.E. ... (continued).
Believe me I am most grateful for your kind attention.
                                                            Yours sincerely,
                                                                (signed) B.S.

This letter shows a moderate degree of thought disorder. The puns and flight of ideas are not typical of thought disorder—they may be seen more characteristically in the talk of hypomanic patients—but the letter does have a *looseness of association* that illustrates the thought disorder. Often there is a connection between one sentence and the next, but over the course of two or three sentences any thread is lost, so that it is not at all clear what the writer is trying to get across.

This situation is seen in real life when one gradually realises after, say, an hour's interview that one is still no further forward in finding out why the patient came up in the first place. It may be not until then that one suddenly realises that the patient was talking 'thought disorder'. The letter quoted above, not the grossest form of thought disorder, illustrates this point quite nicely.

In categorising a sample of speech or writing as thought-disordered one is making a judgment. In doing so an assumption is involved—that the person *intended* to communicate logically in the first place. In the case of poetry this may be an unwarranted assumption. The fact that much modern verse looks like thought disorder does not make the poet schizophrenic—he may have been wishing to communicate at quite another level—even *wanting* to produce a word salad. Similarly, in composing a letter the person writing may just wish to string together snippets of information and opinions and random musings.

In addition to making assumptions, the judgment is a subjective one. On reading it, one says, 'I do not understand the drift of this'. The letter quoted above will be much more intelligible to someone knowing the patient than to a stranger. Close acquaintanceship with a patient may bring about clearer understanding of the references, allusions and symbolism that are used. This does not gainsay the central feature of thought disorder, which may now be restated as a form of expression in which there is a less obvious connection between the elements than one would expect under the circumstances.

A schizophrenic patient is most likely to use thought disorder in a situation that is itself unstructured. In an interview in which the professional person asks a series of questions demanding the answers of 'yes' and 'no', there is clearly little opportunity for thought disorder to be manifest. The best way to elicit the phenomenon is to ask open questions of the sort, 'What do you think about . . .?' or 'Tell me about . . .'. As far as possible the question should be designed to start the patient talking freely without interruption. It may be for this reason that the thought disorder is often seen at its most florid when the patient writes a letter. Nevertheless, in some cases with persistent thought disorder the looseness of association may come through even in a structured interview.

Case 17 Miss V.R.

Miss V.R. was being interviewed by a student. The following sequences occurred during the interview:

1. Student: Do you enjoy washing up?
   Patient: I like clothes from Marks and Spencers.
2. Student: Have you been in the gardens today?
   Patient: I was in a pub in Hammersmith Broadway 10 years ago.
3. Student: Where were you born?
   Patient: I lived with my mother.
4. Student: How did you get that scar (on the arm)?
   Patient: Somebody told me there was a baby in the scar.

With knowledge of the patient this was an example of thought disorder. Alternatives could have been that she was deaf, that she did not understand the questions (perhaps because of receptive dysphasia) or that she understood but could not express herself properly (*e.g.* because of expressive dysphasia). In fact she was not deaf, and there was no evidence of organic brain disease.

Some of the answers illustrated, and many of her other answers, showed that she had understood the questions. In fact, some of her replies contain an oblique reference to the subject matter of the question. One has to refer to a looseness of association rather than a complete absence of association.

Sometimes the schizophrenic patient will make up completely

new words. These are known as *neologisms*. We have talked about looseness of association between sentences and looseness of association within sentences (word salad) and now we come across a further degree of non-understandability with the very word itself. The following is a letter written to me by a patient which shows thought disorder, neologisms and delusions, and it is difficult to disentangle the different features from each other.

RE. = DOCTOR R.G. PRIEST   CODE = = RADAR No 13
                              = (84)

                                         (Name and Address)

INVESTIGATION OF "INVALIDITY" BUGS   (Date)
NONE—Phonical=Aerial Radio Bugs
SPACE=NONE PHONE + —INVALIDITY—

Dear Dr. R. G. Priest,

                         It was nice to have seen you in regard to my invalidity caused by the want of concern for my "Radar". Condition Based Purely on Physical lines of an Unusual type of Radio Isotope Bug Radar Sub-Atomic Wave form Transmissions of "Invalidity" owning to the Fact of the "Absence" of Exsternal Applied Phone's and anode's as to some kind Civilised Characteristics of Applied, and removed co-herence, and co-ordination, Meaning and Genetical disfiguration Imprisenment and Persecution, of the Human existance. I Dare say with phones and Anodes Applied to the Suit, or Harness, or Equipment, then its use's in Way are enormous and very Far and Wide. Example = Outer Space Programe's and Uropa Space Programe. ect, ect, (only a Few years from now.) (Under Sea, ect. ect.) With the Proper Equipment Anodes stuct elastic down Harness on Nerves of "Anatomy" If Caesium Quarzts Crystal Isotopes can be used & Aerial Radio or Space Radio = Then the Very Same Used in Anode's and "Anode-Phones" – "placed"on"Nerve's" via Wires and Eqipmend Then is much more Valuable in –"Recordings–"Para'psychology and Analytical Diagnosis, ect, in perhaps eqipment such as

"Detection EQUIPMENT" such as * Spectrosizemagraph
                                       Recorder"*
                              (=Stress and Vibrations=)
                              ="Detection" and "Senatizer"

also =* "Monitor=Micro Spectrosizemagraph*
          (Objects and Elements) *Detection Recorder"*

But possibly some certain "specialists" in these "Electro =Medica=Researche's. might be best advised sort for, their attention in the "Detection" and "E.S.P." Although you yourself might and will Do the Electro encellegraph as you have these skills so as you have assured me. "yourself personally" when I saw you and together with your suggestions, with intents to get my Bug trouble removed and in all Vigilance, Broad and Wide. About the more medical Advantage's could quite be possible and more possible with the Co-operation. N.B.of some "Rare" "Exsperts such as "Para-Psychical Scientists' E.S.P. ect.

Ex=None–Phonecal Bugs Radio clerial type Cause Split Mind in the victim. But the Phonical Type is externally applied and removed= say in (ten minutes within) and No Damage.

About Inventions of and in psychial Science which I myself can including physical.P.S.I.Telegrephy (phones) But could Discuss this privately regards Time Benifaction and Message's, also regards=Past,=reserve Foreknowledge interjection outside of assistant Expossive Research Worker. (18 years ago.) (Claims for Exspense's ect) Could be some reservation here (on the Finanial Matter "Telephathy.ect") About the Neutron Fissons and Special Tunner's Only I myself in co-operation would say what these are if only we knew of the Rare Experts in psychic physical science, or, para-psychology=physical= I would most like these Bugs out of my System. And not someone else using me under one's capacity. At the same time I would like an understanding regard past outside of myself (reservations as mentioned)

In Time Benifaction Reserve mean's =there=Electro Atomic Reactors

ect, ect, =Experts=

*Some Rare *Exsperts* in

Plant life =Experts,=

* psychical physical*

Radio Signal Time Benifaction

= "Communiques" =
(Systems in Physical sciences's)

Past back into the Past
Externally,

"Some" Mediums" possibly additional

ect.

Regards Messages, ect,
(Inclosing some letters =herewithin=) (You Think + me Thinks)
Yours sincerely
Best Wishes   (Name)

P.S. I might mention that instantaneous Fissons of Neutrons of Alpha in the "Trillionley Cycle's " interjections into the nuclei of the Radio Waves commonally, and what more the same sizemagraph in Isotopes friquency fixtures by way of photoelectric photocellic that is to say regulated rata by way of neutron cycle rythum the same then is placed in two parts whatever the Transmis-

sion One— 1 — then the same Isotope is used in the receiving
Valve's. Simple Wave Balance
   Show this to any =Top Exspert" and see if he wants me to tell
the World. Please if you would be so kind

One has the impression that the letter is written in a private
language understood only by the patient. This sums up the disorder
of the form of thought that one finds in schizophrenia—what is
said or written appears to satisfy the need of the patient to express
himself without apparently paying the usual degree of attention to
the need of the listener to understand. Some psychiatrists would put
it more strongly, and suggest that the idiosyncrasies of speech pur-
posely (though unconsciously perhaps) avoid free communication,
placing a barrier between the patient and those around him, and acting as one means of avoiding close personal involvement.

Possession of thought

Disorder of the possession of thought refers to a phenomenon that
is seen in schizophrenia, although in only a minority of patients
with this disease. It takes one of several forms. It may mean that
the patient believes literally that he is being dispossessed of his
thoughts—that they are being taken away from him by somebody
or something; this is known as *thought removal*. A converse belief
may also be found—that thoughts are in some magical way being
generated in his mind—*thought insertion*. A third phenomenon is
the conviction that whatever he thinks can be heard by those
around him—*thought broadcasting*.

   When they are present, these features are important evidence of
schizophrenia (provided that organic disease has been excluded).
They are not seen in the affective psychoses.

   Although it is convenient to separate them off into a category of
their own, these subjective experiences could all be subsumed under
the heading of false beliefs, or delusions. As such they could
equally well be included in the following class of abnormal thoughts.

Disorders of thought content

1. *Delusions* The most striking of the disorders of thought content
is the delusion. This is basically a false belief. Often the fact that a
patient has delusions is the main evidence for labelling him as psychotic. Various attempts have been made to define a delusion more

closely. There are various false beliefs that do not imply that the person holding them is psychotic, and the detailed definitions try to ensure that these are excluded. Firstly, if one has a belief that is false only because one is not aware of the evidence to the contrary, then that is not what we mean by a 'delusion'. One of the lessons that we can learn from history, surely, is that the cherished beliefs of one generation are discarded by subsequent generations. Most of us would agree today that the earth is not flat, but centuries ago one would scarcely be thought of as deluded for thinking that it was. Today we have evidence to the contrary that is readily available, direct, and convincing. In a way this is a poor illustration: I do not personally know any educated adults who do believe that the earth is flat, and if I did I would suspect that they were argumentative rather than psychotic. Nevertheless, this example serves to make the point that a false belief is not a delusion unless it is a *demonstrably false belief.*

We can now add to our definition of a delusion the rider that it is not only a false belief but one that is held *despite proof to the contrary.* In theory a belief should not be categorised as delusional unless the patient has been presented with what would normally be convincing evidence that it is not true. In practice it is often easy to tell that a belief is delusional without going through this process: most of us would probably accept that a firmly held conviction that the central heating radiators were inhabited by little men is a belief that must be intrinsically delusional.

If one is a member of one of the recognised political parties, and holds the entrenched view that the rival party is quite mistaken, then it would not be really fair to say that these rivals were psychotic. One may be sure that they are wrong, and may even feel that they are flying in the face of proof that they are mistaken. Nevertheless it would devalue the term 'delusion' to use it to describe the beliefs of one's opponents and competitors. Similarly, one is not entitled to stigmatise the devoutly held religious beliefs of other sects as delusional. The same reservation applies to folk belief and superstition.

On the other hand, in a different context a religious or superstitious belief may provide a clue that the patient's mental health is impaired. For instance, a life-long belief in witchcraft could not be said to be evidence of psychosis in a native born West

African. But if a native of Edinburgh, in middle age, suddenly develops the belief that his food is being mysteriously poisoned by an enemy living 400 miles away, then it would be naive to deny the possibility that the belief was mistaken and as likely to be a psychological as a forensic problem.

What we have to try to exclude from the definition of a delusion are those false beliefs (whether political, religious superstitions or whatever) that are normal for the population that we are considering. We end up with a definition that is slightly cumbersome, but which is quite workable in practice: *a delusion is a belief which is held despite proof to the contrary, that is not entertained by persons from the same cultural background as the patient.*

The delusions that are found in schizophrenia are very varied. It is difficult to think of a belief that could not be held in this disease. Commonly one comes across patients with schizophrenia who are prey to convictions about their personal wickedness or guilt, their own unworthiness, or (especially) their affliction with physical disease that would be thought of as more typical of the delusions that are found in depressive psychosis. One may equally meet delusions that sound hypomanic in quality, e.g. a firm belief by a patient in his elevated occupational status or his long line of noble ancestry.

2. *Bizarre delusions* Although these delusions smacking of affective psychosis are frequently encountered, what one thinks of as more characteristic of schizophrenia is the bizarre delusion. The strange belief, neither particularly depressive nor especially elated in quality, the significance of which may be quite obscure, is the type of conviction that makes one think of schizophrenia as the diagnosis.

Examples
Mrs. C.R. believed that someone had dropped urine on her head, and it had gone right through her, so that she was full right up with urine. Another patient believed that her feet were nailed to the floor—despite the fact that she walked about the floor freely.

Miss H.L. believed that some electrical power had inserted into her body iron and steel shares (of the stock market type).

Mr. F.G. had a longstanding belief that his right eyelid was 'broken', that there was a piece of metal in the shape of a ring in his left ear, and that a length of thread connected the two.

3. *Delusions with a symbolic meaning* Often one can see meanings in the bizarre delusions. The delusions are saying something in a metaphorical or symbolic manner. For instance, the patient who believed her feet were nailed to the floor was a long-stay patient in a mental hospital. Although she was in a sense free to go, being an informal patient in an unlocked ward, under no restrictions, in another sense there was no realistic possibility of her going at all. She was so psychotic that if she had walked out of the hospital she would have been quite unable to cope with ordinary life outside. It was as if at some level she realised this and resented it, and so was pointing out to us that figuratively her feet were nailed to the floor.

Often one can think of an expression in everyday speech that comes very close to expressing a patient's delusion. It is only that the patient clearly means the saying literally that separates it off as a delusion. Such cases are the patient who believed her children really were 'little angels', others who claimed that their relatives were 'ten feet tall' and races of giants or princes of royal blood (we do not usually mean it literally when describing people as gigantic or regal).

One of the examples above proved to be a remarkably precise symbolism. The man with a 'ring in his ear' had disease of the middle ear on that side which no doubt gave him noises of a buzzing or ringing type. He was later found to have a condition of his right tear duct which required treatment. If the eyelid was not literally 'broken', it would be fair to say that it was not completely sound either. It is possible that these two conditions had a similar origin—as complications of previous infections of the upper respiratory tract. The middle ear and the tear ducts on both sides are connected to the nasal passages (in a similar way to the nasal sinuses), and just as sinusitis may result from a severe common cold, so may infections of the middle ear and the tear duct. Thus, in a sense, there is a thread connecting the two.

There are psychiatrists who believe that delusions always have a symbolic meaning. If this is so then it is not always clear what the significance is. The patient who was saying she was full of urine may have been trying to tell us she was fed up and discouraged. As far as her situation was concerned, she had 'had it right up to here' or she was 'pissed off' with it. Such an interpretation remains conjectural however.

4. *Are schizophrenic delusions non-understandable?* The reader should be aware of the fact that there is a dispute going on at present between psychiatrists on the question of delusions in schizophrenia. There are those who maintain simply that you diagnose schizophrenia using the evidence of bizarre delusions that are not clearly depressive or hypomanic and that are not intelligible as a straightforward way of communication. It is, in their view, the non-understandability of these delusions that stigmatises them as schizophrenic. The opposite camp maintain that, if you get to know the patient well enough, you can always see the symbolism or meaning behind the delusion, and that the delusions are therefore always understandable.

I hope that the reader will be able to discern a grain of truth in both positions. By standards of normal speech, neurotic speech or even the speech of manic-depressives, the utterances of the schizophrenic *do* tend to be oblique, strange, obscure and unusual. It may be that if we look hard enough then we can find, too, that in terms of the private language of the patient the statements are full of intense meaning. They are 'non-understandable' in the sense of having an abnormally low communication value when considered as part of an ordinary conversation; they may be 'understandable' in terms of having a deep emotional significance for the patient.

Psychiatrists who champion the 'non-understandable' point of view are probably interested in sharpening the diagnostic distinction between schizophrenia and other mental illnesses. Psychiatrists who propose the 'understandable' approach are devoted to highlighting the individual differences between patients, irrespective of diagnosis.

Both schools of thought passionately defend their positions, and we may give them the benefit of the doubt in supposing that they both feel that they are trying to say something important about helping psychiatric patients. Can we see what it is? Their motivation will no doubt be complex, but I would like to try to extract at least one positive point of emphasis from each extreme.

We learn from the first camp that we should be on the look-out for non-understandability in our patients. It is very important to diagnose and treat schizophrenia as promptly as possible—the prognosis is much poorer in the chronic stage. We should not wait, therefore, for statements that are frankly bizarre before considering the diagnosis. We should think of the *possibility* of schizophrenia whenever we find it difficult to understand our patients. By further observation we should be able to tell whether our suspicions are correct. This needs to be said partly because it is easy to miss the diagnosis. In one study in the Armed Forces it was found that, of cases found to be schizophrenic when seen by the psychiatrist, only twenty-five per cent had been diagnosed as such by the medical officer who had referred them (Thompson, 1967).

Until recently there has been, too, a tendency to try to avoid the diagnosis of schizophrenia at all costs, by leaning over backwards to find an alternative diagnosis into which the patient's symptoms could be fitted. Psychiatrists wished to avoid labelling the patient as schizophrenic. Their argument would run as follows: 'Schizophrenia has such a terrible prognosis. When people hear that the patient is schizophrenic they give up hope. Psychiatrists and other mental health professionals lose interest. There are countries to which the patient diagnosed as schizophrenic, or even his relatives, will not be able to emigrate. Other sanctions are exacted by society against the schizophrenic. Let us avoid placing the stigma of this diagnosis on him as long as there remains any possibility that we can force his particular symptoms into another category.'

Since the advent of more effective methods of treatment for schizophrenia this attitude is changing. It is now realised that it is important to be as accurate as possible about the diagnosis in order to select the most appropriate form of treatment—giving the schizophrenic antidepressant drugs for his bizarre hypochondriacal delusions is not generally considered to be the best that could be done for him, so it is important to recognise the bizarreness of the delusions rather than saying 'they are hypochondriacal delusions, so we'll assume he has a depressive illness'. It is also realised that this business of delaying a diagnosis of schizophrenia until it was no longer possible to think of an alternative produced a circular argument. You start from the belief that schizophrenia has a bad prognosis, you avoid diagnosing it in the cases that clear up promptly, and you find later that those cases that have become chronic are those that you diagnose as schizophrenia. It is realised nowadays that many cases of schizophrenia have a good prognosis, and it can be made even better if it is treated after prompt recognition.

This, then, is one way of looking at the behaviour of those psychiatrists who pay great attention to the *'non-understandable'* qualities in schizophrenic speech. Train yourself to spot these, they might say, so that you pick up cases of schizophrenia early or at least avoid having on your conscience large numbers of patients to whose diagnosis you blinded yourself for fear of giving them the nasty label of schizophrenia.

Secondly, now, let us take the opposite camp of psychiatrists —those who emphasise the *understandability* of schizophrenic delusions. What can we learn from them? They would complain that if we emphasise the non-understandable qualities we are distancing ourselves from the patient. We are saying that the patient is a psychotic, a man apart, whose words can be ignored because they have no meaning. Furthermore, in concentrating on the delusional form of his speech (rather than listening to what he is saying) we are tempted to put *all* such patients in the one category, thus neglecting the differences between the patients. There is no doubt that this is a salutary warning. There is a danger that if we think of schizophrenia as a single entity, with one form of treatment, we may think of our latest patient as 'the seventeenth case of schizophrenia this year'. This might go along with a tendency to a mechanical or veterinary approach, where the emphasis is on diagnosis, and after this has been made all patients with the same diagnosis are treated similarly. It can be seen that this would tend to become a treatment by numbers, or at least lead to a less human and more insensitive attitude towards the patient. The alternative is to think of the patients by their individual differences—Mr. A., who is preoccupied with such-and-such, Mrs. B. is the one who had the delusion about so-and-so, etc.

It should be pointed out that the first of the two alternatives (emphasising non-understandibility) is likely to be associated with an emphasis on physical methods of treatment. If drug X is good for schizophrenia, then let us sharpen up our diagnostic skills to make sure that every schizophrenic gets it early in their illness. It is therefore the psychiatrists who strongly believe in the importance of drugs and other 'medical models' of treatment who have this approach. The importance of the second alternative—understanding the communication—comes into its own with the psychotherapeutic approach. Schizophrenic patients may or may not all need drug X but one's psychological approach to each of them will be varied according to their individual differences. This will be emphasised particularly by those who feel that concentrating on the particular background of that patient is not just a means of respecting his individuality but is also essential to his treatment. In other words psychiatrists will espouse this attitude when they believe that the psychotherapy is more important than the drugs.

At this point it may be more helpful to the reader if I stop trying to give an impartial account of both sides of the coin with Olympian detachment. Perhaps I should say where I stand myself. I do not believe that in the hands of the average psychiatrist psychotherapy alone is the treatment of choice for schizophrenia. I think that the use of psychotherapy as the prime method of treatment for schizophrenia is difficult, complex, and fraught with danger. That is not to say that it is impossible in theory and there are possibly a few psychiatrists who can achieve it. Even so, it would be extremely time-consuming, and therefore uneconomical for the vast majority of patients.

By contrast, I believe that drug treatment can produce a radical and beneficial change in the course of the disease, and this can take place even with a relatively unskilled psychotherapeutic approach, certainly where the therapist has a moderately sympathetic way with him (and probably even in the absence of that).

Nevertheless we remain indebted to the second group of psychiatrists. By emphasising the individual differences they remind us to treat the patient as an individual and to respect his dignity and the fact that he is unique. In fact, when the patient is being treated with the appropriate drug, he may be much more amenable to a psychotherapeutic approach. Where I (and many other psychiatrists) would take issue with the more extreme proponents of the 'understandability' school is when they forbid the patient the benefit of medication as part of their doctrine. I see no reason why the schizophrenic patient should not have the advantage both of physical methods of treatment and (where he can get it) psychological methods of treatment simultaneously—and in fact I see every reason *for* such a procedure.

We have followed up an important point that arose in connection with the question of how 'non-understandable' we should consider the delusions of schizophrenia to be. Let us now return to the phenomenology of schizophrenia.

5. *Disorders of possession of thought* We have seen that, with delusions, the more bizarre and 'non-understandable' they are the more likely they are to be regarded as evidence of schizophrenia. I have written as though there is no sharp demarcation along the spectrum from the typical delusion in, say, depressive illness to the most schizophrenic-sounding delusion. I certainly believe that there are all grades of delusion in between. Nevertheless, one does not always have to have an agonising debate about the diagnostic implications of a delusion; some delusions are accepted as being, of themselves, diagnostic of schizophrenia (always providing that the patient is not suffering from organic brain disease). That is to say, if we have narrowed down the range of diagnoses under consideration to functional psychoses, then the elicitation of certain delusions will make us have no hesitation in regarding the patient as schizophrenic.

The first of these is the delusion of *thought broadcasting.* This is the belief that other persons around him can clearly hear the patient's thoughts. A related belief is the delusion that other people can put thoughts into his mind—*thought insertion.* Clearly this delusion needs to be carefully distinguished from normal beliefs about the extent to which others affect one's own thinking—most of us would accept that our thoughts are influenced by others to a degree, otherwise why would you be reading this book? To be classified as a delusion, the phenomenon of thought insertion requires that the insertion takes place in a magical or improbable way.

A similar belief sometimes encountered is that the patient can hear other people's thoughts: it is not always possible to distinguish this from auditory hallucinations.

The first two of these delusions (thought broadcasting and thought insertion) are sometimes grouped together with thought withdrawal under the heading of *disorders of possession of thought.*

Case 18 Mr. J.Z.
Mr. J.Z., a black immigrant, presented himself for treatment as an emergency. He was suffering from a recurrence of symptoms that he had first experienced five years previously. He had become increasingly convinced that passers-by in the street were jeering at him. He believed that he could hear other people's thoughts and that they

could hear his. He described an uncontrollable desire to laugh though he felt no humour, and a sensation of fear though he was not afraid. He also had pains in his body for which no cause could be found. He felt shy and embarrassed in company.

He had experienced a deprived childhood, which was unusual in his country of origin, and his parents had been divorced when he was three years old. An older brother was at present in gaol for drug offences. The patient had done well at school, and had strong religious views. He had never cared much for girls, but had married, and left his wife and their one child back home when he came to this country eight years before. He had worked in menial jobs by day in order to study at evening classes.

His first mental illness had come on insidiously until finally, three years after immigration, he had been admitted to a mental hospital grossly hallucinated and excited. His symptoms remitted after two months, but eighteen months before his present episode there was a short period during which he believed television and radio programmes were directed at him personally.

For the current episode he had considerable insight into the abnormal nature of his symptoms, and with appropriate treatment in the hospital he improved. He joined in the social activities, and his symptoms subsided one by one, the last one to go being the pains in his body. Arrangements were made for continued treatment as an outpatient.

In the case of Mr. J.Z., the diagnosis of schizophrenia is not in doubt when one hears the history as set out above. At various times in his illness it might not have been possible to be quite so certain, but if one had interviewed him at the time when he was suffering from his delusion that other people could hear his thoughts, then one would have been categorical in the diagnosis—whether one knew the rest of the history or not (there was never any suggestion of organic brain disease). Incidentally, he described his symptoms with unusual sharpness, and in particular the picture he gives of the subjective component of incongruity of affect was exceptionally clear; it is possible that this manifest insight was made possible largely by his high intellectual ability.

6. *Passivity phenomena* The final type of false belief to be considered in this section is that of *passivity phenomena*. Here the patient believes that he is under the influence of outside powers which make him do things against his will. The powers are often mysterious and indefinite, the patient describing himself as if he were a robot or a puppet, acting out the behest of a superior force.

The precise nature of the outside force is something that is likely to be conceptualised according to the cultural background of the patient. Currently patients may believe that they are under the influence of radio waves—a belief that would have been impossible before such waves were known. An older patient (Mrs. H.L.) believed that she was influenced by a 'power machine' in the basement, which was switched on by the engineer or at other times, she said, by the electrician. In times past a passivity feeling might have been attributed to the effect of witchcraft or spirits.

Case 19 Mr. B.D.

Mr. B.D., at the time that I saw him, was not a psychiatric patient at all—in the sense that he was not receiving psychiatric treatment or indeed any medical attention for his mental state. I came across him during the course of a research study, during which I was interviewing men who lived in common lodging-houses—in the U.K. known as 'doss-houses' and in the U.S.A. as 'flophouses' or 'Skid Row' hotels. Like the other men, his name was picked out strictly at random. He was described by the lodging-house manager, on seeing whom I had chosen, merely as a 'fresh-air fiend'—a reference to his habit of walking about this northern British city (where I was working) in all weathers in an open-necked shirt.

The subject was a 65-year-old man, but looked fit and only half his age. He admitted a history of mental hospital admission but that was 25 years previously, and he had had no treatment since. I had introduced myself as a hospital doctor doing research, and he asked to see my credentials (remarkably enough the only subject that ever did so out of over a hundred interviewed). He eventually agreed to be interviewed when I was recognised by the University teaching unit in General Practice, a hundred yards down the road, and they allowed me to use an office there. Seated with me in the room there, and apparently satisfied that I had a *bona fide* story, he talked openly about himself in an over-anxious fashion, stuttering and using mime. One of the questions I asked him (designed to elicit ideas of grandeur) was if he was a more important person than others seemed to think. He responded positively to this and claimed that he had designed the building in which we were sitting, he had put the Russians into space, he had written a current hit song, he had started the 'Twist' and the Beatles (the interview took place in the mid-1960s) and he had 'created miracles better than Jesus'. He went on to say 'I'm the greatest!' At this point I was taken aback; I felt that this sounded like plagiarism. Possibly my concern showed in my face, because he went on to say spontaneously 'I wrote to Cassius Clay and gave him that patter'.

So far the grandiose picture would be compatible with a nonschizophrenic diagnosis (such as hypomania). However, he went on to describe passivity feelings, although it seemed that he was groping for the right way to put it. 'I'm under this juju, this radio, this psychiatry.' He felt controlled by the 'radio' and that it made him do things. I had the impression that the 'radio' also took the form of auditory hallucinations. He believed he had experienced precognition, and claimed to have forecast (remarkably) Pearl Harbour and (with bathos) Errol Flynn's divorce.

The feature that passivity feelings all share is what is sometimes called the *loss of self*, particularly the loss of that part of the self that is responsible for doing things, initiating behaviour or acting in a certain way. The loss of the idea of the self as agent has been stigmatised as the central feature of the most severe form of schizophrenia, as far as the thought content is concerned.

Perception

Psychologists have shown that we do not all perceive things identically. Our interpretation of what our senses take in depends on our environment and our mood, and can be distorted.

Users of L.S.D. and other hallucinogenic drugs actively seek out such disorders of perception, hoping to acquire new insights. Under the influence of these drugs familar objects take on a new appearance; they are vivid and related to other subjects in a way previously unseen.

A similar distortion of perception has been described in patients with acute schizophrenia.

Illusions

Case 20 Mr. A.C.E.

Mr. A.C.E. was an undergraduate studying psychology. He presented to the psychiatrist with a primary complaint of disordered perception. He described clearly the confusing brilliance and distortions of what he saw, and spontaneously went on to say that it was as if he were looking at Van Gogh paintings all the time. He was admitted to a psychiatric hospital (part of the teaching hospital complex) for further observation and treatment. The same evening the junior psychiatrist carried out a physical examination and then spent a long time taking a history and performing a thorough mental examination.

The patient, later on that evening, was sitting in the lounge of the observation ward. Things were quiet, and the only other person around was the male student nurse sitting a few feet away. Suddenly the patient leaped up, rushed to the bathroom, broke open an earthenware utensil, and slashed at his throat and wrist with a sharp edge.

He had made dangerously deep incisions before anyone could get into the bathroom to stop him.

His life was saved at the nearby general hospital, and gradually his wounds healed. He was treated with phenothiazine drugs and group therapy.

He made a very early and complete recovery from his psychiatric disorder.

The Van Gogh description is a well-known simile in psychiatric and psychological circles as a means of describing the acute schizophrenic perceptual state. It seemed that this student realised what his diagnosis was, and feared that he was being consigned to a mental hospital for the rest of his days.

The type of perceptual disturbance that we have been considering is probably best classified as an *illusion*: it is a distortion of an image that is actually received by the visual senses.

Hallucinations

We come now to consider *hallucinations*—which are conjured up in the mind even in the absence of any relevant visual stimulus.

The reader will recall how a delirious patient will be able to see animals and other objects even though looking at a blank wall.

1. *Auditory hallucinations* In schizophrenia the most common hallucinations are auditory in type. They may be rattles, bangs or other elementary hallucinations, but the distinctive ones are of human voices, talking about the patient. They may be male or female, loud or soft, intelligible or mysterious.

The message may be simple, such as 'Be happy' or 'She is a slut', or it may be complex and even thought-disordered. The voice may be unidentifiable or belong to a relative—alive or dead. It may make the patient angry, or it may be accepted. The patient may carry on a conversation with his 'voices' and be seen standing to one side of the room or in a corner taking part in one side of the conversation, or shouting and gesticulating. It is presumably this phenomenon that has given rise to the common saying that if you talk to yourself you are mad. Of course, there are many situations where to talk to oneself is understandable and normal, but in an uncommunicative patient it may be indicative of auditory hallucinations.

Hearing 'voices' is, in any case, not diagnostic of schizophrenia. For a start, one has to consider the possibility that it was not a hallucination but an illusion—such as hearing one's name called in a busy street, often a misidentification of some other noise or shout.

Secondly, even if it is a hallucination, it is not necessarily a sign of illness. One type of hallucination that is often seen in normal persons is the hypnagogic hallucination. This occurs when the subject is about to drop off to sleep. It is of no sinister significance.

Thirdly, auditory hallucinations occur in other illnesses. They may occur in organic brain disease—especially when this affects the parts of the brain concerned with hearing that are found in the temporal lobes. In addition, patients with functional psychoses other than schizophrenia may hear voices. In depressive psychosis, for instance, the voices may tell the patient things that reflect ideas of guilt, unworthiness and disease, saying 'You will die' or 'You are wicked'.

The auditory hallucinations that are diagnostic of schizophrenia (in the absence of brain disease) are those that talk about the patient in *the third person*—'She does so-and-so . . .' or 'He is such-and-such'. A particular instance of this is where the patient hears a continual running commentary on his behaviour.

So if a psychiatrist is satisfied that the patient has no underlying brain disease, he will accept auditory hallucinations in the third person, occurring in clear consciousness, as good evidence of schizophrenia. In fact, in patients who are diagnosed as having schizophrenia, other hallucinations may be encountered as well, just as the schizophrenic may have symptoms of any of the other functional mental illnesses. Often one may be quite sure, on other grounds, that a patient is schizophrenic whose voices are always in the second person—'You——this . . .' and 'You——that . . .'. But it is only the third person type of hallucination that is of itself diagnostic.

Case 21 Mr. J.L.

A 31-year-old man, Mr. J.L., was admitted to hospital, tense and restless, repeatedly trying to escape from imaginary pursuers. He felt they would try to cut him up. He could hear the next-door neighbours talking, even though (in the hospital) they were miles away. The man and wife who lived next door appeared to be arguing, and talking about the patient.

He responded poorly to treatment and has remained in hospital until the present time. After the lapse of fifteen years he still hears the voices. They say to him 'He hasn't suffered enough', 'His mother is dead' and 'We'll murder him if he comes out'.

At this point in time there is no doubt about the diagnosis, and the clinical diagnosis of chronic schizophrenia is confirmed when one elicits these hallucinations of voices talking about him in the third person. Nevertheless, not all of his hallucinatory experiences are in the third person—the voices will also say 'You've got hostages', 'We'll kill you stone dead', 'You've had your treatment, you've had your protection, we'll kill you all anyway' and 'Go on, then, tell the doctor'.

At one time his illness could have been construed as a depressive psychosis. At the beginning of his (currently) fifteen-year-long admission to hospital he described how he entertained 'improper thoughts' about the woman next door and it does not take much imagination to guess the particular retaliatory way in which he feared they were going to 'cut him up' (later on in his illness he was quite explicit that he was afraid that they would cut off his genitals). One could have said, then, that he was depressed and preoccupied with guilty ideas. The persecutory delusions would have been acceptable as part of his depressive illness since they were based on guilt. However, even at that stage there were features suggestive of schizophrenia—bizarre delusions that his mind would get mixed up with hers, and a belief that she would overhear things *he* said (while in hospital) and could read his thoughts.

Case 22 Miss Rosemary Gore

Miss 'Rosemary Gore' (my fictitious name for the real patient) was only 18 years old at the time of her first admission to mental hospital. She believed that people were influencing her mind and interrupting her thoughts, reading her mind and inserting ideas into her brain. 'My mind has been used by people through telepathy.' She heard voices that told her to leave the country. 'I dare not tell you any more or they will kill me.' Some of the symptoms had been present for eight months, and she had heard the voices for five weeks before admission. She was treated with phenothiazines and became free of all psychotic symptoms within three weeks—her parents said she was 'better than she has ever been'.

Unfortunately this medical triumph was short-lived. Within a few months the auditory hallucinations returned, and on one occasion the voices told her to kill herself. Her mother was in time to stop her from cutting her wrist with a knife. The dose of medication was increased with partial success but she relapsed as the voices came back 'with a wham'—less than five months after her original admission. They said 'Your mother's a whore' and, she explained, 'I had to kill myself because other people knew what I was thinking'. The voices also said 'You are a sod' and

'You are a whore
Rosemary Gore.'

She showed no improvement on increased doses of medication alone, but made a partial remission when she was given three electro-convulsive therapy (E.C.T.) sessions as well.

She remained out of hospital for nearly four years. For most of that time she remained auditory hallucinated, but her condition became worse after the birth of her baby, and she was readmitted. The voices continued to say obscene things, and also had repeatedly told her to commit suicide—a course she had attempted on several occasions. She spent six weeks in hospital this time.

Eighteen months later she came in on her fourth admission. She had undergone a termination of pregnancy and sterilisation 6 months previously. She was now separated from her husband and living with her parents. She complained of auditory hallucinations which were sometimes male voices and sometimes female. They said unpleasant things and ordered and 'controlled' her actions.

The voices, at the height of this relapse, used the first person plural (we) for themselves and the third person (she) for Rosemary.

'Rosemary should be dead—we are in charge now.'
'We won't let Rosemary come back—poor Rosemary.'
'We will use her hands for nursing, we will speak with her voice.'
'She used to be a nice girl.'
'Her body may save the world like Mary—that's why we had her sterilised.'

The voices at this time spoke about Rosemary as though she were someone who used to inhabit the same body but did not do so now. The patient showed the same confusion of identity when speaking about herself. She said that Rosemary was not her but 'her', pointing to her abdomen. She would refer to herself as 'Rosemary' or 'We'.

When partially improved she discharged herself from hospital and went off to live with one of the male patients, leaving her child in the care of her mother.

2. *Tactile hallucinations* Hallucinations can affect any of the senses. Earlier in this chapter tactile hallucinations were referred to, in the case of the homeless man who talked of 'missiles and kicks'. It is often difficult to disentangle such hallucinations from the

delusional system of which they form a part. A burning sensation on the back of the head was attributed to mysterious rays directed at the patient. Another patient believed that her burning sensations were caused by acid that dropped on her during the night. By the time she was drawn to our attention she had built up an elaborate arrangement of plastic sheets on her bed and other methods of protecting herself while she slept.

A woman who experienced sensations in her genitals attributed them to sexual interference by an evil man. Another woman who had pricking sensations in her skin thought they were due to tiny arrows being fired at her by someone who resided behind the walls of her apartment.

3. *Gustatory hallucinations* Gustatory (or taste) hallucinations are not often prominent in schizophrenia. They are certainly not very helpful in the diagnosis. When marked, they raise the possibility of an organic lesion in the temporal lobe. In less dramatic forms they are found in other disorders; for instance, a 'bad taste in the mouth' is quite common in depressive illness.

4. *Olfactory hallucinations* Olfactory hallucinations also raise suspicions of temporal lobe disease, but are quite common in uncomplicated schizophrenia nevertheless. A patient rushed through the ward breaking all the windows that he could to 'let out the gas' that he could smell so strongly.

Another patient had a preoccupation with her own body odour that was either delusory or hallucinatory—it is difficult to say which. When she first presented she suffered from florid paranoid schizophrenia. A native of Scotland, she first noticed excessive perspiration when she went to a warmer country. She became paranoid there, it seems, and was convinced that the persecution was because of her offensive body odour. She was treated on return to her home country. With the administration of phenothiazine drugs her illness cleared up completely, and she was discharged from hospital. Although she had been advised to continue on the phenothiazines she secretly stopped taking them, and during out-patient sessions it became clear that she had relapsed. She eventually required re-admission with a further period of intensive treatment. Again full remission was obtained. Warned by this experience, it was possible for the psychiatrist to tell, when she came up to the out-patient clinic, whether or not she was taking her medication. If she stopped her tablets, then first of all she would 'admit' to excessive perspiration. If at that stage she agreed to take her drugs again this symptom would clear up. If not then she would progress to the stage of 'admitting' an offensive body odour, and it became a matter of urgency to persuade her to take the phenothiazines before she again became frankly paranoid. It is not often, though, that one has the convenience of such finely graded series of symptoms to provide one with a sensitive indicator of early stages of relapse.

5. *Visual hallucinations* Visual hallucinations will by now be familiar to the reader as a characteristic feature of organic brain syndromes, particularly delirium. They do occur in schizophrenia. In one investigation of mental-hospital patients who were schizophrenic, the authors found that fifteen to thirty per cent of these subjects admitted seeing 'visions, or people, animals or things around [them] that other people did not seem to see' (Foulds and Hope, 1968). Such visions are, however, by no means diagnostic of schizophrenia and they can occur in patients who are suffering from other functional mental illnesses.

Intellectual ability
Tests of intellectual ability rest, for the most part, on the assumption that the subject is doing his best. In an intelligence test he will be asked to solve a puzzle as quickly as possible, or to answer questions as accurately as he can.

A patient in the acute stage of a schizophrenic illness is unlikely to be able to function at his usual level. His answers to questions may be obscured by formal thought disorder and distorted by delusions. He will often find it difficult to show complete co-operation.

Under these circumstances clinical psychologists will often feel that the application of standardised test procedures is invalid, and will report that the task had to be abandoned. When psychologists have been able to complete their assessment on the more tranquil patients in the *chronic* stage of schizophrenia, they have reported results that are not grossly different from normal. The average intelligence quotient (I.Q.) of a group of chronic schizophrenic patients may be expected to be 90, say, rather than the more usual 100.

On a day-to-day clinical level, the impression is that patients with schizophrenia retain the use of many of their intellectual powers. The patient with acute schizophrenia may be severely disturbed, out of touch with reality, unable to communicate coherently and apparently preoccupied with his delusions and hallucinations. Alternatively, he may be mute and stuporous. Nevertheless, when his illness is over, and he is able to talk intelligibly about his experience, it may become apparent that he was able, during the height of his illness, to perceive what was going on around him, that he was oriented correctly, and that his memory for the events is relatively unimpaired. Certainly he may forget a certain amount of what went on, as if it had been a bad dream, but the point remains that his potential intellectual ability seemed to have remained intact throughout.

Testing *orientation* with the disturbed patient is difficult. One patient gave her age (when asked at different times) variously as 500 years old, 34, 43, 3,000 or 100. Another gave her age as 3,022.

Other patients will give inaccurate replies as a result of their delusions. In working with patients with chronic schizophrenia in the long-stay wards I have found that one of the commonest of false beliefs (or at least false replies) is found when one asks a female patient her age. The culturally-fostered desire to be less than one's chronological age, common enough in normal women, takes on interesting proportions in these women. Although the bizarre answers given above are unusual, it is common for the patients to give answers which represent only about half of their true age. The element of wish fulfilment in this fantasy is conspicuous.

A 58-year-old gave her age as 41, a 67-year-old said she was 61, and a 79-year-old woman claimed to be 26. These were all women with chronic schizophrenia, with no evidence of organic brain disease. (The same phenomenon may be observed in patients with senile or arteriosclerotic dementia, but it is then often difficult to disentangle from memory disorder and true disorientation. A 101-year-old patient claimed she was in her teens!)

Making allowance for his florid symptoms, it does seem that the average schizophrenic patient remains remarkably well-oriented in time, place and person. If one can obtain his co-operation, it will eventually be found that other intellectual faculties are also preserved, such as his ability to perform arithmetical tasks and his comprehension of vocabulary. On testing memory function, if his concentration and attention can be mustered sufficiently to register the material (*e.g.* a novel name and address), then it is likely that his retention and recall will prove adequate. General knowledge will remain intact unless the patient, for instance with chronic schizophrenia, shows gross withdrawal of interest from the outside world.

The test of new learning referred to earlier in Chapter 6—the Brief Paired-Associate Test (*see* Appendix I)—has proved to be a valid method of distinguishing between patients with organic brain disease and chronic hospitalised schizophrenia, with the obvious exceptions of those schizophrenics who are mute or suffering from severe formal thought disorder.

The term 'schizophrenic dementia' is unsatisfactory, since the word 'dementia' is usually taken at the present day to refer to an *irreversible* loss of intellectual ability. Cases of schizophrenia who have been grossly disabled for a decade or more, then to make a full recovery, are well known, and it is probably justifiable to regard the intellectual faculties of the chronic schizophrenic as lying dormant rather than having been irrevocably destroyed. *Dementia praecox* (*i.e.* precocious dementia) was the diagnosis that historically preceded schizophrenia. As a means of indicating a different type of illness to the organic brain disease of old age it served its function. It may now be abandoned.

Insight and judgment

It is said that in psychiatric illnesses in general, and in schizophrenia in particular, insight is impaired. This can be a misleading statement, and it should be considered carefully. Statements in case notes that record insight as being 'lost', or alternatively as 'preserved' miss the point. Like other assertions that are based on subjective impression, any comment should be accompanied by the supporting evidence (and preferably verbatim reports of the patient's speech).

Patient's insight into his illness

We have to ask ourselves what this insight is into. Are we referring to the question of insight into his state of health? Some psychiatric patients, especially when in a hypomanic mood, will claim that they never felt so well, and will challenge any suggestion that they may be suffering from an illness. Many schizophrenics will take a similar stand if one asks them bluntly if they are suffering from an illness, but the majority of patients with acute schizophrenia will admit to what amounts to an excessive number of anxiety and depressive syptoms if asked in the right way. Some, of course, will in any case complain of excessive anxiety or depression, but a large number will spontaneously respond positively to individual questions on whether they suffer from excessive trembling, perspiration, palpitation, loss of energy or sleep disorder. Although they may deny that they are ill, they will admit to so many symptoms of emotional disturbance that they are clearly no longer in the psychologically well sector of the population. Is that evidence of lack of insight? If so, then there are many men and women in the street who are similarly blind. Although schizophrenia itself is not the commonest of diagnoses, epidemiological studies have shown that there are many persons in the general population afflicted with psychiatric symptoms which go unrecognised and untreated.

So the fact that some schizophrenics do not regard themselves as ill is of limited significance. What about insight into the *nature* of the illness? Even if he does regard himself as anxious or depressed, is he lacking in insight if he does not regard himself as schizophrenic? It is difficult to answer this sort of question if one does not know the background of the patient's general knowledge. If a psychiatrist were schizophrenic and did not know it, this would be evidence of impaired insight. Otherwise it is conjectural. Many patients are never told that they suffer from schizophrenia, for fear that they read a gloomy account of the prognosis and become depressed or even suicidal. Is it evidence of lack of insight if the patient does not know that he is psychotic? We can substitute for the word 'psychotic' the nearest lay equivalents of 'insane' or 'mad', to get a sideways look at this question. There is an old wives' tale that if you are worried about being insane, then you are not mad. The conclusion that only the sane are worried about their sanity appears to be based on the notion that if you are mad then you are oblivious to this fact.

The saying, the assumption and the conclusion are all questionable. The saying is certainly not literally true—many patients diagnosed as schizophrenic admit to fears about their sanity. Foulds and Hope (1968) found that although the proportion of schizophrenics that were worried about being insane did not quite come up to the rates found in anxiety states, they certainly exceeded by many times the rates found in their control (normal) population.

One might feel on firmer ground in judging insight when one comes to the question of delusional beliefs. Surely here one can confidently state that insight is impaired? Suppose that a man, as part of his schizophrenic illness, holds the delusion that he is the rightful heir to the British throne, then this clearly has a *prima facie* case for being considered as evidence of loss of insight. Even here, though, the picture is not quite so sharp as one might imagine. The afflicted man might stoutly defend his assertion if one tried to argue him out of it, but on the other hand it is common to find that much of his behaviour suggests that for most purposes he regards himself as Mr. Smith from Balham rather than royalty. In particular you may observe that he consults a psychiatrist about his condition rather than a lawyer. This and other evidence shows that many psychotic patients do not behave whole-heartedly or consistently as if their delusions are true, much as they deny alternative possibilities.

Patient's insight into his current circumstances

We have so far considered the nature of a patient's insight into his *illness*. We can now go on to consider his insight into his *current circumstances*. Does the person realise that he is a patient in a hospital? The commonly expressed lay view that patients in a 'lunatic asylum' do not know where they are is largely false.

Illustration

As a junior psychiatrist in a large mental hospital it was my job to provide the day-to-day care in a ward which happened to be one of the worst in the hospital. Worst, that is, in the sense that it was a long-stay ward for patients who, despite having had a full course of treatment, remained psychotic and actively disturbed, and who needed to remain in a locked ward (or at least a securely guarded ward) for the protection of themselves or other people. One could not enter the ward without being confronted with baleful glares, importunate requests or bitter complaints. The demands were the harder to meet because of the common irrational content. I thought that it might be therapeutic to have a regular ward meeting at which the patients would have a chance to discuss their problems—not in itself a very original idea. The scenes that resulted were rather remote from one's idea of a typical committee or boardroom meeting, and not much closer to standard small-group therapy for patients with neurotic character disorders. The course of the meeting was usually chaotic and difficult to steer.

On one particular occasion it was difficult even to start the meeting. There was a continual hubbub and it was impossible to make oneself heard in an ordinary conversational voice. At this point one patient took it upon herself to campaign for a respectful silence. She herself was considerably disabled. Her diagnostic summary might read something like this: 'A personality-disordered schizophrenic with marked manic and depressive swings, suffering from a partial post-leucotomy syndrome.' She shouted at the top of her voice to make herself heard.

'Shut up you lot', she bellowed. 'It's like a bloody mad-house in here.' About half the patients smiled, tittered or in other ways showed their amusement at this gratuitously apposite turn of phrase. Manifestly they understood how ironic the expression was. It was equally clear that, in this respect, they had not lost insight into their general situation.

Judgment

There is no doubt that schizophrenics often show evidence of impaired judgment. Their behaviour, we have seen, may be bizarre, and their talk inappropriate. They often come out with things in everyday speech that are obscene or shocking, frequently of a sexual or violent nature. It is not just that most of us would not say such things, it is that they normally would not even rise above the unconscious level of the mind. There is thus said to be a lack of *censorship* in the mental workings of the schizophrenic.

Nevertheless, there can be few schizophrenics who do not do *some* appropriate things (*e.g.* sitting, eating, sleeping, watching, grasping, standing, walking, etc.) and so the extent to which their judgment is impaired is always relative. As one found with 'insight', there is no place for the sweeping statement about a patient that 'judgment is impaired'. Comments about judgment should be buttressed with concrete examples.

Formulation

Under this heading the psychiatrist will include a brief diagnostic summary, often mentioning the personality of the patient as well as present and past psychiatric illnesses. Where possible he will add comments on the aetiology of the mental state or on the response that has been shown to treatment.

Example

'This patient is a plumber of above average intelligence suffering from recurrent episodes of paranoid schizophrenia. From a background of a dominant mother and passive father, he has homosexual tendencies in his past behaviour, and shows extravert and hysterical personality traits. On previous occasions his paranoid psychotic features have responded well to phenothiazine drugs, but he has refused to take medication during follow-up after discharge from hospital. One of his six sisters suffers from catatonic schizophrenia.'

In the following chapters we shall go on to consider the different types of schizophrenia, aetiological factors, treatment and management.

SUMMARY

Compared with other functional psychoses, in schizophrenia the patient is further removed from reality and the symptoms and signs are less understandable. The terms 'bizarre' and 'incongruous' come to mind. With certain provisos, features that suggest the diagnosis include catatonic postures, formal thought disorder, thought-blocking, peculiar delusions (especially passivity feelings and those to do with the *possession* of thoughts), and hallucinations of voices talking about the patient in the third person. The affect may be incongruous or blunted. In 'schizophrenic dementia' the intellectual faculties seem to be dormant rather than destroyed.

9 Schizophrenia—types, causes and treatments

What is the difference between paranoia and paranoid schizophrenia? What can you do with a chronic, mute patient? When is a drop-out sick? Why is schizophrenia seen most often in the centres of cities and the lowest social class? Are schizophrenics more or less sensitive to their environment than others? These are some of the questions we try to answer in this chapter.

TYPES OF SCHIZOPHRENIA

Four main types of schizophrenia are described—paranoid, catatonic, simple and hebephrenic. Depending on the time elapsed, the schizophrenic illness is referred to as acute or chronic. A distinction is also made between the inexorable 'process' schizophrenia and more fleeting 'schizophreniform psychoses'. Let us now delve into the significance of those different expressions.

Paranoid schizophrenia

The term paranoid almost literally means 'beside onself'. More particularly it means that the person so described believes himself to have a *special* relationship with other people. The person may be rather grandiose, but at the present day the word has come to have the connotation of meaning preoccupied with ideas of being *persecuted*.

Feelings of being persecuted are not very unusual in normal persons. In times of difficulty most of us probably find it easier to blame others. We may feel that our own progress or advantage has been blocked by the selfish or hostile attitude of someone else. Sometimes, of course, it has been. It is not always easy to know when one's own judgment of the rights and wrongs are correct, since we are naturally biased towards our own point of view.

The tendency to ascribe failure, not to our own shortcomings, but to those of other people, is known as *projection*. It is similar to the mechanism referred to in the adage, 'The bad workman always blames his tools'.

Paranoid delusions

Let us move, though, from the degree of self-deception found in neurotic or even normal persons to that found in psychoses—the paranoid *delusion*.

'That car standing there across the street', she might say 'just looks like an ordinary car, but in fact those men in it are plain clothes detectives, trying to work up a case against me'.

Such ideas frequently crop up in organic brain disease. There it is sometimes difficult to know how much is plain delusion and how much is based on the misperception and misunderstanding that are part of the brain's malfunction.

Paranoid delusions may also be found in the *affective* psychoses. In fact it was a patient in the throes of a depressive psychosis who made the above statement to me. In her case the paranoid idea was in turn based on a delusion of guilt. She was convinced that she had committed a serious crime, and that the police were now catching up with her. At the opposite extreme, paranoid ideas are common in *hypomania*. Here the mechanism seems often to be based on the grandiose approach. The hypomanic patient might argue, 'it is strange that such an important person as I does not receive the respect and admiration that I am due. Why are people withholding it? It must be that they have secret hostile feelings towards me—they are against me.'

Either of these types of belief may be found in schizophrenic patients. What is more characteristic of schizophrenia, however, is the paranoid belief that is inexplicable in ordinary terms. Let us take the example given above of the plain clothes detectives sitting in the car. If such a delusion were typically schizophrenic, then when one asked the patient how he *knew* that it was so, he might reply 'because the car is red'. He would be unable to explain how the fact of the car being red was at all relevant—it would be convincing for him in a way that was not dependent on guilt feelings, or grandiosity, or any other understandable logic.

Like other delusions in schizophrenia the paranoid delusion may be bizarre. Many of the illustrations given in the previous chapter could be construed as paranoid—having someone drop urine on one's head, having one's feet nailed to the floor, suffering under the influence of a power machine in the basement.

Case 23 Miss H.L.

Miss H. L., who was the patient who complained of the power machine in the basement, had a number of other preoccupations.

When she was admitted to hospital 30 years previously at the age of 39 she had said she had Crippen in her medicine. Her conversation contained references to the Bible, pins, rays, wires and currents. Within the next 10 years she developed her ideas about the engineer and the power machine. Thirty years after admission she still talked about the power machine; she also complained that there were 'steel shares' in her body, she had been branded 'like signing a cheque on my body'.

On one occasion, talking to a stranger, she introduced herself as 'I'm the woman who had the war on my body, and all the law courts and a pain in my leg and left foot (pause) . . . and all the crippled power in it'. When asked how she got that way she reverted to the engineer and the machine.

The patient, Miss C. R., who complained that someone had dropped urine on her head also had a number of other bizarre delusions, many of which were paranoid in quality.

Case 24 Miss C.R.

Miss C. R. was admitted to the hospital in 1947 at the age of 25. She had a delusion that she had venereal disease affecting her throat, and accused 'her husband' of sexual perversion and infidelity. Over the years she had a number of different delusions. She complained that people were 'gnawing' her back, or trying to put a lump on her back. She said that her mother came up from the grave and scratched her legs. 'The witch is boring my eyes out.' She also said that her mother kept eating at her eyes through the wall—the pupil disappeared and the eye became painful. She repeatedly talked about witchcraft.

The mechanism of projection (as exemplified by paranoid delusions) is common in schizophrenia, and it is possible to see auditory hallucinations as having a similar psychodynamic basis. 'It isn't me that is thinking these thoughts', the patient might be saying, 'it is those other people saying them to me.'

Paranoia paraphrenia and paranoid schizophrenia

Paranoid delusions, on their own, do not necessarily signify that the patient is suffering from schizophrenia. A person may suffer from one delusion only, without hallucinations, formal thought disorder, passivity feelings or any other features of schizophrenia. Where do we fit this in the diagnostic classification? It is sometimes just given a separate status—a functional psychosis called *paranoia*.

A further concept is that of *paraphrenia*. Here, too, the patient does not have categorical features of schizophrenia. There are none of the features that were described in the last chapter as being diagnostic, and in particular the patient will not suffer from delusional passivity feelings nor from formal thought disorder. The illness does not produce a severe disruption of his personality—his mind is not 'fragmented' as the term schizophrenia would imply. The clinical picture is dominated by preoccupation with paranoid ideas and delusions that affect only one sector of his life. It is only, say, when he is at his workplace that he is suspicious and fearful. Alternatively he may function well at work but become psychotic in his interpretations when he is at home.

The three conditions of paranoia, paraphrenia and paranoid schizophrenia have been likened to a bad cake. In paranoia, it is just one cherry in the cake that is bad. In paraphrenia one whole slice of the cake is foul. In paranoid schizophrenia the whole cake is rotten. This type of classification of paranoid states does not satisfy everybody. Some psychiatrists will point out that many illnesses that are first seen in the form of paranoia or paraphrenia later develop into fully-fledged schizophrenia. It seems to them that these illnesses are all of the same ilk, and that it is pettifogging and pointless to try to distinguish one from another.

A variant of this view is that, granted that the illnesses have a great similarity, it is important to note the distinction in the way in which persons are affected by them. It has been observed that if an illness of this family strikes a young person in his teens, the effect will be much more disruptive than if it occurs for the first time in middle age. Thus, while florid schizophrenia is characteristically seen in the young, a paraphrenic picture tends to occur in the older patient. It is as if the young, malleable mind is more vulnerable to a distorting process, whereas in middle age the personality is well formed and entrenched in fixed ways of thinking and more rigid behaviour patterns.

We shall see later that these distinctions do not materially affect the type of treatment that the patient will be prescribed, so one could ask what is the practical importance of such hair-splitting. One possible answer might be in the prognosis that one has to give. There is a sense that florid schizophrenia is a more sinister illness than paraphrenia or paranoia. However, it is likely that a patient with florid schizophrenia who presents within a few days of the sudden inception of his illness has a far better prognosis than a patient who presents a year or two after the insidious development of paranoia or paraphrenia. Evidence on the malignancy of individual symptoms of the illness (taken as prognostic indicators) is very conflicting.

Under these circumstances many English-speaking psychiatrists are content to regard the majority of paranoid psychoses as similar in nature to schizophrenia in general, excepting perhaps the very isolated single-delusional illness.

Phenomenology of the paranoid psychoses
1. *Features of the paranoid psychoses* Apart from the persecutory delusion itself, what are the features that one may see clinically in the paranoid states? There are a variety of distortions to be found in the *thought content*, but a striking delusion is that *of reference*. With this the patient falsely believes that an event has a particular significance for him individually. Watching television, he may believe that the events described by the newsreader are oblique references to his own life. Conversations that he overhears in a shop are, despite superficial appearances, really about him. The newspapers say things about him in code. There is a special

meaning for him in the nods and glances exchanged by others on the train.

Ideas of this sort, short of delusional conviction, occur to many of us. If we leave a crowded room and return promptly for something we have left behind, a sudden silence greets us. Were they talking about us? Depending on how important to us is the reality of our acceptance by the group, these ideas tend to be fleeting—unless they are in fact true.

With the paranoid psychotic they become entrenched beliefs, tinged with sinister meaning, and reinforced by signs which only he can read.

The persecutory beliefs and the element of mystery combine to produce a preoccupation with *plots* to kill or injure the patient. The culprits may be unknown, or may be members of religious or political groups. In England, paranoid subjects often attribute their troubles to Freemasons, communists or Roman Catholics. It is interesting that these patients, feeling so vulnerable themselves, pick out minority groups for suspicion.

One patient, living in a capital city, was convinced that when he went out into the busy street all the vehicular traffic converged on *him*.

If the patient does not 'know' who is involved in the plot, it may seem safer to trust nobody. One sometimes comes across cases where the person loses a great deal of weight for no obvious reason. It later transpires that he believed he was being poisoned, and was suspicious of food from any source.

Another way in which the events of peculiar significance may be understood by the patient is that he is destined himself for a particular fate. It may dawn on him that the signs and portents are revealing to him his own special mission in life. This may be a humdrum or vague notion, but more typically the patient has messianic beliefs that he has the answer to the world's problems. This links with the ideas of grandeur that are so often part of the paranoid picture. He may secretly nurture beliefs in his own exceptional powers, convinced that he has abilities which are not appreciated or perceived by those around him.

Often he does not attempt to realise these powers, content in the comforting knowledge that he has them. Sometimes, however, he feels obliged to fight the forces of evil, and may then come into conflict with the law. Alternatively he may feel the fight is hopeless and panic.

Case 25 Mr. E.O.

Mr. E.O. was a 30-year-old man from Ireland. He was admitted to hospital in 1972 at the height of the hostilities. His parental home was just on the Republican side of the border, and his family of origin worked on the British side of the border. He was a Roman Catholic, but not in favour of Irish nationalist aims, and in particular had made no secret of his criticism of the Irish Republican Army (I.R.A.). He had travelled widely in the English-speaking world.

He became preoccupied with the idea that the I.R.A. were after him. He walked 'all over' London thinking that he was being followed. At times he thought his food was poisoned. He was admitted to hospital following an overdose of sleeping tablets.

He told how on one occasion he rushed out of the shop where he was eating, convinced that the men working in the restaurant were from the I.R.A. They were in fact all Indians in a curry restaurant, established for years in the neighbourhood.

At times he thought that his mother in Ireland had sent people to spy on him and to try to get him to go back home. He sometimes heard her voice saying to him 'Give us peace'. One night, while in hospital, he got up and locked himself in the lavatory. He had woken up with the conviction that his mother was there in the bed with him. He ran to the men's toilet—'I felt sure she wouldn't follow me in there'—and spent the next 3 hours there.

After a stormy course he lost his delusions (he was treated with phenothiazine drugs). There was, however, a further suicidal attempt before his recovery was complete. Eventually he developed insight into the irrational nature of his ideas and was no longer prey to them. He found a steady job in London.

Although patients sometimes try to strike back at their 'tormentors', it is surprising how seldom innocent bystanders are hurt in the course of a paranoid psychosis. It is as if the mind of the paranoid psychotic is working at two levels. At one level he thinks about, talks about and to some extent acts out his paranoid delusions. At another level he retains some control over his behaviour which is governed by reality, so that he will not seriously harm those who have not really hurt him. Sometimes he may be more drastic. A common paranoid belief is that the neighbours are conspiring to annoy one. A woman reported that her neighbours always hung out their washing at the same time as she did, as some sort of secret signal. Another reported that the paint smudges under a neighbour's window were clearly a derogatory phrase (although the patient's own husband affirmed that no lettering was to be described). She went on to reveal her belief that a box she had seen in the neighbour's window was really her (the patient's) coffin. Under such provocation patients will sometimes retaliate, but more commonly they just shout abuse or draw attention in some way to their emotional disturbance until the police or a doctor is brought in.

2. *Detection of the paranoid psychoses* How can one detect paranoid psychoses at an early stage of their development? It is understandable that many persons so afflicted will be embarrassed at the idea of talking about their peculiar beliefs, and may not voice them freely. If someone does not spontaneously mention ideas of persecution, it is still sometimes possible to get an indication that they might be present. One clue is that the person will reveal that he is concerned that people are looking at him or talking about him. With either of these hints it is worth exploring further for evidence of belief in hostile attitudes from others or in ideas of reference. Of course it often turns out that these preoccupations with the behaviour of others towards him are merely signs of exaggerated self-consciousness of the degree found in normals or neurotics.

There are two general points of contrast between the thoughts of paranoid psychotics and the thoughts of non-paranoid forms of schizophrenia. The patient with a paranoid psychosis feels intensely *responsible for his actions*: he is alone, fighting against a hostile world. The patient with non-paranoid schizophrenia, typified by the passivity feeling, seems to feel that he is no longer primarily in control, but is subject to outside forces that force him to behave at their whim. This is closely bound up with the other point of contrast, which is to do with interpersonal relationships. The paranoid patient is intensely preoccupied with his *relationship to other people*, bad though this relationship may be. The non-paranoid schizophrenic with passivity feelings feels that he is under the influence of a power that may be a disembodied force or, if a person, then anonymous.

These are generalisations and are given as food for thought. Many mixed or indeterminate delusions will be found. A well-known belief, falling uneasily between the two, is that the patient can identify a person who makes him do things against his will by influencing his brain or his thoughts in a mysterious way. Nevertheless both contrasts can indicate a further degree of distortion of mental action. One can see that there is a sense in which it is more disturbed to believe one is controlled than it is to believe one is fighting enemies, and similarly there is a sense in which it is less disturbed to believe that one's relationships with other persons are bad than it is to have been forced to abandon interest in relationships with other persons altogether.

It is for this type of reason that many psychiatrists will place the type of schizophrenia with passivity feelings in a more severe category of illness than the paranoid psychoses.

Catatonic schizophrenia

Features of catatonic schizophrenia

If paranoid schizophrenia is categorised mainly by features of the *thought content,* then catatonic schizophrenia is diagnosed mainly on the patient's *behaviour.*

The patient may stand for hours in a bizarre posture. If one of his limbs is moved into a different position, he will keep it there. He may automatically obey commands: alternatively he may resist even the simplest request (negativism). He may repeatedly carry out complicated stereotyped movements, such as banging the parts of his chair in a certain sequence symmetrically with both hands.

The patient is likely to be uncommunicative, and may even be mute for periods of weeks or months. All motor behaviour may be inhibited (stupor) or alternatively he may break out into an inexplicable burst of overactivity (catatonic excitement).

Many of these items of behaviour are reminiscent of other mental states and are therefore not diagnostic of schizophrenia when taken on their own. Individual features may have to be differentiated, for instance, from the stupor of hysteria, the excitement of mania, the retardation of depression, the compulsive behaviour of the obsessional, or the mannerisms of normal persons.

The diagnosis involves a certain amount of judgment on the part of the observer, especially if only a few catatonic features are present.

Case 26 Mr. J.B.

Mr. J.B. was admitted to a mental hospital in 1968. At that time he gave a history of recurrent admissions to mental hospitals, and his alleged diagnoses on these occasions included 'hysteria' and 'hysterical stupor'. He was not very communicative on admission, and within 3 days became quite mute. Although he sat in the chair with his head down in a withdrawn way, he would make his own coffee. He made a partial recovery on E.C.T. and was prescribed phenothiazine drugs. When he did talk he was still unable to give a coherent account of himself, and his conversation would be fragmented and contain irrelevancies.

Four months later he had relapsed completely and was again mute and withdrawn. E.C.T. was prescribed but the patient refused to sign the consent form—though apparently knowing what it was about.

After much discussion it was decided to go ahead with the treatment with the permission of his nearest relative and the consultant concerned.

He again made a partial recovery although his condition fluctuated from week to week. He did not show any inclination to leave the hospital. A year after his admission, at a typical interview, he would not look at or talk to the doctor. He resisted physical examination and was generally negativistic. He went to great lengths to keep himself to himself.

He used the hospital as his home, but would absent himself for long periods during the day. He still went to his flat at weekends—although since he had paid no rent he had no right to be there (and eventually the landlord changed the lock). There was an impression of wilfulness about his behaviour. When he was not completely mute he would talk to other patients but not to the staff. He would not reply to a greeting, but when asked to come to an office for interview would do so fairly readily, and then refuse to co-operate further. Even in phases when he would reply to the physician's questions he sat hunched up, avoiding looking at the doctor; gazing downwards but alert.

In 1971, 3 years after admission, a turning point came. He ate little and was noticed to be losing weight. Although he was below average height, he looked rather emaciated by the time his weight was down to 80 lbs. (36 kg) and when he suddenly refused to eat at all it was clear that intervention had to take place. Meanwhile it had been noticed that he always visited the lavatory soon after being given his medication (even when he was nominally eating), and it was suspected that he was not swallowing his tablets (phenothiazines).

He was transferred to a ward for the physically ill, and in addition to being fed he was also given a particular phenothiazine (fluphenazine) by injection—a drug whose effective duration of action spans several weeks. His physical state improved, and as a bonus he accepted the injections that were given at intervals of 2 to 4 weeks. After a few months had elapsed his mental state was quite different. He spontaneously asked for interview and asked about future treatment prospects. He talked freely and on his own initiative. He no longer avoided the gaze of the doctor. He admitted his improvement, only claiming that it was due to the passage of time rather than the injections.

He began to work well both in the ward and in the Industrial Therapy unit. He was sociable. By mid-1972 he had once again obtained a job in his own profession. A year later, at follow-up, he remained well, out of hospital and still holding his job (at £4,000 per annum).

This patient illustrates a number of features of catatonic schizophrenia. These included mutism, stereotyped posture and negativism. He also illustrates the difficulty one has in arriving at a diagnosis purely on terms of behaviour. Many observers would have given him a different label if they had seen him merely at one point in time, and some would possibly even disagree with the diagnosis of catatonic schizophrenia given the complete history. It is not my purpose now to attempt to justify the diagnosis in this particular case, but it is worthwhile taking the features that he showed and discussing how catatonic (or how schizophrenic) they are.

Let us first take the fact that he was mute. This can arise from organic brain disease, but that is not applicable to this case. We are really thinking of alternative possibilities that are *less* pathological than schizophrenia. Of the other functional psychoses, hypomania, we can agree, is hardly likely to strike a person dumb, but depressive psychosis might well do so. There are several ways in which the silence of depression differs from that of catatonic schizophrenia. Mutism is rarely the first sign of depression: almost always the patient will express a great amount of depressive thought content both before he gets to the stage of losing his speech and also after he recovers it. The silence is not usually absolute, and it is consonant with the apparent degree of depressive affect. In favour of such a diagnosis in the case of Mr. J.B. was the hang-dog body position and (at least in one stage) the failure to eat properly. However, when he did talk he never expressed ideas of guilt, unworthiness, poverty or disease and he certainly never complained of feeling low in his spirits.

Apart from depressive psychosis, what else could the diagnosis be? Of the neuroses, hysteria is the best candidate. If the silence were a way of lowering his anxiety levels (the 'primary gain') then it could be accepted as a form of conversion hysteria. However, in hysteria this usually takes the form of *aphonia*, in which the patient can whisper but not talk properly. Furthermore, there was never any convincing evidence while he was in hospital that the silence did operate as a primary gain, with one possible exception. This is that being schizophrenic, the silence helped him to maintain his distance from other persons. It can be seen that this argument might be applied to any case of catatonic schizophrenia, and does not alter the diagnosis *from* schizophrenia.

The final alternative is that he was not suffering from any form of psychiatric disorder. One could argue that, given that he was antagonistic towards the staff, he was merely showing his surliness by not talking to them. Many of us will punish those around us with silence when we have fallen out with them. But this is not an adequate explanation either. There did not seem to be in his case any particular reason why he should be more hostile to the staff than anyone else. And if there were some idiosyncratic reason why he should be, why could he not do something more positive about it? He was an intelligent man, and might be expected to present his case with effect. If all else failed, why stay at all? For much of the time he was in the hospital he was an informal patient in an unlocked ward—indeed he spent much of his time out of the grounds as it was.

We end up in the situation that, although the proof that the mutism shows that he is suffering from catatonic schizophrenia is lacking, alternative hypotheses are no more certain. Much the same could be said about the negativism that he showed, and the stereotyped postures were not really *good* evidence of catatonic schizophrenia to start with. Why give him as an illustration? There are several reasons. Firstly, in real life one does not always have the evidence to say beyond reasonable doubt what is the exact diagnosis. Secondly, this applies particularly to catatonic schizophrenia. Thirdly, he illustrates the sort of reasoning that one has to apply in testing the differential diagnosis. Fourthly, he provides an opportunity to look at the *point* of making a diagnosis. The point is to give a clue to the best method of treating him.

Treating him as a 'normal' person, one with no psychiatric abnormality, was presumably not applicable at the time of his admission to hospital, and certainly was not an option he wished to avail himself of in the open ward—he stayed. Treating him as suffering from conversion hysteria makes little sense when one has no idea what anxiety it is he is defending himself from by his behaviour.

Treating him as schizophrenic, at least when injections were used, did coincide in time with his clinical recovery. Incidentally, the diagnosis of schizophrenia also takes care of his withdrawn, autistic behaviour, his opting out from working or functioning in society, and the 'non-understandability' of the whole episode.

It has to be confessed that there is not in his case the final crunch of satisfaction of independent evidence of the firm accuracy of the diagnosis that sometimes happens.

Case 27 Mrs. C.O.

Mrs. C.O. (also referred to on p. 160) was admitted in a mute state. A diagnosis of catatonic schizophrenia was made clinically on grounds that were easier to feel than to explain verbally. Partly it may be that the impression of alertness militated against depressive retardation. Partly there was no logical or normal reason that one could see for her silence.

She responded promptly to the appropriate treatment and further information came to light. An immigrant from a European country, she had had several previous hospital admissions with a diagnosis of schizophrenia, and had been treated with phenothiazines in her country of origin. She revealed that while she had been silent she had had fears of persecution. These included suspecting that her food was poisoned. She also had ideas of reference and thought that people were watching her. On a previous admission she had heard voices, and believed that evil men were coming to take her from the hospital to kill her. She felt that people were following her on the ward, and that the police were coming after her.

In more florid cases, the phenomenon of waxy flexibility (*flexibilitas cerea*) may be seen. Here the patient's limbs have an abnormal quality of muscle tone. They may be placed in grotesque positions, and moreover they will be retained there. This is similar to the feature of automatic obedience: the traditional way of eliciting this sign is to ask the patient to put out his tongue; the examiner then lunges at the tongue with a hat-pin. Incredibly the patient does not withdraw the tongue in self defence, but imperturbably leaves it projecting.

It can be seen that in catatonic schizophrenia a central problem of the patient is that of the *will*. Instead of giving an appropriate response, the patient responds to requests, invitations or commands with unnatural obedience or surprising resistance. With the two examples quoted the negativism was more prominent than automatic obedience. A certain amount of unco-operativeness is understandable, and in an institution the spirit of avoiding compliance to authority may even be admired. 'Negativism' is likely to be the word that comes to mind when the resistance is arbitrary (even capricious), wholesale, or extreme.

The more florid examples of bizarre postures or stereotyped movements seem to be much less common today than they were 50 years ago. It is interesting that the form that mental illness takes changes with the years—among the neuroses the numbers of cases of gross hysteria have also dwindled. One particular posture that used to be observed in catatonic schizophrenia was that of the 'psychological pillow'. Here the patient would lie on his bed for long periods of time with his head 6 inches or so above the pillow. It is said that charge nurses (presumably with their own personal quirks) would line up a row of such patients for amusement. The two case histories of Mr. J.B. and Mrs. C.O. are more illustrative of the less flagrant examples that are seen presenting with catatonic schizophrenia these days—and even at that degree this is an uncommon illness.

Simple schizophrenia

Features of simple schizophrenia
This term is used for describing patients who lack such overt signs of schizophrenia as hallucinations, paranoid delusions or catatonic behaviour. The diagnosis is made from a consideration of their *emotions* and their *drive*, rather than abnormal thought content and perceptions.

The simple schizophrenic, then, will typically show flattening of incongruity of affect, with loss of drive. He will be emotionally cold and callous, unmoved and impassive, given neither to despair nor elation in response to everyday events. He will be unconcerned with the feelings of others, apathetic and lacking in initiative. During interview there may be a conspicuous lack of *rapport*, the examiner failing to achieve any empathy with the patient. The life style will be unproductive, with an apparent lack of concern on the part of the patient about the fact that he is not working, or playing, and not apparently achieving anything.

If one accepts that such persons exist, then it probably only remains to consider whether or not such a state should be regarded as one of *mental illness*. In some this will have been their temperament for the whole of their lives, and then it seems inappropriate to use the term 'illness'. It would seem more legitimate to regard it as part of their character make-up, and these are the cases described as having a *schizoid personality*.

In other cases there seems to be a significant change in their lives. Take a man who until his mid-30s, say, has led a productive and prosperous life, with an apparently normal pattern of friendship and social relationships. If he suddenly, for no obvious reason, fails to turn up to work, no longer socialises, is indifferent to the consequences, and drifts into poverty and squalor, what is one to make of it?

Diagnosis

Where there is a picture as described at the beginning of this section on simple schizophrenia, which arises out of the blue as a convincing change in behaviour, then this is the type of case that is *diagnosed* as simple schizophrenia.

It is clearly in many ways an unsatisfactory diagnosis. It highlights the fact that in making allocations to diagnostic categories we were very dependent on what the patient tells us about the content of his thoughts. Suppose a patient has hallucinations and delusions but chooses to deny them, how are we to know? Unless he is shouting at himself in a corner or suspiciously refusing his food, he may be able to keep his secret life to himself. One cannot know the numbers of persons who have schizophrenic conceptions and ideas but who never tell anyone about them.

Another unsatisfactory aspect of the diagnosis of simple schizophrenia is the difficulty in distinguishing it from disorders that are not schizophrenic, or from normality itself. It is conceivable that someone might choose to make a change in his life style as described above and not wish to discuss his cogent reasons for doing so. Such a story is intriguingly similar to that of some well-known artists, except that they usually have something creative to show as a result of the change.

A final hazard of the diagnosis is that, unless a good description of the previous life style is obtained from the patient, one may have to rely heavily on the description of isolated and biased observers, such as the spouse. One can think of cases where the spouse might be motivated to paint a blacker picture of this progression than could be justified.

Maybe I am being too scathing about the diagnosis. It is certainly one that I do not make great use of myself. What about the 30,000 men living in common lodging houses in Great Britain; or the even greater number of men living in 'Skid Row' hotels in the U.S.A.; the *Landstreicher* of Germany; the *clochards, errants* and *vagabonds* of France? It is possible that many of these men have simple schizophrenia. I have examined such men. A great number suffer from clearly diagnosable *overt* schizophrenia, but of those remaining it is difficult to know from their own vague story whether they have had a gross personality change or whether they have always been apathetic and inert.

The diagnosis probably does have some value in clinical practice in patients who fulfil the description given at the beginning of this section on simple schizophrenia, who are wanting help, who clearly have psychological problems of some sort and for whom one needs some sort of focus in thinking about their treatment or management.

Hebephrenic schizophrenia

This is the core concept of schizophrenia. Most of what was written in the last chapter on schizophrenia in general could equally well have been said about hebephrenic schizophrenia. The term essentially connotes a schizophrenic illness starting in *youth*. It also carries with it the idea of insidious onset and relentless progression. Enough was said in the last chapter to make it clear that relentless progression cannot necessarily be predicted from any one individual symptom (except perhaps that the case has shown relentless progression so far) so that the clinical features of hebephrenia are those of schizophrenia in general.

The four types of schizophrenia described so far are not mutually exclusive. There is nothing to stop a patient with a paranoid psychosis showing catatonic features at the same time, and a patient who seems to be in one category may show predominantly the features of a different category at another point in time.

On the whole psychiatrists diagnose such patients as having 'schizophrenia', only adding the epithet 'catatonic' or 'paranoid' if the appropriate features are particularly prominent, and in many cases not specifying which category at all.

The terms *acute* and *chronic* are used in their general medical sense. Acute just means that the illness has lasted a short time, and chronic merely means that it has been going on for a long time. Acute, then, refers to a duration of days or weeks, and chronic to months and years.

The contrast between a *schizophreniform psychosis* on the one hand and *process schizophrenia* on the other was discussed in the last chapter, though without using those terms. The concept of process schizophrenia is one in which the illness is relentlessly progressing to chronicity and destruction of the personality. The term 'schizophreniform psychosis' implies a psychotic illness that seems to be just like schizophrenia at one point in time, but is not 'really' schizophrenia. How, you may ask, can one tell it is not really schizophrenia? Well, the reply runs, it got better so it couldn't be, since real schizophrenia has a relentless chronic course, etc. I have already made it clear that I find this distinction unsatisfying. The reader should merely be aware that there are two possible points of view on this subject. Luckily, although the proponents of the different points of view argue over the theory, in practice they both seem to agree on the treatment, so the schism is not too serious.

Two other diagnoses that the reader may come across are firstly *pseudoneurotic schizophrenia*, and secondly *schizoaffective psychosis* (or *schizoaffective schizophrenia*). They illustrate a principle that was alluded to in early chapters of this book. We saw then that we could construct a ladder or hierarchy of diagnoses, and at any rung of this ladder the diagnosis situated there could show any of the symptoms above it, or could in turn itself merely be a 'symptom' of the diagnosis below it. Thus, anxiety symptoms could constitute a diagnosis of their own (anxiety state) or could be merely features of a depressive illness. Similarly, depressive symptoms could constitute their own affective illness, or just be symptoms of schizophrenia. In turn schizophrenic symptoms may form the basis of a diagnosis of schizophrenia, or may be themselves features of organic brain disease.

Let us accept, then, that a case of schizophrenia may show many symptoms of affective illness (depression or hypomania), or strong anxiety, hysterical or obsessional features.

Moreover, one appreciates that not all schizophrenics confess to their delusions and hallucinations. If we take these two facts in conjunction, we can see that there may be patients who are in fact suffering from a schizophrenic illness, who deny psychotic symptoms but show instead affective features or neurotic features.

Thus the patient with *pseudoneurotic schizophrenia* will be treated in vain for his neurosis until it is realised that he suffers from schizophrenia. The proof of the pudding is in the eating, and if treatment for schizophrenia works where treatment for neurosis fails then this is a powerful argument.

In *schizoaffective psychosis* the connotation is slightly different. This diagnosis is applied (by those who use it) to patients who certainly seem to be schizophrenic on the usual criteria, but in whom the affective array of symptoms is unusually prominent and dominates the clinical picture. Here the diagnosis is said to carry implications for prognosis (unlikely to become chronic) and for the treatment (E.C.T. is very successful) as well as being graphic. There are patients who, in the absence of any definite schizophrenic features, are diagnosed as suffering from depressive illness, but for whom conventional antidepressant therapy is of no avail. Some of these clear up promptly when treated as for schizophrenia, and one cannot help thinking that they may in some sense be 'really' schizophrenic, although the schizophrenic symptoms have failed to manifest themselves. This is not a very satisfying concept from the semantic point of view, and the precise way of talking about it is not important provided one remembers that there *are* patients who respond in that way, whatever one calls them.

AETIOLOGY OF SCHIZOPHRENIA

Heredity
It is widely believed that there is some hereditary tendency to develop schizophrenia, and this belief can give rise to pessimism, gloom and an attitude of mind which looks on the illness as untreatable. This bias is understandable but unwarranted.

It is agreed that the chances of developing a schizophrenic illness are higher if one of the parents has had the illness. Furthermore, this has been shown to be the case even when the child has been separated from his family soon after birth, so it appears that there is a genuine hereditary effect. Twin studies confirm this impression. One can compare non-identical twins and identical twins. Non-identical twins are born at the same time and usually brought up together, but are no more alike in their chromosomes than are two ordinary siblings. Identical twins are born at the same time and usually brought up together, and in addition their chromosome make-up is identical. Many studies have found concordance rates for schizophrenia that are higher in identical twins than non-identical twins. That is to say, if we take the case where one of the twin pair has schizophrenia, then the chances of the other twin having schizophrenia are higher when he is identical than when he is non-identical. Since the main difference in the two cases is in the chromosomes, this suggests that hereditary influences play a part in the inheritance of schizophrenia.

Dominant inheritance

Therefore there are few psychiatrists who would deny that the genes and the chromosomes may be loaded for schizophrenia in the children of schizophrenics. The room for argument is on the extent of the influence that this has.

It is certainly not as great as in Huntington's chorea. You will recall that in this condition if one parent is affected, then fifty per cent of the children are likely to be affected. This is the pattern of *dominant* inheritance, which is not what is seen in schizophrenia. Mark you, even in Huntington's chorea not all experts are pessimistic about finding a cure. They point out that although the average time of onset is at about 40 years of age, some persons develop it at 20 years and some at 60 years. If one could find out some factors in the environment that delayed the onset then one would be well on the way to therapeutic intervention.

Recessive inheritance

A different pattern of inheritance is found in *phenylketonuria*. Here it requires both parents to carry the gene, neither of whom actually show the disease themselves. This is known as the *recessive* mode of inheritance. It is explained by the fact that each person has two complete sets of genes and one set is passed on to the child. (The strong influence of a dominant gene overpowers the action of the other gene in the dominant form of inheritance, and there is a fifty-fifty chance that any of the children will get this gene.) The recessive gene does not dominate the other one, and *both* have to be affected before the disease shows up. This means that one has to get one affected gene from each parent. It can be calculated that the chances of this happening, even when both parents unwittingly carry the gene, are only 25 per cent cent for any particular child. And in practice one does see that roughly a quarter of the children of such couples are affected, on average.

So this is less serious than with the full dominant inheritance. We saw earlier in the book (pp. 122–3) that even with such a categorical pattern of inheritance as in phenylketonuria one can intervene, in this case with a diet, to avoid the disease showing itself.

To return to schizophrenia, the percentage of children affected where one parent has the illness is not even 25 per cent, let alone 50 per cent. The precise figures vary from study to study, but are usually below 20 per cent and may even be as low as 10 per cent. The pattern of inheritance is therefore a relatively weak one, although still a factor that cannot be ignored. It is not certain what form the mode of inheritance takes. It may not even be a single gene—it may be more the effect of a number of different genes on the personality—similar to the inheritance of height.

Tuberculosis

It could be that as our methods of treatment for schizophrenia become more effective we shall become less preoccupied with the hereditary influence. To illustrate this idea we can take the case of tuberculosis. We are so accustomed nowadays to thinking of T.B. in terms of bacteria and antibiotics that it takes an effort of mind to realise that many people used to think of it as hereditary. One is tempted to scoff, and point out that we now know that parents may have been infecting their children. But this is not the whole story, and in a sense it is hereditary. For instance, the concordance rates in twins bear a remarkable resemblance to those for schizophrenia—concordance rates are much higher for identical twins than they are for non-identical twins. Nowadays we would not say

T.B. was hereditary, we would rephrase it, something like 'the tendency to develop into a frank clinical case of tuberculosis, after having been exposed to infection, is much greater for some constitutions than for others'. In plain words, though, we are saying that whether or not you get T.B. depends on hereditary factors, admitting that it also depends on your environment whether your hereditary weakness is exposed.

The tremendous fall in the number of cases of T.B. in western countries has not taken place just because we have better treatment: almost certainly environmental factors have played an enormous part, so that one can cut down the infection rate by altering social factors (overcrowding, slum conditions, public manners, etc.) and increase resistance to infection in other ways (improved diet and standard of living, decrease in working hours, etc.).

There is no reason why, given the hereditary tendency to schizophrenia, one should have to sit back and leave the outcome to fate.

Demographic factors

It is known that the proportion of schizophrenia in the population varies, depending where one looks. The rates of incidence and prevalence have at one time or another been said to vary with age, marital status, social class, location (town or country), degree of geographical mobility, residence status (native-born or immigrant), religion, nationality and ethnic group.

Many of these findings have proved unstable, and have not been confirmed by further studies. The two associations that have been displayed over and over again are those with social class and the centre of cities.

In the 1930s, it was shown in Chicago that the highest rates for schizophrenia in the sprawling city were for the *very central parts*. At least judged by mental hospital admissions for a diagnosis of schizophrenia it was the central areas that were producing the highest numbers. This finding has been confirmed elsewhere, and has since been replicated in the United Kingdom.

After the Second World War, investigators in the New Haven area of New England found a relationship between schizophrenia and *social class*. They found higher rates in social class V, comprising poor unskilled labourers. Again, similar findings have been obtained in Great Britain.

To many observers this suggested that poorer living conditions, especially in central urban areas, was a breeding ground for schizophrenia. The constant nagging worry of poverty, it was argued, and the vicissitudes of slum dwellings would be enough to drive you mad in the end.

A competing hypothesis was put forward. It was suggested that the above interpretation was not justified by the facts. Those behavioural scientists who favoured organic factors (such as heredity) for the main cause of schizophrenia tended to argue as follows. If a person is becoming schizophrenic, or has become schizophrenic, then this will impair his ability to function in society. His working skills will deteriorate, and he will join the ranks of the unskilled and that body of anonymous urban residents who inhabit boarding houses, single rooms, cheap hotels and common lodging houses which are to be found in central city zones.

Both the 'breeding ground' theory and the 'downward drift' theory were logically tenable, and psychiatrists sympathised with one or other view according to their bias and their preconceived notions.

Eventually studies were carried out to test the relevant hypotheses. To take the social class observation first, some British investigators argued quite simply that if the 'breeding ground' hypothesis were correct, then the parents of the schizophrenics should show a pattern of social class that over-represented social class V, similar to that of the schizophrenics themselves. They analysed the social class of male schizophrenic patients on their first admission to hospital together with that of their fathers. Once again they confirmed the observation that the schizophrenics themselves were to be found in social class V. They found that the fathers did not show this tendency, but showed a pattern of distribution like that of the general population (Goldberg and Morrison, 1963).

There was an element of unfairness in this simple study that the research workers themselves admitted. The fathers were that much older than the patients. It might be, then, that it was not reliable to compare their social class structure with that of the patients. After all, many of us hope to be promoted in the course of our careers. Some of us may arise from teaboy or filing clerk in our teens to managing director in our fifties. At least the ordinary workman may eventually become a supervisor—much higher in the social scale. The investigators found an ingenious way of dealing with this problem. When a birth is registered in the United Kingdom the details of the occupation of the parents are recorded at the same time. By choosing schizophrenics (on their first mental hospital admission) within a certain age range they were able to collect a group whose fathers would have been, when the patients were born, of the same average age as the patients were currently. They were then able to compare the occupational status of a patient with that of his father at the same age. They confirmed their original finding. Even with this precaution, the fathers did not show the excess in social class V that was found in the patients.

As far as the 'centre of the city' observation goes, the crucial test has been carried out by Professor Dunham, one of the original team that made the observations in Chicago in the 1930s.

He altered his focus of attention to Detroit for his further studies. There he chose two areas of the city for analysis, one of which had an admission rate for schizophrenics that was three times that of the other. He argued as follows. If people become schizophrenic through living in a certain place, then to some extent the longer you live there the more effect it will have. So he compared admission rates for those who had lived there for more than 5 years against those who had lived there less than 5 years. He found that residents who had been there more than 5 years showed no difference in admission rates between the two parts of the city. The difference in admission rates arose solely from persons who had *recently* moved into the respective areas (Dunham, 1965).

Professor Dunham himself had originally subscribed to the 'breeding ground' school of thought, so the results seem to have come as a bit of a surprise to him, and therefore carry the more weight for that reason. (When scientific studies prove what the author strongly believes from the start, they are always subject to criticism—not that the books were necessarily cooked, but that the research design might in a subtle way have made it more easy to prove one thing than another.)

These two studies, one on social class and one on urban locality, both provide strong evidence in favour of the 'drift' theory. It looks as if the epidemiological findings that have proved to be so consistent are themselves the *results* of the schizophrenia, rather than the cause of it. Drift down the social scale, or towards certain areas of the city, happens either because of the social incompetence caused by the illness or (according to a related theory) as a result of changes in the personality that precede the actual illness itself.

If we accept these conclusions we see that the epidemiologists have so far not provided us with much evidence of causal factors in the environment to explain the development of schizophrenia. This does not mean to say that there is no environmental element in the causation of schizophrenia. It is possible that the factors that they have looked at so far are too crude and broad. After all it is known that schizophrenia occurs in all social classes, so an association with poverty could never have been more than a partial explanation of its origin. If the association with the centre of the city had been a causal link it would still have needed more work to find out exactly what it was at the centre that made it produce the schizophrenic illness.

If we cannot find the environmental causes of schizophrenia in a wide scan of the landscape, maybe we should look nearer home for some clues.

Family environment

Many schizophrenics never marry and so they fail to develop a family of their own. Observations of family interaction in adult life have often been about the patient who has already developed the frank illness. Theories have been developed, however, on the type of relationships in the childhood of the subject that predispose him to schizophrenia in later life.

The double-bind theory

One of the best known of these is the theory of the 'double-bind' relationship. It is said that the schizophrenic as a child was treated by his mother in a very particular way. In brief, her non-verbal behaviour does not match her verbal behaviour. She will say something like 'Come to me, darling, mummy loves you' in a way which sounds fierce, hostile and repelling. To hear her tone of voice you would get the message that she is angry and rejecting and wishes the child to go away. However, the words she is saying are commanding him to approach to receive love. What can the child do? It is a very frightening business to go near the mother who is sounding so menacing, yet if she goes away he is risking the mother's reproach for disobeying her and spurning her offers of 'love'.

There is obviously no right answer. If a child spends his formative years in the presence of such a mother one might predict certain features of his later behaviour.

1. He will find the whole idea of relating to other people difficult and may even avoid close interpersonal relationships.

2. He will experience emotions that are not necessarily the usual ones in any given context, or he may have developed a protective psychological shell to defend him from emotional stress, and show little emotion at all.

3. He will find it difficult to make decisions, particularly in answer to the approaches or demands of other people. He will be in great doubt as to the right way to respond to them.

4. He may avoid committing himself in speech and, when giving a reply, may give an answer that actually says very little, is vague, or difficult to understand.

These features, on the one hand, can be easily understood as habit patterns or defensive mechanisms that are built up as a response to the long-continued influence of the mother. On the other hand they are very similar to some of the clinical features that one observes in adult schizophrenics. The behaviour described under 1 would correspond with the withdrawn or solitary patient often described as autistic. Heading 2 covers the disorders of affect referred to as incongruence or flattening. Category 3 reminds one of the disorders of volition known as ambivalence. The vagueness and unintelligibility of 4 is reminiscent of the loosening of associations that in the schizophrenic is called (formal) thought disorder.

It is interesting that long before the 'double-bind' theory was promulgated a world famous psychiatrist, Bleuler, had attracted many to his viewpoint that the four fundamental findings in schizophrenia were autism, ambivalence, disorders of affect and defective associations of thought. He thought of such things as frank delusions and hallucinations as being secondary characteristics, which were not necessary to the diagnosis. He considered that they were merely reactions of the individual to the disruption of his personality caused by the four primary features. Although he has a wide following, his views have not been adopted by all psychiatrists, possibly because there must be such a large subjective element in the judgment about identifying Bleuler's four primary features—it is much easier to decide if the patient has delusions and hallucinations, and there is more likely to be unanimity of opinion about whether he has such beliefs and experiences than whether his solitary habits are schizophrenic autism or just ordinary shyness. It may also be that to make the diagnosis according to Bleuler's criteria requires a lot more time to be spent going into the patient's background than most psychiatrists have available.

To return to the double-bind theory itself, it requires some elaboration to explain why a person should suddenly break down in a schizophrenic illness in adult life, which then recovers or progresses. Presumably one can postulate that although the child adopts the protective reactions in the first few years of life, while under the domination of his mother, he will develop more normally when he goes to school, for instance, and interacts in more normal relationships. One would then suggest that, as a response to emotional stress in adult life, he reverts back to his infantile defenses as a primitive method of coping—a common enough argument used in psychiatry to explain neurotic illnesses.

Objections to the double-bind theory

Thus far we can see that the theory can, at least in some cases, fit the facts. Unfortunately it remains far from being proved. There are several objections to it. Firstly, there is the intriguing if rather weak reservation that the 'double-bind' type of maternal behaviour is quite common among normal parents of normal children. Many mothers try to temper the wind to the shorn lamb, and utter terms of endearment when they scold their children. The start of the sentence may be furious, and the end of it conciliatory, for example, 'John, *for goodness sake* put that vase down, darling'. This is seen the more so when the mother herself feels guilty about any anger she expresses towards her offspring. Such guilt may be a relic of her own moral or religious background, or it may have been engendered by those psychiatrists who have given the public the idea that any personality deviation, behaviour disorder or mental illness is directly the fault of the parents' handling of the patient as a child.

Such degrees of mixed message and (to the child) confusing emotions are commonplace, and luckily most of us do not subsequently suffer from schizophrenic illnesses. However, I described it as a weak reservation because clearly there are double messages and double messages. Some can be much more difficult for the child to deal with than others.

It is when we go on to the more extreme forms of double-bind that we come across the next potential flaw in the theory. If a mother is irrevocably warping a child's mental health by the persistence or intensity of her 'I love you and/or hate you' communications, then what sort of mother is she anyway? Doesn't the mother herself have serious psychological problems? In fact, isn't she expressing ambivalence, inappropriate affect, obscure verbal communication and gross difficulty in interpersonal relationships? It sounds, in fact, as if she has been tarred with a very similar brush. If we admit that, then we also have to admit that the behaviour we are observing is not *necessarily* a result of early environment, but may be something that is governed by genes and chromosomes. We are in the all-too-familiar position of asking ourselves which came first, the chicken or the egg.

A third possible objection to the theory is that we do not always (or even, some would say, often) elicit a history of obvious 'double-bind' behaviour in the mother when we see our schizophrenic patients. This merely illustrates the difficulties in proving a theory of this sort. It is not always possible to get a good account of what the mother's behaviour was during the patient's infancy. Certainly the mother and the patient themselves are likely to be biased witnesses, and so are the other relatives and friends whom one sees. It would be very difficult to carry out the experiment of rating a random sample of mothers from the population for double-bindedness and then follow up hundreds of children to see which ones developed schizophrenia. Until someone does do this, one's belief in the theory remains a matter of faith rather than observation.

My own personal view is that the double-bind aetiology seems to operate in *some* of one's schizophrenic patients, but not in the large proportions that were described in those states of the U.S.A. where the theory was first promulgated. Nevertheless it is worth considering the implications of the theory in the social management of the average schizophrenic patient. This will be discussed later under that section but, put briefly, short of attempts to produce a radical *change* in the patient's psychodynamics, one can at least recognise his problems in a practical way. When considering the plight of the schizophrenic when he is discharged from hsopital, for instance, one may judge that the intense personal relationships of the parental home may be too much of a stress for him to bear at that time, yet on the other hand consider that the privacy of a flat, apartment or bed-sitter would err too much on the side of isolation, encouraging further withdrawal. One is searching for what has been called the *optimal social distance* for such a schizophrenic patient (Brown *et al.*, 1958). A suitable solution for the time in question might be hostel accommodation, for instance, where ideally there would be company (but non-intrusive company) and supervision (but not overpowering authority).

Biochemical theories

Many people have had a hunch that schizophrenia must be based on an abnormality of the body chemistry, and the scientific literature on the subject is full of discarded or unproved theories. However, there is a lot to be said for such an idea.

L.S.D.

We know that subjects can be made to experience psychotic symptoms as a result of taking drugs. Possibly the best known example of such a drug is lysergic acid diethylamide (L.S.D.). This can produce distortions of perception up to and including hallucinations. It can also produce delusions. Interestingly enough L.S.D. does not seem to produce true physical dependence, but it can prove dangerous in two ways. Firstly, under the immediate influence of the drug the subject may feel that he has supernatural powers. His subsequent behaviour may prove dangerous to himself or others. If he believes he is able to fly, and cheerfully leaps out of the fifth floor window the damage will be to himself. If he thinks he is endowed with divine protection and drives down a busy high street at 100 m.p.h. then the disaster is likely to involve others as well.

The second way in which L.S.D. is said to be dangerous is that it appears that it can precipitate frank mental illness. This is difficult to prove (it may always have been a coincidence) but some subjects not only get a 'bad trip' from taking 'acid', they do not come out of it in a few hours, but remain psychotic for days or weeks or until they are treated.

Having said this, it must be admitted that the features of L.S.D. intoxication, especially in the acute phase, do not closely resemble any of the common functional psychoses. The hallucinations and delusions may sound superficially like schizophrenia, but the man on 'acid' is likely to be more disoriented and suffer a greater disturbance of consciousness and of awareness of surroundings than is usually seen in schizophrenia. The picture produced by 'hallucinogenic' drugs like L.S.D. carries some of the qualities of an *organic* psychosis.

Stimulants

A picture more closely resembling schizophrenia may be produced by the *stimulant* group of drugs, including the amphetamines. These 'pep pills' were used during the Second World War to keep air crew awake during long bombing missions. In addition to keeping the subject alert and preventing sleep, they also severely inhibit appetite for food. They, and drugs like them, have subsequently been used as appetite suppressants for people trying to lose weight. Unfortunately they do prove to be habit forming, and some patients become addicted to them. They crave the tablets, and take increasing doses as time goes on. They may wangle excessive prescriptions for the medication—in the form of amphetamines, dexamphetamine, mixtures of amphetamine with barbiturates or (particularly as a solution for intravenous use) methylamphetamine. Alternatively they buy the tablets illegally in pubs and bars as 'the blues', 'black bombers', 'purple hearts' (these mauve heart-shaped tablets containing a mixture of dexamphetamine and amylobarbitone are no longer manufactured because they were so easily recognisable) or as 'speed'.

A proportion of amphetamine addicts become psychotic. The psychosis typically includes persecutory beliefs, and mimics paranoid schizophrenia so closely that there is no known way of distinguishing the psychotic symptoms of amphetamine psychosis from those of paranoid schizophrenia. The clinical picture may even include auditory hallucinations. Amphetamine psychosis is diagnosed by the history of ingestion (or injection) of amphetamines, finding the presence of amphetamines in the urine, seeing injection marks in the fold of the forearm over the veins, or by such clues as insomnia, loss of appetite and loss of weight, and other incidental effects of the drug.

Amines

A further argument in favour of a chemical basis to psychotic symptoms is provided by the nature of the drugs that we have been discussing. Many 'psychotomimetic' drugs are members of the chemical class known as *amines* (*e.g. amphetamine*). Amines do occur in the human body, two of the most important being called serotonin and (the more familiar) adrenaline. These two naturally occurring amines, or compounds closely similar, are found in the brain, and are believed to act as chemical messengers between nerve cells, as an intimate part of the process of communication between one part of the brain and another. One can readily see how taking drugs which may cheat the brain (into thinking it is receiving genuine messages) can bring about psychotic symptoms. The fact is that *most of the well-known psychotomimetic drugs resemble either serotonin or adrenaline.*

The proponents of the chemical theory of schizophrenia would argue that a small abnormality in the body chemistry could convert the naturally occurring adrenaline or serotonin into a psychotomimetic agent. It is known that the body has processes (enzyme systems) that could easily be switched to do this. It has not yet been proved to everyone's satisfaction that in real life it happens. Sometimes one reads that a certain laboratory has found psychotomimetic breakdown products of amines in schizophrenic patients: so often one hears later that other laboratories have failed to confirm the original observations.

It is certainly possible that more evidence will come to light in this area in the near future. It should be borne in mind that a chemical theory, if proven, would not necessarily put a psychological theory out of court. This point will be elaborated later.

Neurophysiological theories

Many investigations have shown that there is something odd about the state of *arousal* of schizophrenic subjects. It is a complex situation—in some ways the state of alertness of schizophrenics seems peculiarly vulnerable to incoming stimuli, and in some ways it appears resistant. The resistance is perhaps more obvious—the apparent indifference that schizophrenics show to other people, the affective blunting, the obscure language. On the other hand experienced psychiatric nurses will often explain a schizophrenic patient's temporary exacerbation by pointing out that the atmosphere in the ward at that time was too 'stimulating'. It is possible that these patients are basically vulnerable to stimulation, and that the resistance is a secondary defence.

Whatever the explanation may be, psychologists agree that the field of arousal is a fruitful area for investigation. Much of the research carried out so far has been fairly academic, but some ties up with what was written in the previous section (on chemical theories). An important organ of arousal within the brain is a network of nerve cells at the base of the brain called the *ascending reticular formation*. To recapitulate a little on an earlier chapter, you may recall that three things happen when someone stamps on your toe.

1. A message passes up to the part of the cerebral cortex that deals with the big toe, so that you say 'I have a sensation in my big toe'.
2. A message passes up to the part of the brain that deals with pain (the thalamus) so that you say 'it hurts'.
3. A message passes to the ascending reticular formation so that you become alert, aroused, startled, galvanised into activity—whether the activity is jumping on one foot, shrieking, pushing the person doing the stamping away, or just looking surprised and at a loss to know what to do.

The state of activity of the ascending reticular formation, and therefore the state of arousal of the subject, depends not only on stimuli arriving from the peripheral sense organ and the organs of special sense (eyes, ears, etc.) but also on stimuli coming from other parts of the brain itself, probably including the frontal lobes.

There are two pharmacological observations that suggest that the arousal mechanisms may be involved in schizophrenia. The first we have just considered in the previous section—the action of amphetamine. We saw there that amphetamine produces a near-perfect imitation of paranoid schizophrenia. There we were focussing down on the chemical nature of amphetamine. If now we stand further back and look at the *effect* of amphetamine on the activity of the nervous system, we can see that amphetamine is an *alerting* drug, one that above all increases the state of arousal of the subject taking it.

Now let us switch our attention to a drug with the opposite effect. Taking chlorpromazine (Largactil, Thorazine) as an example of that group of tranquillisers called phenothiazines, we have here a drug which is known to be one of the most powerful in *removing* the symptoms of schizophrenia. The action of chlorpromazine on the nervous system has been analysed, and we find that it reduces the input of ascending nervous messages into the reticular formation (the third type of message that we considered above in the case of the hurt big toe). A person taking this drug will still be able to detect sensations, will remain able to identify their origin and their nature, but will get less worked up about them (less aroused).

Se we have a drug which increases arousal that is guilty of producing schizophrenia, and a drug that decreases arousal that clears up schizophrenia, between them providing quite strong evidence for disorder of arousal being a causative factor in the aetiology of schizophrenia.

Relationship between the theories
The various strands of evidence that we have looked at so far can now be considered together. Although we have discussed them as different theories, and although the proponents of one theory often do not see eye to eye with the proponents of the others, much of the evidence is not so much in conflict but rather looking at the situation from a different perspective.

We can see this in the case of the effect of *amphetamine*. Looked at in one way, it is an example of an action at the chemical level. If we consider the situation on a different level, and ask what is the sum of all the chemical actions at the nerve junctions, then the total effect may be seen to be one of arousal.

An increase of arousal in itself is not sufficient to cause

schizophrenia, and only a proportion of amphetamine addicts, for instance, will develop the psychosis. It is possible that a person does not develop schizophrenic symptoms unless his pattern of interpersonal relationships is already abnormal—maybe as a result of a double-bind relationship with his mother or other morbid earlier experiences.

Schizophrenia is likely to have at least as complex an aetiology as tuberculosis. At present we do not seem to know enough about it to produce that dramatic fall in the incidence of schizophrenia as has happened in the case of tuberculosis. It may come soon. It is not so long since large hospitals were full of chronic cases of tuberculosis, regarded by outsiders as hopeless.

TREATMENT OF SCHIZOPHRENIA

One can say that both psychological and physical methods are important in the treatment of schizophrenia, as with most other forms of mental illness. One has to admit, though, that most psychiatrists throughout the world would feel that it is the physical treatment which at present makes the most crucial difference to the outcome.

Psychological methods

There are some therapists, particularly in the United States, who seem to be effective in treating schizophrenia by psychological methods alone, but they are rare. Most psychiatrists would not claim to be able to provide the definitive treatment in this way: they would rely heavily on physical methods of treatment, and in particular on the set of drugs known as the neuroleptics or major tranquillisers.

My own attitude is that I prefer to use both methods together. I find that I get nowhere in trying to treat schizophrenic patients with 'talking' methods of treatment if they are not at the same time receiving neuroleptic medication. In addition I believe that it is important to administer these drugs as soon as possible after the onset of the illness—there is little scope for a wait-and-see philosophy. If a patient has to wait months or years before receiving his physical treatment, then the chances of a complete remission of symptoms are reduced: in plain words, if you wait too long, he may never get better again.

With this proviso, then, what are the important features of psychotherapy for schizophrenia? The first, and most important principle, is that one should *not* use the classical form of psychoanalytically oriented psychotherapy: the removal of defences and use of uncovering techniques are fraught with danger in schizophrenics, and may even precipitate overt schizophrenia in previously borderline or latent cases. Secondly, the use of *supportive* techniques of psychotherapy are generally considered to be valuable at best, and harmless at least. In this context, specific aims will be to help the patient to use the healthy part of his mind that remains to retain his contact with reality, to enlarge the scope of this area of function, to encourage a conscious dismissal of 'strange' thoughts, putting psychotic material to the back of his mind, and with the aid of face-saving ways of talking about his experiences to make the maximum use of what insight he has.

This may sound rather abstract, so let us take a simple example at the expense of being a little obvious. A schizophrenic with residual symptoms (*e.g.* grandiose ideas) may be quite incapable in practice of returning to his old white-collar job. Left to himself he may reject the idea of any occupation which is not of as high a status as his old job. The consequence would be long-term institutionalisation or the degradation of unemployment. Let us imagine that at some level he knows what the score is, despite his grandiose talk. If the idea of taking a humble job, well within his capabilities, can be put to him as a 'fill-in' job just 'for the time being', or as a welcome rest from the rigorous demands of his normal occupation, then he may accept this face-saving way of construing the situation and take the job. One anticipates that in many cases this will enable him to lead a relatively normal life, free from acute poverty, with some satisfaction from occupying a role in society, and in addition will enable him to avoid the loss of self-esteem involved in remaining in the mental hospital, or whatever is the alternative.

This rather simple illustration may not deserve the title of 'psychotherapy', but perhaps does something to show in practical terms what is meant by the abstract concepts of employing the healthy parts of his mind to contact reality, and to use what insight he has with the aid of acceptable descriptions of his situation.

Physical methods

When we come to the *physical* methods of treatment the results are seen most impressively in the treatment of the acute attacks of illness. One can often walk into wards into which patients are admitted at the height of their disorder to find them quiet and peaceful—in fact rather dull. There is rarely raving, seldom shouting, and violence has practically vanished. Within weeks, if not days, the patients lose the most florid signs of their sickness.

The impact of this on psychiatric wards has been undeniable. What about the longer term? Admitting that the neuroleptic drugs are more useful than previously used sedatives (such as barbiturates) do they have any long-term effect? This is more difficult to demonstrate, and it is difficult to know in any individual patient to what extent drugs are contributing to his continued good progress (rather than psychotherapy, good management, social measures, therapeutic atmosphere, passage of time, etc.). One way of testing this is to substitute inert dummy tablets for the real thing. In one study where this was done (Caffey *et al.*, 1964), during a period of several months after stopping active medication nearly 50 per cent of the patients relapsed. A comparable group who continued on active medication showed a negligible relapse rate. (We return to this finding towards the end of the chapter.)

In addition to medication some patients receive electroconvulsive therapy (E.C.T.). It has been shown scientifically that this will slightly improve the results that would otherwise be obtained by medication alone. In most centres it is not given as a routine, however, but is reserved for special cases in whom the drugs are not proving successful in the short term, or for patients who are particularly distressed by concomitant depressive symptoms.

This has been a fairly brief account of the treatment that patients with schizophrenia receive. Further details of major tranquillisers have already been given in Chapter 2, and more details about E.C.T. are given in Chapter 9. Later in the book a special chapter is devoted to psychological methods of treatment (Chapter 12). With these additional contributions many readers will now have learned as much as they need to know about the subject. They may skip the rest of the chapter with impunity. For those readers who are going to come into close and frequent contact with schizophrenics in the clinical situation we shall now look in more detail at some of the problems that doctors face when they are giving psychotropic drugs to schizophrenic patients.

Treatment with neuroleptic drugs

The basis for using neuroleptic drugs in schizophrenia is em-pirical—they were just found to work. Various theories have been brought forward to explain why they might work and on the whole they may be thought of as complementary to one another rather than as rivals. At the level of *behaviour* it is known that these drugs impair conditioned reflexes but leave unconditioned reflexes intact (as opposed to the sedatives which inhibit both types of reflex). If psychological illness is considered to be a form of faulty learning or conditioning, then the drugs may be seen as cutting out the faulty conditioned responses.

At the neurophysiological level schizophrenia may be seen as a disorder of *arousal*. This theme is attended to elsewhere in the Chapter (pp. 222–3). Drugs that *increase* arousal (like amphetamines) may produce a schizophreniform picture. Drugs that *decrease* arousal, such as phenothiazines, are beneficial in schizophrenia.

At the neuroanatomical level neuroleptic drugs may be seen as damping down the activity of those central areas of the brain concerned with emotions—such as the hypothalamus. At the neurochemical level they may be correcting the abnormal effects of compounds important in the activity of the nervous system (e.g. amines related to adrenaline such as dopamine).

Although this situation may change as discoveries take place, at present the day-to-day management of patients on neuroleptic drugs does not depend on the truth of one particular theory rather than another. What is taken for granted is that, for one reason or another, they do work.

To illustrate their use we shall refer to the *phenothiazines*, since this is the group about which most is known, but most of what is said could equally apply to the butyrophenones, the Rauwolfia alkaloids, or to other more recently introduced neuroleptic drugs.

Apart from the knowledge that it works, the next thing a physician likes to know about a drug that he is using is what the *disadvantages* are. Let us consider these now.

Side-effects of phenothiazines

1. *Extrapyramidal effects* The main side-effect that is attributable to abnormal action on the extrapyramidal system (*see* p. 83) is that of *parkinsonism*. The patient becomes rather rigid-looking with mask-like facies and reduced spontaneous movements. *Tremor* may be a distressing feature. Other curious extrapyramidal effects may be associated with the parkinsonism. Firstly *akathisia* may appear: this is a pathological restlessness or inability to sit still. Since many patients may be restless to start with, it is important to note carefully the precise time relationships of the onset of the restlessness. If the patient was restless *before* starting on the medication, then current restlessness and agitation may mean that the patient is not having *enough* of the tranquilliser. If the restlessness started after going on to the drug it may be a sign of excessive dosage. Sometimes if the situation is obscure (particularly if no-one can remember whether the patient *was* restless beforehand), then it becomes necessary to abandon the medication for the time being and later start all over again.

A second side-effect associated with parkinsonism is the *oculogyric crisis*. This may suddenly come upon the patient without warning, and in the attack the eyes become deviated strongly upwards, with a painful spasm of the muscles around the eyes. (Oculogyric crises do not usually occur in the common form of Parkinson's disease but do occur in the type of parkinsonism that sometimes follows encephalitis.)

Apart from these two disorders of movement a number of other abnormalities of muscular action occur in the extrapyramidal syndrome which are lumped together as the *dystonias* (abnormalities of tone) and the *dyskinesias* (abnormalities of movement). In the dystonias the patient may adopt curious postures, including grimaces. A troublesome form of dyskinesia affects the mouth and face, producing protrusion of the tongue and chewing movements (*orofacial dyskinesia* or *tardive dyskinesia*).

2. *Autonomic effects* The autonomic nervous system has not so far received in this book the attention that it deserves. As its name implies, it is an independent system—not directly under the influence of the will. The nerves in it control the secretions of many glands in the body (for instance the salivary glands) and the activity of involuntary muscles. These involuntary muscles (sometimes

known as 'smooth' muscles) in turn control such things as the movements of the intestine and stomach, the size of the pupils, the depth of the lens of the eye, and width of blood vessels—and therefore the blood flow to the affected organs.

The autonomic nervous system is divided into two parts—the sympathetic and the parasympathetic. Sympathetic nerves are called into play when the body prepares to meet an emergency ('fight or flight' reaction). Characteristically they act in short bursts. In contrast the parasympathetic nerves typically have a long-continued, gradual effect repairing the body and aiding nutrition and digestion.

The phenothiazine drugs tend to cut down the activity of both sympathetic and parasympathetic nervous systems, but because the parasympathetic is in action more consistently its *inactivity* is so much more conspicuous. For instance, in the human body there is normally enough saliva regularly secreted to keep the mouth moist, the intestine is usually on the move in some part of its length, and the eyes are altering their focus at frequent intervals. It may be very irritating if, as a result of taking a phenothiazine, the mouth is dry, the vision is blurred and the person affected becomes constipated.

Inhibition of the sympathetic nervous system can produce dramatic effects. When one rises from the sitting position to the standing position complex changes in blood flow take place. If the sympathetic is out of action these changes do not occur, the blood pressure falls, and the patient faints or feels dizzy. A bodily event that may be said to take place suddenly under circumstances of intense nervous stimulation is that of ejaculation of semen, and it is not surprising to find that this activity is also under the control of the sympathetic nervous system. Failure of ejaculation is occasionally complained of by men taking phenothiazines.

3. *Miscellaneous side-effects* Government regulations require pharmaceutical companies to warn doctors of potential side-effects of their products, and these are printed on pieces of paper that are included in the packages of drugs sent to pharmacies. They make fascinating reading. The drug firms often lean over backwards to avoid leaving out an alleged side-effect that someone has complained of at one time or another. Looking at these lists it is difficult to keep a sense of perspective and make out which of the side-

effects listed are of frequent occurrence and practical importance, and which are so rare that during his lifetime the average psychiatrist is not going to hear of a case, let alone see it happen to one of the patients.

A common side-effect is *drowsiness*. This is so common as to make one ask if it should properly be regarded as a side-effect or should perhaps be seen as an essential action of the drug. A better question might be—to what *extent* is drowsiness an inescapable result of treatment with phenothiazines? Earlier in the chapter (p. 223) we saw that phenothiazines tend to block the nerve impulses that have an alerting effect on the brain.

You can easily see that, in the absence of incoming alerting stimuli, it is quite easy to fall off to sleep at the drop of a hat. By this effect the tranquilliser does not *make* you sleep, it *allows* you to sleep. You can easily be woken up by a vigorous enough stimulus which breaks into consciousness. This contrasts with the effect of such drugs as barbiturates and similar sedatives. In small doses the barbiturates make one drowsy: in large doses they produce unrousable sleep, coma and even death. This effect of barbiturates in producing sleep is known as their *hypnotic* action. Although phenothiazines probably all *allow* one to go to sleep more easily, they vary in the extent to which they produce drowsiness. Trifluoperazine (Stelazine) seems to have little such action —patients taking this drug appear to complain less often about drowsiness than do patients on chlorpromazine (Largactil, Thorazine) and thioridazine (Melleril, Mellaril). So on low doses most patients on trifluoperazine do not complain of drowsiness at all, and many do not feel sleepy even on large doses. Even with large doses of chlorpromazine and thioridazine, if the patient does tend to drop off to sleep he can almost always be woken very easily, in contrast to someone taking large doses of sedative or hypnotic drugs.

As a side-effect of phenothiazines drowsiness is an irritation to the patient, then, rather than a danger.

Patients on phenothiazines tend to *put on weight*. Two factors here are fluid retention and fat deposits. In the early stages of phenothiazine treatment a patient may retain more fluid in his body than is usual, producing a marked increase in weight in a short time. A more prolonged increase in weight sometimes follows, resulting from increased appetite and food intake. It is not certain whether this is a secondary effect of increased well-being and relaxation—the patient eating more because he is less worried—or whether the drug has a direct action on the part of the brain that regulates appetite (in the hypothalamus).

There is no medical reason why the patient should not try to avoid this deposition of excess fat by dietary control, but sometimes there are psychological reasons why he should not do so. After all, a reducing diet is a form of deprivation, and this may be more than the patient can bear.

Some phenothiazine groups have their own special side-effects. Chlorpromazine has been associated with jaundice and also with photosensitivity—patients taking it tend to burn easily in the sun. Persons taking thioridazine have developed tiny deposits in the eye, which can interfere with vision: this usually only occurs when the patient is taking very large doses. This is not to say that chlorpromazine is the only drug, say, that produces photosensitivity, and so on. What it does mean is that chlorpromazine, and other phenothiazines closely related to it, are more likely to do so than less closely related drugs (like thioridazine and trifluoperazine). Very rarely patients taking phenothiazines develop anaemia and other disorders of the blood.

The importance of side-effects
There is no drug that does not do harm to some patients—even aspirin and penicillin have their problems. The administration of any form of medication, then, is a matter for considering the pros and cons.

By most standards phenothiazines are comparatively safe drugs. It is practically unknown for a patient to become addicted to a phenothiazine and there are rarely any withdrawal effects when the drug is stopped. It is difficult for someone to kill himself by taking an overdose. In the majority of patients any side-effects experienced are easily reversible on reducing the dose.

As drugs go, then, the phenothiazines are fairly harmless. It is important to keep this in mind when considering the damage that is done to the occasional patient.

1. *Eye deposits and blood disorders* Which of the side-effects are not so easy to reverse? The eye deposits and some of the blood

disorders are among those that affected subjects are not likely to recover from within a few days of stopping the drug. The blood disorders may in fact prove fatal: the problem in interpreting the degree of danger resulting from this is that these disorders are seen so rarely it is difficult to know whether they were caused by the drug concerned, some other drug the patient has received, or by something else that was nothing to do with their drug therapy.

2. *Lowered blood pressure* The results of the lowered blood pressure may be permanent. If an old lady with hardened arteries has a sudden drop in blood pressure she may fall and break a fragile bone. This may heal up, or it may result in permanent damage. The bone often affected is the femur, and it is notorious that after going to bed with a fractured femur many patients in old age never get up again, and die from complications.

3. *Extrapyramidal symptoms* As far as extrapyramidal symptoms are concerned the patient will normally lose these side-effects when taken off the drug. In some patients however this does not occur. For instance, an elderly patient with oro-facial dyskinesia may continue to show the grimacing, mouthing and chewing movements after the drug is stopped. This usually occurs only in the patient with organic brain disease. However, we have seen that patients with organic brain disease may in any case develop extrapyramidal symptoms as part of the clinical picture of that disease. So the question asked is—does the permanent extrapyramidal symptom represent a permanent side-effect or a coincidental symptom of the underlying disease? To the best of my knowledge the crucial experiments to distinguish between the two possibilities have not yet been carried out.

4. *Jaundice* Similar elements of doubt also concern the question of jaundice. In the early years after chlorpromazine was introduced it was widely accepted that jaundice (sometimes with fatal liver complications) was a recognised hazard in its use—though only seen with the occasional patient and then usually in a mild form. In deciding which phenothiazine to give a patient, this chance of liver complications would make many clinicians avoid chlorpromazine when otherwise it would have been the drug of choice. The special effects that chlorpromazine was supposed to produce in the liver were worked out in detail. Something has now happened to alter this situation. Psychiatrists are now less preoccupied with the

danger of producing jaundice when prescribing chlorpromazine. If you ask them why, they often say that they do not see jaudince so much nowadays—they can't think of a case that they have seen recently. How can this be explained? No-one knows for sure. It is certainly not because physicians have given up prescribing chlorpromazine—it is still one of the most widely used of the phenothiazines.

There is one other change that has taken place that might just explain it, which can be set out as follows:

1. There is a form of jaundice that is infectious, thought to be caused by a virus.

2. One way of transferring infection is by hypodermic syringe and needles—if the syringe is used for patient harbouring the virus and then for a second patient, the second patient may later get jaundice.

3. The period of incubation is long (months) so the injection, or the significance of it, may be difficult to recall when the jaundice appears.

4. Although the virus can be destroyed by sterilisation of the syringe, it takes much more sterilisation (*e.g.* heating) to destroy it than is needed to kill off the ordinary bacteria that one worries about.

5. In recent years this danger from the use of syringes has received more prominence, and sterilisation may have been taken to further lengths as a result.

6. The use of disposable syringes has become widespread.

The reader can draw his own conclusions. Many psychiatric patients have been given an injection of chlorpromazine in the acute stage of their illness. Injections of trifluoperazine do not seem to be so popular, and it has been difficult for the manufacturers to produce an injectable form of thioridazine. Now, once the patient has the injection of chlorpromazine this tends to be the phenothiazine that they continue to be given in the form of tablets. Some time later, when they develop jaundice, the medication is blamed rather than the now forgotten injection.

However, the liver changes in viral jaundice are not the typical liver changes found in chlorpromazine jaundice. The above suggestion can therefore be considered as no more than a plausible theory. It is brought to the reader's attention to make it clear that the significance of side-effects attributed to a drug is very difficult to assess—it may be years or even decades before their importance can be put into perspective.

Management of the medication

Deciding to put the patient on a particular phenothiazine is not the end of the problem as far as medication is concerned. The next question is—what dose? In a crisis situation a large dose, maybe by injection, may have to be given.

There is a wide-spread belief in non-medical circles that there is a 'correct' dose for medicine. The notion of a fixed dose of each drug that is correct for every adult is an idea that is false. Human beings vary widely in their response to different chemicals—alcohol is a familiar example—and if possible the dose should be gauged by the effect that it produces on that particular individual.

So when we start off with a small regular oral dose, we may get some patients who over-react even to that—patients who are un-usually sensitive to the drug. They may get the side-effects that one normally associates with very large doses. In that case then even their small dose should be cut down. Often they will obtain as much benefit from their tiny dose as another patient would from an enor-mous one.

Suppose, on the other hand, that if we started off on a larger oral dose level the patient had no response at all. Of course one explana-tion might be that the patient was not taking the drug! Many patients fail to take the medication that they are prescribed. Even apart from problems with memory or delusions about being poisoned, many people have a 'thing' about tablets—a rooted objection in principle to putting themselves in danger from taking the doctor's potion. Maybe as many as a third of patients who are supposed to be on tablets are in fact not taking them at all. This is particularly true of patients 'on tablets' in their own homes or com-ing up to out-patients' clinics, but it also happens with in-patients in hospitals. Even though they take the tablets under the eyes of the nurse who hands out the drugs, they can secrete the pill for the time being in a corner of the mouth and spit it out later. They may even accumulate a stock of tablets that they are thought to have swallowed—such stocks are sometimes used for suicidal overdoses.

Let us assume for the sake of argument that our particular patient is co-operatively swallowing all the tablets he is given, but that there is still no response. He shows no side-effects. The next step is obviously to increase the dose, and to go on increasing it gradually until something happens.

What we do next depends on whether the something that happens is (a) an improvement in his clinical state or (b) a side-effect. If it is improvement that we notice, then the dose can be maintained at that level. If it is a side-effect that is observed, there are two courses of action open to us. We could reduce the dosage to a level that fails to produce the side-effect. Alternatively we could carry on giving the phenothiazine in the same dosage, but *in addition* give the patient an antidote to the side-effect. This is commonly done when the patient experiences extrapyramidal side-effects, such as parkinsonism. There are many drugs available that are active against parkinsonism.

You can see the logic. If no benefit had been obtained even with a dose that produced side-effects then a way had to be found of continuing the drug to give the patient a further period of time in which to have a chance of responding. There is no doubt that many patients who do not respond at first will do so if the drug is given for longer.

Even so, psychiatrists are not all agreed that the policy of giving an antidote in these cirumstances is the best one. Why not reduce the dose and persevere at the lower level? There is a general principle in drug treatment that wherever possible you avoid giving the patient two drugs when one will do and another that the smallest effective dose is the best dose.

There is disagreement over another course of action as well. Parkinsonism is such a common side-effect of phenothiazine treatment that many psychiatrists give the patient anti-parkinsonian drugs simultaneously with the tranquilliser right from the start of treatment. If you reproach them, and remind them that they are guilty of *polypharmacy*—prescription of multiple drugs—they have a ready answer. It is very distressing, they say, for patients to experience the symptoms of parkinsonism at all. Far better that they should never have to suffer the leaden limbs, the involuntary shakes, and the distinctive zombie-like change in appearance.

Personally, if I were putting pen to paper for the prescription, I would prefer not to give the anti-parkinsonian drug at the start. I feel that the dose can usually be raised slowly enough for any symptoms of parkinsonism to be noticed at an early stage and dealt with promptly then. Generally they can be inhibited promptly by stopping the drug for 24 hours and starting again at a lower level. The body is slow to destroy and excrete phenothiazines, so the patient is not without treatment entirely for the 24 hours as might be supposed. Even at the end of that interval, nearly half of the drug may still be lingering in the tissues of the body, continuing its effect.

I would be the first to agree that mine is merely one point of view, and I have not proved that the other course of action is inferior.

If parkinsonism does make its appearance, and is distressing to the patient, adequate doses of the anti-parkinsonian drugs are given until the phenothiazine level is reduced to tolerable levels.

One more point on this matter of combined drugs. There are some psychiatrists who believe that the patient is always given the best chance of benefiting from treatment if you give him doses that produce parkinsonism, and they aim to increase the dose of phenothiazine rapidly to the appropriate levels—adding the antidote when necessary. I regard this motion as unproven. Again, they are both tenable points of view, until someone is able to settle the issue with appropriate scientific experiments (more difficult than you might think).

When should the drug be stopped?

Let us assume that the patient has made a good response to phenothiazine treatment. The patient has lost all the symptoms that we thought he would (there are some that no drug will help) and everything is going well. How do we decide when he no longer needs the drug?

At present there is no way of telling for sure, and all that is possible is a well-informed guess. What it comes down to is that you stop the drug and then see if the patient shows any signs of relapse. If not, you made the right choice. If he does, then you start him on the drug again for a further period.

This is obviously a rather unsatisfactory situation, the more so because in a disturbed state during the relapse the patient may opt out of treatment, or even if he once more accepts treatment the response may not be so good a second time. The consequence of this state of affairs is that many doctors take a conservative approach and encourage the patient to stay on the drug for as long as is possible. Times of up to 2 years are not uncommon.

Shorter times will be advised when the patient had only a short length of history before presenting for treatment, when the symptoms responded dramatically to the drug in the first place, and when the improvement has been consistently maintained since.

Having taken the decision to stop treatment, how long is it before one can be sure that the patient will not relapse as a result? In the case of phenothiazines the answer seems to be a long time—about 6 months. In one experiment (see Fig. 20) the patients

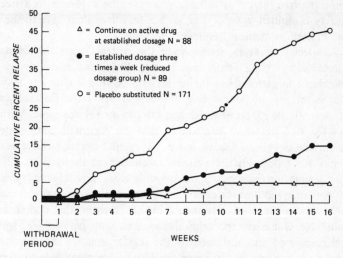

Fig. 20. Cumulative percentage of clinical relapses.

were split into three groups. Each were given similar looking capsules. One group had capsules containing their original medication in the same strength of dosage. The next group had capsules with half the original dose of medication. The third group were given dummy capsules.

The first group had an acceptably low rate (about 5 per cent) of relapse, and it was not much higher (15 per cent) in the group continuing on half strength medication. In the group with the dummy capsules about half of the patients relapsed, but it can be seen from the curves obtained that even after 4 months have gone by the relapse rate has not levelled off in the group without active medication (Caffey *et al.*, 1964).

With the co-operative patient this predicament can be explained to him and he can be encouraged to report back promptly if there is any suggestion that his symptoms might be returning. So often it happens, however, that the patient is unconvinced that medication is required, or even that it had anything to do with his recovery in the first place. Such patients may repeatedly relapse for want of taking their drugs, and require numerous admissions. It is difficult to compel a patient to continue on treatment at the stage when he is symptom-free, and it is a basic principle that a person in a free society is entitled to be ill if he wishes to, rather than have to subject himself to medical treatment.

A special situation arises when the patient is on the whole agreeable to having medication for his illness, but is merely unreliable or forgetful about taking his tablets. In this case one may use injections of long-acting phenothiazines (*e.g.* Depixol or Modecate), the effects of which last for 1 to 4 weeks or more. With this form of treatment one knows that the patient is getting the prescribed dose—no less, no more. The regular injections have as a bonus for follow up the systematic contact of the patient with the helping professions. Some psychiatrists have claimed that depressive symptoms (or even suicide) are more likely to supervene with this method of treatment, but at present the matter is debatable. One may expect that there will be some patients who will feel comforted and sustained by the regular contact and discrete treatment, and others for whom the idea of not being able to stop 'taking the tablets' at their whim will be an intolerable loss of independence. The latter group may become depressed if they are unable to voice their resentment and feel overwhelmed by the control that is imposed upon them. Nevertheless there is no doubt that, with the type of patient who is wholeheartedly willing, this form of treatment is often a notable advance. It could be a very important factor in cutting the relapse rate.

SUMMARY

Schizophrenia may be paranoid, catatonic, simple or hebephrenic in form and acute or chronic in course. Schizophreniform psychoses are contrasted with process schizophrenia. Interesting varieties are pseudoneurotic schizophrenia and schizoaffective psychosis.

The hereditary component in aetiology is not necessarily damning (compare that of tuberculosis). Family upbringing, biochemical balance and neurophysiological mechanisms have all been implicated in the causal events leading to schizophrenia, and the theories are not necessarily mutually exclusive. Amphetamine psychosis gives a close imitation of the illness. The high rates of schizophrenia in the centres of cities and the lowest social classes are probably explained by the effects of the disease rather than illustrating its causes.

10 The affective psychoses

In patients with reactive depression there may be a precipitating cause that is irrevocable, such as a serious loss or disappointment. In patients with endogenous depression the cause is obscure. In spite of these obstacles we shall see that depressive illness is one of the most readily treatable of all the mental disorders.

In this chapter we look at the different forms of treatment—psychotherapy, drugs, E.C.T., brain surgery and so on—and ask if they leave lasting damage, if they are painful, if they respect the dignity of the patient and if they are worse than his disease.

Hypomania is often thought of as the opposite of depression, yet we find there are many features in common. The hypomanic illness, too, responds fairly soon to treatment, but in the interim there can be problems in trying to manage the overactive, interfering, bossy patient.

First of all we look at depressive illnesses.

DEPRESSIVE PSYCHOSIS

We saw earlier, in Chapter 1, that an episode of affective psychosis is likely to take one of two forms. In depressive psychosis the spirits are low, energy reduced, and the thoughts dismal. In hypomania (or the more rare mania) the mood is elevated, energy abundant, and the thoughts extremely gratifying.

Of the two types of illness, depressive psychosis is much commoner than hypomania. In patients with recurrent illnesses, the
three patterns seen, in order of frequency, are recurrent
depressions, manic depressive psychosis (attack of depression at
one time and hypomania at another) and recurrent hypomania.

Finally, in some illnesses there is a mixture of features, some
depressive and some elated. These illnesses are referred to as *mixed
affective states*.

Clinical features

In depressive psychosis, as in depressive neurosis, the patient loses
his interest in things around him. In the neurotic illness this may
not be conspicuous—it may be that one is not aware of it until
asking the patient if he still cares about the things that he did in the
past. Only then does one find that he has lost interest in work, hob-
bies, sex, family and friends. In the psychotic illness the withdrawal
of emotional investment is often very evident. The patient may
neglect her appearance, with hair ungroomed, or with undyed ends
showing for several inches in a startling way. Make-up is carelessly
applied or abandoned. Washing becomes too much of an
effort—one patient was admitted to a general hospital ward in a
gross state of neglect. Her clothing had not been removed for weeks
and her stockings adhered firmly to her legs. In hospital she sat
dumbly in a chair with a vacant expression. (She was at first
thought to be demented by the general physicians.) Not only is
work abandoned, but pleasures too. *Retardation*—the slowing up
of movements—may become so extreme that the patient either sits
doing nothing or even just lies in bed ignoring his surroundings and
needs for food and hygiene, in a form of stupor.

As an alternative to the retarded picture, the patient may present
with extreme restlessness, pacing up and down with agitation, and
moaning and wringing his hands. Although the two conditions of
retardation and agitation appear superficially different, they both
have in common the end result that there is less *useful* or productive energy available.

Loss of appetite is common, and loss of weight often results,
amounting to 10, 20 or 30 pounds. The patient may complain of
severe constipation, going days between successive evacuations of

the bowel. *Insomnia* is the rule. This may take the form of the difficulty in getting off to sleep ('initial' insomnia) that occurs commonly in psychiatric illnesses but the form of sleep disturbance that is characteristic of the severe forms of depressive illness is *early morning wakening*. The patient wakes at 4 or 5 a.m., sometimes earlier, and is then unable to return to sleep at all that night.

The fact that the spirits are manifestly low is rarely denied by the patient. The depression may be subjectively different in quality to that experienced in the past, as well as quantitatively more severe. The mood may remain low uniformly over the 24 hours, but more characteristically fluctuates, being worst in the morning and least bad in the evening. The combination of this *diurnal variation in mood* with early morning wakening leads to the situation where the patient wakes in the early hours of the morning only to face the blackest period of the day. At this time suicidal attempts are often made.

Going along with the loss of interest in things is a profound loss of energy. The simplest task is an effort. One patient was able to cope with her dirty dishes only by having a rest between washing them and drying them. It is this loss of energy, no doubt, that accounts for the retardation that is seen. Short of actual immobility, the patient moves slowly, walking with leaden footsteps, slow to initiate movement and slow to accomplish it. The loss of energy is not just for physical activity but for mental activity as well. The patient will complain of absentmindedness, difficulty in concentration, impaired memory and difficulty in thinking clearly. A very common feature is *loss of confidence*, associated both with difficulty in making decisions and a loss of the normal satisfaction with the correctness of the decision once it has been made. In depression the description of an 'agonising reappraisal' is not a metaphorical one.

It must be difficult to take decisions in the general belief that the outlook is black whatever one does. The prevailing pessimism of depression takes many individual forms. The profound hopelessness may lead to suicidal attempts, or merely to the passive contemplation of suicide. In many patients the idea of killing oneself is anathema on religious or moral grounds and suicidal feelings will not actually reach consciousness, or will be denied. Such patients will often admit, however, that they feel, as they go to bed at night, that they would not mind if they never woke up again.

Otherwise the hopelessness may show itself in inability to cope with (and the lack of will to cope with) minor problems, or a feeling that the future is pointless, or bouts of crying may be experienced.

Psychiatrists tend to think of the loss of energy as resulting from the withdrawal of interest. Similarly, in contrast with what might seem obvious, they tend to think of the beliefs of the depressed patient as stemming from the low mood, rather than the other way about. One has to admit, though, that the beliefs held by depressed patients would be enough to make one feel depressed if one were not so initially. The beliefs are commonly in the realms of disease, guilt, unworthiness and poverty.

The preoccupation with *disease* may be merely a more enduring variant of the fears that strike all of us from time to time. Lung or abdominal cancer, heart disease and brain tumour are common preoccupations of the depressed patients as well as being common transient fears in healthy persons. In depressive psychosis they reach delusional proportions, and despite physical examination, X-rays and special tests the patient retains his convictions.

It is not always easy to tell whether the patient's preoccupation with bodily symptoms is delusional or not. Sometimes the belief is incompatible with evidence available to the patient, such as that held by the woman with regular bowel motions who maintained that her insides had all rotted away. When a patient says that his legs have been 'turned to lead' it seems more likely that he is talking metaphorically.

Rather odd-sounding beliefs may be expressed when depressive ideas are combined with ideas of *depersonalisation* and *derealisation*. Feelings of depersonalisation can occur in many different psychiatric illnesses (or even in a relatively pure state on their own). The patient with these ideas feels that his own body is no longer real, or is changed in some way, so that it has lost the sensation of belonging to him, or feels strange. His actions seem mechanical and his ability to savour his emotional feelings may be lost. In *derealisation* it is not his own body but the environment that seems unreal. As if he is in a dream, he can no longer be confident that things around him are what they seem, and these things may be referred to as vague or unnatural. In depression, feelings of depersonalisation coloured by the mood are expressed as 'my mind is dead'.

Case 28 Mr. J.H.

Mr. J.H. was an architect in his 50s. He had worked for various firms, but opened up his own practice 6 years previously. His business failed and over a period of 3 or 4 months he developed a severe depressive illness. Among the usual symptoms was that of insomnia: 'I just want to lie down in bed, and when I lie down I want to get up again'.

He was accompanied by his sister, who mentioned that one of the patient's frequent complaints at home was that his 'brain had gone'. This appeared to refer to the great subjective difficulty in memory and concentration that he experienced.

Objectively there was no abnormality. He registered a complicated name and address correctly at the second attempt, and recalled it perfectly after 12 minutes. A consultant neurologist could find no sign of organic brain disease.

On antidepressant drugs and supportive psychotherapy he improved slowly but steadily. He was symptom-free 5 months later. After 9 months he remained well (after discontinuing his treatment) and had managed to obtain a well-paid job, again being employed as an architect for a large firm.

The loss of energy and difficulty in movement may be brought out in concrete terms. The patient complains of his legs being 'weak', 'turned to water' or aching. Pains are common.

Case 29

A man aged 50 complained bitterly of backache. It was very severe and difficult to endure. Although he was behaviourally depressed, he denied any problems or worries. Physical examination and investigation failed to reveal any local reason for his back pain.

He was treated with E.C.T., and not long after he improved behaviourally his backache also disappeared. He still denied any problems that might have precipitated the illness, but it was noted that he led a remarkably restricted life. Not only was he able to mention no problems, but it also appeared he had no interests and no friends. The relationship between the patient and his wife seemed a rather abnormal one, and it is possible that an exacerbation of difficulties here had led to his illness. In the face of such staunch denial of almost all emotional aspects of his mental life it was difficult to explore this or any other possibility, and one had to be content with having provided him with symptomatic relief at least.

Passing on from feelings of pain and incurable disease, the next constellation of ideas we consider is that of feelings of *guilt*. Here the patient has no difficulty in knowing why he feels the way that he does—it is a punishment for his wrong-doings. Persons who may or may not be particularly religious in the ordinary way become convinced that they have committed an unpardonable sin and are henceforth condemned. Something that they have said or done (which may seem to the listener to be quite insignificant) will, they think, have serious repercussions.

Case 30

A middle-aged woman was admitted in a distressed and agitated state. She had a number of problems, and she knew that they all stemmed from a wicked act that she had committed. It did not seem strange to her that her current difficulties arose from this isolated act of 20 years previously. The action itself was one of theft. She had stolen a plant from the neighbours' garden. The neighbours had long since gone away and the garden was derelict. Nevertheless to our conscientious patient this was the heinous crime for which she was now suffering.

This same patient demonstrated another feature that is sometimes found in the thought content of depressive patients—paranoid ideas. In her case, as is the rule in depressive illness, the paranoid ideas were in turn based on ideas of guilt. It was *because* of the crime that she had committed that she was now being hounded. She was convinced that she was being followed by plain-clothes detectives who were trying to 'build up the case' on her.

Preoccupation with guilt and wickedness is not a preserve of the pure in heart.

Case 31 Mrs. T.N.

Mrs. T.N. was in her late 50s at the time of the admission to hospital that we shall quote here. She suffered from manic depressive illness, and she had had repeated admissions in the past. She drank excessively when she was depressed, and again when she was elated. She showed life-long promiscuity, which was not obviously related to her affective swings.

Preceding the present admission she had become miserable, with poor appetite and loss of energy. She felt guilty about her past behaviour. She felt unloving and worthless, wicked and undeserving of help.

She felt that she was a false and superficial person and often wondered if she were responsible for her son's (very real) misfortunes. She felt guilty about her sexual behaviour and said that she had been banned from pubs in the area because they said she was a prostitute. She admitted sleeping with twenty to thirty men in the previous few years. She was agitated, pacing the floor and twisting her hands, and wondered whether to take her life.

Ideas of *unworthiness* are widespread in depression. They are often conveyed in the humble or self-effacing manner of the patient, which may reach masochistic proportions—much of depressive behaviour carries a risk of damage to the self or at least injury to self-interest. When ideas of unworthiness are put into words, it may be in the form of 'Don't bother to try to help me, I'm not worth wasting your energies on'. Such statements might in other circumstances appear sarcastic, or a manipulative nudge for further help, but in depressive psychosis they are spoken with sincerity. Similar thoughts are expressed when the patient reveals that he 'feels a burden' to those around him.

In the presence of a low mood state *worry about money* is common. It varies from merely an excessive degree of concern or preoccupation with what is in fact a real but minor problem, to a full blown delusional belief.

Case 32
A woman in her 60s was admitted to the amenity bed section of a mental hospital suffering from depressive psychosis. She was retarded and lacking in spontaneity. Conversation with her revealed that she was concerned about her financial position and believed that she was insolvent. Superficial enquiry suggested that this was not only untrue, but on the contrary she was a woman of considerable wealth, who had currently tens of thousands of pounds in her bank account.

It is a general principle of the management of psychiatric patients that one avoids getting into an argument with them. As a rule, this means that one does not dispute their delusions. The relatives of such patients often either are not aware of this principle or wish to ignore it. In the case of this patient her next of kin was her nephew, and in an attempt to reassure his aunt on her financial position he brought up to the hospital the statement of account from the bank to show her. Predictably this did not sway her belief. Logical argument is the last thing that is likely to dispel a delusion.

Perception
In depression the world looks black. Nothing gives delight. Sometimes the patient presents after a holiday. Noticing his lowered spirits everyone had said 'Never mind, you'll feel better for the holiday'. In fact things got worse. It is painful to see others enjoying themselves, and to realise that one is getting no pleasure

oneself. It is then that the patient realises there is something serious afoot.

The future looks black and the patient is pessimistic. In addition the past looks black and herein lies a danger for the unwary observer. If you speak to a patient who is in a depressive psychosis and ask him how long he has felt like that, or how long such and such an unpleasant feature has been present, the answer may be 'always', or at least it may exaggerate grossly the length of time involved. This can be misleading in assessing the timing of the illness in relation to external events, and therefore distort the observer's judgment on possible aetiological factors.

False perceptions are not characteristic of depressive illness as of schizophrenia, but auditory hallucinations sometimes occur. The voices speak to the patient in the second person accusing him of wicked acts or of shameful thoughts. The projection of the patient's own sense of guilt and unworthiness is usually clear.

Intellectual function

We have seen that the patient with a depressive illness may complain of difficulty in thinking, impaired concentration, faulty memory and absentmindedness. On testing his powers of memory one often finds little or no objective evidence of impairment despite his genuine subjective difficulty. The best physical analogy is probably with the contrast between weariness and paralysis.

One test of memory, mentioned on p. 46, is that of remembering a new name and address over a period of, say, 10 minutes. To do this the subject has to pay attention in the first instance, concentrate, memorise (register) the name and address, retain it over the 10 minutes (during which time it is usual to distract him) and at last either recall the address without aid or at least recognise the elements from a choice presented to him (*e.g.* was it Mr. Green, Mr. Black, Mr. White or Mr. Brown?).

With organic brain disease various parts of this process may be affected. In depressive psychosis the retention over the 10 minutes typically remains intact. If one can induce the patient to attend, concentrate, memorise and later make the effort to try to recall or recognise, then his retention will be found to be unimpaired. In fact patients often do amazingly well on what appear to be fearsomely complicated addresses. In practice they do not seem subsequently to be reassured by the demonstration that their suspect memory is after all intact. They are still left with the problem of sustaining the *effort* needed to ensure the function of their intellectual powers.

There are cases when it is difficult to tell whether the poor test performance is the effect of depressed mood and drive or whether it is the result of early organic brain disease. Here the position is usually clarified by treatment. If the patient is retested after his mood state has improved, then if the impairment was due to the depression the test results will now be satisfactory. One of the most dramatic demonstrations of this is when the patient is treated with electroconvulsive therapy. This usually produces a convincing improvement in depressive psychosis, but at the expense of some (temporary) disruption of brain function. Despite the fact that patients may complain afterwards of memory difficulty, in depressive psychosis the memory tests typically show an improvement in function after E.C.T. In organic brain disease without depression the E.C.T. can hardly be expected to improve matters.

Alcoholism and depression

The relationship of alcohol intake to affective illnesses is a complex one. People may spend more money on drink when they are high, or they may drink more to console themselves when they are depressed: clearly for some people any change is a good enough excuse for a drink.

Some patients (including Mrs. T.N. to whom we referred earlier) actually stop drinking when they are severely depressed. This is similar to the loss of interest in other appetites like food and sex that also occurs in depressive psychosis.

Case 33 Mr. J.J.

Mr. J.J. was admitted to a general medical ward in a hospital with a convulsion. It was discovered that this was a withdrawal fit in a person addicted to alcohol. When seen by the psychiatrist he was initially not very co-operative, but later agreed to answer questions about the way he felt. In addition to life-long anxiety symptoms he now had a number of depressive features. In reponse to direct questions he admitted believing that he was a condemned person, that his sins were unpardonable; he wished he could stop worrying about having hurt other people's feelings with things he had said. He believed he had not lived the right kind of life, that he could not overcome his difficulties, and that he was lacking in self-confidence. At times he felt useless, that he was no good at all, and much of the time he felt that he had done something wrong or evil. He had trouble sleeping, he had lost weight, he currently had crying spells, he was constipated and he got tired for no reason. The future seemed pointless.

He did not make much of these symptoms. They had not been recognised by the staff on his general medical ward. They were discovered incidentally as the result of thorough psychiatric questioning.

Suicidal behaviour

Feelings of hopelessness are common in depressive illness and it is no surprise that such patients from time to time make suicidal attempts. It is my belief that, as far as depression is concerned, death from suicide is to a large extent preventable if only one can be sensitive to the message and the needs of the patient. It is to some extent preventable in other patients, but this is difficult in for instance schizophrenia, when the attempt is so unpredictable, or in some forms of personality disorder, when the attempts are repeated again and again, or in subjects with no psychiatric disorder, before their plight comes to the attention of the helping professions or agencies.

Whether a patient attempts suicide at a particular point in time depends on the phase of the illness, his relationships with other people, and his own personality make-up. The phase of the illness that is most dangerous is not necessarily that period when he appears to be most depressed. To understand this one must recall the tripartite division of mental process into thoughts, affect and drive (or behaviour). At what, objectively, one would normally consider the worst point of the illness all three aspects are likely to appear equally bad. The patient is typically pessimistic in thought, low in his spirits, and retarded in his behaviour. Now, suppose as a result of treatment (or even spontaneously) the drive starts to improve before the other two features, what happens? At his worst, our despondent patient was feeling desperately low and hopeless about the future, but was paralysed into inactivity. Now his energy is coming back he is able to express the way he feels in action. It is at this point that suicidal behaviour notoriously occurs.

Although he may feel desperate, it is a rare patient that is not influenced by real factors in his environment, which brings us to a consideration of his relationships with other people and their effect on his behaviour. The patient may read into their attitudes the message that his worst fears are correct, and as a result be the more firmly committed to a path of self-destruction. Alternatively, he may derive from them the feeling that *perhaps* things are not as bad as they seem, and, though scarcely convinced, he is prepared to bide his time before making the final decision.

The tyro soon finds in dealing with such a patient that bland reassurances that all will be well are at best met with tolerant incredulity. Worse, the patient may feel that such statements merely reflect a lack of understanding on the part of the therapist or even a lack of concern. One can imagine the patient thinking 'You are telling me it will be all right just as an attempt to shut me up. You can't be bothered with me really'. (There may even be a grain of truth in this. Reassurance generally needs to be a more subtle affair with such critical patients.)

The patient may become more certain that his suicide is inevitable by the reaction of those around him. There was once a widespread practice in mental hospitals of searching patients when they were admitted for knives, scissors, razors or any other potential suicidal tools, and removing them from the patient's possession. In the realisation that this actually suggested to the patient that suicide was what was expected of him this custodial behaviour has now largely been given up. For many hospitals it was not easy to abandon. Understandably the authorities felt vulnerable to the gibe: 'You allowed this patient to kill himself with his own razor—it was reprehensible of you not to have removed it'. It was difficult to establish statistically that the improvement in atmosphere that accompanied a more relaxed approach in fact paid dividends.

What about talking to the patient on the subject of his suicidal feelings? Might that not also encourage him to think that he is expected to kill himself? It is possible that this is sometimes the case—depending on how it is done. There are still doctors who treat the subject as taboo for this reason. The circumstances in which talking about his suicidal ideas could increase the risk of suicide might be as follows. Supposing the therapist asks the patient if he is suicidal and is answered affirmatively. The therapist goes on to find that the patient is actively considering taking his own life, and has worked out how he will do it. If now the therapist changes the subject, treats the patient in a cavalier way, and makes no firm commitment to try to help the patient, disaster may follow.

The patient may think: 'I've told him I feel like killing myself. He either doesn't believe me or doesn't care. I'll show him'.

Many psychiatrists believe, on the other hand, that discussion of the patient's suicidal feelings can be used therapeutically, and I share this conviction. Suicide may be considered as a form of 'acting-out-behaviour', in which the patient expresses his feelings. If he can be given the opportunity to express himself in a less drastic way, the irrevocable act may be avoided.

The details of management using this principle will be discussed in the section on treatment (*see* pp. 266–282). Briefly, *if the patient admits to suicidal feelings*, the therapist encourages him to put into words how desperate and hopeless he feels. After allowing the patient to ventilate his feelings, the therapist makes a point of emphasising his appreciation of the serious state of the patient's emotion, so that the patient can see that he has got the point across. The therapist then makes a firm commitment of further help. In this way the patient is less likely to feel the need to *act* out his problems, having had the opportunity to *talk* them out.

In England and Wales about 5,000 persons kill themselves every year. Death by suicide is no longer statutorily notifiable to the police, and in any case coroners are likely to vary in the degree of ease with which they give verdicts of suicide, so it is difficult to be sure of the exact number of deaths that were brought about by the mood state of the person involved. There is a roughly equal number of road traffic deaths. How many of these were acts of 'carelessness' occurring in persons who did not care much whether they lived or died?

Can one predict suicide attempts? If one could say that certain persons were in a state in which they were very likely to kill themselves, one could direct one's energies accordingly. Admitting that there always will have to be reservations about the statistics of suicide, certain findings remain fairly consistent. Suicide has been found to be more common in males, with increasing age, in those who have had a broken home in childhood, who suffer from physical disease, and who are employed in the occupations of student, lawyer, physician or dentist. It is more frequent in big towns, especially in those districts with high population density, with over-crowding, in areas of boarding-houses or cheap hotels, and amongst the immigrants and foreign-born. Suicide is more likely in those who are not currently married; that is to say, amongst the single, the divorced, the separated and the widowed. The incidence is great in those that are childless. Suicide is common in persons with a high standard of living, particularly in times of economic crisis (as typified by those hurling themselves from Wall Street offices during the depression). It is also common among those with mental disorder (such as depressive illness and schizophrenia), among drug addicts and alcoholics, and among criminals. It is often found in those who are socially or geographically mobile.

Suicide is more likely to occur after bereavement or retirement. It can occur after the loss of one's job, or after any break of routine that involves the loss of the normal role in life.

Suicide is *less* frequent among the devoutly religious, among those with a large number of children, and in times of war.

Despite all this information, biographical data alone are a poor guide to whether a particular patient is likely to kill himself. For instance, suicide is one of the commonest causes of death in middle-aged men, but this fact is of little value in clinical practice as a guide to whether an individual middle-aged man is suicidal at any particular point in time. It has been claimed that a number of features in the *current* life situation should raise the suspicion of the professional helper that the patient or client harbours suicidal thoughts. These include preoccupation with disease—particularly the possibility of having cancer, being liable to a heart attack, or some form of disease usually accepted as potentially lethal; worries about sleeplessness, fears of losing control, lack of sympathy in the relatives, dreams of catastrophe, failure of treatment, panic reactions, and such symbolic actions as giving away possessions ('I shall not be needing these any more'). Among these, sometimes oblique, hints, one may see recurring themes which on reflection can be reasonably expected to be related to suicide: the preoccupation with death and (symbolic) sleep, feeling abandoned by relatives or helpers, inability to control one's reactions to fear, a sense of impending doom, and the central features of the suicidal state—*hopelessness* and *desperation*. One can be hopeless without feeling desperate, and *vice versa*, but the suicidal person is likely to be both.

So far we have considered the statistical or biographical data, and we have tried to sense the feeling state. The reader may feel that the first is too impersonal as an indicator of suicidal potential, and the last too intangible. There are two items to be considered now that are quite concrete and down to earth, and they are by far the two most important pieces of information in enabling one to decide how dangerous the patient is to himself. They may appear to be so simple and elementary that they are self-evident, yet sometimes they are left out of consideration by the unwary.

The first is a history of a previous suicidal attempt. Most of the biographical factors that are associated with increased suicidal rate enhance the likelihood by a fraction, or possibly mean that the person concerned is twice or even three times as likely to kill himself as the average member of society. A history of attempted suicide, on the other hand, increases the risk concerned *tenfold*, or even more, according to those studies that have looked into this aspect. Attempted suicide itself is reaching epidemic proportions. Compared with the annual rate of suicide of 5,000 for England and Wales, the rate of attempted suicide was 16,000 in 1957, but by 1964 had jumped to 50,000 and is still rising. Attempted suicide, mainly in the form of drug overdose, accounts for about 7 per cent of all admissions to general medical and surgical beds. Despite this enormous increase the rates for suicide (*i.e.* deaths) are not increasing. This is probably due to a number of factors, amongst which are improved medical treatment of the comatose patient, the prescription of safer drugs as sleeping tablets by general practitioners, the activities of the Samaritans, improvements in psychiatric care (including the follow-up of patients who have already taken an overdose), and possibly the detoxification of household gas.

Apart from a *history* of attempted suicide, the most important factor in assessing whether a patient is suicidal is whether they are *thinking and talking* about attempting it. Although this may seem perfectly obvious, it has been denied in the past. There is a myth that 'those people who talk about killing themselves never do it'. This is certainly not true, and it cannot be refuted too strenuously. The truth is quite the opposite. We saw that the risk of suicide in someone who has already made an attempt is of the order of ten times that of the man in the street. For someone who is currently talking about feeling suicidal, the risk is certainly as high as ten times average, and may be as much as a hundred times that of the next man.

If this is the case, how has it ever been possible for doctors (and others) to claim that it is the person who talks about it that never does it? It is clear that such an assertion flies in the face of the evidence. Thus, to make such an unrealistic claim, two factors probably operate. One is that those responsible are able to ignore the evidence. This is not too difficult since, fortunately, in any one doctor's (or social worker's, or nurse's or clergyman's) experience suicides are rare, and even when it occurs, *sometimes* it is in a person who has not publicly proclaimed his feelings. The second factor is one of attitude. To allege that those who say it do not do it suggests that the allegation is made by someone who wishes to minimise the dangerous state of the patient, who even wishes to imply that the person talking about suicide is hysterical, making a fuss, trying to draw attention to himself, exaggerating, play-acting, and trying to get his own way by devious means. In our society people who behave in this unrestrained manipulative way are not popular, and arouse the hostility of their would-be helpers. In the medical world persons who have such behaviour patterns as their character traits are labelled as 'hysterical personalities' and despised. The doctor's own reaction to the patient may colour his judgment, make a misdiagnosis more likely, and render it difficult to feel sympathetic.

It has to be admitted that many episodes of drug overdose appear to contain an element of manipulation of relatives or friends of the patient, of 'getting his own way' by raising the anxieties of those around him. It is, after all, a form of primitive, non-verbal, acting-out behaviour.

Nevertheless, it is a serious mistake to think of it as *just* manipulation or *just* attention-seeking. There are many other ways of seeking attention or of manipulating that do not carry the risk to one's own person that overdosage does. In all but the most trivial instances there must be entertained the thought that in addition to the antagonising hysterical elements in the behaviour there are also the self-destructive patterns. If badly (or unsympathetically) handled, the person who has made a suicidal 'gesture', or who is making apparently empty and exaggerated threats of suicide, may go on to take the lethal overdose that (in his eyes) proves those who have pooh-poohed his seriousness to have been fools.

We must accept, then, that *talk* of suicide must always be taken very seriously. The opposite is not the case. The fact that a person *denies* suicidal feelings cannot always be taken at face value. A patient may have most of the features of a severe depressive illness, and on other grounds may be judged to feel hopeless and desperate, and may yet deny suicidal feelings right up to the final act of self-destruction. One particular case of this, long known to be highly dangerous, is the condition known as 'smiling depression'. The patient, who may have admitted to insomnia, loss of appetite, loss of weight, loss of energy, lack of interest and inability to cope, brightly denies feeling depressed. It is obvious to an observer that the patient suffers on any realistic criteria from a disabling emotional illness in which depressed mood is to be confidently expected, but the sufferer staunchly denies any lowering of spirits. Clearly for some reason it is not acceptable to this particular patient to be 'depressed'. It may mean to him such weakness of character that it is beyond his belief, so that this mood state never reaches consciousness, is rationalised away, or is too shameful to be frankly admitted. In one case where the patient mysteriously evaded admitting his feelings it was later found that a close relative had committed suicide some years previously. The patient manifestly wished to avoid identification with such a fate. Other patients find suicidal thoughts unacceptable because of their religious background.

One must beware the 'smiling depression' because it is so unpredictable—one may not know when such patients are getting worse, and in particular when they are getting so desperate in their brittle state that they will suddenly break.

We have noted earlier in the chapter that if the patient becomes more *active*, without a corresponding improvement in mood, then this is a potentially dangerous period. Sometimes an improvement in mood itself indicates danger. This relatively rare event occurs when the patient, who has endured unbearable tension, has taken the deliberate decision to take his life. Waiting his opportunity to make absolutely sure of his bid, he becomes calm and relieved, knowing that his term of distress is soon to be over. His advisers and helpers may be misled into thinking that a true improvement has occurred. The resulting self-destructive act is likely to be particularly irrevocable—if an overdose then the dose of tablets will be high, and the chances of discovery small.

Fortunately not all claims to be free of depression are false, and in fact the vast majority may be taken at face value. If the claim is specious, there are usually clues for those who have eyes to see. One particular instance of loss of depressed mood is very striking. Some persons, having taken an overdose (or committed some other self-destructive act), when their lives are saved lose their depression. The suicidal attempt itself is said to have a cathartic effect. It may be that they have, in a way, had their say, and no longer have the bottled-up emotions pressing for expression. It may be that they have thrown their fate into the lap of the gods, and having survived, feel that the gods may be smiling on them after all (as if they are 'meant to live'). Thus, irrespective of the environmental situation, the patient often feels better after the attempt. Of course, improvement in mood is to be expected when the situation of the patient has changed as a result of the overdose: if a teenage girl in a frustrated angry mood takes an overdose because her parents will not allow her to do something, and if subsequent to the overdose they relent, then there is no mystery about the relief of the depression.

From this account of suicidal behaviour it will have been seen that depressive psychosis is by no means the only condition to lead to attempts at acute self-destruction. Not all suicides (let alone attempted suicides) have shown evidence of mental illness of any sort. Of those that have shown evidence of depressive illness, the illness would often on other criteria have been judged to be of neurotic (rather than psychotic) degree.

If we look at the situation from another point of view though, the risk of suicide in patients with affective psychosis is substantial, and it has been estimated in the past that of manic-depressive patients 15 per cent will eventually kill themselves. Suicidal attempts in these patients are often made with near foolproof methods, leaving little chance either of recovery or of discovery in the interim. What is especially tragic is the situation where the suicide note makes it clear that the patient is killing himself because he is suffering from incurable disease, and autopsy later shows that his belief that he had such a disease was mistaken—and merely another facet of his depressive illness.

Affective illness and society
Affective illnesses are typically acute. Chronic hypomania is

extremely rare, and patients diagnosed as such by some psychiatrists would almost always be diagnosed as schizophrenics by other authorities. Chronic depression was less rare in the past, but it is a very unlucky patient nowadays who does not recover, if not within weeks then at most within a few months of the onset of his depressive psychosis. Affective illnesses are well recognised as coming and going without leaving a permanent impairment of the personality. Even where a patient suffers from recurrent attacks, he will most typically revert to his normal personality between episodes. The concept of relentless deterioration, considered with the diagnosis of schizophrenia, is not associated with manic-depressive psychosis.

Furthermore, many patients have a single episode of depressive psychosis with no recurrence. Others will have only one or two further episodes in the course of their lifetimes. This means that the effect of the illness on the patient's home life, his employment, and his relationship with friends and relatives is often merely a fleeting one.

Such an episode of illness (which will possibly be referred to as a 'nervous breakdown') may prove to be, if not completely forgotten, certainly seldom brought to mind, and the disruption of the patient's life will be minimal. It can be allowed to remain in the background unless the coals are raked over by an application to emigrate or by investigation as a candidate for high office.

In the past such illnesses were not always dignified with the title of 'depressive psychosis'. If the delusions were florid, or the patient's behaviour provoked anxiety in those around him, he might suffer the stigma of mental hospital admission. Otherwise he may have been allowed to stay in bed for weeks or months at home, with or without medical attention, until spontaneous recovery took place. Sometimes a conveniently significant physical 'diagnosis' was invoked to explain the loss of energy (what about post-influenzal debility?) or sometimes the patient was given a course of relatively non-toxic glandular treatment (*e.g.* thyroid extract) on the premise that he was suffering from a deficiency of this hormone. The degree to which the primary care physician was aware of the real state of affairs will no doubt have varied from case to case.

It is when we come to the *recurrent* affective psychoses that we see that disruption of the patient's adaptation becomes difficult to avoid. Depressive psychoses, with their highly-charged content of guilt and self-criticism, frequently occur in individuals who are at the best of times liable to high degrees of conscientiousness. If this habitual behaviour is not carried to extremes it may make them valuable members of the community, as they discharge their duties thoroughly and meticulously. If a person is regarded with favour at his place of employment, and is hard-working, punctual and painstaking, then his employers may be loath to replace him. Such a person may have episodes of illness lasting a month or two every year, and still be welcomed back to his old job when he has recovered.

If at home he is an attentive and diligent husband, his temporary absence from the home is met with concern and his relatives and friends will wish him a speedy return to the domestic hearth.

Such a picture is not universal. A business firm may welcome an episode of illness, particularly 'mental' illness, as an excuse to rid themselves of an out-of-favour employee. If the person concerned has been of rather inadequate personality, slow at his job, of unsatisfactory intelligence or aptitude, or merely unpopular, then after one episode of illness he may recover his mental health only to find that he has lost his job.

If there is marital friction then the patient may, as a result of his illness, incur further contempt or hostility from his spouse. If his relationship with relatives and friends is at all prickly then they may subsequently avoid him or break off contact with him.

The patient with organic brain disease may be faced with early retirement, and the patient with chronic schizophrenia may have to take on a menial task far inferior to his normal position. The patient with recurrent affective illness, by contrast, remains able to work at his previous level between illnesses if he is allowed to do so. If he is sacked whenever he has an episode of illness he will clearly have *changes* of job, but it may be possible for him to remain at the same level.

Several factors can interfere with such a relatively satisfactory employment situation. If his profession is one that depends on promotion along the career ladder at frequent intervals, then this may prove difficult. If he requires references from previous employers then his prospects are vulnerable. In a small community his repeated illness may engender an unsympathetic response.

His social life will be at risk in the same way. It will remain satisfactory if he avoids the pitfalls mentioned above, and avoids the possible complications of the illnesses. For instance, if excessive drinking is part of the picture of either his depressive spells or his hypomanic swings, then his reputation may suffer. Similar (and also unfair) gossip may mar his social life as a result of excessive spending or promiscuity during hypomanic illnesses. His friends may have been worried by suicidal talk during the depressive phase.

Sometimes these 'stigmata' are even more concrete. One patient, in her melancholic state, grasped the heating element of an electric fire apparently in order to electrocute herself. She failed to do so, but for ever afterwards had gross deformities of the hands as a result of the loss of some fingers and scarring of others. The disfigurement was a permanent reminder of the illness to her and her friends.

Until recently in the United Kingdom mental illness was not a sufficient ground in itself for divorce. It had to carry with it the further stipulation that the patient had spent 5 years continuously in an institution and was not expected to recover. Affective psychosis did not often behave in this way and was therefore difficult to use as a basis for divorce action. Now, with the criteria being merely one of irretrievable breakdown of marriage, it is possible that we may see more use of it in evidence. In matrimonial cases, one feature that the Court may be interested in is the ability of the parent to take custody of the children. It is difficult to make universally applicable statements about the effect of manic-depressive illnesses on others. One knows of reports that a patient kills first his family and then himself (or attempts to) because he feels the world is such a wicked place. These events are rare, though. It will probably be necessary to point out to the Court, when it is coming to its decision, the episodic nature of affective psychosis, and the distinction that should be drawn between the personality traits of the subject in ordinary life and the behaviour that is shown during the active phase of the illness. In the average case one usually rests on the maxim that the best guide to future behaviour is that person's past behaviour.

Treatment of depressive illness
We have seen that it is possible to think of depression, in the sense of a mood state, as the emotion that is concerned either with something unpleasant that has happened to the person or that will inevitably happen. This is in contrast with anxiety—the mood state to do with a threat of a *possible* disaster in the future. The psychological approach to the problems in treatment is therefore different. In anxiety states the patient may, with successful judgment or advice, avoid the dreaded catastrophe. If depression follows a disappointment or a serious loss then the environmental deprivation may be irretrievable (*e.g.* death of a parent).

We have to distinguish between the unpleasant events that have triggered off the depression and the unpleasant matters that are on the mind of the patient. One does meet cases of depressive illness where there seems to be no psychological event that preceded the illness, and these are cases labelled as 'endogenous depression'. In many cases of depressive illness there are to be found life events that preceded the illness, though by definition to be considered as pathological the depressive state has to be inappropriate (in duration or degree) to the stimulus.

In anxiety states the patient may see in his mind's eye as enormous and devastating problems that would in fact be trivial and easily dealt with even if they did occur. Similarly, in depressive illness the patient may dwell on psychological blows as if they were major tragedies rather than normal misfortunes.

On the other hand the distressing thoughts of the patient may have nothing to do with real life events—and this is the distinction which was mentioned above. This can be seen most clearly where the patient has clear-cut *delusions* that preoccupy him. Here, then, is the scope for treatment, even when the illness is not an 'endogenous' one. Firstly, one can aim at removing the concern with purely *illusory* misfortunes (or frankly delusional beliefs). Secondly, one can try to cut down the *real* losses to size in the mind of the patient, so that he does not suffer excessively from them.

We have now provided ourselves with two aims of treatment. The course still appears formidable. We are faced with an illness which (in the reactive type) may have a cause that is irrevocable, or (in the endogenous type) a cause that is obscure. We know that it is fruitless to argue with a patient about his delusions in the hope of inducing enlightenment by means of logic. In spite of these obstacles, we shall see that depressive illness is one of the most readily treatable of all the mental disorders.

Methods of treatment

The two main types of treatment are psychological and physical. Psychological methods involve talking to the patient and (possibly more important) listening to him. Physical methods involve such measures as drugs acting on the brain or direct electrical stimulation of the brain. There is no doubt that in the layman's mind higher prestige accrues to the psychological methods. Indeed, such terms as 'drugs' and 'electric shock treatment' have a decidedly negative connotation. They conjure up a picture of a white-coated establishment figure brutally or unthinkingly reducing the patient at best to a position of silence or at worst to a senseless cabbage-like state.

Furthermore, it does seem illogical to treat a condition that may have been precipitated by psychological trauma with physical therapy. It would look, at first sight, as if psychological treatment were not only the more elegant approach but also the more direct. One would think that the physical treatment would be palliative and the psychological treatment, if not curative, at least radically approaching the sources of the problem.

On the other hand one knows that physical methods are widely used by doctors for depressive illnesses. What is the rationale for their use by those physicians who are not brutal and unthinking? The answer, briefly, is that such methods work. Particularly with those depressive illnesses that are of psychotic degree, many patients respond quickly and gratifyingly to physical methods who have responded poorly to psychological methods. This simple statement sidesteps many questions. Let us leave further discussion of the *relative* merits of the two main types of treatment until after we have seen what is involved in each. Then we shall be in a position to discuss such questions as whether the treatment is better than the disease, whether it is painful, whether it leaves lasting damage, and whether it respects the dignity of the patient.

Psychological methods

Techniques that involve using the interaction of the therapist and the patient as persons, including making special use of verbal contact, are known as *psychotherapy*. The different forms of psychotherapy themselves may be broadly divided into supportive methods and insight-oriented methods.

1. *Supportive psychotherapy* Sympathy, reassurance, affection, understanding, advice and explanation are some of the constituents of *supportive* psychotherapy. This approach may have been tried by friends and relatives of the patient before he consults a professional helper, but the prestige of the professional may enable these techniques to be more effective, even if they are disdained when given by mere acquaintances.

Such methods look very attractive. At first sight it would seem that everyone should have some. They are indeed among the safer forms of treatment, and at least enable one to obey the exhortation that, in treating our patients, if we cannot do them any good at least we should avoid harming them. Even these benign techniques, however, are not without their disadvantages.

Let us start by considering *sympathy*. Effusive expressions of concern may be quite coldly received by the patient. If the therapist's warm and active overtures are rebuffed, this creates a tension in the relationship that is awkward for both therapist and patient. The therapist should be aware that some depressed patients cannot *take* the strain that even a positive approach like this makes on their slender capacity for sustaining interpersonal relationships. It is like the child who falls over and hurts himself, who responds to attempts to help him with anger and impatience rather than with touching gratitude. At a more directly psychological level, some of us will recall, after disappointments or other causes of unhappiness, feeling that we just cannot be bothered being nice to people, or even wanting company at all.

Many patients do well without the therapist expressing any sympathy. The fact that frequent appointments are being offered is possibly sufficient implicit indication of the seriousness of the therapist's concern. In other cases the quietly spoken 'It must be very difficult for you' is more effective than more elaborate statements.

One is apt to fall into the error of thinking 'If I felt depressed, I should like someone to be sympathetic toward me'. For a start, many patients have had difficulties in interpersonal relationships that long antedate the onset of their illness: their 'normal' personality structure (in the sense of 'usual for them') includes traits of prickliness, oversensitivity, undue self-criticism or criticism of others, paranoid attitudes or a habitual inclination to blame others for their situation. Add to this such features of the depressive state as a smarting loss of self-esteem, inability to cope with anyone (let alone do-gooders), loss of confidence and a profound lack of energy or the inclination to care or bother, and it is small wonder that the patient greets one's vibrant hail-fellow-well-met outpourings with mute silence.

The danger is not so much that the 'sympathy' produces no benefit. It is that the patient realises the great gulf that exists between the response that he is capable of giving, and the reaction that is expected of him. It is clear to him that the therapist does not really perceive how different from normal he feels. This only confirms his pessimistic fears that no one really understands or can help him, and the therapeutic relationship is hampered from the start.

A slightly different case is that of offering gratuitous reassurance. The patient is assured 'Everything will be all right, don't you worry', or 'Soon you'll be feeling better, you'll see'. This may be uttered with the best intentions in the world, but it may backfire for two reasons. Firstly, it may be met with complete incredulity. The depressed patient is convinced that the worst is going to happen. Entrenched in his pessimism, your statements of optimism seem quite foreign and either seem to him to mean that you have not been listening to what he has been saying, or you are ignoring what he has been saying (it is rather like arguing with a patient's delusion). Secondly, it is eminently falsifiable. You may believe at the time you make the statement that it is true, that he soon will be feeling better, that everything will turn out all right in the end. But what happens when next day or next week he is feeling temporarily worse, or he hears of some slight misfortune that has happened to a member of his family? The result is that you have disappointed him. His trust in you, fragile from the start, is broken. He had difficulty in believing that anyone could *really* help him—you claimed to, and now you have (in his eyes) been proved wrong. Of course, there is the added factor that in the black mood of depression, many developments will be seen as setbacks that the outside observer would not see as such. The upshot is, then, that the depressed patient is in the mood neither to accept reassurance nor to see it borne out in events.

We can now sum up two of the problems associated with using supportive psychotherapy in severely depressed patients. Attempts at providing sympathy, understanding and affection miss the boat by emphasising to the patient how ill he really is, as shown by his inability to respond in the usual way to such overtures, and by highlighting the gulf that seems to be fixed between him and the therapist. Efforts directed at reassurance, advice and explanation are fraught with the attendant danger of turning out to be false—if only in the pessimistic interpretation that the patient provides for subsequent events.

The reader may feel that my account of these methods has itself been rather an unduly pessimistic and gloomy one. To a certain extent this is fair criticism. It is a side of the picture that needs to be examined, however, in view of our own tendencies to want the opposite to be true. We would like to believe that the patient is not *really* as sick as all that, and that our own therapeutic efforts will be powerful and promptly rewarded. In our own wish-fulfilling fancy we want to believe that the patient will feel better if we sympathise with him and reassure him. That is the direction in which we tend to deceive ourselves.

If my own prognostications have been too pessimistic, we can now try to balance the picture. We have agreed that the methods of supportive psychotherapy are relatively safe. If we feel an urge to apply them in a particular case, then it may well be a good idea provided that, firstly, we bear in mind the possibilities of its going wrong, and secondly we are reasonably sure on introspection that we are doing it for the patient's benefit and not just to make ourselves feel better.

So, if we offer sympathy, we avoid the gushing warmth that may be difficult for the patient to accept. In fact we offer the sympathy in a form that he can ignore if he likes without slapping us in the face. As he pauses in his narrative, after pouring out his tale of woe, a matter-of-fact 'That must have been very hard for you to take' will test the temperature of the water. His response will show whether he is ready for sympathy or wishes to ignore it. The bare statement may be enough on its own just to show that you are on his side.

What about reassurance? This is a more difficult venture. It is a sad sight to see the badly depressed patient with such a gloomy outlook, and one is often tempted to try to tell him that it will not turn out as terribly as he thinks. A common fear he expresses is that he will never recover. One knows this is highly unlikely. Should one not share this knowledge with him?

Provided the therapist, once again, is not doing it just to make *himself* feel better, and he realises the difficulty of reassuring a depressed patient, it is sometimes worth a try. One must explicitly avoid attempting to effect a deeply-felt change of opinion on the part of the patient. It will have to be sufficient that he knows that *you* believe he will get better.

Sometimes the communication from the therapist can be rather contorted: 'I think you *will* get better. Most patients with your illness improve a lot in the course of a few weeks. I don't expect you to be able to believe me, the way you are feeling, but I want you to know my opinion'. This suffers from being too lengthy for an ideal psychotherapeutic remark. It is also liable to apparent falsification in the short term and it is frequently met with in-difference by the patient. At least it has the virtue of making little demand on the patient's allegiance, with the explicit let-out that the patient is not necessarily expected to believe it. It can therefore be used to assess the patient's overt response to attempts at reassurance, so that the therapist may know whether he is being too cautious or too bold. All patients are different, as are all therapists, so it is impossible to make inviolate rules or formulae. Instead of the elaborate statement quoted above, the therapist may get away with presenting the gist of it with a brief '*I* think you will get better'.

2. *Insight-oriented psychotherapy* Supportive psychotherapy needs a modicum of skill and careful consideration to avoid the pit-falls outlined above. Insight-oriented psychotherapy for severely depressed patients is an even more difficult task. Our unconscious motivations are usually less flattering than our conscious reasons for doing things and their revelation as a result of psychotherapy can be sobering if not distressing. The depressed patient is already preoccupied with real or imagined misdeeds and shameful acts, and the last thing he needs is to have someone give him a glimpse of as yet unimagined weaknesses in his character.

Certainly a full-blown psychoanalytic approach would be difficult, if not dangerous, with such an illness, and the patient might have to go for many months without subjective improvement. Most psychiatrists would feel that it was unwarranted to offer the patient an analysis while in the active phase of a depressive psychosis.

Such techniques as exploring unconscious processes, removing ego defence mechanisms, and analysis of the transference are, then, to be avoided.

In my opinion the therapist need not feel ashamed if he offers no direct attempts at insight therapy to the patient with such a psychosis. It is a risky business in any case, and there are other ways of helping. Some skilled therapists do, nevertheless, seem to be able to enable the patient to look at what he is doing in the here-and-now situation and to correct unproductive behaviour patterns. This needs a great deal of tact and ability to present the confrontation in a supportive and non-threatening way.

3. *Listening* One of the basic techniques of the analytic type of therapeutic approach is that of free association. The patient is instructed to tell everything that comes into his mind, even though it might in other circumstances be deemed shameful or embarrassing. To the extent that such a request might encourage the psychotic depressive to dwell on his self-critical thoughts this technique is contra-indicated, but let us see what the psychotherapist does next.

If the patient stops, the therapist does not leap in with a piece of counselling, or words of consolation and reassurance. What he says (supposing he talks at all at that point) is 'Tell me some more about . . .', 'I was interested in . . .', 'You say that what happened to you was . . .', etc. Such phrases are an explicit or implicit invitation to carry on speaking. In a very high proportion of instances the patient (or client) will respond as is expected of him and go on talking.

If the responses of the therapist are analysed, it may be found that a high proportion of his contributions are merely of this 'come on' type, rather than interpretations. The lay fantasy of the psychotherapeutic process may be that of the patient making a statement, followed by a wise response from the therapist giving the patient instant insight. The truth is probably more like the patient being asked to talk, and when he stops being nudged into talking some more.

It is generally agreed that patients and clients of varied descriptions find this talking helpful in itself, whether or not interpretations are given. The reasons for such benefit are not clear. The reader will probably be able to make some inspired guesses himself.

There would seem to be no reason why these 'come on' methods should not be used to get the patient to speak in other forms of management and treatment. The basic technique of allowing the patient to talk, and if he pauses offering mainly statements encouraging further talk, may be used as a basis for giving diluted forms of insight-oriented therapy, or supportive psychotherapy, or just be used on its own until the therapist is sure exactly what he *does* want to do.

This approach is not always applicable to patients with depressive psychosis. Some such patients are suffering from so much retardation that they may be silent or talk hardly at all in the first instance. They are difficult to treat with any form of verbal psychotherapy, unless the therapist is prepared to justify sitting there and talking away at the patient in a one-sided fashion.

Then again the patient may be so depressed that, although he is able to speak, his efforts are slow and laboured, or it may be that to speak about almost any topic causes him distress. These are extreme cases. At the other extreme are patients for whom talking about their problems gives them immediate relief, and whose treatment may be based entirely on this premise. In between are patients who obtain only partial help from this opportunity, and those who can talk only for 10 or 20 minutes before showing to the wary observer signs that the technique is becoming stressful.

Encouraging the patient to talk freely is then a process that helps many with severe depressive illness, but it must be remembered that there are some for whom even this gentle way of baring the soul is too upsetting.

Physical methods of treatment
The main physical methods of treatment used for depressive psychosis are antidepressant drugs and electro-convulsive therapy (E.C.T.).

1. *Electro-convulsive therapy* The story of how convulsions came to be used to treat depressive illness is a curious one. It

started from the observation early in this century that epilepsy and schizophrenia, though both common conditions in the large mental hospitals, rarely occurred in the same patient. From this observation was derived a hypothesis, that there was a biological incompatibility between the two conditions. It then followed that *producing* convulsions in a schizophrenic patient might drive away his illness.

This was tried, and to a certain extent it was found to be true. Many schizophrenic illnesses do show improvement or even remission on treatment with induced convulsions. It was noticed that the schizophrenics who did best were those with a large *affective* component to their illness (usually depressive) and the treatment was then tried with depressive psychosis. It was found to be even more successful with depressive psychosis than with schizophrenic illnesses.

There are two riders to this story, one a theoretical point and one a practical point. The theory was probably wrong in its first stage: the observation that there is a negative association between schizophrenia and epilepsy has not been confirmed. In fact the latest evidence suggests that if anything patients with epilepsy are slightly *more* likely than others to suffer from schizophrenic symptoms. Readers of this book will, I hope, not be surprised at this evidence. One of the main themes in earlier chapters was the proposition that organic brain disease can produce *any* symptom of functional mental illness, including 'typical' schizophrenic symptoms. Since epilepsy itself is often produced by a lesion in the brain it is small wonder that the two clinical pictures can co-exist. Why was the original mistake in observation made? Probably because the patients in the hospital were not thought of in relation to the population from which they were drawn. If you have a hospital full of epileptics and schizophrenics, it might seem remarkable that 'only', say, 5 per cent of the epileptics suffered from schizophrenia. But if in the general population less than 1 per cent of the population suffered from schizophrenia, then this 5 per cent is more common, not more rare.

The practical rider that one must add to the story is that the original treatment was not E.C.T. The convulsions were induced, not by electricity, but by injecting certain stimulant drugs into a vein. The method did work, but for one thing the timing and

number of the fits produced were unpredictable. The other drawback was that the method was literally horrible for the patient.
Before producing the fit (and loss of consciousness) the drug would
bring about a state of intense horror. This is not a necessary accompaniment of epilepsy, but was a feature of the action of this
type of drug.

It was found that applying a brief electric current to the scalp
was sufficient to cause a fit, and the results were more predictable
(for instance, the intravenous drug method might produce a
delayed fit, or more than one fit, neither of which are likely with the
electrical technique). The modern method of E.C.T. includes a
number of further refinements. The two most important are the use
of a general anaesthetic and a muscle relaxant. The general
anaesthetic (an injection of a *sedative* drug intravenously,
producing rapid loss of consciousness) avoids any unpleasant sensations for the patient during the procedure, and is also needed on
humanitarian grounds for the use of the muscle relaxant. This
muscle relaxant is also injected intravenously and causes a paralysis
of the voluntary muscles of the body. This avoids large muscular
contractions during the fit itself (which could cause fractures of the
bones if it were violent). Thus the modern method avoids much of
the mental trauma and a lot of the physical distress that might
result from inducing a fit.

E.C.T. is given as a course of treatments, one every 2 or 3 days
to start with being the usual frequency. In cases of desperate urgency it is given daily; in more leisured circumstances, or towards the
end of the course, it is given weekly. It is customary to limit a
course of E.C.T. to no more than twelve treatments, and to avoid
repeating a course within 6 months. These are arbitrary limits, and
need not necessarily be rigidly adhered to, but they make a point.
In fact, the vast majority of patients with severe depressive illness
will remit on less than twelve treatments, and the vast majority will
not relapse within the following 6 months. The self-imposed limits
have the salutary effect of making the physician pause and reconsider whether in prescribing so much E.C.T. he is doing the right
thing for the patient.

What are the ill effects, then, of E.C.T.? They are real, but surprisingly few. Like any procedure that is carried out under general
anaesthetic (even dental extraction) there is a mortality rate.

Estimates vary on the mortality rate for E.C.T., but it is probably less than 1 in 10,000. One would like to see it even safer, but this particular rate makes it already one of the safest anaesthetic procedures to be found.

What about physical damage to the body? This, too, is uncommon, but depends to some extent on how well the fit is 'controlled'. The amount of muscle relaxant used clearly determines the amount of paralysis. If a large amount of this curare-like drug is used paralysis will be virtually complete, the patient may take many minutes to recover from the dose and require artificial ventilation with oxygen. Some patients will complain of pains in the muscles after treatment and this is thought, too, to be a result of the action of the muscle relaxant. If on the other hand too little is used, the patient will show appreciable movements of the limbs during the fit, which is then said to be 'poorly controlled'. Fractures of the long bones or of the spinal vertebrae are nowadays rare, but the patient may clench his jaw during the convulsion and loosen any irregular teeth.

Probably the most noticeable unwanted side-effect of E.C.T. is loss of memory. This varies widely from patient to patient—some scarcely acknowledging it even when specifically asked. Others will complain that after the E.C.T. they have trouble in registering events for a period of an hour or more. A few patients experience difficulty for weeks even after the course of E.C.T. has ended, and will have to write down their shopping list on a piece of paper to avoid forgetting various items when they go out. The fact that patients suffer at all from these difficulties with memory suggests that the treatment has produced an impairment of brain *function*, but there is no convincing evidence that E.C.T., administered as described here, is likely to produce permanent brain damage.

2. *Antidepressant drugs* The other main method of physical treatment is by drugs whose actions are neither sedative nor tranquillising but directed specifically at depression. There are two main categories. Firstly there are the *tricyclic* antidepressants, so called because of the three-ringed structure of their chemical molecules. Secondly there are the *mono-amine oxidase inhibitors*, M.A.O.I.s for short.

The tricyclics are widely used and probably fairly safe. They are not liable to produce addiction. They do have a number of side effects, resulting from their action on the autonomic nervous system (composed of the *sympathetic nervous system* and the *parasympathetic nervous system*). The sympathetic nervous system has the function of preparing the body to meet an emergency (fight or flight reflex) and is concerned with maintaining a normal blood pressure. If its action is impaired then the blood pressure will be low and fail to respond to changes in bodily posture. Drugs that interfere in this way may cause the patient to feel faint and fall to the ground.

Among the diverse actions of the parasympathetic nervous system are those allowing the pupils to contract in response to light, enabling the lens of the eye to focus on near objects ('accommodation'), stimulating the salivary glands to keep the mouth moist, and facilitating the action of the bladder and bowel. Drugs that interfere with the parasympathetic may cause blurred vision, dry mouth, constipation and sometimes difficulty in emptying the bladder.

Most of the tricyclic antidepressants are liable to cause one or more of these side-effects. If they are experienced by the patient then the dosage of the drug should be kept down to a level where the side-effects disappear, or are trivial, or are at least acceptable to the patient as preferable to the depression. There are no absolutely fixed doses of these drugs, and although there are recommended starting doses the number of tablets taken by the patient has to be determined by his response. These side-effects disappear on stopping the drug, and permanent damage by the drugs is rare in moderate use. When taken in suicidal overdose they may be lethal, and some persons taking them for very long periods of time have developed abnormalities of cardiac rhythm. They may be dangerous in the presence of coincidental heart disease.

The effects of taking these drugs for very long periods of time—2 years or more—are the most difficult to evaluate from the safety point of view. Their action is different from that of sedatives—which make the patient feel better after each dose. Antidepressants take several days or weeks to produce their maximum benefit, and it may be weeks after stopping them before a patient who needs them relapses.

When antidepressant drugs are prescribed for a patient he is told that it may be 10 days or so before he notices an improvement. In the absence of improvement at this time it is worth continuing the drug for a month or 6 weeks because some patients respond later than others. If the patient makes a good response, and loses his symptoms, it is customary to recommend that he continues to take the tablets for several months. The reasons for this are as follows. It is impossible to know when a patient can stop his medication with no risk of relapse. Suppose that a patient were to stop his tablets as soon as he felt better, and then relapse again. Once more back in his depression, with everything again looking black, he may find it difficult to recall clearly those few days when he did feel well. He feels that he has been depressed all along, and pessimistically believes that nothing has helped him. It may be very difficult to persuade him once again to start taking the medication that he regards as a hopeless failure. On the other hand, if he has had a month or two of a return to normality, he is less likely to forget this, and will be more likely to see the connection between the relapse in his mood state and the discontinuation of the tablets. Studies have shown that there is no doubt of the efficacy of antidepressant medication in tending to prevent the relapse of a depressive illness, whether the original illness was treated with E.C.T. or the tablets themselves.

There are various types of M.A.O.I., of differing chemical structure. They have in common the ability to inhibit the action of an enzyme known as mono-amine oxidase. This enzyme is found in the human body, in the brain and other situations. The action of the drug is to prevent a rapid breakdown of certain amines which are compounds derived from proteins in the diet.

This property, which may be part of their beneficial action in depression, also confers a considerable disadvantage in their clinical use. Some amines, notably *tyramine*, can cause a dangerous rise in blood pressure. Large quantities of this amine are liberated into the bloodstream when such foodstuffs as cheese are digested. Normally the amine-oxidase enzyme system breaks it down rapidly enough to avoid too high a concentration in the blood. In the absence of the action of this enzyme the blood pressure rises and the patient is liable to experience a severe headache. The high pressure also reveals any weaknesses in the circulatory system and may cause heart failure. A proportion of persons in the population have small balloon-like expansions in their cerebral arteries called *aneurysms*. The wall of the blood vessel is weak at this point and the lesion, which from its size is usually referred to as a 'berry aneurysm', is vulnerable to higher arterial pressure. In these circumstances it may rupture, allowing a sudden jet of blood to escape. Even if it escapes only into the fluid surrounding the brain—a 'sub-arachnoid haemorrhage'—the rise in intracranial pressure may be dangerous. Sometimes the jet of blood may penetrate the brain itself, causing permanent damage and some patients go into a coma and some die. On the other hand, some recover completely and some recover with partial paralysis.

Suspect foodstuffs include (beside cheese) meat and yeast extracts, broad beans and some alcoholic beverages. A large number of *drugs* are also contraindicated. Some of these are drugs that might be used in emergencies or operations. Others are included in medicines, tonics or 'cold cures' that are sold over the counter at the retail chemist's shop.

Patients for whom M.A.O.I.s are prescribed are now given a card with the latest list of banned foodstuffs and drugs printed on it. They are told to inform any new doctor who treats them about the M.A.O.I, and are warned not to take drugs other than those prescribed.

In addition to the above hazards some of the M.A.O.I.s are addictive, but since they come from a variety of chemical groups, some have shown no tendency to habit formation at all.

3. *Precipitation of hypomania* When a depressive illness is being treated either by E.C.T. or antidepressant drugs the patient's mood may be elevated past the normal level up to elation, and a state of frank hypomania may follow. This is rather unpredictable, and it remains a matter of opinion whether the treatment actually increases the chances of the patient swinging from one extreme to the other (after all, such a fate is well recognised as happening even without therapeutic intervention). At the present time it is probably true that most psychiatrists regard it as a complication of treatment. A certain number, on the contrary, regard it as a sign of improvement and continue with the same line of treatment! The use of E.C.T. for hypomania is considered later in the chapter.

Brain operations

The measures described so far may be relied upon to enable the vast majority of patients with depressive illness to lose their symptoms, or at least to have them reduced to acceptable levels.

A small proportion fail to improve. This is generally an indication that one should review the diagnosis. It may be found that further investigation reveals unsuspected schizophrenic symptoms or signs of organic brain disease. An alternative finding, fortunately rare, is a physical illness which either produces the symptoms of weakness and lethargy directly or, for instance, malignant disease (which the patient may have suspected all along).

Having excluded alternative explanations for the symptoms, how does one treat the severe depressive illness that fails to respond to drugs and psychotherapy? One resort that is considered at this stage is the brain operation.

The most notable of these operations is the prefrontal leucotomy. This has been referred to in previous chapters. The aim of the operation is to destroy the connection between the supervisory, regulatory areas of the frontal lobes and the central areas of the brain concerned with emotion. The disadvantages of earlier operations included haemorrhage and death in some cases, and severe impairment of the personality in others. Although a vegetable-like state of inertia, lack of initiative, and loss of self-control might be preferable to a life of prolonged mental agony, such risks limited the applicability of the operation.

Recent advances in selection and in surgical techniques have improved the results, but it is still only a tiny minority of psychiatric patients who are advised to have brain operations. Patients with refractory depressive illnesses are among those considered, and a good proportion have done well. Doctors are reluctant to consider patients for the operation unless, prior to the illness, the patient has shown an adequate ability to cope with life's demands without impulsive behaviour or loss of control. Alcoholism and drug addiction are regarded as contra-indications.

Having ensured that the patient is of a previous 'good' personality, the operation will be offered only to those who have suffered conspicuous distress for a long period of time (usually years) and for whom other measures have proved ineffective.

Instead of a broad cut through the connecting nerve fibres within the frontal lobe, nowadays small, accurately placed lesions are made. These may be sited within the frontal lobe, or within the central parts of the brain that are concerned with emotion. Instead of relying on the surgical incision to interrupt the fibres, small lesions may be made by implanting radioactive Yttrium seeds that kill off that area of brain immediately around them, or by freezing the brain tissue. In co-operative patients an operation can be done under local anaesthetic, and the part of the brain considered for surgery is first stimulated electrically. If it is confirmed that that part produces signs of emotional stimulation (including changes in respiration and so on), then that point and an area about a third of an inch (1 cm) in diameter surrounding it are frozen. This method does not seem to be associated with the haemorrhage that complicated earlier operations.

The initial location of these probes is facilitated by X-ray techniques combining air studies with a specially designed frame fitted to the patient's head for the operation, and such precise operations are referred to as 'stereotactic surgery'.

In modern operations, then, the disastrously severe effects on the personality are largely avoided. Since the operation is much safer it can even be repeated if the first set of lesions proves to be ineffectual. Many patients, when examined closely 4 to 8 weeks after the operation will show dramatic benefit. Unfortunately this benefit is sometimes lost over succeeding months. The exact place of stereotactic surgery in the treatment of depressive psychosis is still to be decided.

Strategy of treatment

When a patient is first seen in a psychiatric out-patient department suffering from a depressive illness the average psychiatrist will probably prescribe an antidepressant drug (usually a tricyclic). The reasons are not difficult to find. The patient may well have had treatment by supportive psychotherapy before being referred, since all cases (or almost all cases) seen routinely at the N.H.S. out-patient clinics have been sent there by another doctor—the patient's own G.P. or a physician from another department of the hospital. Some patients have already been told to 'snap out of it' or to pull their socks up. Those for whom this approach works presumably will not need to see a psychiatrist, and so do not appear at the clinic.

In any case the prescription of drugs does not preclude further supportive psychotherapy from the psychiatrist. Some patients will have had some antidepressant tablets from the G.P. before coming up. Often the course has been at a low dose, or taken only for a very brief period, so that it is worth trying the effect of a longer, stronger course.

What happens if after a month on the tablets, at satisfactory dosage, the patient has not made a substantial improvement? There are several avenues open.

Continue for even longer on the same medication
Patients are not always obliging enough to produce their main improvement in the first 4 weeks.

Review the diagnosis
Also remember that an unknown number of patients will say they have been taking their prescribed tablets when in fact they are failing to do so.

Switch to a different type of antidepressant
On the whole, if one tricyclic has not proved effective, it is not considered very likely that another tricyclic will work. This type of switch *can* be made if none of the other alternatives are attractive but it is at this stage that a *changeover to a M.A.O.I.* is often considered.

There are various reasons why it is usual to try the effect of the tricyclics first. Firstly, they are usually considered to be safer. Moreover many tricyclics are incompatible with M.A.O.I.s, and the average psychiatrist (treating the average patient) will not lightly consider prescribing them together. The peculiarities of the action of the M.A.O.I.s on the body chemistry mean that, if one has prescribed *them*, to be absolutely free from the danger of interaction one should wait for as much as 2 weeks after stopping the drug before giving a tricyclic. The relevant effects of the tricyclic drugs, on the other hand, are over in a couple of days. The upshot is that one can go from tricyclic to M.A.O.I. with a much shorter delay than going from M.A.O.I. to tricyclic.

Consider the psychological effect on the patient. Suppose one had put Mrs. Smith on an M.A.O.I. at her first visit. After 4, or even 6, weeks she says she is no better. It seems likely that it is not worthwhile persevering, and one wishes to try a tricyclic. Mrs. Smith has just been saying how depressed she still is, she feels hopeless, life is not worth living, she can't see how she can go on, she feels desperate. 'Well, Mrs. Smith', one tells her breezily, 'we must change your treatment. It means that you should not take any tablets at all to help your depression for the next 2 or 3 weeks.' You can imagine the effect of *that*!

M.A.O.I.s *are* given as the treatment of choice (and therefore the first treatment) by a school of thought that recognises a certain type of depression (paradoxically called 'atypical depression') which is said to respond better to M.A.O.I.s than to tricyclics. Personally, I do not find the description of such a group of patients sufficiently clear-cut for me to have the confidence to prescribe M.A.O.I.s from the start. In any case, for the purposes of this book, they do not sound like the typical depressive *psychosis*, whatever else they are.

Treat the patient with insight-oriented psychotherapy

In the milder depressive illnesses it may be clear by this stage that the difficulties that the patient is suffering from are arising largely out of his own life-long character traits and habitual patterns of behaviour, and that physical methods of treatment are not the answer. If the patient is a suitable case, and the therapist has the time available, then the long (and sometimes painful) procedure of insight-oriented psychotherapy may be considered—perhaps on a basis of an hour once a week. Some idea of the length of time that is considered necessary for this type of treatment is given by the fact that a method lasting 40 weeks is described, almost apologetically, as 'brief psychotherapy'.

For patients with the more severe degrees of depressive illness it does not seem warranted to keep them waiting so long for relief from their symptoms.

Admit the patient to hospital

There are several reasons why it might be desirable for the patient to be admitted to a psychiatric bed. Admission can be very valuable in the case of a suicidal patient. For a start it relieves the anxieties of friends, relatives and those treating the patient and relieves the tension surrounding his management. Secondly, the patient feels that people are taking him seriously, that they care, that something is being done for him, and at least in one part of his mind he may begin to believe that perhaps the situation is not hopeless after all. Thirdly, in hospital close supervision can be given. One would not want to make this too obtrusive—if it seems to the patient that everyone is expecting him to take his own life then he may oblige. On the other hand, the suicidal feelings should not be completely ignored. If a patient, saying life is hopeless, is admitted to a room on the sixth floor with a wide open window, or a secluded room with a long cord dangling from the light fixture or window blind, then he may feel that he is not being taken seriously. If the happy medium is found, and the patient receives the appropriate degree of supervision and concern, then everybody can get on with the business of treating the depressive illness. Usually admission to a psychiatric bed will immediately result in a dramatic lowering of the suicidal potential of the patient.

Admission to hospital may be desired in order to administer E.C.T. Although it is not absolutely necessary to be an in-patient to have this treatment, there are advantages in giving it this way. The frequency of treatments can be adjusted more finely to the patient's progress and the transient memory disturbances matter less. There is less danger of the patient's clinical state changing unnoticed to either hypomania or to that combination of energy and desperation that was mentioned earlier in the chapter in the discussion of suicidal stages in treatment.

A patient may be admitted to hospital because it is wished to give him intensive treatment of other sorts, such as high dosages of drugs.

Often a patient who is brought into hospital for one or other of the reasons mentioned makes an impressive recovery that does not seem to be at all related to the physical methods of treatment, or occurs even before they have been started. In these cases the conclusion is often that the patient's depression had stemmed directly from his environmental circumstances in a way that had not been appreciated before he was removed from them. In some hospitals a conscious effort is made to ensure that the whole ambience or atmosphere of the ward is in itself therapeutic—the *milieu* therapy or therapeutic community type of approach. Patients are encouraged to help one another, to participate in the administrative management of the psychiatric ward (or mental hospital), and to join in frank, open group discussion about their problems. The degree of personal involvement expected is too much for some patients with depressive illness, but others find it helpful.

If full hospitalisation is not acceptable, then various forms of partial hospitalisation are available. The most common is the day-hospital, where the patient attends during working hours, 5 days a week, or even more than this. An alternative is to consider night-hospital, but this is usually less suitable for depressive psychosis, and more useful for those patients whose problems do not prevent them working during the day. The current pattern of hospital care that is being encouraged is the provision of day-hospitals linked closely to in-patient units. Here the in-patients spend most of their time using the day hospital facilities—occupational therapy, recreation, dining, group rooms and so on. Since exactly the same facilities are being used by those patients who are living at home and coming in just during working hours, there is a less abrupt distinction between in-patient and day-patient status.

E.C.T. should be considered

There are a relatively few psychiatrists for whom this form of treatment is still anathema. They belong especially to the psychoanalytic schools of thought. To some extent the difference of opinion between them and most general psychiatrists can be explained by the different types of patient that each sees. The analyst sees financially and educationally better-off patients, often self-selected, with relatively minor problems. The general psychiatrist is usually seeing the most disturbed and acutely ill patients from his catchment area.

We may say that, apart from those that see only a selected type of patient, most psychiatrists would not delay too long before considering E.C.T. for the patient with a depressive psychosis which has not responded to drugs. Indeed, in the most severely depressed patients many would advocate E.C.T., either alone or in combination with drugs, right from the start. The severity of the depression may be variously judged for this purpose. Certainly a patient would be considered if retardation were so profound that he was not fulfilling the basic life-maintaining behaviour of eating and drinking. Subjective distress, agitation and suicidal feelings would also rank as important. Perhaps more debatable would be the urgency to be attributed to such overtly psychotic features as delusions: these might be regarded more seriously if they were accompanied by evidence of impulsive or unpredictable behaviour.

Other forms of management are occasionally invoked
The place of *brain operations* has been discussed. They are not used very often, and then only after exhausting other methods of treatment, and consideration by more than one psychiatrist. Prolonged narcosis is carried out in some centres, with the patient being kept asleep by a combination of sedatives and tranquillisers for most of the day, weeks at a time. Sleep deprivation over one or more nights a week is also under evaluation. *Combined antidepressants* are sometimes prescribed for depressive psychosis, the tricyclic and M.A.O.I. antidepressants being prescribed simultaneously. This is regarded by many psychiatrists as dangerous, but clearly it may be warranted if the suicidal patient with refractory depression is at even greater risk, or it may anyway be regarded as a worthwhile risk if the distress is great, and does not respond to more conservative methods.

The use of *lithium compounds* will be discussed further in the section on hypomania. Lithium is used as a prophylactic to prevent recurrences of depressive illness, particularly when they are frequent, severe and apparently endogenous. It is occasionally used for the treatment of the acute illness as well.

Relative merits of the various treatments
Earlier in the chapter we said that after considering each of the main methods of treatment, psychological and physical, we should be able to answer such questions as

1. Does the treatment leave lasting damage?
2. Is the treatment painful?
3. Does the treatment respect the dignity of the patient?
4. Is the treatment worse than the disease?

As far as *lasting damage* is concerned, both antidepressant drugs and E.C.T. may produce irreversible toxic effects, but very rarely. Death is even rarer. Psychological methods of treatment are more difficult to assess in their long-term hazards; they may raise unjustified hope in the mind of the patient that all his personality problems and character traits can be dealt with, as well as his current problems, and he may spend much of the rest of his life in a disappointing search for this holy grail. Psychotherapy is likely to cause death only from suicide (if the mood of the patient is misjudged) or from depression itself (lack of eating, infection, loss of will to live) if it is allowed to go on too long in an absence of symptomatic improvement.

As for *pain*, E.C.T. involves no more pain at the time than the prick of the needle for the anaesthetic, but patients may have a headache afterwards. Drugs may produce physical discomfort (not usually frank pain) from their side effects, but this can be abolished by reducing the dose. Psychological methods of treatment may produce mental pain if the uncovering process and removal of defences are pursued too vigorously, or involve a prolongation of the agony of the depression if they are given at the expense of more comforting methods of treatment.

What are the effects on the *dignity* of the patient? Here the physical methods of treatment can do badly. If the patient does not get a full hearing, and is given antidepressant medication as a means of shutting him up; if he is referred from the G.P. to the specialist only to get the same treatment; if he continues to attend the psychiatric clinic only to be told 'Just keep on taking the tablets': then he may feel that he is being treated as a lump of meat. If he waits for his E.C.T. in a long queue, and rarely sees his therapist between these treatments, he may feel that he is a veterinary patient, a cypher. Individual psychotherapy, on the other hand, is uniquely tailored for the patient, and is likely to fail to satisfy his need for respect as a person only if he feels he is not getting enough of it. Group psychotherapy will fall somewhere between the two.

Is the treatment worse than the disease? The reader will now be in a better position to judge under what circumstances he might think so. In fact, for the vast majority of patients, they vote with their feet to continue the treatment. They continue to attend the clinic and talk about their problems until they are well, they do not discharge themselves from hospital rather than have E.C.T., many take medication regularly for long periods of time with only the doctor's word for it that it is helping them. There are some notable exceptions: but if the various treatments are given with skill and humanity, they should be acceptable to most patients, and help to cut short much suffering.

HYPOMANIA

Hypomania is in some ways the opposite of depressive psychosis and yet in some ways very similar to it. The phenomena, the symptoms and signs, of the acute state are at the opposite pole to those of depression, with cheerfulness, animation and optimism taking the place of gloom, fatigue and hopelessness. The course of hypomania, the rapid response to treatment, the return to normal personality between episodes, the fact that attacks are likely to occur in someone who has already suffered a depressive illness, and that sometimes the same treatment is used successfully for both of the affective illnesses, all serve to point out the relatedness of the two conditions.

Case 34 Mrs. J.A.
Mrs. J.A., a woman in her 50s, presented to the general physicians with abdominal pains. No physical cause was detected, and in fact she was found to be suffering from a depressive illness. She continued to have the conviction that she suffered from an undiagnosed abdominal disease until her depression cleared.

Three years later she was brought to the hospital in a state of considerable excitement. She was overtalkative and verbally aggressive, critical of those around her and accusing people of wrong acts without any evidence. She had threatened her husband with a knife. By the following day she was still talkative but more obviously cheerful, and trying to make people laugh. Her conversation would flit from one topic to another. She showed relatively little insight into the fact that she was ill. During her stay in hospital she bought items from nearby shops for which (according to her husband) she could have no use.

Clinical features

Over a short period, sometimes just a few hours, the patient experiences the onset of an elation of mood, or persons close to him perceive a change in behaviour.

Mood
The *mood* may in fact be the least conspicuous of the abnormalities.

Although some patients become extremely cheerful, and reach a state of ecstasy, other are less clearly happy. They will certainly deny being depressed or low in their spirits, but at the same time may appear irritable and impatient. The most important factor here is their usual personality. In a person who is as a rule rather subdued and pessimistic by nature, the hypomanic mood may be sufficient merely to bring him up to the upper ranges of normal as perceived by an observer meeting him for the first time. The marked change will be obvious, though, to his friends and relatives. On the other hand, the mistake is sometimes made of continuing to treat a patient as if he were still hypomanic, when in fact his abnormal mood has subsided and he is just back to his usual bustling, jocular self, particularly if he is being seen for the first time.

Thought content

The *thought content* of the hypomanic is sunny. He is intensely enthusiastic and confident. He believes that he is a person of great importance. The patient may make it clear that he feels he has the right to respect and deference, but frank *delusions of grandeur* are not so common nowadays. It may be that it takes time for grandiose feelings to be organised into a particular delusion that, for instance, he is Napoleon, Jesus Christ, the Prime Minister or the monarch. He may be content with believing that he is the head of the hospital, or of his place of employment. An intriguing variant is when he decides that he is the doctor, and the medical staff are the patients.

More often, however, there is an attitude of superiority or a regal air rather than a specific identification.

The grandiosity may be tinged with paranoid ideas. The patient sees himself not only as a very great person but also as subject to persecution. Sometimes the paranoid ideas follow the line of reasoning: 'Since I am so important, why do I not seem to receive the respect that is due to me? It must be because people are against me'. Alternatively, the patient may be so extremely egocentric that he sees everything around him as having a special significance for himself, and so suffers from ideas of reference. Reading hidden meanings into the actions of those around him, sometimes he will find these flattering, but at other times they will give rise to suspicion.

The grandiose ideas can be contrasted with the ideas of unworthiness or the self-deprecation to be found in depressive psychosis. In hypomania the match for delusions of poverty is also found. The patient believes he has unlimited funds, and will spend generously and lavishly. Vast debts may be incurred with bouncing cheques, by borrowing from friends and acquaintances and exploiting credit accounts.

Whereas the patient with depressive psychosis is preoccupied with ideas of guilt, the hypomanic patient acts in a remarkably conscience-free way. He appears to be carefree, reckless or even abandoned. Again, rather than be concerned with imaginary illnesses, the hypomanic tends to deny those illnesses and disabilities that he really does have.

Behaviour

The *behaviour* of the hypomanic patient is typically energetic. He is restless, and busily starts one project after another. Whereas the hypomanic *personality* may reap the fruits of his ventures, the person with hypomanic *illness* does not have the consistency to follow through his initiative to ensure its completion. He will start a dozen schemes one after another, but not actually finish any of them.

The activity may continue well into the night, and be relentless during the day. Eventually the physical health of the patient suffers as a result of continued exertion, lack of sleep and lack of proper diet. Serious illness or even death may then occur.

Short of this the patient may act in ways which he will subsequently regret. He will certainly be in a sad plight later if he grossly overspends and the pathological freedom from guilt may result in an orgy of promiscuity, or an indulgently excessive intake of alcohol.

In his relationships with other persons, the hypomanic is likely to prove meddlesome. Partly this will arise from his consistently high level of energy and activity. The reader may well be able to call to mind acquaintances who have a hypomanic type of personality. Full of humour and high spirits, they are great fun to be with for a short period of time, as long as their mood is infectious. After a time, however, particularly if one is not feeling particularly jovial oneself, they become rather tedious or even irritating. Another reason why the patient with hypomania is so interfering is that he is sure he knows best. He can't bear to see the ordinary mortals about him struggling in their ignorance and inefficiency. He feels obliged to show them how to do things properly, or tell them the real facts.

Case 35 Mrs. N.F.

Mrs. N.F. was 35 years old at the time of her admission to hospital. She was a woman of African origin who had lived in this country since she was 20 and who spoke good English.

On admission she was overactive and excited and her rambling speech at that time was difficult to understand. When interviewed by the doctor she drank his tea, resented the cups and saucers being taken away from her afterwards, and insisted on leaving the room to go and wash them up. (Later she cleaned all the ward lavatories and was prepared to go on doing so indefinitely before she was stopped.)

She came back into the interview room as requested. She carried on pouring out tea and fussing around saying 'I am with the Gods, God supplies us with our needs'. Eventually she sat down. She replied to a few questions, but for the most part rambled on, ignoring what was said to her. Later her conversation became more coherent, but she still jumped from one topic to another. At the end of the interview it was difficult to persuade her to leave the room. Eventually she did so, but she insisted on taking the tea tray with her.

The patient's mood may show itself in the way he dresses. He may be extraordinarily venturesome in the brightness and colour of his costume. Rings, gaudy jewellery, flowers and flashy ties are the order of the day. This is particularly noticeable if the patient has normally been conservative and sober in his sartorial habits.

The speech of the hypomanic is said to show *pressure of talk*. He speaks excitedly and rapidly, as if he can't get the words out fast enough. This appears to reflect his thinking, which is also fast and under pressure, and the patient may declare that his thoughts come faster than he can get them into words. He will dart from one topic to another in a bewildering fashion, a pattern referred to as the *flight of ideas*.

Hazards of hypomania

If the 'patient' feels so well, and does not complain of his condition, then is it warranted to describe his state as an illness and offer him treatment for it? It does seem a shame to spoil his apparent sense of well-being if he is so happy. In fact many psychiatrists will avoid doing anything very active if the patient is merely mildly 'high', and no one is suffering from it. Personally, I think this is often reasonable provided that the patient is under fairly close supervision, for instance with relatives who will report any deterioration of his condition.

There are risks in this *laissez-faire* approach, though. If the patient does become rather more elated, it may be so much more difficult to treat him—or even to persuade him to accept treatment. If he is not treated in the frank hypomanic phase, what then?

We have already seen one main danger—that he may do things he will bitterly regret afterwards. The promiscuity, alcoholism and excessive expenditure of money come into this category. The infuriation which he causes other people is also of this order. We have seen, too, that escalation of the overactivity may cause exhaustion and serious illness, if not death.

Another less obvious hazard is that of an abrupt change in his emotional state. Spontaneous remission does occur—probably sooner with this type of psychosis than with any other. However, sometimes the mood state descends from the heights of elation only to plummet to the depths of depression. Unknown to those trying to help him, the patient, within a few days perhaps, goes from feeling confident and successful to feeling hopeless and desperate. Apart from the obvious mental suffering, there is also the danger of suicide.

Treatment of hypomania
In dealing with the hypomanic patient physical methods of treatment and psychological measures are both important. It will be helpful to consider the physical methods first.

Physical methods
Drugs are extensively used. Sedatives, such as barbiturates, and anti-anxiety drugs (minor tranquillisers) are of little use. Major tranquillisers are quite effective, and on the whole the same range of drugs is used as was considered in the section on the treatment of schizophrenia. The first type of major tranquillisers, the *phenothiazine* group, has been in widespread use for about 20 years now. In many cases of hypomania it will reduce the elation and overactivity quite promptly and dissipate the delusions. Apart from the intrinsic side-effects of the drugs, which are described

elsewhere (Chapter 9) a disadvantage is that quite often the patient's mood descends from elation not just to normal but even deeper, into a state of depression.

The second type of major tranquilliser, the butyrophenone group, has been introduced more recently, and includes such drugs as haloperidol and trifluperidol. These seem to be even more effective than the phenothiazines in bringing down the elated mood. They are valuable drugs for use in the difficult management problem, but unfortunately they also seem to be more likely than the phenothiazines to produce depression.

It had been found with these two groups of drugs that the acute attack of hypomania could be readily controlled in the majority of cases. What one then needed was something to stop relapses occurring. Such a substance appears to have been found in *lithium* which, given in the form of one of its salts, replaces sodium in the body fluids. There is convincing evidence that, if this is given on a long-term basis, it will substantially reduce the frequency of attacks of hypomania suffered by the individual. It is a potentially toxic drug, and can damage various organs in the body, so that a check has to be kept on the precise level that is reached in the blood, and the dosage altered accordingly. A virtue of lithium is that it does not increase the likelihood of the patient going into a depressive phase—and is in fact used for the prevention of depressive psychosis. It is regarded as a *mood stabiliser* rather than a tranquilliser or an antidepressant. If there is no desperate urgency, then it is sometimes used as the definitive treatment in the acute episode of hypomania, and not merely as a prophylactic after the attack has subsided.

Apart from drugs, E.C.T. is also used for the treatment of the acute illness. In fact, it is often brought into service in addition to drugs if the latter are not producing their effect rapidly enough. It does seem paradoxical that E.C.T., regarded as the most effective physical treatment for depressive psychosis, should also be used for hypomania. It may be that, like lithium, it acts as a mood stabiliser. Perhaps it is not so strange that some treatments are of benefit to both high and low mood states of pathological degree. It was pointed out at the beginning of this section on hypomania that both it and depressive psychosis have a lot of features in common. Some investigators have gone as far as to say that they are merely different *degrees* of the same illness, with hypomania being a more severe degree than depression. Many analysts believe that hypomania represents a form of adaptation of the individual to (or a defence against) depression—a form of whistling in the dark: 'Look how cheerful I am, I can't be depressed'.

Psychological methods

This brings us to a suitable point at which to discuss those methods of dealing with hypomania that do not rely on drugs and E.C.T. One hesitates to call it psychotherapy for various reasons. On the one hand one hardly gives supportive psychotherapy in the usual sense—the patient does not apparently need sympathy or reassurance, and is unlikely to thank one for advice. Certainly it seems an inappropriate time for insight-oriented psychotherapy, and the patient will probably not be able to discipline himself to the requirements of either individual or group psychotherapy. It is, in fact, a rather chaotic experience to have a hypomanic patient as a member of a group.

The nature of the interpersonal transaction is perhaps best described as *management*. It may be debated as to who manages whom, but we shall describe it from the point of view of the therapist trying to manage the patient. It is likely that first of all, with any but the mildest illness, the person with hypomania will need in-patient care. Control is difficult enough then, but is practically impossible as an out-patient. So the first difficulty one will have to overcome is that of getting the patient into hospital.

The easy way out is to have him sent to hospital on a compulsory order under one of the sections of the Mental Health Act (*see* Chapter 13). It does seem a pity to stigmatise the patient in this way if it can be avoided. Often it *can* be avoided, but not without difficulty.

How does one persuade him to accept hospitalisation on an informal basis? After all, he says he feels well. He is actively denying his disability, so it is an uphill struggle to get him to accept treatment for it. One is not likely to get very far by informing him point-blank that he is psychotic.

Well, like patients of many descriptions who maintain unreasonable positions, they will assert their position at the level of the direct statement, but at another level (often that which is implied or just left unsaid) they tacitly accept reality. Thus, although the hypomanic patient will deny, if you challenge him directly, that he has any form of psychiatric illness, he will often agree eventually to enter a psychiatric ward. If one is tactful enough not to point out to him that this in itself is illogical, his admission may form the basis for treatment.

There is, then, a question of finding some common ground— something to agree upon. Clearly, whether it is expressed or not, the patient is maintaining that he is well and the therapist that he is ill. It is usually best if one manages to avoid getting into an argument about this. If one talks to him for long enough, however, it may be possible to find a reason that the more realistic part of his mind can motivate him to accept, provided it is couched in sufficiently face-saving terms.

For instance, after discussing with him his immediate future, it may be possible to get him to agree to come into hospital because he is 'tired'. Admittedly, it may take an hour or two of conversation to get him to accept this, since most of the time he will be talking rather than listening—such interviews are laborious struggles.

What happens once he is in the hospital? One's troubles are by no means over. In his overactivity he tends to explore the precise limits that are set on his behaviour. If he is allowed to make a 'phone call, he will then make call after call. He will want to see how loudly he can play records, or how late into the night.

The reaction of both staff and fellow patients is not just a function of the continued demands made by the patient. In general, he will be able to make quick superficial relationships with those that he meets, and it may look as if he is insensitive to the personalities of his contacts. There is no doubt, though, that sometimes the hypomanic patient will be very clever at getting his way with others by exploiting their guilt feelings, their sense of pride, or whatever other weaknesses they have.

The relationship may start with the patient flattering the other person and suggesting that he (that is therapist, patient, staff member) has remarkably fine qualities. This, together with the out-going manner, the wit and good humour, make him seem very attractive. As he then uses the other person to get his own way, the other gradually feels manipulated and outdone. Repeatedly he finds that the patient has somehow got the better of him. Even experienced staff members may find that the patient has somehow out-manoeuvred them in extracting concessions. When things go wrong the hypomanic patient is adept at clouding the issue and shifting the blame, so that one is not quite certain what *did* happen. In these ways the patient sows seeds of dissension and arouses the hostility of those around him. He may well have produced the same effect on his own family before his admission.

The first step in effective management of the hypomanic is to recognise that these processes are going on. If the staff can recognise that they are being made angry by the effects of the patient's behaviour, then they can relax and see their own reaction as a feature of the patient's illness. They may still feel the emotion, but since they no longer take it personally there is not the same urge to act it out.

There is no doubt that a lot of self-control is required in managing the hypomanic. He repeatedly makes difficult demands, leaving one feeling guilty about a conservative decision. It is particularly difficult for those professionals who pride themselves on a liberal approach when they repeatedly find themselves being cast in an authoritarian role.

One needs self-control because under these circumstances one is tempted to resolve the tension either by setting arbitrary limits and refusing to budge, or by abandoning all attempts to set controls for the patient. One knows that neither course is ideal, but the intermediate pattern is difficult to achieve. For the best management of the patient, however, there is no substitute for a careful consideration of his demands, followed by a deliberate decision, which is then adhered to despite entreaty. One must be sure that it is a reasonable decision in the first place, of course, but then one must have the courage of one's convictions and not give in to feelings of guilt or heartlessness that the patient will engender by his attempts to gain concessions.

The patient can be relied upon, having been given his limits, to try all the time to extend them. If denied an extension, warmth and charm will turn to irritability and impatience on his part. Inevitably the therapist feels that he is not making his patient happy, and will tend to feel bad. He will do his patient the best service he can by remaining reasonable but firm. It is important for the therapist to remember to avoid arguing with the patient. This is a lesson that is easier to learn when dealing with frank delusions—one soon learns neither to confirm nor deny them.

With hypomanic behaviour one can readily slip up. With his superficially plausible manner, the patient can make the therapist forget that he is dealing with a case of someone who is mentally ill, and start discussing the demands on a point by point basis. It is easy to slide into an argument on details that the patient is likely to be better armed for, and the therapist is in danger of ending up quibbling. After giving his considered opinion the therapist should not be seduced into an acrimonious debate, but should be prepared to maintain his position without demur.

A further way in which the patient will produce management difficulties is by dividing the staff against each other. Judicious use of flattery of the present staff member, criticism of the absent staff member, and a partial account of the situation may exploit existing differences of opinion among the staff, towards which the patient often glides with uncanny sensitivity.

This calls for frequent meetings of the staff to discuss the management problem and to recognise the way in which they are reacting to the patient. Within the staff group, as well as within the individual member of the staff, it is important to make sure that one is not merely acting out the patient's psychopathology on his behalf.

The puzzle of the management of the hypomanic patient can be kept within acceptable limits, and even converted into an enjoyable task, if one anticipates the varied problems that are likely to crop up, and avoids taking them personally.

AETIOLOGY OF THE AFFECTIVE PSYCHOSES

Reactive and endogenous depression

In psychiatry there is widespread use of the contrast between *reactive* and *endogenous* depression. Reactive depression follows an unpleasant event, or series of unpleasant events. In endogenous depression no relevant loss or disappointment is found and the onset of the illness is attributed to some sort of biochemical or physical change in the body: what in turn produced the physical change is unspecified.

So far there is little disagreement. The next part of the thesis is that reactive depressions and endogenous depression, defined by aetiology, in fact produce different clinical symptoms and signs (phenomena). There is general assent to this proposition too, and though individual psychiatrists might not agree exactly about the phenomena concerned, suggested features include (for the *endogenous* depression) early morning wakening, diurnal variation in mood (worst in the morning), loss of appetite, loss of weight, and response to physical methods of treatment.

The concept as stated so far is acceptable. But when one tries to apply it to the total prevalence of depressive illness agreement breaks down. What is the proportion of endogenous to reactive cases? Can one in fact *see* endogenous and reactive cases as fairly distinctive groups? Many psychiatrists would say that, though the *concept* is useful, in fact what one comes across is a spectrum of different degrees of admixture, with relatively pure endogenous cases at one end, and fairly obvious reactive cases at the other, but the majority in between showing a mixture of the two types. In terms of descriptive statistics, the question is whether the distribution curve of incidence on the endogenous–reactive axis is unimodal or bimodal. There is at present active debate on this issue. As far as the non-psychiatrist is concerned the facts are:

1. If the 'spectrum', unimodal psychiatrists are right, then it follows that there are many cases that are not clearly either pure endogenous or pure reactive in type.
2. If the 'separate entity', bimodal psychiatrists are right, then there are many (other) psychiatrists who are unable to classify their individual patients into the correct groups.

In either case, the non-psychiatrist will not need to feel ashamed if he is unable to sort them out either.

There is one further obstacle to clear thinking. It is generally accepted that cases of depressive *psychosis* tend to be distributed towards the endogenous end, and cases of depressive *neurosis* go to the reactive end. Unfortunately there has grown up a not very happy habit of talking about depressive illness as either 'endogenous' or 'neurotic'. This is clearly, on consideration, an invalid distinction. One can logically make a contrast between endogenous and reactive, or separately between psychotic and neurotic, but to use *endogenous versus neurotic* is like saying that there are two types of human beings: those that live in the U.S.A. and those that do not have cars.

In addition, the term 'neurotic' is used in a rather derogatory sense, to carry with it the possible implication that the patient has had a life-long history of maladjustment in interpersonal relationships—and how can the poor psychiatrist expect to cure *that* with a few tablets? The nice endogenous depression (only some of whom will be psychotic in the sense of being frankly deluded or hallucinated) will be expected to get better rather gratifyingly and completely.

If we take the two dichotomies, endogenous versus reactive and neurotic versus psychotic, we can split cases of depression, in theory at any rate, into four categories (*see* Fig. 21).

	NEUROTIC	PSYCHOTIC
ENDOGENOUS	A	B
REACTIVE	C	D

Fig. 21. Classification of depression.

No problem is posed by those in group B (psychotic and endogenous) and those in group C (neurotic and reactive). If depressions always fell in these two groups then there would be no harm (except bruises to logic) in referring to depressions as *either* neurotic *or* endogenous.

What about those in group D, reactive and psychotic? Can it happen that a depressive illness of psychotic degree is precipitated by psychological (environmental) trauma? There is no coherent reason for supposing that this is impossible. In fact many psychiatrists believe that, in the majority of depressive illness that they see, of whatever degree, there are relevant factors in the recent history of the patient, in the form of losses, disappointments or other blows. One can argue that in smaller doses, or with relatively stable personalities, either no depressive illness will be produced, or the illness will be of only neurotic degree. As the psychological trauma continues the depression will deepen to the stage of physical phenomena (loss of appetite, loss of weight, early morning wakening, constipation, etc.), of severe retardation or agitation, and of false beliefs.

If this is the case then it is a paradox that such deep depressions appear to respond *better* to physical methods of treatment than do the reactive depressions in a less severe stage. This difficulty is not impossible to resolve, but the answer has not been proven. One has to postulate that it is the *physical symptoms and signs* that respond best to physical methods of treatment. At an early stage, before the depressed patient has developed such phenomena, the anti-depressants will have less effect. At the severe stage, the patient is so impressed by his response that his hopelessness disappears, the vicious circle of depression–despair–further depression is broken, and the patient is able to make the progress back to normality without much difficulty. It has been demonstrated that patients with physical phenomena do show the best response to drugs and E.C.T., but as far as I know the rest of this argument has not been empirically tested.

Let us now look at category A. Is it possible that there are endogenous depressions that only reach the neurotic level of severity? There seems to be no reason why this could not be so. Possibly many of the minor psychiatric illnesses that are treated in general practice are of this sort. They may not even be labelled as depressive illness: they may be called anxiety states, or no one may realise why the patient is in an unusually pessimistic and lethargic frame of mind. If so, then, these minor endogenous depressive illnesses will be very similar to the states that follow influenza, virus infections or treatment with certain drugs.

In these latter categories one can see that the illness is only endogenous in the sense that it does not result from psychological precipitants. There may be external agents (viruses, drugs) affecting the chemistry of the body.

Biochemistry of depression
Chemical changes in the body are known to occur in depressive illness. Alterations have been shown in the amount of hormones relating to the adrenal glands, the balance of sodium ions, and

possibly the concentration of amines in the cerebrospinal fluid (C.S.F.).

It is well known that the adrenal glands secrete hormones (such as adrenaline and cortisone) in response to stress. It will be recalled that the balance of sodium ions in the body is affected by salts of lithium.

As far as the amines are concerned, the activity of such amines as noradrenaline, dopamine or 5-hydroxytryptamine (5HT, serotonin) in the nervous system is thought to be affected by both tricyclic antidepressants and by the mono-amine oxidase inhibitors (M.A.O.I.s).

These chemical changes, then, certainly seem relevant to depressive illness. Their place in the aetiology of depression has not yet been firmly established, however. Firstly, it is possible that the changes that have been demonstrated arise as a *result* of the depressive illness. For instance, the changes in hormones relating to the adrenal gland might come about because of the undoubted stress of the depressive illness itself.

Secondly, even if the chemical changes are part of the chain of events that *lead* to the depressive state, it is still possible that they in turn are brought about *either* by psychological factors *or* by physical factors, just as flushing of the face can be produced by an increase in heat production or by a rise in the metaphorical emotional temperature. The demonstration of changes in biochemistry does not tell us what proportion of cases are endogenous in the sense used in this chapter.

Just in case by this time the water seems to be too muddied, let us finally clarify the various types of depressive illness one may find, according to aetiology.

1. Depressive illness in patients who at other times suffer from hypomania. These are likely to fulfil the criteria of the endogenous type most clearly.

2. Depressive illness, identical phenomenologically to those in 1, of a recurrent pattern. Since hypomania is a relatively rare manifestation of affective illness, many patients could have an identical aetiology to those in group 1.

3. Depressive illnesses following treatment with certain drugs (*e.g.* reserpine) or illnesses (*e.g.* virus infections). These, too, are

typically similar to those in group 1.

    4. Endogenous depressions not in categories 1 to 3.

    5. Depressive illness, in association with clear-cut, over-whelming psychological trauma of environmental origin.

    6. Many cases in which there is psychological trauma that one can see in the environment, but where it is debatable whether it is sufficient to account for the illness.

Depressive psychoses following childbirth or the menopause

These are no longer thought to be separate illnesses, unconnected with other mental illnesses (*e.g.* puerperal psychosis, involutional melancholia). They seem to be similar to depressive illnesses found at other times.

There is no doubt that the incidence of mental illness is high in later life, but whether this can be attributed to the menopause is conjectural, and even for those illnesses immediately following the menopause the aetiology could be:

    1. the effect of hormone changes in the body at that time;

    2. the psychological effect of realising that one is past reproductive age;

    3. neither of these—a coincidence.

During the childbearing age women show a pattern marked by a relatively low incidence of psychosis during pregnancy and a relatively high incidence in the weeks immediately after delivery. Again it is not clear whether the main influence is endocrine or psychological. Schizophrenic illnesses seem to show this pattern as well as the affective psychoses.

It has been found that *treatment* with hormones is fairly un-successful for depressions at these times (as it is at other times too) but orthodox treatment for depressive psychosis usually works very well. This does not necessarily demolish the case for an endocrine aetiology, but it makes the consideration of it rather academic for the average psychiatrist.

SUMMARY

If we accept that depressive psychoses may be precipitated by either psychological (losses, disappointments) or biological (drugs, viruses) stresses, then we have a wide range of treatments to choose from. Psychotherapy, antidepressant drugs (tricyclic and M.A.O.I.), lithium, E.C.T. and (rarely) brain surgery all have their advantages and their dangers. Hypomania is in some ways the opposite to depressive illness, in other ways very similar to it. Not only does it usually occur in the very same patients, but remarkably it often responds to similar treatments. If anything, hypomania responds more promptly to treatment than depression.

In depression, suicide is a risk, especially in patients who have made a previous attempt, and particularly if they are currently talking about the possibility of an attempt. Critical times are when energy is returning. Dangerous patients are those who smile through their sadness.

The hypomanic patient, if uncontrolled, may carry out acts that he will seriously regret after recovery. Attempts to control him as an in-patient are met with persistent efforts on his part to extend the permissible limits of behaviour which may cause endless recriminations between staff members. This has to be dealt with by anticipation and by frequent intercommunication.

With or without energetic treatment, depression may be a sudden complication of the hypomanic illness, and hypomania may ensue upon the depressive illness.

Both types of illness tend to remit without permanent damage to the personality. For this reason the effect on the social life of the patient need not be severe if employers, friends and relatives do not take too harsh a view of the episodes.

11 Other psychoses

To what extent should the epileptic be regarded as psychotic? Why are some people said to be 'as mad as a hatter'? What is wrong (if anything) with taking L.S.D.? Can yet get a psychosis with cannabis?

In which society do some patients 'run amuck' and others repeat word for word what is said to them? What terrifies a Chinese who has *Koro*? Can dieting be a psychosis? In this chapter we look at those psychoses that do not fit into the neat patterns that we have described so far.

At this point in the book we have already considered the typical features of the organic psychoses, schizophrenia, and the affective psychoses. This forms a basic framework into which we can try to fit other psychoses as we come across them. Life being what it is, we shall come across illnesses which do not fit into such a simple classification.

PARANOID AND SCHIZO-AFFECTIVE PSYCHOSES

Some, you may recall, we have already alluded to in passing. Should the paranoid psychoses that do not show unequivocal *schizophrenic* features nevertheless be included in the slot for schizophrenia? Or should they just be given a slot of their own?

The paranoid psychoses are easy to define but difficult to place.

The schizo-affective psychoses are not even easy to define, and there is a school of thought that believes that one should not use the term. The concept is an easy one—an illness that lies on the borderland between an affective psychosis and schizophrenia. This description fails to be of use as a definition, since we have already seen that we are entitled to expect to see any *affective* symptom or sign in acute schizophrenia anyway. So we are left with a rather unsatisfactory outline of our meaning—something like 'a psychosis in which the affective phenomena are prominent compared with the schizophrenic features'. Although unsatisfactory logically this category does seem to work in practice, in that it throws up a group of patients with conspicuous features in common (such as the gratifying response to E.C.T.).

EPILEPTIC PSYCHOSES

Both the paranoid psychoses and the schizo-affective psychoses are illnesses that, while functional in type, lodge uneasily in the cleft between schizophrenic and affective groups. The *epileptic psychoses* hesitate in their loyalty to functional illnesses on the one hand and organic disorders on the other. If one slices open the brain of an epileptic patient one may or may not find an organic lesion to account for the features of his illness, and it is by no means always possible to guess from the clinical phenomena in life which category he will come into at autopsy.

Opinion on the psychiatric disorder that results from epilepsy is changing. In the past textbooks have described a particular set of psychological characteristics that were said to mark out the epileptic. Nowadays that is thought to be too over-simplified a picture. This is a shame for those that like their psychiatry cut and dried, since a simple description is always easier to learn than the complicated ifs and buts. To try to keep it as straightforward as possible, what one has to do is first consider what *type* of epilepsy the patient has, and then to reflect on what has happened to the patient as a result of his brain dysfunction.

We can divide epilepsy into three main types: *petit mal, grand mal* and focal epilepsy.

Petit mal

In *petit mal* the signs are likely to start during childhood. The clinical picture is clear: the child has attacks lasting a few seconds in which he will pause in what he is doing, lose contact with his surroundings, and then carry on as if nothing has happened. These episodes are known as *absences*. The diagnosis can be clinched by the E.E.G., which shows the absolutely characteristic 3 cycle per second spike and wave abnormality. There is no gross brain disease, the condition is treated symptomatically with drugs, and the frequency of attacks can be reduced. The child may be affected psychologically by the concern of his parents, disruption of his schoolwork, and the dulling sedative effect of the drugs. Although disabling, these features hardly constitute a psychosis, so we will pass on to the remaining categories of epilepsy.

Focal epilepsy

In *focal* epilepsy abnormal psychological phenomena may easily be produced by the discharge. Depending upon which area of the brain is the source of the unco-ordinated electrical activity the patient may experience morbid sensations (hallucinations), strange behaviour or surges of emotion. Where the episodic nature of the disturbance is recognised (the single attack should last for seconds rather than hours) then the diagnosis is not especially perplexing. If attacks recur frequently or are at times confluent, the situation may be more difficult to unravel. We have already seen (Chapter 5) how temporal lobe epilepsy in particular may produce phenomena very similar to other psychoses. When a patient with abnormal behaviour is found to have an electroencephalographic abnormality in the temporal lobe it is sometimes difficult to know how much of the behavioural disorder can be ascribed to the epileptic focus.

Grand mal

For the patient with *grand mal*, if attacks are at infrequent intervals, and do not require large doses of drugs, then it may be possible to lead a fairly normal sort of life—it is even possible to get a driving licence under certain circumstances (currently with the proviso that there have been no seizures for over 3 years). If the *idea* of having epilepsy has not produced disastrous personality changes, and the patient is able to hold down a job and make friends, then there is no reason why he should not be free of psychological symptoms. But think of the alternative. Let us imagine a patient who has frequent fits that are difficult to control. Furthermore, let us take a patient who has spent, at the age of 50, most of his life in a mental hospital. What of his psychological status? Many factors will have interacted to produce the final result. The brain damage produced by repeated falls and injuries, the stultifying action of the drugs, the depressing awareness of the repeated seizures, institutionalisation from being cooped up all that time, and possibly more specific phenomena if the seizure, though a general one, spreads initially from a focus (*see* p. 107). There may be, too, the disability of the original brain lesion that produced the liability to epilepsy: at this stage in time it may be difficult to distinguish the cerebral pathology that is responsible for the fits from that which has resulted from them.

The epileptic and society

There are two more factors that must be considered, both of which concern the patient's relationship to society. To a great extent they are not specific to epilepsy, but are relevant to all disorders that may take a patient into the mental hospital. Firstly, not all patients who suffer from fits are taken to a mental hospital—far from it, only a small minority are. Secondly, as control of the fits, and symptomatic treatment for the behavioural changes take place, the patient may be expected to leave again in due course. It is found, for instance, that phenothiazine drugs will often work wonders in melting away the behavioural disorders associated with epilepsy, a benefit that may outweigh their tendency slightly to increase the frequency of the fits. So the population of patients with epilepsy in mental hospitals is a highly selected one. It may be expected that the physical severity of the pattern of seizures will not be the only factor in picking out those patients who remain, and they are also likely to be those most rejected by their relatives. It is also the hostile family, or the family at the end of its tether, which will be the first to insist on having its epileptic member being admitted to the hospital.

It is this unrepresentative section of epileptics that may have formed the basis in the past for the descriptions of 'epileptic psychosis' or 'epileptic personality' that appear in the older textbooks.

Character traits of the individual which are liable to make him more likely to stay in the mental hospital are those of passivity, dependence and 'inadequacy'. The patient who still behaves as a dependant, and treats the staff as parent figures, may fear the cold wind that blows in the world outside, and may actively resist discharge. At present only a small percentage of patients in hospital are compulsorily detained. Among the long-stay population the proportion is minute. The problem of the patient who will not go is much greater than the problem of the patient who would not stay.

These facts are relevant to the selective retention of *chronic schizophrenics*, but since these people tend to eschew close interpersonal relationships the character traits are not so noticeable in one's day-to-day dealings with them. The dependency needs of those *epileptics* who stay are more overt, and they tend to adhere to one in the ward, buttonholing visitors and regaling them with their symptoms, physical and mental, and showing a reluctance to break off the conversation. The need to please parent figures may also play a part in the *religiosity* that they have been noticed to show.

DRUG-INDUCED PSYCHOSES

It is accepted that psychoses sometimes follow, and appear to be precipitated by, the administration of drugs. According to the definition used in this book many do not show the essential characteristic of organic brain disease—gross visible (macroscopic or microscopic) changes in the brain—but rather produce disorders closely similar to schizophrenia and the affective psychoses. Nevertheless some psychiatrists would like to extend the concept of organic psychosis to include these drug-induced illnesses.

It is possible to produce *frank brain pathology* by using some drugs. They will poison the brain, and besides producing paralysis, ataxia or parkinsonism they also give rise to an organic brain syndrome (delirium, dementia, etc.). Carbon monoxide, plant alkaloids and industrial solvents have been incriminated. Lead poisoning causes fits rather than insanity, but other metals may cause psychological symptoms: the expression 'mad as a hatter' may have arisen from the liability in days gone past for those concerned with hat-making to become poisoned by the metal they used in the process (which was mercury). In general it is the toxic substances which produce fits, coma or death when taken in large amounts that will produce delirium or other organic psychoses in smaller amounts.

L.S.D.

Important as such overt states of poisoning are, it is of great fascination to turn to the drugs that mimic the functional psychoses. The term 'psychotomimetic' or 'hallucinogenic' is often used for L.S.D. but it is questionable whether this drug produces a very good imitation of a functional psychosis. Closer mimicry is produced by reserpine and amphetamine. We have seen how reserpine can precipitate an illness (Chapter 10) that is indistinguishable from a depressive psychosis, and which may result in suicide. We have also seen how amphetamine (Chapter 9) can produce a psychosis that is indistinguishable from schizophrenia of the paranoid type. The only thing stopping one saying that it *is* paranoid schizophrenia is that one knows that the symptoms and signs usually clear up on withdrawing the drug, and it does not seem right somehow that schizophrenia should be so easy to cure. The depressive illness that follows administration of reserpine does not necessarily abort so promptly, and is likely to require treatment in its own right.

What sort of psychosis is produced by L.S.D.? *Delusions* may certainly be conjured up. Some of the tragedies result from this. The belief that one can fly may induce the subject to launch himself from a high window; a conviction that he has superhuman skills may lead him to drive his car through a busy shopping area at high speed. *Perception* may be distorted, producing curious visual effects on the contrast between a figure and the background (sometimes likened to the paintings of Van Gogh) or overt hallucinations may occur. On a good trip the phenomena will be joy-inspiring, on a bad trip depressing or frightening. But one cannot call it an affective psychosis, because much of the content can be bizarre and incongruous. A schizophrenic illness, then? Many have talked as if it were a model for schizophrenia, but it has more of the delirious disorientation than is usual in a schizophrenic illness. The types of phenomena vary from person to person, and according to the mood and environment at the time when the drug was taken, at one time the emphasis being on the affective state (*e.g.* elation), another time being on the perceptual disorders, and yet another time on the disorientation. The L.S.D. psychosis is not in fact a convincing imitation of any one psychosis.

Other hallucinogenic drugs
Other hallucinogenic drugs, whether naturally occurring (*e.g.* mescaline) or synthetic, appear to have similar effects to L.S.D. Cannabis is sometimes included under the same category, but evidence at present available suggests that the euphoria produced is more usually comparable to that produced by alcohol or sedatives. There may be exceptions to this generalisation, especially when the subject has recently taken a more powerful hallucinogenic drug, such as L.S.D., under which circumstance a reappearance ('flashback') of the phenomena of the previous trip may occur.

PSYCHOSES OF OTHER CULTURES

Drug-induced psychoses
When one looks at psychiatric disorder in different environments one finds some that are found only in a particular cultural background and others that are universal. We have just been looking at the effects of *drugs*: obviously a disorder that is described in terms of use of a drug is only found where that drug is available—alcoholism or barbiturate addiction are examples. The same type of problems that make a man dependent on alcohol in Western Europe *may* lead to opium addiction in the Far East, but one cannot assume that they will always manifest themselves that way, nor that the underlying problems of addicts in different cultures are identical. Other disorders that are highly influenced by the culture probably include attempted suicide and antisocial behaviour. The extent to which traffic accidents are a manifestation of psychological disorder is a matter on which the reader will no doubt make up his own mind.

Psychiatric disorders
At the opposite extreme there are psychiatric disorders which are indubitably universal. Among these are the organic brain syndromes. The clinical pictures of delirium and dementia are recognisably similar in whatever part of the world they appear. In

delirium, the content of the visions will differ, but not the fact that in many cases of delirium visions will occur. In dementia, loss of ability to button a waistcoat in one culture will be matched with loss of skill in draping a sarong in another, but loss of faculties will be characteristic of the disorder.

Functional psychoses

What about the functional psychoses? As time goes by, there is less tendency to deny that they are universal. In the past there have been claims that certain cultures are free from (functional) psychosis. The attractive idea of the noble savage and the disenchantment with the stresses of modern society both tend to make one want to believe that it is true, but in fact further investigation usually proves such claims to be false.

Taking *schizophrenia* first, this is recognised among all ethnic groups of any size. Its manifestations do vary, though. Even taking into account the fact that a varying amount of weight is placed on one or other of the symptoms and signs in arriving at the diagnosis, countries far apart seem to have a differing proportion of the individual features of the illness. In one country religious delusions are common, in another rare. In one part of the world suicidal ideas are rife, in another homicidal ideas are to be expected.

Depressive illnesses are even more variable. Partly this may be because it is difficult to distinguish depressive psychosis from other severe depressive illnesses, and so on through to the minor depressions of ordinary life. The thought content of even frank depressive psychosis is variable, though, from country to country, for instance when we look at delusions. The four categories of guilt, disease, poverty and unworthiness are found in different proportions, guilt being relatively common in those societies that have been strongly influenced by European beliefs.

Exotic mental illnesses

There are mental illnesses which are not seen here at all. Probably the best example is *Koro*. This is a state of intense fear, intimately bound up with a conviction that the penis is shrinking. This illness is found among the Chinese, and almost never seen outside South-East Asia. A terrifying part of the delusion is the belief that when the penis finally disappears the patient will die. The pathetic subject may present clutching at his organ in a desperate attempt to avoid this fate. The state of high sympathetic tone that accompanies anxiety is likely to cause contraction of the involuntary muscle in the penis and reduce it to its smallest size in any case, so there may be additional evidence to feed the delusional belief.

Witigo is found among the Eskimo. Here the delusion is that those persons in his immediate vicinity are conspiring to kill the patient. He decides to save himself by killing them first.

Amok is found among people of Malaysian race, and is the origin of the expression 'to run amuck'. The afflicted subject rushes around in a frenzy, wielding the traditional long chopping knife (the *parang*). He will strike out at anyone blocking his path, injuring or killing them, and frequently ends up by attempting to kill himself. *Latah* is seen in the same ethnic group, and is less sensational. The patient, often a young female, appears to be in a daze, and responds to other persons in a stereotyped way, either repeating their statements (echolalia) or copying their actions (echopraxia).

The place of these exotic disorders in a classification of mental illness is debatable. *Latah* might not be considered a psychosis at all, but more akin to hysterical behaviour. *Koro* could represent a depressive delusion. It would be difficult to say more about *amok* without having the results of a mental examination on a series of cases: it is conceivable that this is like those cases of agitated depression that one sees closer to home where the patient, convinced that the world is a terrible place to grow up in, kills his family and then tries to kill himself. *Witigo* sounds like a patient beset by ideas of reference in an acute paranoid crisis; alternatively a cynic might suggest that the story was a convenient tale to cover up a murder carried out for other reasons—particularly if only the 'non-afflicted' survivors are there to tell the tale, having 'defended themselves' and killed the supposed patient in the process.

PSYCHOSOMATIC DISORDERS

Those physical diseases that are thought to have psychological factors as a dominant feature in their aetiology are referred to by some psychiatrists as forms of psychosis. This is not a popular view, and it certainly seems that a man with a peptic ulcer or asthma is rather a different kettle of fish from the man with schizophrenia.

The concept is more acceptable, however, when applied to that paradigm of psychosomatic illness, *anorexia nervosa*. In this condition, typically affecting an adolescent girl, carbohydrate restriction (aided where necessary by vomiting) serves to achieve a profound weight loss, so that the patient looks like a walking skeleton. The determination to keep up this dieting pattern is carried out with such conviction that its place in the realm of behaviour is reminiscent of the effect of a delusion in the realm of belief. Otherwise such patients do not suffer from delusions or hallucinations, and their actions may be regarded as wily rather than bizarre. But it may not be unfair to regard such a condition as a psychosis when the person places her health in such jeopardy, with a mortality of anything up to 10 per cent, and a chronic morbidity (permanent dietary idiosyncrasies) of up to 50 per cent. Long after the acute episode is over, perhaps decades later, such patients may be shown to have a quite abnormal body chemistry as a result of their curious diet, their vomiting, and their purging.

SUMMARY

So far we have followed a logical classification of mental illnesses in this book. Now we look at the misfits.

Somewhere uneasily between schizophrenia and the affective psychoses we have the schizo-affective disorders, with features of both, and the paranoid psychoses, with features of neither. Epilepsy lies on the borders of organic and functional disorders: here the problem is that one can get similar clinical pictures in one patient with visible brain pathology and in another patient with none. The child with *petit mal* is scarcely psychotic; the temporal lobe epileptic may have hallucinations, delusions and disordered behaviour; the patient with poorly controlled major fits may develop an organic brain syndrome.

Poisons may produce classical delirium or dementia. Other chemicals can mimic exactly the clinical syndromes described earlier in the book—as in the association between reserpine and depressive illness, and amphetamine and the paranoid schizophrenia picture.

The picture produced by L.S.D. is not that of a pure clinical form, and shows features of both schizophrenic and delirious states. Cannabis intoxication produces a distortion of reality that falls short of psychosis (at least when used in low dosage on isolated occasions): the exception is when the subject has already taken L.S.D. in the past, when psychotic 'flashbacks' may occur.

The intriguing psychoses indigenous to other cultures include delusional states (*Koro*), abnormal behaviour (*amok, latah*), and mixtures of the two (*witigo*). With *anorexia nervosa* one could argue the case for such life-threatening behaviour to be regarded as psychotic.

12 Psychological methods of treatment

It is fairly easy to find accounts of the laws of psychology or the principles of psychotherapy. What is not so easy to find is a psychiatric textbook that tells you what to *say* to the disturbed patient. I presume that the reason for this is that what one says is in practice governed by so many factors that to write down actual words in black and white may either give a misleading impression or even look downright foolish.

All the same, I feel sure that many readers would like to have *some* hints on how one can talk to disturbed patients, so I have grasped the nettle. In return, may I ask readers to expect some statements that are trivial, some controversial, and some homespun. In practice what one will say to patients will reflect not only circumstances and value judgments but also the unique individuality of the patient's personality.

It is customary to compare *curative* treatment and *symptomatic* treatment, with the former being regarded as superior. This contrast rather oversimplifies many real-life situations and, what is more, leaves out other aspects of treatment. These include *prevention* (in the sense of avoiding getting the illness in the first place) and, at the other extreme, *management*—dealing with the patient in such a way as to avoid further complications (but without necessarily improving the situation positively).

GENERAL PRINCIPLES OF
PATIENT MANAGEMENT

If the patient is managed well, then the course of his illness is not marred (more than is avoidable) by feelings of distrust towards the hospital staff, he does not feel he is being neglected, he does not think that those treating him are fools, rogues or arrogant heartless creatures, and he does not resort to acting out his distress by breaking windows, discharging himself prematurely or attempting suicide.

This does not mean to say that good management is the same thing as a smooth bedside manner, civility, supportive psychotherapy or maintaining a positive transference. It is all these things at times, but at times each of them must be discarded. *The essence of managing the patient well is detecting his current emotional needs and responding to them.* In the case of a therapeutic milieu it is similarly finding out the corporate emotional needs (of either the ward or whatever is the entity of the therapeutic community) and making the appropriate response. This does not necessarily mean gratifying them, but it does at least mean *recognising* them.

They way in which one recognises these needs varies from case to case. It often requires the therapist not only to realise what is going on himself, but to make it clear to the patient in some way that he has perceived it (and, in psychotherapy, making what may have been a non-verbal communication available for discussion). Let us take an example.

Case 36 Mr. H.C.

Mr. H.C. was an in-patient in a general hospital psychiatric ward. Now aged 40, he had been illegitimate, and his mother became an alcoholic. He wet the bed until he was 15 years old, and was bullied at school.

As an adult his problems were with his homosexuality and his dependence on drugs.

At one stage during his in-patient admission it was found that during his frequent excursions to his home he was picking up further supplies of drugs. This information came from another patient—let us call him Mr. B.

Mr. B. felt he had been told in confidence and though he thought it was important that the staff should know, he did not want Mr. C. to hear that he (Mr. B.) had spilled the beans.

This put the junior doctor in charge of the case into a dilemma. He was annoyed with the patient for taking non-prescribed drugs, and wanted to have it out with him. However, if he confronted the patient with his knowledge, he was afraid he would have broken the trust of Mr. B.

The problem was thrashed out at the case conference. It seemed likely that the taking of non-prescribed drugs was an important communication from Mr. C., and it was very possible that either consciously or unconsciously, he had *intended* the information to leak back to the medical staff.

Mr. C. was seen, told that there were rumours that he was taking such drugs, and asked if it were true. He hesitantly agreed. It was put to him that this was seen as his not being happy with the way he was being treated at that time, and the topic was thus made available for further discussion. The junior doctor did not express his annoyance, and Mr. C. did not ride his high horse on the subject of being caught by a confidence given to a fellow patient.

There are several points to note about this case.

1. The patient was in fact suffering from a paranoid psychosis, but that did not mean that he could not be talked to as a rational human being when off the subject of his delusions.

2. The reader may believe that the subject should not have been discussed with Mr. C.—that respecting the confidence of Mr. B. was more important. In this case it was not thought so, but the dilemma is real. With *better* management the staff might not have got into this position in the first place.

3. Supposing the interpretation was right—that he had been taking his own drugs because he was dissatisfied with the treatment he was receiving—then, since he seemed to need to act out this problem (not all patients have the temerity to criticise the treatment they are given directly to the staff) the *recognition* of it may have prevented his going to further extremes to express his displeasure. Given that the majority of the patients are in a depressed frame of mind when they are admitted, the way they express their resentment is often *intropunitive* in direction, turning their hostility in on themselves in a masochistic way. Thus they will discharge themselves against medical advice (aggravating the difficulties they are having with treatment) or they may take an overdose of drugs.

4. The junior doctor did not vent his spleen on the patient. It

is rarely good management to express affect-laden negative feelings towards a patient. (The only time it may make the patient feel better is when the patient himself has deliberately been trying to provoke such a reaction—and in those circumstances to gratify his psychopathology is likely to be the wrong *treatment*.) It is likely that he was angry partly because the patient had ruined the scientific value of the doctor's observations on the results of treatment so far (now he had no idea whether the patient's changes in behaviour were due to official treatment or the patient's own drugs) but also partly because he detected at some level the criticism of therapy implied by the patient's resort to private relief.

To express his anger, then, might merely have demonstrated his own sensitivity to criticism. It could certainly have been taken by the patient to mean just that. One has to learn to be aware of one's own feelings towards the patient, and to try to understand their origins before acting upon them. This is easier said than done, of course, and the doctor in this case was lucky, in a way, that he heard about the patient's behaviour at a time when the patient was not with him.

5. Although there was the danger of resentment being incurred in confronting the patient with his behaviour, it is also possible that Mr. C. derived much satisfaction from the demonstration that the staff were fully aware of what he was doing and what was happening to him. He would take this as positive evidence of their concern—rather more valuable to a suspicious patient than endless verbal protestations of their interest and sympathy from the staff. At least he does not feel neglected.

6. Discussion of the events with the patient showed that the staff were not fools. What does one want of a therapist? One wants him to be sympathetic or at least understanding. One also wants him to be reasonably intelligent. Let us consider the case of Mr. C. logically. He was taking his own drugs. In his mind either the staff knew about it or they didn't. We have considered what might have happened if they did not seem to get the message—he would probably have gone on to make it even more plain. Suppose, though, that in his fantasy the staff *do* know about it, Then, if they don't respond, they are either fools

or they are callous. Either they do not realise he is trying to say something, or they realise it and they could not care less. Much of what psychiatric patients do can be interpreted as testing whether their therapists are bright enough.

7. None of the previous points mean that the management described was particularly *therapeutic*. It was designed to avoid falling into traps for the unwary, so that the relationship between the patient and staff was not worsened, and so that the patient was not pushed into further acting-out behaviour. To the extent that it smoothed his path, it made continuation of therapy possible, but it was not a specific form of curative treatment in itself.

MANAGEMENT OF THE PSYCHOTIC PATIENT

The case quoted above illustrated some general principles of patient management, but they might equally have applied to a patient who was not suffering from a psychotic illness. Let us go on to consider the problems that are encountered because of the psychosis itself. What should you do when a patient tells you about his delusions?

It is tempting to point out to him the obvious fallacy in his logic, if only as a way of reassuring him that his fears are not true. This is usually poor management. You may find yourself drawn into an argument. It is usually a bad policy to argue with the patient, and the chances of your convincing him are slender. After all the delusion arises from roots in his psychopathology, and

'A man convinced against his will
Is of the same opinion still'.

The alternative is that he does not argue with you. It is a terrible feeling to see the look of sadness that comes over the patient's face, and to realise that you have disappointed him, when he thought that he had found someone at last that understood him.

The other temptation is to agree with him explicitly. 'Yes, I believe that your food is being poisoned.' 'I expect that the people on television are talking about you.' Again, the patient is likely to think you are a fool. Although he states such beliefs himself, and may even act on them up to a point, one has the impression that many psychotics do not entertain their delusions at all levels of consciousness. Although some patients complain to the police or the B.B.C., others take themselves to doctors or social workers, and still more can be persuaded to seek therapeutic help with tactful handling.

So where are we left? If it is wrong to argue with him, and wrong to collude with him, what *can* we do? The solution is simpler than it may appear. *When talking to the patient about his delusions one neither confirms nor denies them.* One can say, 'Tell me about these feelings you have about your food being poisoned' or 'I would like to hear more about the sensation you get when watching television'. Ideally one conveys to the patient that one believes that his distress, and often his perceptions, are genuine without commenting on his interpretation of them.

Suppose, you may ask, he specifically demands to know whether you believe him or not? How do you get out of that? In fact it is noteworthy that the patient is seldom unkind enough to put you in this difficult position. Somehow the majority of patients play fair. If you do not challenge them, they will not challenge you. This situation is likely to occur only when you have expressed some incredulity. However, let us suppose that you are landed in this predicament, whether or not with hindsight you could have avoided it. Answers are difficult, but not impossible.

For a start, you could say 'I believe that your distress, and probably your perceptions, are genuine but I do not know about your interpretations'. I would not really recommend such an academic approach though, particularly as it seems to end up with a good lead into a protest on the part of the patient that his beliefs are true. The patient may allow you to get away with 'I can see that what has gone on has been very upsetting'. This does not answer the overt question, but may really be answering the hidden question ('Do you really care about what is happening to me?'). Similar replies are 'I can see that you have had a hard time recently, and I would like to help you' or 'Well, I realise that you are very distressed and I would like to try to find the causes for it'.

It has to be admitted that some patients are cruel enough not to let you get off the hook so easily. What if you feel you are really obliged to give a direct answer? You can say 'I do not know whether your beliefs are true' if there is a shadow of doubt. If not, then one may be forced to admit that one does not really agree with the patient about the interpretation of events.

Now this last contingency is fraught with danger. It may result in the patient's breaking off treatment. This cannot always be avoided, but in many cases it can. The aim is to find some common ground on which the therapist and the patient agree (usually not impossible), and to try to keep the conversation to that area. One may even make this explicit with the patient.

'We do not really agree about (your belief in so-and-so), but I would still like to help you. Can we talk about your job situation for a bit? . . . .'

There are ways of avoiding giving a direct answer even when given the straight question, and some of these techniques are explored in the following paragraphs.

Distraction
The essence of distraction is changing the subject. This can be done in a fairly compelling manner, so that despite himself the patient's attention is diverted away from the original subject.

In a way it is not playing fair by the ordinary rules of conversation, and one should only use it when the alternatives are worse. For instance, one sometimes gets quite unreasonable requests from psychotic patients. One of the commonest in a mental hospital is 'Can I go home now?'. That the question is unrealistic is often made all the more obvious by the fact that the patient is in an open ward, and there is no physical reason why he should not just leave the hospital the next time he has a pretext to walk through the door. (Admittedly there may be moral constraints but let us assume for the purposes of the illustration that there are none in this case.) What is one to do when repeatedly the patient's opening remarks are couched as a request to go home?

On the first few occasions one will try to give a straightforward response. One will deal with it objectively, sympathetically and with concern. Possible replies might be:

'Well, are you feeling better now then?'
'Do you feel you will be able to cope?'
'What is the situation regarding your accommodation?'

and as a result of the answers the conversation can become a constructive discussion on whether discharge is currently appropriate, or alternatively on what steps have to be taken before it is indicated.

If attempts along these lines show that the repeated question is quite unrealistic, one may change tack and respond to the feeling tone behind the question rather than the specific question itself:

'I can see you are feeling impatient to get out of here'

'I expect you are feeling homesick'

'You must feel cooped up'

or a similar response which opens up the possibility of the patient's ventilating his frustration and at least ending up with the impression that you understand how he feels.

Sometimes even this fails to help. The patient keeps on reiterating 'I want to go home'. Obviously one should not neglect to explore the possibility that he is right and the staff are wrong—that in fact it *is* possible or even desirable that one should make a special effort to get him home by some means or other. However, let us return to the case where it is still an irrational and inconceivable request. Some patients just seem to use the demand as a stick with which to beat the staff, with no rhyme nor reason behind it, and without responding to any of the above attempts to deal with it.

At this stage one is entitled to consider using the technique of distraction. A very real possibility at this point is that by trying to use other methods of psychotherapy and failing, one will simply engender a negative attitude between the patient and oneself (possibly in both directions).

So, the next time you meet him and he importunately asks you 'Can I go home now?', you may reply. 'How are you sleeping?'.

This does not sound completely irrelevant—presumably it would be nice if you had cured his insomnia before he went—but in fact you know that he usually wishes to discuss his sleeping habits so eagerly that the chances are it will be possible to slide off the subject of his going home without giving any offence or sounding brusque and unsympathetic.

Of course the danger of this technique is that, if the patient tumbles to the fact that you are treating him this way, he will think of you as devious, patronising, insincere or possibly worse, and you may lose some of the trust you have been trying to build up on the basis of fair dealing. It is only if the alternative is that of a stand-up argument, or the patient's acting out his frustration, that you would consider it worth the risk.

Answering with a question
The technique of distraction is worth considering on its own, but it is just one example of the general case of answering a question with a question. Although it sounds artificial it is in fact used in ordinary conversation.

    1. *Q.* Where is my jacket?
       A. How should I know?
    2. *Q.* Where are you going now?
       A. Why do you ask?

It is a way of continuing the conversation without giving a direct answer. It is often legitimate, if further information is required before a precise answer can be given, but it can also be used in a hostile manner, to express resentment or non-cooperation.

It is used clinically when the therapist wishes to avoid committing himself, or wishes the patient to reflect on his own behaviour or to take responsibility for it.

    Q. Am I getting any better?
    A. What do you think yourself?

Such a reply is acceptable if used sparingly, but the patient is liable to get irritated and frustrated if he feels he never gets a straight answer.

There is a current joke—'Why does a psychiatrist always answer a question with a question?'. The joke is completed when the person making it (who has to be a psychiatrist) replies with one of a number of alternative questions, depending on the sense of humour of the audience—'You're asking me?', 'How should I know?', 'Is it true?', etc. (The same joke is found with one or other ethnic group name substituted for 'psychiatrist'.) I am aware that in cold print it is likely to appear as a remarkably unamusing joke. I present it to show the extent to which the technique of answering a question with a question is being exploited currently in psychiatric circles.

The reflective answer
A similar phenomenon is the reply that, while not being a question, continues the conversation without in fact answering the question.

1. *Q.* Why am I in here anyway?
   A. I imagine you have some idea yourself.
2. *Q.* What is going to happen to me?
   A. I wonder what you are afraid might happen.
3. *Q.* Why can't you see me more often?
   A. It seems that you feel I am neglecting you.

This type of answer is used frequently for the same reason as answering with a question. It clearly has much the same effect. It is not quite so open-ended as the 'question' answer, and it may be used to lead the patient onto a particular train of thought with such words and phrases as 'Perhaps you believe . . .' and 'I wonder if you feel that . . .'.

Interviews

Structured and unstructured interviews

When starting an interview a therapist normally asks an open-ended question rather than a closed question. He is more likely to say 'What is the problem?' or 'How are you getting on?' (to which there could be innumerable different replies) than 'Is your date of birth January 5th 1943?' (to which there are few common acceptable responses).

During the first part of the interview with a patient it is customary to ask the patient in general terms why he has come up for consultation, what is bothering him and so on and then to ask further open ended questions, *e.g.* 'What was that about your mother?' or 'What other worries do you have?', to get the patient to paint in the picture. Later on in the interview the therapist will wish to tie up loose ends and get particular details by asking specific questions ('How many brothers and sisters do you have?' or 'How old were you when your father died?') and at that time the interview may become more structured, even to the point of the therapist completing a check list of questions.

With the average patient this works very well. The patient feels that he gets a chance to express himself in the first part of the interview, while the therapist at that time gets to observe the patient's more obvious patterns of speech and behaviour and hears his current preoccupations. During the second part of the interview the therapist can systematically go through various questions in his own mind and ask relevant questions on, for instance, whether the patient is suicidal or homicidal, whether he is taking medication, whether he has symptoms of psychosis, and other factors that may not have come up spontaneously in the unstructured part of the interview.

These two different types of interviewing can produce different emotional reactions from the patient. Apart from the fact that, short of a veterinary approach, it makes sense to hear what the patient himself is worried about before deciding what to ask him, it also fits in with the patient's needs. He may be bursting to pour out his troubles, and obtain the relief of telling them to another person, who may hear them with understanding and compassion. It will dampen his spirit for the therapist to intervene and show interest in only certain aspects of his mental life, especially if the patient sees the questions as arbitrary or irrelevant.

This aspect of the difference in emotional reaction of the interviewee is easily appreciated. What may be less obvious is that many psychotic patients do not feel this way. They find the lack of structure disturbing. They feel expected to talk, but don't know what to say. They are not particularly keen, anyway, to bare their soul. They may fear the interviewer, be suspicious of him, or feel spied upon. They may have fantasies that he can read their thoughts. In the unstructured interview they do not know what is going on, and any paranoid fears are worsened. It is often during this type of interview that thought disorder becomes apparent: it is possible to construe the emergence of this as a defence mechanism (*see* Chapter 3).

During the structured interview they know better where they are. They have a specific question to which they can say 'yes', 'no', 'I don't know', or to which they can refuse to reply. It behoves the examiner to be alert to possible distress during the unstructured interview (which may manifest itself in subtle or bizarre ways) and either to switch to a more structured approach, or alternatively take steps to wind up the interview as soon as possible.

Negotiations with the patient

There is usually a third part to the interview. After the first, unstructured part, characterised by open-ended questions, and the second, structured part with the finite questions, comes the negotiation. A bargain is struck. Often it is a very simple agreement.

'See you next week, then?'
'Yes, all right.'

Sometimes it is more complex—for instance if the therapist is recommending admission to hospital. Before agreeing to this the patient may wish to be assured that it will not be a locked ward, or that he will not be in the company of violent patients.

Case 37

A 20-year-old patient was in a gynaecological ward after an operation. As a result of the operation she had lost her libido. She also felt that she had an undiagnosed complication and repeatedly complained of pain. She was requiring heavy sedation to get to sleep and also needed pain-killing injections by day. She developed a number of dramatic symptoms after being told she was due to go home.

At the psychiatric interview she said she could not face going home to the boyfriend with whom she was living as she was not able to entertain the thought of physical proximity to him in her present state. She had a number of features of anxiety and depression, and talked in thinly veiled terms about the possibility of attempted suicide.

She had had psychiatric treatment in the past which she had broken off. It seemed reasonable to offer her a bed in a psychiatric ward.

Although she appeared to welcome the suggestion (and one felt she was almost pressing for it) she needed reassurance on a number of points before she accepted it. Would she have to spend her day building coloured wooden bricks? (A curious notion, possibly a fusion of some elements of an intelligence test with the idea of occupational therapy.) No, we were able to tell her that arrangements for occupational therapy were flexible. Would she be prevented from going out when she wanted to? Well, she would be an informal patient in an open ward. Her next demand was that her boyfriend should not be told that it was a psychiatric ward. We would not agree to this one. We were reluctant to start treatment on a basis of deception anyway, but it seemed to be a forlorn hope on her part that he would not discover the truth from some chance remark on the part of a patient or a member of the staff. Despite the fact that we would not grant her this request she still accepted the bargain as a whole.

On the whole patients respect their bargains, with the proviso that they must have made them wholeheartedly in the first place. If an in-patient wishes to go home for the weekend, it is sometimes difficult to know if he is ready for it. If the request is neither unrealistic on the one hand, nor clearly overdue on the other, then it may be impossible for the person in charge of management to make a definite decision purely on the basis of the remaining signs and symptoms of the illness. Some patients who are still far from well manage to cope, others who have few remaining features of their illness find that they make a mess of things and return early or have an exacerbation of their illness.

The single most useful piece of information in predicting the outcome is the response of the patient when asked simply if he feels he will be able to handle the problems he may face on the weekend. Unequivocal affirmative replies suggest that the weekend will in fact go well, ambivalent responses bode ill. It is not just that the patient is likely to know best what his own attitudes to his environment are, there also is an element of nailing his colours to the mast. If he has told the therapist that he thinks it will be all right, then he feels, consciously or unconsciously, obliged to make that amount of extra effort to ensure that it does work out well. If he has not given any such reassurance, then he feels under no obligation to try, and may in fact get some pathological satisfaction from proving that the staff were misguided in letting him go at that stage. Rewarding this last morbid trait can be lessened. If the patient seems set on going, or the weekend is agreed to despite an element of lingering doubt, then pointing out to the patient that one is not absolutely certain that it is the right thing to do cuts down any satisfaction he may get from proving the staff to be fools. This can be done more supportively by adding that he should feel free to return to the hospital if things do *not* go well.

If the patient is too psychotic to negotiate explicitly along these lines it is usually obvious at the time. The clue will be given by thought disorder or irrelevant replies, returning to the subject of the delusion, or lack of interest in the topic under discussion. Nevertheless it is remarkable how, within the limits of their psychoses, even severely disturbed patients do keep their implicit bargains.

The suicidal patient

When a psychotic patient is suicidal the therapeutic attention to the underlying psychosis is probably the most radical way of actually *treating* the suicidal feelings. Nevertheless the feelings themselves require particular attention while waiting for the psychosis to be brought under control.

Some aspects of the management of the suicidal patient were considered in Chapter 10. Suicidal feelings are not the prerogative of the patient with depressive psychosis, however, and they may occur in the patient with schizophrenia or in the patient with organic brain disease, personality disorder or indeed in any of us. Some general aspects of the management will therefore be considered here.

The practice of searching patients for potential suicidal weapons has been seen to be itself a double-edged sword. One has to set against the physical advantages of this policy the psychological disadvantage that the whole procedure may *suggest* to the patient that this is the type of behaviour that is expected of him. Though the force of suggestion might have little effect on a well person, in the patient who already feels hopeless and who has uncertain control over his behaviour, an act of desperation may beckon compellingly.

The main principle used in the management of the suicidal patient is that *talking out his problems is likely to minimise the need to act out his problems.* It is common experience that a person with a load of despair can often obtain relief by talking about his woes to a willing listener. Although at the end of the day there is no tangible improvement in his environmental circumstances, he feels better for having unburdened himself, and goes on his way with fresh spirit.

When a patient hints that he feels that life is no longer worth living, the skilled therapist will not make soothing noises and reassure him. Instead he will allow the patient to ventilate to the full his pessimism and desperation.

It seems that if the patient really believes that he has conveyed his feelings adequately, he does not have to demonstrate how he feels. A patient who is regarded as hysterical, attention-seeking or histrionic, and who is treated as if his expressions of woe are insincere, will experience a need to 'show them' so that 'they will be sorry' they didn't believe him. This seems incredible at first, but some patients behave in such a self-punitive way when they are violently depressed it has to be believed.

The patient, then, is allowed or even encouraged to pour out his feelings of hopelessness, so that he does not feel any need to prove that he has them. What then?

Many inexperienced therapists shy away from such an approach for the very reason that they do not know how to handle the situation when they have allowed it to develop. Important guidelines at this time are that the therapist:

1. does not have to offer dramatic solutions;
2. does not have to persuade the patient that the future *is* worth living;
3. should avoid being persuaded by the patient that his situation *is* hopeless;
4. should implicitly or explicitly keep hope alive;
5. should ensure that any form of suggestion in his statements should be to the effect that he expects the patient *not* to kill himself (though without appearing unsympathetic);
6. should make help available to the patient on a regular basis and at times of crisis.

The resulting response does not have to be complicated. In a mild case the simple invitation, at the end of the interview, to come for another talk the following week (with a number to 'phone if a crisis develops) may fulfil all these requirements.

In a patient with a florid psychosis the management may well have to be in hospital. Let us take the guidelines one at a time.

1. *No dramatic solutions* Members of the helping professions tend to have a crusading urge to solve all the problems of the world, and get frustrated or lost when this proves impossible. What happens if you cannot see an obvious solution to the person's problems? Try saying sympathetically: 'You really seem to feel that your problems are insuperable at the moment'. (If, in fact, there *are* obvious solutions to his problems then by the same token it is worth hesitating a while before suggesting them—there may be a good reason why the patient has not tried them himself.)

2. *Persuasion is not necessary* The suicidal ideation is of the same quality as a delusion. It is pointless arguing with the patient about it—he will merely regard you as antagonistic or without understanding. It is sufficient to accept it as an indication of the feeling tone of the patient.

3. *Avoid being persuaded* It is sometimes easy to fall into the trap of feeling that the patient is right—he would be better off dead.

This is dangerous as it may communicate itself to the patient.

A patient may have all sorts of unpleasant things happening in his real life. The unguarded therapist can easily see himself in such a situation and realise that he might feel the same way under those circumstances. He should remember that it is virtually certain that in a short space of time his patient will have lost his suicidal feelings and feel differently about his problems. If you *then* ask how he sees his life he will talk, if not cheerfully, at least constructively and realistically about how he intends to surmount these hurdles, now that the will to do so is there.

It is sometimes argued that human beings have the *right* to kill themselves and that it is an unwarranted intrusion with their freedom to take away that right. In fact one sees so often that the suicidal feelings are transient that it appears reasonable to allow patients a chance to recover from their black mood of despair before letting them go ahead.

4. *Keeping hope alive* Partly this is similar to item 3—avoiding a collusion with the patient that all hope is gone. In addition one should avoid saying anything to the patient that might be construed as meaning that all hope is lost. One should be careful, when sympathising with the patient, to avoid saying 'Yes, the future does look black' and instead say 'Yes, I can see that *you feel* at present that the outlook is black'.

5. *Remember the power of suggestion* The patient is influenced by what he perceives the therapist to believe. If the patient thinks that the therapist really expects him to kill himself before the week is out, then his pessimism and despair is confirmed.

The practice of removing sharp objects, ties and belts was mentioned earlier. Though there may be circumstances in which this is necessary, there can be little doubt that it may act as a form of suggestion to the patient—a psychological force that makes him more likely actually to believe that he is doomed. With the era of active treatment a similar dilemma crops up with the use of antidepressant medication. Taking two tablets, three times a day, then 4 weeks' supply will amount to a bottle of 168 tablets. In a fairly typical case of depressive illness, where the patient has had some thoughts of life being not worth living, but not appearing to need urgent hospital admission, should a doctor blandly give the patient so many tablets to take away with him (or a prescription for them, which amounts to the same thing)?

What are the alternatives? The doctor could entrust the tablets to a relative, to be handed out dose by dose. He could prescribe just 2 or 3 days' tablets at a time.

In my opinion, in the average case none of these solutions is correct. The problem is that one extreme is foolhardy and the other is fraught with suggestion. Just sending a patient off with 168 tablets after he has told you about his feelings of hopelessness may be interpreted by him as meaning either that you do not believe him or that you do not care what he does: in his bitter, inturned, depressive anger he may take his own life 'just to show them'.

The other extreme, of dispensing the tablets a few at a time, is strongly suggesting to the patient that you believe his suicide is imminent. He may find the strain of this vote of no confidence too much to bear.

How do we escape from this dilemma? One answer, with many patients, is to allow *them* to make the running. The majority are not going to take an overdose, so it is often reasonable to point out to the patient that the total number of tablets is 168, and to ask them if they feel comfortable in accepting such a large number. Usually they will affirm their willingness to do so, sometimes with a smile—of pleasure that you have recognised what they have been saying—or possibly of amusement that you thought they were *that* bad. If they show any hesitation in accepting this deal then one has to think again.

An alternative, supposing that one feels the risk is more serious, is to ask them if *they* feel that they would like someone else to look after the tablets, or if *they* would prefer the pharmacist to release the tablets a few days at a time. Although the danger of suggestion is obviously present to some extent with this approach, it is not of the same order as with the earlier alternatives considered. If you had issued the decision as a command, the patient could end up with the fantasy that you are certain in your own mind that he is destined to kill himself. Discussing it with the patient as a possible course of action is more likely to allow the patient to believe that you are merely considering all avenues.

One loses little by sharing the decision with the patient. As a rule even severely depressed patients will indicate which alternative they prefer. Having committed themselves to it in an uncoerced fashion they will stick to their side of the bargain subsequently.

There are exceptions, of course. The patient who assures you too over-emphatically that you are quite safe to leave the tablets in her hands is a worry. This evidence of insincerity was recognised by Shakespeare:

> 'The lady doth protest too much methinks'
> (Hamlet, Act III, Scene II).

6. *Make help available* There is a natural revulsion to hearing someone talk about suicide in the same way as one is repelled by the idea of a patient wanting to talk about his cancer. What do you say to someone in that position?

The novice will be afraid of getting into a conversation on such topics partly because they are unpleasant in themselves, partly because he feels unable to offer any useful solutions, and partly because he just does not know what sort of responses to make during the conversation.

We have already discussed some of the things that can be said to a suicidal patient. In general they are those things that will encourage the patient to speak even further about how badly he feels. Well, you may ask, after we have done this, what do we say next? Even if practically the whole of the interview is taken up with this technique, what do we say at the end? We can't just walk away into the sunset.

We have already seen that no dramatic solutions are called for. It is difficult for the beginner to believe that he does not have to say *something* constructive, to make *some* suggestion of how things could be improved. He will soon find, if he tries, that he merely receives a metaphorical slap in the face from the severely depressed patient, who remains convinced that the future is unremittingly unpleasant.

Of course, one cannot just get up and go. Sometimes one can think of appropriately constructive things to say which are appreciated by the patient. But one should not feel obliged to sit racking one's brains for a brilliant suggestion. All one needs to say, as a rule, is something like, 'Well, I would like to talk to you some more about this. Can we meet again tomorrow (or next Friday, or next week)?'. The patient has probably been helped by feeling understood, by ventilating his despair, by being accepted, and possibly by feeling comforted that there is someone who does not share his pessimism. He does not need to have all his problems solved at a stroke, and he is usually content to accept the offer of another meeting which holds out hope for him that solutions will be found eventually, and also means to him that someone cares.

There is always the chance, clearly, that a fluctuation in mood may bring an exacerbation of his suicidal feelings before the following appointment comes round. For this reason he should be given clear instructions on how to obtain help if this occurs—for the out-patient a 24-hour telephone number (or preferably more than one), for the in-patient a positive invitation to tell one of the staff members or (with milieu therapy) one of the other patients that he is feeling worse.

It will not surprise those well acquainted with human psychology to learn that the more one leans over backwards to make sure they know how to get help, the less they actually have to test out the situation and apply for help as an emergency. The knowledge that they can get it is therapeutic in itself.

It is my belief that, if handled carefully, a large proportion of suicides are preventable. This is less so with severe personality disorders, alcoholics and drug addicts, many of whom make attempt after attempt. Among psychotics the schizophrenic patient is probably the most unpredictable. A patient with a severe depressive illness will sometimes surprise one with the timing and impulsiveness of his suicidal attempt, but on the whole if he communicates freely then one can do a lot to avoid his untimely death.

MANAGEMENT OF THE DIFFICULT PATIENT

Psychiatric training

Patients may prove 'difficult' for a variety of reasons. They may be violent, unco-operative or inaccessible. The extent to which patients behave in a violent or unco-operative way depends a great deal on the way that they are handled. In hospital practice whether or not the nurses are psychiatrically trained makes a dramatic difference. A patient who has proved quite unmanageable in a general ward may quieten down and become peaceful and calm when he is transferred to a psychiatric ward, without any specific measures at all. How is this done? It is difficult to describe, but it clearly has something to do with the attitude of the nursing staff and their behaviour.

If the staff on the ward panic and show their fright, the situation is aggravated. Clearly it is difficult to know exactly what is going on in the mind of the severely disturbed patient but it may be that the fearful expressions on the faces of the staff look like hostile expressions (fear is different from, but very close to, anger). Possibly the dimly perceived knowledge that not only is he out of control of himself but also that those around him do not seem to be masters of the situation either is a frightening realisation.

In those general hospital wards where disturbed patients are a rarity, and where psychiatric training has been inadequate, fear and concern may show themselves all too clearly in the behaviour of the staff, and this is perceived in the above ways by the patient. By contrast, on a well-run psychiatric ward, if the staff are afraid of the patient they will try not to show it, and they will continue to be firm but considerate towards him. They will take pains to help him with his controls over his behaviour, to set down simple, clear limits if possible, and on the whole treat him as if it is *he* that has the problem of fear, rather than they.

To some extent the success of these policies breeds its own success. The confidence gained in having handled aggressive patients makes it all the more easy to deal with future situations without panic. Until this happy state arises, though, the advice just given may be difficult to follow. It is rather like being told that a lion does not attack if you gaze at him staunchly. I am not even sure if that is sound advice—as far as lions are concerned. One shares the hesitation of the small boy who was told that the lion is not supposed to attack if you stare him in the face, and asked 'Does the lion know that?'. One has more direct experience of human beings, and the patient has to be very disturbed indeed who is so out of touch with his surroundings that he is not influenced by suggestion. If one demonstrates the *expectation* that he will fight and be difficult he is more likely to behave that way than if one conveys the expectation that he will settle down again.

Of course, ideally one does not get into this situation in the first place. One must be alert, particularly with new patients, for any hint that they may be fearful or suspicious, and one must lean over backwards to avoid precipitating a crisis. The experienced members of staff will automatically provide (in generous doses) reassurance for the fearful, information for the paranoid, clear-cut instructions for the ambivalent and structure (whether in conversation or in the day's activities) for the perplexed.

Patients who are self-critical

In dealing with psychiatric patients one should start off by assuming that they are experiencing high levels of hostility feelings that will mar their interpersonal relationships. Foulds and Hope (1968) have shown this to be true for the majority of patients recently admitted to psychiatric hospitals whom they examined (using formal questionnaire techniques). The hostility may be present in various forms. It may be directed outwards or inwards. If directed outwards it takes the form of criticism of others, an urge to act out one's problems, or a tendency to blame one's problems on others ('projection'), sometimes in a paranoid delusional way. The hostility may be turned inwards in the form of guilt or self-criticism.

The patient whose hostility is intrapunitive in direction presents less of an overt management problem. Unless he is actually suicidal, the main difficulty for the novice is likely to be in carrying on a conversation in which the patient repeatedly says things like:

'It's all my fault anyway'
'I know I'm no good'
'Nobody likes me, I'm so selfish' and 'I've always done the wrong thing'.

So long as one remembers neither to confirm nor deny the patient's delusional or over-valued ideas, this is not too difficult to learn to deal with.

Patients who criticise others

If the hostility is directed outwards in the form of an urge to act out problems, we have seen earlier that getting the patient to *talk* out his problems takes away some of the need for acting out.

An excessive *criticism of others* is a feature not confined to psychotic patients. It can be very difficult to manage. There are two conspicuous reasons why this should be so. Firstly, the criticism may be directed at oneself, and one's indignant reaction may bring about difficulties with achieving an objective handling of the situation. Secondly, it is not always obvious to start with that one *is* being criticised—it may be a more subtle implication that just leaves one with a dissatisfied or puzzled feeling. The next time you have the nasty sensation, at the end of an interview when the patient or client walks out of the door, that he is no further on or quite unhelped by the interview, ask yourself what has happened. It may be, of course, that this is a realistic objective appraisal—you were of no help. Often, however, the neurotic (or psychotic) hostility levels of the patient operate as a veiled criticism of all that you are doing, and leave you feeling nihilistic yourself.

The way to deal with such patients, whether the criticism is overt or subliminal, is not difficult in theory but in practice may take a long time to accomplish. Firstly, one must become sensitive to such emotional communications, so that one can readily detect and mentally label them. Secondly, one must learn to avoid indulging in the natural reflex of returning the patient's hostility. It is obviously bad to let one's own anger towards the patient influence the relationship. In time you can learn not to show your annoyance at the criticism, to regard the criticism as the patient's problem rather than your own (after all, he probably spreads his criticism round about on most of those he meets), and in the long run you may even not *feel* the anger in the first place, but be able to see the criticism as a weakness of the patient rather than a pointer to your own weakness.

Suspicious patients

We now come to the problem of dealing with the *suspicious* patient. In line with earlier policy, one does well to assume as a matter of course that psychiatric patients may find it difficult to believe others, wonder about hidden motives, and in general have difficulties in readily developing a relationship based on warmth and trust. Assuming this, one will start the first interview with a new patient in a way that does not rub salt into the wound. One will not gush warmth in an initial approach as this will be difficult for the patient to respond to, and will only heighten his sense of inability to cope with personal contact. Instead one adopts a more neutral approach, not making any demands on the patient to return a smile or an effusive greeting.

The interview with the patient is likely in itself to prove helpful—a powerful method of minimising the tendency to paranoid beliefs is the provision of information. So provided that the therapist does some of the talking, the patient will get to know him. This applies to that part of the transaction when therapist and patient are face to face.

It often happens that one has to talk to other persons about the patient. The patient can easily get the impression that one does not really have his interests at heart, but that one is conspiring with his relatives or the authorities against him. This can be dealt with by interviewing his relatives always *in his presence.* At first sight this might appear to be an unattractive proposition. It is not popular with the relatives, it might limit what they can tell you about him, and in any case is it not futile, since the patient does not know whether you are seeing them when he is not there? In practice it works quite well. It is surprising how rarely one misses any information of consequence because the relatives are inhibited by the presence of the patient (one might even argue that this technique is a means of inducing a more healthy adult frankness between relatives and patient). No doubt the patient is reassured not only by the tangible evidence that the relatives, on that occasion at least, are talking to you in front of him, but also by the fact that you are taking trouble to avoid any suggestion of going behind his back.

When dealing with employers, local authorities and general practitioners one can telephone them with the patient in the room (having obtained his permission—usually readily granted under these circumstances). One will start off the telephone conversation with 'I am speaking to you about Mr. John Smith, who is in the room with me . . .'. Again it is remarkable how little this inhibits genuine communication with the third party, or how little the patient appears to resent hearing only one end of the conversation. Naturally one will tell him what was said at the other end after putting the receiver down, but the extent to which this is an edited version is something of which he knows he remains ignorant. A little embarrassment can occur sometimes when the third party, despite being told of the presence of the patient, talks loudly on a clear line in terms which they would almost certainly not use if they knew the patient could hear. Sometimes they are quite audible to the patient. I can recall on occasion pressing the receiver more and more firmly to my ear to try to blot out the uncensored words. Admittedly I cannot remember a case in which the unexpected revelations seem to have done any harm.

Uncommunicative patients

Turning to the *uncommunicative* patient, we are now in a better position to understand him and to manage him. Why does a patient fail to talk to those who wish to help him? This can be seen as an example of intropunitive hostility—cutting off his nose to spite his face. It certainly occurs in depressive illness, and no doubt both masochistic urges and lack of interest and energy (retardation) play their part. Here the therapeutic attack will need to be on the underlying depression itself. It can also occur with the suspicious patient—he does not really believe that the staff wish to help him. Here management on the lines referred to above—providing information and avoiding 'confirmation' of his suspicions—will pay dividends. Other patients are silent (or relatively so) out of pique. Because they resent some way in which they have been handled they display their anger in this self-defeating way. Often such patients have the habit of hurting themselves when angry with others as a life-long personality trait. This is analogous to the teenage girl who takes an overdose when angry with her father, or to Harlow's maternally deprived monkeys who (instead of showing normal aggression) sit and bite their own arms.

How does one deal with the 'silent treatment' handed out by such a patient? In psychoanalytically-oriented methods of psychotherapy a silence will be interpreted directly to the patient as resistance to treatment on his part. In some cases this will have a dramatic effect in bringing the situation to a head. The patient will break his silence, possibly to deny the suggestion, but maybe to discuss his feelings constructively. However, in many psychotic patients insight-oriented interpretations are either contraindicated or irrelevant. Here a more supportive approach may be tried.

If one suspects that the above interpretation—the patient resists treatment—is true, one can base supportive treatment on it. At the simplest level one might try:

'It must be very difficult for you to talk under these circumstances.'
'Don't worry if you are not able to say anything yet.'

'There is plenty of time, it doesn't matter if you can't talk at the moment.'

or other comments exhibiting various degrees of sympathy, understanding, advice and encouragement.

It is probably desirable to end such a one-sided interview after a few minutes, rather than going on for a long time and entrenching the position.

More delicate approaches can be made when the *cause* of the silence is known. If this is resentment of the management so far, then this can be recognised by the therapist explicitly and dealt with specifically in his supportive remarks.

With practice, the patient's non-verbal communications can be utilised to cut short the period of silence. Some of these gestures and postures may be non-specific—for instance the averted gaze that does little more than confirm the significance of the silence. Other communications can be used to build up a rapport. Hand movements, grunts of assent, shakes of the head can be responded to until almost by accident the patient finds himself talking.

With the best will in the world there will be some patients who remain unaffected by these psychological manoeuvres on the part of the therapist. The patient described on p. 200 was one. In catatonic schizophrenia, for instance, the therapist may find that his supportive psychotherapy falls on deaf ears until the illness itself is modified with the effect of phenothiazines or other drugs.

PSYCHOTHERAPY

Definitions

Although the make-up of the word 'psychotherapy' does not seem to mean anything other than treatment-of-the-mind, it has come to be used for those particular methods of treatment that involve talking with the patient rather than those that rely upon physical methods of treatment. It is in that sense that it is used here.

Theory on the subject has in the past been dominated by the psychoanalytic school of thought, the followers of Freud and the neo-Freudians. Adherents of this school sometimes talk, in fact, as if the word 'psychotherapy' means only 'psychoanalytically-oriented psychotherapy'. This seems to be an unnecessarily parochial limitation, and I am sure that those who use it in this way would be the first to understand the motivation that lies behind such behaviour.

In this book the term psychotherapy will be used as a generic term to describe all forms of treatment that rely upon talking, interviewing and interpersonal relations rather than upon drugs, E.C.T., etc. It will be seen that there is an unavoidable overlap with much of what has been described earlier in this chapter.

Two techniques of psychotherapy

As defined here, then, psychotherapy covers a wide range of techniques. In order to try to simplify the description I shall first of all contrast two typical forms of psychotherapy. These two forms are in some ways poles apart, and having spelled them out we shall be in a position then to describe other forms of treatment as lying somewhere along the spectrum between. At one extreme we have the treatment mentioned above, *psychoanalytically-oriented psychotherapy*, sometimes known as *insight-oriented psychotherapy*. At the other extreme we have *supportive psychotherapy*. In general, insight-oriented psychotherapy aims at uncovering reasons (for psychological symptoms) that are not fully appreciated by the patient. The uncovering process may be painful and very time-consuming, but the intention is that the cure should be a radical one.

In supportive psychotherapy the aim is usually to relieve the mental anguish immediately. The intention is that the patient should *feel* better, and it is not claimed that it deals with the cause of the distress. The procedures that go to make up the two techniques are illustrated in Fig. 22.

To clarify the effects of the differing methods let us take a simplified example. A woman goes to see her general medical practitioner with a wart on her hand. She is worried that it might be a form of cancer. He examines it, pronounces it to be harmless, and the consultation ends.

She goes back to see him the following week, again worried that it might be malignant. He examines it carefully and again states quite definitely that it is benign. He may say something like:

'I know these things can be worrying. I imagine that you keep looking at it and wondering what it really is. In fact those little

PSYCHOANALYTIC PSYCHOTHERAPY	SUPPORTIVE PSYCHOTHERAPY
Exploration	Reassurance
Uncovering	Sympathy
Removal of defences and resistance	Explanation
Interpretation	Advice
Insight	Encouragement
Analysis of the transference	Understanding

Fig. 22. Contrasted types of psychotherapy.

clear areas make it quite certain that it is an ordinary wart. These warts are caused by virus infection. It will disappear without any treatment in time, but why don't you just cover it with a sticky plaster, then you may not worry about it so much.'

These statements combine various elements of supportive psychotherapy—reassurance, sympathy, explanation and advice.

Let us now imagine that our patient goes back to her G.P. for a *third* visit. She is still worried that she might have cancer. The G.P. could now take even further steps to make his supportive therapy more effective.

Grasping her arm in a friendly way, he says 'Look, Mrs. Smith, you've known me for a long time, and I've never deceived you so far. Trust me. I've seen hundreds of warts like this and they are nothing like the lumps that you get with serious tumours. I promise you faithfully there is absolutely nothing to worry about'. In this way he steps up the intensity of his reassurance. Other G.P.s might at this stage refer the patient to a specialist for reinforcement of the diagnosis—another method of obtaining reassurance.

If the patient is able to trust and believe the doctor, she will go home comforted and relieved. Of course, no attempt has been made to go into the reasons why Mrs. Smith should be excessively concerned about her wart.

What reasons could there have been? Maybe her mother had died from cancer starting in the skin. Maybe the patient was pathologically depressed and would worry about anything. Maybe it was just a transient concern, but the G.P. irritated her and his reassurance was not only ineffective but provocative—how could he be so sure it was benign from a superficial examination? Maybe the wart had some symbolic meaning. Maybe she had worries at home, her marriage seemed to be breaking up, and her concerns about the future were displaced into her wart.

A different type of G.P. would have investigated some of these possibilities at an earlier stage. When she came up on the second occasion, or even the first, he would have asked some probing questions:

> 'Have you any other worries on your mind?'
> 'How are things at home?'
> 'Do you know anyone who has had a serious skin condition?'

This sort of approach has its difficulties. It may antagonise the patient—'You're treating me as if I'm neurotic'. In a state of resentment the patient may deny her problems, and resist further enquiries. If the doctor is sufficiently skilled he may be able to deal with such resistance and eventually see for himself the real cause of her problem. At this stage he can make his interpretation: 'You are worried about this innocent wart because your mother died of skin cancer'.

If the patient accepts this insight she may be able to deal with her concern objectively and consciously, and not require any further assistance from others.

Psychoanalytic psychotherapy

At one extreme (of the spectrum of psychotherapy that we have been looking at) is *psychoanalysis* itself. In a typical form of psychoanalysis the patient will be treated for an hour (or 50 minutes to be more precise) once a day, 5 days a week, for several years. During the treatment sessions he will lie on a couch, with the analyst sitting out of his range of sight. The patient will be asked to 'free associate', that is to speak freely about whatever comes into his mind, no matter what it is, and go on talking about his thoughts and feelings as subsequent associations reveal themselves. He will be expected to talk frankly even if the subjects are not those usually discussed in polite society.

If in fact he remains silent, or claims that 'nothing comes to mind', this may well be interpreted to him as resistance to treatment. If he insists that he is really trying, it may be postulated that the resistance is caused by unconscious parts of his mind.

When the patient avoids large areas of experience in his verbalisations the analyst may probe such areas and invite him to discuss them. Unconscious motives and resistance to treatment may be put forward by the analyst as the underlying reasons for appointments unaccountably missed by the patient, late arrivals, forgetting what he had said on the previous day's session, and other interferences in the smooth running of the analysis.

There is no doubt that, as unpleasant and unflattering aspects of the personality are revealed, the treatment can be rather painful. Anxiety, tension and depressive feelings may be aroused. Most of us are capable in the ordinary way of distorting reality sufficiently to preserve a flattering image of ourselves. Analysts would claim that such distortions are universal, that we all utilise these *ego defence mechanisms* to preserve our pride, dignity and self-esteem. We are likely, therefore, to feel rather vulnerable as the analyst removes, circumvents or points out these defences.

One of these defences is *repression*. Associated with a painful memory (or series of memories) is a cluster of ideas known as a *complex*. To protect us from the unpleasantness of these memories this complex will be consigned to the *unconscious*, the part of the mind of which we are normally unaware. No doubt this repression is often a very convenient way of making life more pleasant. When the mechanism of repression is unsuccessful, however, and the complex continues to dominate our lives, it may be better to expose the constellation of ideas, feelings and memories to the light of day, and to see if a better adaptation could not be found by going over this material again.

For the most part the analyst is content to rely for his subject matter on the memories of the patient. As time goes on, though, more direct evidence becomes available. The patient's personality is reflected in the way he behaves during the analytic hour. His habitual patterns of behaviour, his way of looking at things, his prejudice and bias, may all affect the way in which he deals with his analyst.

Patients differ in the expectations they carry with them, and the attitudes that they demonstrate. The analyst will be able to see this with his own eyes, or at least hear it with his own ears. He can point out to the patient the extent to which his (the patient's) attitudes differ from the average. If they are unrealistic, it may be possible to interpret them as a transfer towards the analyst of attitudes and expectations he has come to develop towards his parents in the past, or towards other important persons in his life.

The analyst will make interpretations based on these emotional reactions towards him. The unconscious emotions that the patient has towards the analyst are summed up in the term 'transference'. When the analyst interprets these he is engaging in what is called 'analysis of the transference'. This is nowadays considered to be one of the most important parts of the whole psychoanalytic process.

The analyst would be the first to admit that he has his own emotional reactions towards the patient. He may also have reactions of which he himself is unaware, and this is known as the 'counter-transference'. These feelings are potentially dangerous, as they may distort his perception of the patient, and lead to faulty treatment. As part of his training the psychoanalyst will have undergone his own personal analysis. In the course of this he will become more objective, and less at the mercy of the vagaries of his counter-transference.

In *psychoanalytically-oriented psychotherapy* it is common for the procedure to take an hour a week rather than an hour a day, for the therapist and patient to sit facing each other as in an ordinary interview, and for the therapist to be more active in the dialogue than in the typical psychoanalytic session. The principles used and the underlying theory are basically similar.

Supportive psychotherapy
Whereas psychoanalysis, and by extrapolation psychoanalytically-oriented psychotherapy, by now have a considerable body of theory and knowledge built up around them, less is known and written about supportive psychotherapy. The latter tends to be the poor relation—regarded as inferior, unworthy of scientific study.

The truth is that it is much easier for a novice to learn parrot-fashion how to carry out insight-oriented psychotherapy than it is to learn supportive psychotherapy. The latter requires an adaptability and flexibility of style that make great demands on the practitioner. Because it involves a large number of diverse skills it is also very difficult to teach. The current picture is, then, that those who practise it do so to a great extent using features of their own personality, or using techniques that they have picked up over the years in a haphazard and intuitive way.

Let us consider some of the features that are lumped together under the heading.

Reassurance

This, in its crudest form, is the response that is almost instinctive, elicited by someone in distress from a helping person. 'There, there. It will be all right.' 'Don't worry, things will seem better tomorrow.'

When this superficial degree of reassurance works, it does so largely by the good will of the sufferer. Samuel Taylor Coleridge described (in *Biographia Literaria*) poetic faith as the 'willing suspension of disbelief'. Something similar is often involved with this level of reassurance. One can imagine the patient thinking 'I don't believe for a minute that everything *will* be all right, but he's a nice chap trying to make me feel better. I'm grateful for his effort anyway'.

With a serious degree of depressive illness such attempts at reassurance fall a bit flat. For a start, when the attempt is made the patient is not feeling in a sufficiently happy frame of mind to respond in a grateful fashion. Secondly, as time goes by and day after day he *still* feels depressed the reassurance tends to wear a bit thin and becomes still less convincing.

Better results can be obtained with a more subtle type of reassurance in which a favourable outcome is *assumed* or *implied* rather than asserted. Still at a fairly crude level, the simplest technique is to talk as a matter of course in terms of the patient's getting better. A patient complains of loss of confidence, say. After some time has been spent expressing sympathy, the therapist could say:

'I think that as your depression lifts your confidence will return'.

In the case of a patient in hospital, it may not be necessary to make such a bald statement as that; instead the conversation may be moved round to discussing with the patient the situation in which he will find himself on discharge from the hospital. Here improvement is both implied and assumed.

With many patients it is possible to take a still less demanding course. If the patient is uniformly gloomy the therapist may respond with 'I get the impression that you feel you will never get better'.

This statement is clearly designed to allow ventilation of the feeling. It also implies that the therapist does not accept the idea of never getting better as a valid judgment. It is not so challenging as the previous responses, however, as it does not *assume* that the patient is going to get better, and far less does it dogmatically assert it.

The therapist's statements, in a further technique, may not bear directly on the question at all. It may be his actions that are telling. He may hear the patient's tales of woe regularly and continue to make progressive appointments without any overtly reassuring statement. This can nevertheless be extremely reassuring to the patient if he gets the feeling that the *therapist* believes that progress is being made.

By this stage it will be obvious that relying on such a subtle conveyance of confidence can badly misfire. If the therapist misjudges the situation, the patient may feel that he does not care what happens, or that he is trying to prove a theory, or that he has nothing better to do with his time.

To ensure success with this delicate method therefore requires artistic skill and a high level of perception of how the patient sees the situation. It also requires the therapist to convey his own confidence in the patient's eventual good outcome by means of various non-verbal communications—his bearing and demeanour as he ushers the patient in and starts the interview, or as he terminates the interview and sets up a further appointment. The verbal and non-verbal interchange at the beginning of the interview should allow the patient to say frankly how he is getting on. Clearly it is inappropriate for the therapist to beam at the patient and say 'Everything going well, I suppose?'—such optimism is riding for a fall. Equally clearly the therapist should not give the impression of expecting the worst—this would scarcely be a reassuring touch.

In the interests of psychotherapy, then, as much as in the interests of accuracy, the therapist does his best to adopt a neutral, impassive approach as he asks the patient seriously 'How are you getting on?'.

By the time the end of the interview is reached the therapist should have a better idea of the mental state of the patient, and will be able to be serious and neutral on the one hand or perhaps more cheerful and relaxed on the other, depending on what the patient can accept.

There is space to consider one more technique of reassurance. This is to act not exactly as devil's advocate, but judiciously to consider the worst. It is rare that one can say bluntly 'Of course, you may not get better', but one can come quite close to it at times. How can this be reassuring?

In the case where the therapist has been using rather a lot of reassurance, it may not only have been devalued, but the relationship may even have got to the stage where the patient feels anything he says will be met with bland reassurance from the therapist. It is as if the therapist is not responding to *him* but to some inner drive of his own. Under these circumstances (but also at other times) instead of:

Patient: 'I don't think I'll ever be able to get a job again'
Therapist: 'I'm sure you will get one soon',

a more useful interchange may be:

Patient: 'I don't think I'll ever be able to get a job again'
Therapist: 'It must feel like that to you at present. I suppose there is a *possibility* that you could wait a very long time before getting one',

followed by the opportunity for the patient to ventilate his despair.

Here, if the intonation has been correct, the therapist has encouraged the patient to talk about his fear, but has implied that it is a pessimistic forecast, the pessimism stemming from the patient's emotional state.

This approach is sometimes of great value, but does make some demands on the patient. It should be used little, if at all, where the patient either has very high anxiety levels at the time or where the patient has difficulties (because of his psychosis, say) in making the fairly close interpersonal contact required to handle the transaction. It comes into its own when the patient is convalescing from his acute episode of illness.

Sympathy

Sympathy is sometimes distinguished from *empathy*. Empathy means feeling or understanding exactly how the other person feels. Sympathy means having positive feelings towards the person who is distressed.

Thus, if a friend's dog has just been killed in a traffic accident, it may be possible to feel empathy, particularly if you have recently had such an experience with your own pet. On the other hand, you may find it difficult to feel empathy (for instance, if you are not a pet lover) but you may feel sympathy—a positive response to his grief, feeling sorry for him and wishing to comfort him.

Empathy has not been included in the list of techniques of supportive psychotherapy. It certainly is a valuable commodity when treating patients, but firstly it is as useful in management or in insight-oriented psychotherapy as it is in supportive psychotherapy. Secondly, it is not always possible to achieve a high level of empathy in dealing with the psychotic patient, but of course that does not necessarily prevent one helping him on general principles.

Often high degrees of sympathy are difficult to achieve as well. This may be partly because of the emotional cutting off that results from the psychotic patient's affective blunting or inappropriate mood. Often it is because the patient offends one's own system of personal values. Part of the training of the therapist should be aimed at enabling him to relate positively to the patient whom the average layman might regard as selfish, mean, immoral or lazy. Sometimes these features are results of the illness. Even where they are more part of the enduring character traits of the patient they are relevant. Persons who are egocentric, inert, who lack identity with society's values, or who lack generosity are likely to suffer as much as the rest of us, and are in fact probably less likely to find help from their neighbour.

It is very seldom that sympathy is contraindicated on psychotherapeutic grounds. When a patient has uttered his distress, then to say 'That must be terrible for you' or just 'You must feel bad' is almost universally either soothing or at worst neutral (if the patient is relatively inaccessible). One can conceive of circumstances where, if the rapport is bad, the patient might perceive such comments as sarcasm, but this is unlikely.

With a psychotherapeutic tool of such universal application, the reasons for not using it are mainly tactical. For a start one cannot very well use sympathy every time one opens one's mouth: it would not only lose its effect, it would take on a rather farcical sound. There is an art in titrating it in suitable amounts for best effect. Even if it were to be acceptable in large doses, it could be inadvisable in the management of some inadequate patients who might become very dependent on the therapist at the expense of making the necessary effort for their own rehabilitation (though this argument can be exaggerated). A further category in which one might avoid full use of sympathy is where one fears manipulation by the patient, but it is possible to give sympathy *and* avoid being manipulated into an awkward position—and this is probably the ideal response to anxiety-raising manoeuvres by the patient.

Finally there are a few patients who cannot tolerate the therapist being 'nice' to them; these persons, often at a very paranoid and prickly stage of their illness, are so aware of their own difficulties with human relationships that someone else's ability to cope with interpersonal situations makes them feel doubly bad. For them a rather neutral approach is better, enabling them to keep their distance, until they make further progress.

Explanation

It is common experience that an explanation of what is happening has a tranquillising effect. One is not absolutely sure why this should be so. It may be that by 'naming' the unknown one has made it more tangible and less fearsome. It may be that if the therapist gives a reasonable explanation the patient feels that he is in safe hands, that the therapist has experience and knowledge of his condition.

The type of explanation that is appropriate in the supportive treatment of psychosis is not usually that which tells the patient how his character traits derive from early childhood experiences. Such 'deep' interpretations may baffle the patient and appear irrelevant or, if accepted by him, may distress him.

The type of explanation which is more acceptable is that illustrated below.

Case 38 Mrs. E.

Mrs. E., aged 69, was admitted soon after her husband died. They had been very close to each other, so much so that they had cut themselves off from most other human relationships.

On admission she was suffering from a depressive psychosis, as it turned out, although it was so severe that the question of organic brain disease was repeatedly brought up by those looking after her. She was so retarded and uncommunicative, yet at the same time apparently agitated, that it was difficult to make much contact with her. She looked like a frightened mouse.

The physical methods of treatment used were tricyclic anti-depressants and E.C.T. Her recovery was slow in coming, and after some weeks she was more accessible, but still had numerous complaints—she had a pain in her back, she felt that she was becoming deaf and blind, she was petrified by the responsibility when it came to her turn to make the tea in the ward.

She continued in much the same state for some time. It was clear that it was going to be difficult for her to take her place in society again, and it was thought that some of her apprehension and terror might be caused by the thought of having to face the world when she was discharged from hospital. Nevertheless, as tests proved that there was no serious physical cause for her back pain, and that her sight and hearing were excellent, it seemed that there might be some other fear that preoccupied her (not the tea-making—by that time a patient with a different type of problem had taken over that duty entirely).

Because of extreme reticence on her part it was more than usually necessary to watch for hints of delusions or intense ideas which might be worrying her, that she did not mention spontaneously. As a result of the merest whiff of suspicion it looked one day as if one concern that she had might be that of having organic brain disease—a tumour maybe, or senile degeneration. It was not surprising really—the very same idea had preoccupied the staff earlier on in her course of investigation and treatment.

It proved possible to allay her anxiety by means of explanation. I cannot guarantee the exact words, but it went something like this.

> 'Mrs. E., lots of people when they get depressed have difficulty with their memory, get absent-minded, have trouble concentrating, and find it difficult generally to get their mind to work properly. This is just one of the normal features of depression, and all these problems clear up when the depression goes.'

It is not much of an explanation really—it does not rely on any long series of logical arguments. It places the features which concerned her in the context of a functional disturbance rather than the more sinister organic one.

She was much less agitated after this explanation.

Not all severely depressed patients would have been able to derive benefit from such an explanation, especially during the worst of their illness. It is important that this was of value to her when she was already partially treated.

Advice

Many patients actively seek advice and there is little doubt that it is supportive to have someone else's view on the right course of action when one is distressed.

The practice of giving advice to psychiatric patients, however, is fraught with hazards, and the therapist can easily get his fingers burned. This may account for the growing popularity of 'non-directive' forms of psychotherapy.

The sort of thing that may happen, for instance, is that the patient will act on advice knowing that it is bad. If one were to tell a friend that temperamentally he seemed suited to such-and-such a job, and if there were snags in such advice that one had not foreseen but that the friend could envisage, he would point out these snags and one would have to think again.

By contrast, some patients on being given such mistaken advice would go ahead knowing that the snags were there, with disastrous consequences. One is not always sure why they do this. Sometimes it seems they have a perverse wish to prove one wrong ('what a fool that doctor is—a child could have seen it wouldn't work'). Sometimes the patient is behaving with the masochistic, self-destructive pattern so often found in depression. Sometimes he has the curiously compliant attitude that is found with, and contrasts with, strong paranoid feelings.

Whatever the reasons, calamities happen often enough for some psychiatrists to opt out of giving advice altogether, sometimes with the explicit affirmation that it is not their job, 'Don't ask me—I'm just a stupid doctor. Why don't you ask your clever social worker?'. They may see their job as merely improving the patient's state of mind so that he is able to make his own decision.

It is, one would agree, not a good policy as a rule to give advice without some indication that the patient wants it. Gratuitous advice of this sort is particularly likely to prove fallacious. Assuming that the patient *does* want it, are there ways of responding to this demand?

There are some general principles that can be followed, or ignored, but at least which can form the substance of a plan for dealing with the problem of giving advice. The first principle is *to find out what the patient really wants to do and advise him to do it.* I appreciate in penning that sentence that such a path is full of pitfalls, many of which will be obvious to the casual observer. So what is the point of this particular piece of advice to the adviser? At least it makes one think about the motivation and desires of the patient. Whether a particular course of action is the best, in some cold intellectual logical way, is not the point. What *is* the point is his feelings about it. It may be that what he *wants* to do is the last thing he should do, in which case of course *you* will ignore *my* advice as it is clearly misplaced in that instance. Often, however, a patient wants to do something but thinks he cannot do so because of certain obstacles. With support from someone else he may well be able to pursue his goal, and achieve his desire.

The second principle is that more important than the advice itself is the way that it is given. Part of the previous principle as stated was 'find out what the patient really wants to do'. In other words, when he asks a question, you are going to respond with further questions and explorations. How this is done can vary widely. I remember one patient who complained that whenever he asked his previous psychiatrist a question the *only* reply he ever got, time and again, was 'What do you think yourself'.

Not surprisingly, he found this repeated stereotyped response unfriendly and frustrating. Yet if used sparingly, with sympathetic and attentive intonation, at the right time in the interview, such a question might be construed by the patient as helpful and purposive.

If one can convey the impression that one's reply is no idle prevarication then answers to the question 'What can I do?' may include,

> 'What possibilities have you considered?'
> 'You must have thought about this a great deal yourself.'
> 'Do you want to ... (do so-and-so)?'
> 'I expect there would be problems if you decided to ....'

The point of these responses is to open up a discussion of the patient's desires, fears, fantasies and expectations, so that eventual-

ly one can advise him to pursue a line that is really rewarding—or
if there is no easy answer at least allow him to ventilate his
problem.

Encouragement

After having observed the caveats in the preceding section on advice, one may be in a position where one can say to the patient:

'I think if (that) is really what you want to do, then I believe
you will make a good job of it'.

This statement of faith will be encouraging to the patient if he is
in a receptive frame of mind.

Encouragement is not a particularly dangerous manoeuvre, certainly not if one takes the sort of precautions that have been
suggested in the sections above on other supportive techniques. It
does make demands on the personality of the therapist. Some are
just naturally good at imbuing others with energy, enthusiasm and
confidence. Others have to opt rather for the 'soft-sell' approach,
mildly suggesting a solution but relying on the patient's own
resources for the initiative required to embrace it.

A larger problem with both encouragement and *exhortation* is
likely to be the state of the patient. You or I, if we were unsure of
our ability to carry out a course of action, might find it very
heartening to have someone say in a friendly and robust way:

'Of course you can do it. Look, you'll see. You know you can
do it really. Why don't you try?'.

If the patient is in the midst of depressive inertia, however, or
torn with schizophrenic ambivalence, then such an approach may
fall very flat. The secret of good encouragement and exhortation
lies in the accurate judgment of when the patient is ready for it.

Suggestion

The category of suggestion includes a wide variety of techniques.
Some of these correspond fairly closely to the layman's use of the
term—that is, making a suggestion 'Why don't you do so-and-so'.
This is close to the approach we considered in the section on
advice.

More usually the psychiatrist uses the term for a solemn
assurance such as 'You will certainly get better' or 'This red pill is

better than that green pill'. It is known that, in many instances, the very fact of making this assurance influences the outcome, so that a patient is more likely to get better, or to find that the red pill is better than the green one. The psychological factors in the patient that are tapped in this process are referred to collectively as 'suggestibility'.

That there is such an effect can be demonstrated scientifically. One method is to prepare tablets that are identical in chemical composition, differing only in colour or shape (such as the red and green tablets in the previous paragraph). In fact completely inert tablets may have a powerful influence on the outcome, a factor that is referred to as 'placebo' effect.

Perhaps the most striking example of suggestion of this sort in action is in the use of hypnotism. Hypnosis is not a difficult technique to learn. When practising it as a novice, it is uncanny to see that (given the appropriate setting) when one tells the subject that his eyes are closing, they start to close. Even more remarkable is suggesting that one arm is much lighter than the other, and seeing it rise in the air.

There are times when suggestion will not work. Subjects differ widely in their susceptibility and there are those who are quite resistant to hypnotism. One is less likely to respond if one is antagnostic towards (or contemptuous of) the therapist. Suggestion works best, then, when the subject holds the therapist in a position of confidence and respect.

This technique is part of the stock in trade of the traditional family doctor: 'This bottle of medicine will do you a power of good, m'dear'. The power does not necessarily reside in the pharmacological action of the ingredients of the medicine.

Like reassurance, suggestion sometimes works better at a more subtle level. For the sophisticated patient such flowery extravagances of speech may fall flat. The patient may feel he is being treated like a child, or patronised. The soft sell may work better.

> 'I don't know whether you would like to try these tablets. They do have a few transient side effects, but they help in quite a lot of cases. You could take some and let me know what you think.'

To some extent it goes against the grain to use suggestion as it smacks of hocus pocus. The solemn assurance, with steady gaze, that 'all will be well' seems more appropriate to the stage than to the therapist's office. Nevertheless, consciously or unconsciously, in overt speech or in subliminal non-verbal cues, we are probably making use of the forces of suggestion much of the time. It seems likely to be most effective when the therapist genuinely believes in his therapeutic manoeuvre and this is transparently clear to the patient.

Analytic and supportive psychotherapy compared

So far we have considered the apparent *differences* between the two polar types of psychotherapy. They have similarities as well. If one were to compare the two treatments in action one might find that in both of them the therapist was spending the bulk of the time remaining silent. He is not keeping up a steady flow of interpretations on the one hand or of advice on the other; he is *listening*.

Furthermore, when he does talk what he says will often be neither interpretative nor supportive. It may be principally designed to stimulate further talking. These techniques were considered earlier in the section on interviewing methods (pp. 318–21). The patient may be given an open invitation to continue—'Tell me some more about that'. Alternatively, the invitation may be implied, by repeating the last phrase that he used, or by a rhetorical question—'You say your mother died when you were quite young?'—which, given the right conditions, can be expected to start the patient off again.

It will be seen that it is perfectly possible for the comments from the therapist which distinguish him as 'analytic' or 'supportive' to take up only a small proportion of an interview time. If *ventilation*—the pouring out of one's troubles—is therapeutic in itself, then the two techniques may have more effect in common than effects separating them.

Furthermore, psychoanalytically-oriented psychotherapy may be supportive in its effect. The setting of a very long course of treatment with expectation of improvement can be reassuring. Interpretations that imply that the patient himself should not bear the guilt of his misdeeds but that rather he should blame his 'unconscious', his parents or society are likely to be construed as sympathetic, comforting, understanding and encouraging.

Can *supportive* psychotherapy ever be *analytic* in effect? There is no doubt that if psychotherapy is carried out on strictly supportive lines some patients appear to develop an impressive insight into their problems. This may be because they half-suspected what their underlying problems were all along, but at the height of their illness they could not bear to admit them, let alone examine them. However, some patients do appear to be able to develop fresh insights themselves, given a supportive platform on which to stand. The hour a week that is ostensibly a supportive psychotherapy session gives them a time and place to focus their thoughts on their intrapsychic or interpersonal problems, often with impressive results.

The relevance of this for psychotic patients is that even a supposedly supportive psychotherapy session may be seen as threatening. Although the therapist may avoid any form of interpretation or uncovering intervention, the patient's anxieties may rise in his 50-minute 'hour' in which he is expected to talk freely. The sensitive therapist will perceive the signs of tension or the increase of psychotic content in the talk and terminate the interview. For this reason it is often preferable to keep interviews short (20 minutes, even 5 minutes) and to ensure that they are highly structured.

Other forms of psychotherapy
So far we have considered some of the things that can happen in *individual psychotherapy*, a situation in which one therapist sits with one patient to discuss the problems of the latter. There are many forms of psychotherapy, not all of which should be used with psychotic patients.

Small group therapy
In *small group* therapy eight to twelve patients sit with the therapist (and often his deputy, trainee or co-worker). Group therapy became popular in both the U.K. and the U.S.A. after the Second World War, and is continuing to grow. Most of what is known about it comes typically from an out-patient group, with neurotics or character disorders treated in an insight-oriented way. Usually the group will be *closed*, that is to say after starting it up no new members will be accepted into it, and it will run a course of maybe 1 or 2 years. It is customary for the therapist to take a back seat

and encourage conversation between the patient members of the group, rather than between himself and individuals in turn. It is found, if he avoids making interpretations prematurely, that in this atmosphere they will often be made (and sometimes more tellingly) by a patient (or client) member of the group.

Individual psychopathology and individual defences can be observed in the members of the group, but in addition one can describe the dynamics of the group behaviour as a whole, and one can see defences that are not applicable in individual treatment. For instance, two members of the group may talk together for the whole session (usually 60–90 minutes), thus effectively avoiding the more productive criss-cross pattern of within-group communication. Alternatively the group may all address their remarks to the therapist, rather than to each other.

In theory there is nothing to stop the use of group therapy of *supportive* kind for psychotic patients. In practice there are a number of difficulties. It is more difficult for the patient with a psychotic illness to discipline himself to prompt attendance at a regular weekly meeting. Depressed patients are relatively silent, and hypomanic patients tend to dominate the discussion to an unhelpful degree. The communications of schizophrenics are often difficult to fathom and organic patients forget what has gone before. Nevertheless, attempts have been made to use formal group therapy, particularly for in-patients, often using open groups (adding new patients as they are admitted, discharging patients as they leave, and with no limitation on the number of sessions envisaged for the total course). It is difficult with these sessions for the therapist to make out what is going on in group terms—the group dynamics are elusive and difficult to codify. At present they remain an experimental form of treatment which has not been proved to be effective.

The therapeutic community

The group is much larger in *community therapy* or *milieu therapy*. This approach makes the reasonable assumption that the in-patient is likely to be psychologically affected by everything that is happening to him in the ward or unit in which he is being treated. In practice such communities emphasise the idea of patients helping each other both by informal discussions between patients and by the group of patients taking some of the responsibility for their fellow men when his behaviour gives rise for concern. For instance, if they notice that one of their number is preparing to take an over-dose of tablets they will help to prevent him doing so rather than just leaving it to the nursing staff. They will be given more say in the running of the ward, and perhaps have their own committee structure and powers of negotiation as a step towards patient self-government. The medical, nursing and ancillary hospital staff will behave in a correspondingly less authoritarian way.

There is more emphasis on the interchange of information between patients and staff, although it is only with unusually ardent exponents of milieu therapy that one finds the patient's notes available for him to read, and the nurses' reports read out in public. Group therapy frequently figures prominently in the treatment régime and, apart from small groups, an important place in the weekly timetable is reserved for the 'town-meeting' or gathering of the whole community of the unit—patients, doctors, nurses, social workers, administrators, occupational therapists, psychologists and sometimes secretaries and cleaners. Problems in the running of the unit (and there usually are some) are thrashed out with all con-cerned being present.

This contrasts starkly with the traditional system of psychiatric patient care, where the patient was told what to do (or else), com-munications among staff were down a strict chain of command, and passivity was encouraged.

Milieu therapy appears to be more humane, more time-consuming, more modern, less structured, and sometimes chaotic. Many psychotic patients are unable to take on the increased responsibility and seem unhappy with the demands of increased communication. There is a great tendency for patients to be pushed into examining themselves and their behaviour in an insight-oriented way. It is not easy for the staff always to know what is happening with regard to group dynamics: theory and principles derived from small, closed, homogenous, out-patient, neurotic groups are not easily transposed to large, open, in-patient groups of patients with various psychoses and other assorted forms of psy-chiatric morbidity.

However, the principle of a more democratic and responsible role for the patient certainly enables him better to preserve his self-respect as an individual, and avoids some of the dehumanising 'sausage machine' effect that otherwise might result from the authoritarian treatment-by-numbers alternative. It is possible to ensure that the atmosphere and the psychological methods used within milieu therapy are *supportive* rather than uncovering, though this needs constant vigilance. Perhaps the biggest argument in favour of the introduction of therapeutic community methods is not that it influences the outcome of the psychosis directly for better or worse, but rather that it increases the sensitivity and the psychological sophistication of the staff who work in it.

Behaviour therapy

The last form of psychotherapy that we shall consider is that of *behaviour therapy*. This is much more humble in its goals than, for instance, psychoanalytically-based psychotherapy. It does not aim to root out the underlying causes of the patient's mental illness. It merely sets itself to remove those individual pieces of behaviour that are disabling. It is based on the theory of conditioned reflexes (learning theory) and draws many analogies from animal experiments. It treats the unwelcome behaviour as a fault in conditioning—a form of maladaptive learning. There has been much work done on its value in the neurosis, particularly with phobias.

The psychoses are generally regarded as being much too fundamental a disturbance of the psyche to be dealt with in this simple way. Behaviour therapy has been used, though, with patients who have been hospitalised for long periods of time—usually with chronic schizophrenia. The aim is usually not to achieve a complete loss of symptoms, but to produce a significant improvement in their social performance. In *token economy wards* the patients are rewarded whenever they behave at an improved social level. Feeding themselves, making appropriate verbal responses, punctuality, cleanliness and participation in group pursuits may all be reinforced by giving the patient a reward in the form of a token with a given cash value. The patients are able to exchange the tokens for sweets, cigarettes or other items that they find attractive.

After a discussion of the merits of milieu therapy this may sound patronising and naive. The proof of the pudding is in the eating, however, and if patients have previously been degraded by their own squalid or regressed habits, and are enabled as a result of behaviour therapy to achieve more dignity and self-respect, then it is a method of approach that should not be ignored. The extent to which a patient's reaction to the token economy is at all related to the reactions of Pavlov's dog to the sound of bells is another matter.

SUMMARY

Good *management* cuts down unfortunate complications of treatment. The varied techniques are all based on detecting the patient's current emotional needs and in some way acknowledging them. Delusions are neither confirmed nor denied—a better subject for discussion is subjective distress. Distraction of the patient, answering a question with a question, and reflective answers are valuable if used sparingly.

The contrast of structured and unstructured interviews leads to the suggestion that psychotic patients may find the latter upsetting, although they are often able to negotiate realistically. *Suicidal* patients should be allowed to reveal their despair and talk out their problems to avoid acting them out in further attempts at suicide. The therapist will find this easier if he does not feel obliged to have all the answers. The power of suggestion is recognised, hope for the future is implied, and further help is made available.

The behaviour of the *difficult* (violent, unco-operative or inaccessible) patient usually depends on the way he is handled. Violent behaviour may be prevented by reassurance for the fearful, information for the paranoid, clear-cut instructions for the ambivalent and structure for the perplexed. In general, better results are obtained by assuming in advance that psychiatric patients will be burdened with high levels of hostility and difficulties with interpersonal relationships.

For psychotic patients psychotherapy is generally supportive rather than insight-oriented. Most patients benefit from ventilating their problems, but some are distressed by long interviews. Gentle sympathy and subtle reassurance are in order; explanation is helpful but advice is a two-edged sword. Some patients can take encouragement and most therapists use suggestion (wittingly or not). Psychotic patients may sometimes be helped by judicious use of group therapy or behaviour therapy (*e.g.* token economy).

13 Psychiatry and the community

What are the links between the hospital and the community? How are the Social Services and the Health Service organised? What does each provide? How many hospital beds, day hospital places and clinic sessions are envisaged? What does the social worker do for the mentally ill person? How does liaison between the helping professions work in practice? What is the law concerning mental illness? How does it work?

COMMUNITY PSYCHIATRY

Although the term *community psychiatry* has been much discussed and is certainly much favoured in the current conventional psychiatric wisdom it is not a very precise concept. It seems to refer to treatment and management carried out at or near the patient's home, with the help and assistance of such local services as are available as opposed to treatment carried out in a distant, large, impersonal and isolated institution cut off from the patient's normal life. It seems to borrow some meaning from that form of hospital psychotherapy known as 'milieu therapy' or the 'therapeutic community' (*see* Chapter 12) in the sense that both are a commitment by a group of people to use whatever personal and material resources they have to the benefit of the patients. The concept of

community psychiatry also seems to incorporate comprehen-
siveness, continuity, efficiency and *flexibility* and it is this last quality which I consider to be the most important. A good psychiatric
service should provide flexibility of response so that the most appropriate management can be offered for a particular problem, and
should also provide scope for adapting treatment to a changing
situation. It is not long since the only available psychiatric facility
was admission to hospital and thus there was no provision for the
needs of less severely ill patients.

National Health Service reorganisation

For a clear understanding of how the psychiatric services and personal social services now inter-relate it is important to appreciate
how each is organised. In 1974 the whole National Health Service
was reorganised. It will probably take time for the new arrangements to become efficient but the hope is that a more effective
service will result from the introduction of more up-to-date
management concepts.

The basic managerial unit in the new organisation is the *District*
where the health services (*i.e.* hospitals, clinics, health centres)
previously administered separately by local authorities and hospital
authorities are now incorporated so that one authority is responsible
for all the health services in that district, excepting general practitioners. In the District, which contains a population of about
250,000, will be found a *District General Hospital*, which it is
planned will provide not only the usual range of medical services,
but also cater for the mentally ill and subnormal in separate units to
be provided. The hospital, and all other local medical and nursing
services in the District are now administered by a *District Management Team*. This team consists of a hospital consultant and a
general practitioner, each elected by their colleagues, a professional
administrator, a professional finance officer and the senior member
of the nursing profession. The sixth member of the team is the
District Community Physician.

One or more district management teams (D.M.T.s) are responsible to an *Area Health Authority* (A.H.A.), two or more of these in
turn are responsible to a *Regional Health Authority* (R.H.A.). The
R.H.A. is responsible to the Department of Health and Social

Security (D.H.S.S.). The A.H.A. and R.H.A. are statutory bodies and each has teams of officers of appropriate seniority to assist in its work. There are some 200 D.M.T.s, 90 A.H.A.s and 14 R.H.A.s in England and Wales (*see* Fig. 23).

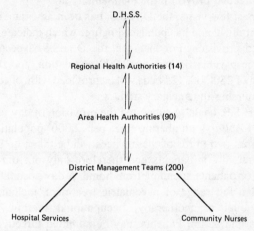

Fig. 23. Structure of the National Health Service.

An important principle which has been established is that the A.H.A. and the corresponding (and likewise recently organised) Social Services Committee are *coterminous* to allow for close liaison between these two services. However, it must be noted that for various reasons the District boundaries do not always corres- pond with their present Areas, so that in many cases, particularly in London, there is overlapping into adjacent Areas with a consequent need for agency arrangements, thus spoiling the coterminosity. Finally, it should be mentioned that no corresponding change was made in the catchment areas of psychiatric hospitals and units at the time of reorganisation. Rationalisation of these sometimes very awkward arrangements is therefore proceeding independently.

Prevalence of mental illness
It may be useful to note that in a population of 250,000, rather less than 1,000 people suffering from schizophrenia will be in contact with specialist psychiatric services in a year. A similar number suffer from affective disorder (mainly depression).

About 15 men and 40 women in every 1,000 attend their general practitioner each year for help with anxiety neurosis. A similar number seek help with depressive neurosis.

Scale of intended provision for the mentally ill

Over the past few years, the D.H.S.S. has been assessing the needs of the mentally ill and has published figures which indicate the scale of intended provision. For instance, the D.H.S.S. expects now to provide one psychiatric bed per 2,000 population, and thus for a population of 250,000, 125 beds will be provided with, of course, appropriate nursing and ancillary staff.

The D.H.S.S. has also suggested the provision of day places (*i.e.* in *Day Hospitals*) numbering 1·2 per 2,000 population. It is expected that two-thirds of these places will be taken up by people who are actually in-patients and therefore only one-third will be available for patients attending from home. A day hospital provides in general a full range of psychiatric treatment, including group and individual psychotherapy, occupational therapy, physical treatments and so on. Patients may be admitted directly to a day hospital or be transferred there from an in-patient unit as a stepping stone to eventual discharge.

Psychiatric *out-patient clinics* are an essential part of any service and can provide either initial assessment and subsequent treatment, or the continuation of treatment after discharge from in-patient or day-patient care. The D.H.S.S. hopes to provide some 15 clinic sessions per 250,000 population.

Another facility available under the N.H.S. is the right that a general practitioner has to call in a consultant to see a patient at home, if circumstances require it, and this service—the '*domiciliary visit*'—is available as readily to psychiatric patients as to any other. In many cases, these referrals may be initiated by a social worker and he and/or the general practitioner may attend the consultation. It is my experience that such visits are of enormous value and reveal very much of the patient's circumstances, attitudes, aspirations and relationships that may well otherwise never come to light.

It is most helpful to have the views of the general practitioners (who in my experience hardly ever do attend) although one must appreciate that they may find a psychiatric interview time-consuming and provokingly passive. Far more often does the social worker come and in the same way his views on the case and account of developments may clarify and inform a situation which would otherwise remain quite obscure. It may well be worth noting that for such domiciliary consultations the Health Service pays a consultant a fee approximately equal to that paid by a local authority for an 'approved doctor visit'.

A further domiciliary service is that provided by a *community psychiatric nurse* who, working in conjunction with the rest of the psychiatric team, visits psychiatric patients in their homes. This service has arisen, I believe, for two main reasons. Firstly, it has arisen because of the increasing use of long-term injections (given on an average every 3 or 4 weeks) in the treatment of those not uncommon patients with schizophrenia who are able to maintain a good standard of health whilst having medication, but who are unreliable with tablets, for one reason or another. Home visits by a nurse who has come to know the patient in the hospital may be helpful not only from the purely pharmacological point of view, but may also provide useful support of a general nature. It may be noted that training courses for nurses who wish to specialise in this work include placement with local authority social work departments.

The second reason for the development is, I think, the demise of the Mental Health Department as a result of the Seebohm Report. I consider that rightly or wrongly the feeling has grown that whereas in the past there was always a willing and expert body of social workers at hand in the town hall to help with psychiatric problems, less assistance is now available. Perhaps the community nurse will grow and develop in the same way as the old Relieving Officer became the Duly Authorised Officer and eventually the Mental Welfare Officer. In other words, through the development of relationships with patients and trusting relatives, a profession may possibly grow.

In the same way that the Health Authorities published their plans for future development, so the D.H.S.S. has made proposals for the development of the *Social Services*. There was a tentative commitment for an annual growth rate of 10 per cent in real terms in the social services, and the total estimated expenditure is £1,500,000,000 (fifteen hundred million pounds) over the decade; these figures have had to be modified in view of the current economic situation.

It was intended to double the number of *field workers* by the end of this period, and to provide 120 day places (*i.e.* in Day Centres) for a population of 200,000; these places should provide both short-term rehabilitation for those likely to return to work and long-term permanent work or occupation for those who are unlikely to be able to return to open employment.

I think it here worth clarifying the difference between a Day Hospital and a *Day Centre*. In a Day Hospital a patient receives treatment and in a Day Centre a client receives care. In practical terms it may be said that in a Day Hospital a person may expect continuous psychiatric supervision.

For the population stated some ten or twelve places should also be provided in a *hostel* with intensive support, together with forty-eight additional places, half of which should be suitable for in-dependent living and the other half where support is provided on a very long-term basis. Suggestions are made in these plans for various staffing ratios and for support services such as meals on wheels.

Many of the people in these hostels and quite a few who live at home require industrial rehabilitation and in a number of areas In-dustrial Therapy Organisations (I.T.O.s) have been set up to enable patients to recover basic working skills. An I.T.O. is set up in con-junction with the trade unions and the D.H.S.S. and can offer a small wage as an incentive.

The Department of Employment run Employment Rehabilita-tion Centres for the rehabilitation of both mentally and physically handicapped people who attend a 6 weeks intensive assessment course. If appropriate, they may go on from here to a Government Skill Centre, a subsidised re-training facility.

Those who are less able may benefit from working in a sheltered workshop such as Remploy or from attendance at a work centre.

Voluntary organisations
No account of the services available for the psychiatric patient can ignore those facilities made available by *voluntary organisations*.

For example the *Mental After Care Association*, whose history goes back over many decades, provides both rehabilitation hostels and homes for those who are unlikely to be gainfully employed.

They have four rehabilitation hostels offering 125 places and seven long-stay homes offering 241 places. These homes are placed pleasantly in the country or by the seaside and they also offer holidays there for more than 200 hospital residents each year. About seventy places fall vacant per annum, forty-three vacancies arising from the rehabilitation of the residents. It should be noted that despite the fact that local authorities are extending or planning to extend their facilities, the M.A.C.A. have a waiting list running into three figures and a keenness and financial ability to extend their facilities hampered only by difficulties caused by failure to obtain planning permission. Local Mental Health Associations have played a vital role in the provision of hostels (in Ealing, the *Association for Mental Health* provides a group home and also flatlets) and also day care facilities. It is estimated that voluntary organisations provided nearly 30 per cent of residential homes and hostels in 1974.

The *National Marriage Guidance Council* offers a great deal of practical help in the field of mental health—by way of the 1,300 marriage guidance counsellors, who not only offer assistance with manifest marital problems and also undertake preventive work, marital preparation work and sex education in youth clubs and schools, but who, in addition, do group work with parents, teachers, clergy and prisoners. They deal with some 20,000 new cases a year in addition to carrying over about 3,000 from the past. It is notable that substantial numbers of marriage guidance counsellors later become social workers or become professional education counsellors in schools.

The Samaritans are a further excellent example of voluntary work in the field of mental health. The movement began 20 years ago and was initiated by a clergyman working in the City of London. It offers a befriending service by telephone (or alternatively by letter or personal contact) to anyone in distress, but particularly aimed at anyone contemplating suicide. There are now 17,000 volunteers organised in 145 branches throughout the country. They deal with 150,000 new clients per annum. The establishment of Samaritan groups in an area apparently reduces the incidence of suicide and although this is disputed the weight of evidence is currently in favour of this suggestion.

So much has the contribution of the voluntary worker been recognised by the D.H.S.S., that both the health and personal social service authorities are advised to make formal provision for utilising their services.

In hospitals there is now very often to be found a Voluntary Services Officer—a paid member of the hospital staff—whose job it is to recruit and co-ordinate volunteers within the hospital, whether members of organisations such as the W.R.V.S. or the Townswomen's Guild or those who come forward independently. A corresponding post will be found in the Social Services Department.

In the health service as a whole, the voluntary organisations have been asked to nominate some members of the *Community Health Council*, one of which is set up in each Health District, as the watchdog of the consumer, with substantial power of entry to hospitals and clinics and with rights of publication.

It is clearly intended that health authorities and local authorities should plan jointly to meet the needs of their areas and co-ordinate their services as much as possible, through *Joint Consultative Committees*. Professional workers at the local authority level will also join in *Health Care Planning Teams* set up to advise the District Management Teams.

Diminution in number of psychiatric beds

No discussion of the services for psychiatric patients can ignore the great diminution in the number of psychiatric beds it is planned to have for the mentally ill. The planned number given is about one-seventh of those available in the 1950s. Critics have pointed out that whereas the number of beds have decreased by 24,000 over a period of 10 years, the number of hostel places provided is little more than 2,000. It is further pointed out that the number of people accommodated nightly at the Camberwell Reception Centre in London has risen from 500 to about 800 and that a very substantial minority are suffering from mental illness and quite a substantial proportion arrive at the reception centre within a week of being discharged from hospital. Of the 30,000 homeless people in Great Britain a high proportion are mentally disordered—possibly 75 per cent (Priest, 1971). There have also been rises in the numbers of prisoners remanded for medical reports and in London one prison reported that 14 per cent of their prisoners on remand had been under care in psychiatric hospitals within the previous 12 months. In fact, the rise in prison population is of the same order as the decrease in the number of psychiatric beds. I am myself far from convinced that the case has been proved that these changes are dependent on one another, and I would need to be convinced by comparable figures taken over a period of time before arriving at the conclusion that the decrease in the hospital population has been a cause of these changes.

The fate of the mental hospital

Concern has also been expressed for the fate of the mental hospital. If in the area traditionally served by any hospital a sufficient number of general hospital psychiatric units is built to deal with all acutely ill patients, it follows that the mental hospital will be restricted to coping with those patients who have failed to recover despite prolonged treatment, and to those patients whose behaviour causes social disturbance such as criminality, noisiness and other disagreeable behaviour. There is, therefore, considerable anxiety that the mental hospital will be left with only the least rewarding and the most unpleasant tasks and that consequently morale will suffer.

The answer must be that the hospital will offer a range of specialised services such as rehabilitation, alcoholism and drug addiction units, adolescent units and possibly secure units, and retain a substantial amount of acute work for as long as possible.

Co-ordination of Health and Social Services

It think it important to describe now how the psychiatric work takes place in my own unit and how social workers and psychiatrists co-operate and co-ordinate their work there. In common with psychiatric hospitals up and down the country, the catchment area has been divided so that particular teams of consultants are identified with particular boroughs. In my own case the principle has been so refined that the consultants are identified more or less with the area offices of a Social Services Department. My own responsibilities are to the people also served by one area office and this helps co-ordination which takes place on several levels. Firstly, I and the social workers who are interested in mental health meet at the area office every few weeks to discuss problems of joint concern, such as the arrangements for admission of patients, the responsibilities of the Mental Welfare Officer, the use of a consultant's time and developments in both services. Social workers will often discuss cases on the telephone informally and/or arrange to meet me on a domiciliary visit.

Furthermore, social workers from both the hospital social work department (now of course local authority employees) and from the area office, attend the weekly ward case conference in which all new and old cases are presented or reviewed. Social workers allocate their cases amongst themselves and implement admission to suitable facilities. They also co-ordinate their work with the community nurse and so play a full part in the *multi-disciplinary team* with nursing staff, doctors, psychologists and occupational therapists. Any social worker with a special interest in a particular patient is welcome to attend this case conference, either to advise or to receive advice.

It would perhaps be useful if I were to give some examples of how these services may integrate.

Case 39 Mr. N.A.

In the case of Mr. N.A., aged 30, the importance of suitable hostel placement had been crucial to his rehabilitation. He gave a somewhat incoherent account of himself, but from what I could gather he had returned from a visit to Cyprus, lasting rather more than a year, some 4 or 5 weeks previously. From that time he had been quite difficult and at times violent to the extent that he had thrown cups at home and overturned an occasional table. His own view of things was that he had a number of isolated problems, including particularly his wish to live with younger people in a hostel. He also indicated that he had some sexual trouble, but it was impossible to discover its nature. The background was that his father was a retired physician aged 80 and his mother was 10 years younger. The patient had a good public school education and when he left went to university where he graduated with a mathematics degree. He wished to qualify as an accountant but was unable to complete his studies since at about that time his illness and admissions to hospital and clinics began. On one occasion, he said, he had 30 E.C.T. and he had been offered a diagnosis of schizophrenia.

He presented as a flat, vague, incoherent, and very disorganised young man. He told me that he had never been auditorily hallucinated or persecuted, nor had he any hypnotic or telepathic experiences. However, he had had ideas of reference and felt from time to time that people were jealous of his advantages. A diagnosis of schizophrenia was tentatively made and confirmed from the case record.

Following the interview with the patient, his parents were asked their views of his difficulties, in his presence, and the ensuing exchange was fascinating. His parents virtually ignored me and indeed in effect put the patient on trial, cross-examining him as to his experiences and their justification for their actions. They were quite cold and unsympathetic in the face of his distress and all-in-all gave a good insight into the family situation as it existed at that time. However, and curiously, as the interview proceeded, the patient stood up very well to attacks made on him and was quite coherent and in fact more dignified than his parents.

In the ensuing two years, the patient's rehabilitation proceeded in conjunction with suitable medication. He was found a place in a hostel which he settled into fairly well and found a simple job in a factory which he did not much enjoy but with which he persevered, thus enabling him for the first time since his illness began, to lead a reasonably well organised and satisfying existence.

In another case, there was substantial uncertainty over the diagnosis.

Case 40 Mrs. L.T.
It appeared that Mrs. L.T., aged 42, had been well enough until a myelogram had been performed (*see* Glossary) after which she became rather distressed and excited. Although unable to give a proper account of her history, she was, however, able to tell me that her parents and fourteen siblings were alive and well in Liverpool. She was born in Ireland, left school at 14, married at 30 and had five children under 12. No better account was obtained from her husband who was rather upset due to his evident anxiety about the patient. She presented in bed, slightly flushed, irrational, labile in her affect, disorientated for time, unable to give an account of current events, failing to grasp questions put to her nor able to reply coherently to them. She gave the ages of her children slightly inaccurately and taken overall gave a typical picture of a patient suffering from a mild confusional state. It did not seem appropriate therefore for her to be admitted to a mental hospital without prior admission to the district general hospital where she was fully investigated. No evidence of brain disease was found and the confusional state was attributed to the myelogram. She recovered fully within a matter of 5 days. In this case the psychiatrist was able to *clarify the situation*, thus ensuring that the patient was admitted to the most appropriate place.

In some cases a psychiatrist is asked to help in order to assist with arrangements already in hand:

Case 41 Mrs. P.L.
Such a case was Mrs. P.L., aged 72. The social worker visited the patient in response to increasing complaints from the neighbours (over the previous 6 months) of her walking down the road bran-

dishing a knife, talking to nobody in particular but everybody in general. When spoken to she immediately declaimed that she was the Queen of England, her son being King and over and above this she herself held the rank of Count. She said she constantly heard the voices of the three families who had moved into the basement below her and they blackmailed her all day, telling her to get out because they wanted her house and calling her all sorts of abusive names. Of her nine children, many were married and she lived with one of them. She had been in hospital 6 and 3 years before for the treatment of a similar condition, which her son said had developed since the Easter uprising of 1916. She had become much worse in the previous 15 years since leaving Ireland. She presented as a restless, excited woman with pressure of talk and incoherence. She was grossly deluded and felt not only that she had great rank and ability, but that she was being persecuted on this very count. It was this persecution which justified her carrying a knife and also contemplating the purchase of two revolvers. She was entirely without insight and refused to contemplate taking any form of medication and it was therefore arranged for her admission to hospital compulsorily forthwith, as tentatively suggested by the social worker, for the treatment of her manic psychosis.

Sometimes one is asked to see a patient for the reassurance of the social worker involved and to confirm that what is being done is both correct and adequate. This is a very proper use of a psychiatrist's time.

Case 42 Mrs. P.Q.
In the case of Mrs. P.Q., aged 78, she complained that for nearly a year she had been depressed, downhearted and anorexic with early morning exacerbation of her symptoms and early morning wakening. Her energy had been poor and she was at her worst 3 months previously, when she was restless and had fallen about. The onset of this condition was associated with the illness and subsequent death of her daughter-in-law, and with her husband's burst ulcer and complications, for which he was 18 weeks in hospital. When he came home, his wife had to feed him through an abdominal orifice for some time. This had fortunately healed and they were both feeling very much better about it. The background was unremarkable. The patient was happily married with two grown-up children and by the time of my visit was beginning to improve. I thought she might benefit from antidepressant tablets, but thought that her heart condition should be further investigated as she had swollen ankles and was suffering from breathlessness. I saw her for follow-up in the out-patient clinic. In this case it was confirmed that the patient could be adequately treated without admission to hospital.

Case 43 Mr. P.W.

Mr. P.W. was a man of 43 whose pre-senile dementia had begun about a year prior to his admission. He had been fully investigated and no treatable cause for his condition was found. He was admitted to hospital because he had become deluded and had refused to eat, and on admission was given a course of phenothiazines after which the delusions disappeared. The problem then arose as to the best management of a man whose wife had as a necessity to go out to full time employment to support her young family. It was decided, in conjunction with the social worker, that a place be made available at the psychogeriatric centre which he began attending whilst still in the hospital and continued to attend on his discharge. He was followed up by the community nurse who co-ordinated the arrangements for his medication and his attendance at the day centre and provided adequate reassurance for his wife.

Sometimes the task of the social worker begins when psychiatric treatment ends, when the patient becomes well enough to cope with those interpersonal difficulties which have contributed to what has resulted in a serious psychiatric disorder.

Case 44 Mr. A.G.

Mr. A.G. was first seen at home when he said that he had always lacked confidence and had been a sad man. He had been much worse in the past 6 months, with tearfulness, poor concentration, diminished energy and early morning exacerbation of symptoms, so that he felt his life no longer worth living. His mother drank a lot and of his three sisters, two had had breakdowns. He had a fairly normal background otherwise, but I noted that he had been in hospital in the North of England in 1962. I decided at that stage to treat him with tablets only and to see him as an out-patient, but his progress was very slow and I referred him then to the day hospital. His progress continued to be unsatisfactory and he was admitted to hospital as an in-patient with a very severe depression. He was ashamed, guilty, actively suicidal and complained of a number of physical abnormalities such as an absent brain, non-functioning kidney and overall muscle spasm. He responded well to electrical treatment but in the course of his stay it became evident that his matrimonial situation was very unsatisfactory. On his discharge, therefore, he was referred to the social worker for further investigation and management of his marital situation which lay behind his very severe depression.

PSYCHOGERIATRICS
Management and treatment

It is well worth considering illnesses of the aged separately as they pose special medical and social problems. There are two main groups of the elderly mentally ill. Those patients who have *functional* mental illness are treated in the same way as the adult mentally ill, will very often be admitted to the very same wards, whether in a general hospital unit or in a psychiatric hospital, and are managed and treated along the same lines.

Those patients who are *demented,* however, present problems which are serious both in terms of numbers and in terms of the particular stresses to family and the community. About 10 per cent of those over retirement age and an even higher proportion of the very aged are found to be demented.

As the overall numbers of the very aged are expected to rise faster (18 per cent) than the aged in general (12 per cent) over the next decade, it is quite clear that there will be a substantial increase in the size of this problem. Since now about 13 per cent of the population is of retirement age, it can readily be seen that there are vast numbers of people with this disability.

For these demented people, the health authorities propose providing between 2–3 beds per 1,000 aged population and a similar number of day places. It has been recognised that for those people who are only mildly affected, *residential care* under the auspices of the personal social services is appropriate, within the overall provision suggested by the D.H.S.S. of 25 places per 1,000 elderly. The mildly demented will be cared for either in special homes or in separate units attached to the normal types of residential accommodation. However, it can be noted that even now, some 30 per cent of persons in residential homes suffer from a significant degree of dementia and that there is nothing new in the proposal to provide for this group of patients.

The question arises quite naturally as to how those who come to the attention of the general practitioner, the social worker or the psychiatrist do so when the vast majority of the patients do not, and whether this gives any clue as to how to cope more successfully with the problems posed. Such patients often come to attention because of the withdrawal of support from relatives, friends or neighbours through illness, death or sheer inability to cope any longer, or alternatively because the patient's behaviour has become intolerable through restlessness, wandering, noisiness or through a deterioration in personal habits.

To offer to deal with these problems, there must be, as always, a range of facilities at hand, either to support or to replace the help given by relatives, which will enable them to cope better or with less strain, as for instance, meals-on-wheels or home nursing. The treatment of symptoms is also important and mild tranquillisers will often control restlessness and noisiness to a degree which makes the situation tolerable at home.

Alternatively, it may become necessary to fully support a patient either part-time or temporarily full-time. I am thinking here of a Day Hospital or Day Centre and of temporary admission to hospital or residential accommodation for say a few weeks, which may enable the relatives to have a well-earned holiday.

Sometimes, however, it will become impossible for a patient to be managed properly at home at all, and such patients can be admitted to hospital. In the locality in which I work, the practice is for virtually all such patients to be assessed by a consultant psychiatrist, jointly with the social worker, and the general practitioner if he so wishes, so that a decision can be made jointly as to the best course of action. Most often this assessment takes place at home.

Psychogeriatric Day Centres
The pivot of the psychogeriatric service in this area is the *Psychogeriatric Day Centre* which has just completed its first year's work. It was purpose built to provide forty-five places for the elderly mentally ill and provides a substantial range of facilities which enables a comprehensive care and treatment programme to be carried out. It was built on a single storey and all parts of the building including the W.C.s and doorways can accommodate wheelchairs. The staff includes two managers, who are qualified occupational therapists, a nurse and a consultant psychiatrist attending on a weekly basis. There are other supervisory and domestic staff. A chiropodist attends and so will a bath attendant. Patients may be referred by psychiatrists, social workers or general practitioners and any patient referred is assessed by a consultant psychiatrist and also by a social worker. The patient will then attend to meet the senior staff, when admission will be discussed.

If the patient is admitted, he will, if necessary, be collected and returned home by ramp ambulance. During the course of his day at the centre, he will join one of four groups which cover a wide range of activities such as woodwork, craftwork, painting and collage.

After lunch (provided for 10p), two groups join in activities aimed at mental stimulation and discussion, including quizzes and ball games, and playing in a percussion band. There are film shows and guest speakers are invited.

What is quite extraordinary is how much even the demented patients are able to join in these activities, and to what extent they enjoy them. Nearly all the clients attending the centre went on a trip on the river recently and this was voted a great success by all.

A formal staff meeting is held once a week and relatives' meetings are held once a month to discuss common problems.

This centre has been an outstanding success. It admitted eighty-four people in its first year of whom forty-three were demented, and a substantial proportion of these were as severely demented as any of the patients in the hospital, and have been coped with at least as successfully.

Not infrequently, ramp ambulances go to the hospital and pick up patients to take them for daily attendance at the centre. This enables full use to be made of the facilities and ensures continuity of care so that when the patient is discharged from the hospital to his home, he continues on the same treatment programme. It would perhaps be as well to illustrate the practice with some recent cases.

Case 45 Mrs. B.T.

I was asked to see Mrs. B.T., a 75-year-old lady who had been blind for 4 or 5 years and under the care of ophthalmic surgeons throughout that time. She had also been cared for by a social worker with special interest in blindness. As is my practice in such situations, I interviewed the relative first to clarify his view of the problem. He told me that over the past 18 months his wife's memory had gradually deteriorated to the extent that he had to look after her in every way, dressing and washing her and taking her to the toilet. He told me that she was never noisy and always conducted herself well socially, except occasionally when she was restless. When I examined her I found her to be a somewhat fidgety but otherwise well-preserved old lady, who told me that she ate and slept well. She was, however, unable to tell me her age, nor the year, nor the month, nor the date, nor the name of the Prime Minister nor the date of the last war, and I therefore came to the conclusion that she was suffering from senile dementia.

In view of the fact that her husband was slightly older than she, I thought it would be as well for her to attend the Day Centre and arranged for this jointly with the social worker. We arranged for husband and wife to attend together on the first couple of occasions to reassure him that she would be well looked after and to enable her to settle down more readily.

I suggested to the general practitioner that if required, small doses of phenothiazines could be prescribed to reduce the restlessness.

Case 46 Mr. L.T.

Another patient I recently saw was Mr. L.T., aged 84, whom I saw at his home with his wife and a social worker. I was told that he had been suffering from Parkinson's disease (*see* Chapter 4) for some while and had had treatment at a Day Centre with special facilities for geriatrics for several weeks, and that he still attended there for review from time to time. He was being looked after by his 77-year-old wife who herself had had a fractured hip. He spent 2 half-days a week out of the house in clubs for the elderly.

He presented to me as an active, well-preserved man, although he did show some degree of tremor and walking disability. He was able, however, to give quite a reasonable account of himself, telling me how long he had been married. He was able to tell me his anniversary date and was well orientated for time and place. He could give me an account of the news and the political situation. Reviewing the case fully with the wife and social worker, it appeared that his problems were mainly those of his physical handicap in that his wife needed help with him in the bath, and that he was also still lonely and his wife felt he could do with more time socialising with people of his own sex. There did not seem to be any substantial reason why he should have to go to the Psychogeriatric Centre and it was arranged to increase the time he spent in social activities and to review the bathing arrangements, including the provision of a bath attendant and bathing aid in the bathroom.

The hospital provides a total of some eighty beds for the care of demented patients (the Departmental norm for 250,000 population is between 65–100). Half of these beds are arranged as an admission unit and one consultant takes charge of this service for the area as a whole. All patients admitted have been assessed by a consultant psychiatrist and great care is taken not to admit patients when any alternative is available. There is no doubt in my mind that it is far better for a patient to be nursed at home if it is at all possible.

The patient on admission is seen at the weekly conference attended by the social worker. Regular reviews are held to assess progress and since quite often the patient will improve in the calm of the hospital atmosphere and with regular attention to his needs, it not infrequently happens that he becomes suitable for placement in a residential home. As soon as this situation is reached, the social worker can proceed.

A further point that has to be borne in mind is that patients can become confused due to some physical ailment and this may be superimposed on a dementia or may occur in an otherwise normal patient. When the acute episode remits, the patient is then in status quo and may be acceptable to his relatives as he was, either slightly demented or indeed quite normal again. If there are no relatives willing to accept the patient it may be quite an undertaking to return him even to, say, a warden-supervised flatlet. In these cases, the fact that the patient is attending a Day Centre and can continue to do so on discharge is a source of great comfort to those responsible for him.

LEGAL ASPECTS OF PSYCHIATRY

Mental Health Act 1959

Quite clearly the legislation which most concerns social workers under English Law is the Mental Health Act 1959, which provides for the compulsory detention in hospital of mentally disordered people under certain circumstances. The most commonly used part of the Act is that providing for compulsory admission for observation under Section 25, whereby an application for admission may be made (either by a mental welfare officer or the next-of-kin) if two doctors recommend, in the prescribed manner, that the patient 'is suffering from mental disorder of a nature or degree which warrants the detention of the patient in a hospital ... for at least a limited period' and 'that he ought to be so detained in the interests of his own health and safety or with a view to the protection of other persons'. Under these circumstances the patient may be detained for a period of *28 days*. If it is necessary to detain the patient further for treatment, the provisions of Section 26 of the Act may be used: in these circumstances the grounds must be that he is suffering from mental disorder:

1. In the case of a patient of any age, mental illness or severe subnormality;
2. In the case of a patient under the age of 21 years, psychopathic disorder or subnormality.

The patient may then be detained for one year.

In an emergency, an application for admission can be made on the basis of one medical recommendation alone (Section 29). This allows the patient to be detained for 72 hours. If by the end of that time a further medical recommendation is made, the patient can be treated as if admitted under Section 25, *i.e.* for a total of 28 days. I think it is worth noting that of the two doctors who make recommendations, one must be approved as having special experience in the diagnosis and treatment of mental disorder; the other will usually be the patient's general practitioner.

The police are given certain powers under the Act (Section 136), namely to remove a person who appears to be suffering from mental disorder from a public place to a place of safety for a period of 72 hours, to enable the patient to be examined by a medical practitioner and to be interviewed by a mental welfare officer. Furthermore (Section 135) a Justice of the Peace may issue a warrant to enable a constable to enter premises where a person is believed to be suffering from mental disorder and neglect, and similarly to remove him to a place of safety.

It is clear from the Act that the signing of two medical recommendations does not *oblige* anyone to make an application for admission, and the mental welfare officer has to satisfy himself of the need for the patient to be admitted compulsorily (and thus be deprived of some of his rights). It is not common for a mental welfare officer to disagree with the general practitioner and differences at this stage can usually be resolved by discussion or sometimes by asking a consultant for an opinion to see if any further light can be thrown on the problem. I am well aware of the distaste felt by many social workers, especially the younger members of the profession, for signing documents which essentially remove a person's liberties from them. It goes against so many of the things that social workers are taught and believe in. However, I think it right to say that I have seen far more harm done by failure to ensure that a patient obtains necessary treatment, than I have seen from unnecessary compulsory admission.

A very real factor in this is that social workers are sometimes not familiar with the hospital treatment facilities available in the area and thus have to rely on their imagination and fantasy for their impressions of what they are arranging for their clients. A lot of these anxieties are allayed when the social worker becomes familiar with the hospital and its staff and, one hopes, learns to trust them.

Ultimately (and of course quite rightly from every point of view) the mental welfare officer, or indeed the patient's nearest relative, has a power of veto.

There has been recent criticism of the operation of the Mental Health Act but I think that in very many ways it is a humane and effective Act given that compulsion is sometimes necessary to safeguard the life and health of the patient and the safety of the public.

Case 47 Mrs. A.B.

Mrs. A.B., aged 53 years, had had previous in-patient treatment for schizophrenia when she complained of mechanical devices by which her neighbours had sexual intercourse with her in her bathroom, and she had later been seen from time to time in and around the neighbourhood of her, by now, neglected home. She came to attention through her neighbours who complained that she was dirty and screamed in a very peculiar way.

Her general practitioner and an approved doctor agreed that she should be admitted, although it should be said that the direct evidence from examination of the patient revealed little as she was extremely secretive. The mental welfare officer, a senior and very experienced man, thought it better to delay the admission until better evidence was forthcoming and certainly until the admission could be arranged with less trauma to the patient. In the event, she was admitted without difficulty soon after, thus justifying the view taken by the mental welfare officer.

A patient may also be admitted under the direction of a court—a 'hospital order' (Section 60), which generally has the effect of a treatment order. Occasionally special restrictions, including the subsequent discharge of the patient, may be made by the court under Section 65 of the Act.

It should be noted that except in the case of patients admitted under Section 65, any patient may be discharged by the consultant in charge of his treatment, by the hospital managers and, in the case of patients kept in under Section 26, by the next-of-kin. A patient may apply to a Mental Health Review Tribunal for review of his case and the Tribunal also has the right to discharge the patient.

The Mental Health Act also advises that a local authority should provide residential accommodation and centres for the mentally disordered; and furthermore provides for the appointment of officers to act as mental welfare officers, which is therefore a statutory office under the Act, the rights and duties being specified in the Act.

Court of Protection

The *Court of Protection* is part of the Supreme Court and its task is to protect and manage the property and affairs of mentally disabled persons. This is a most useful service; whenever it seems that a patient can no longer manage his affairs for any reason, whether that reason be, for example, excessive spending associated with recurrently heightened mood, or through the effects of personality damage in schizophrenia, or because of intellectual deterioration (the most frequent cause in my experience), or for other causes, application can be made to the Court of Protection (25 Store Street, London WC1E 7BP) for the appointment of a Receiver (usually the next-of-kin) who will then be responsible to the Court for management of the patient's affairs to the latter's benefit.

Case 48 Mr. B.M.

Mr. B.M. was admitted to hospital aged 89; he was a widower with no children and was admitted after being found wandering in the streets by the police on numerous occasions. He was a man of means and so arrangements were made for his admission to a nursing home. Because he had no conception of his assets, nor, for instance, did he know the date, the place he was at or the length of time he had remained in the hospital, and was unable to give any coherent account of himself otherwise, the matter was referred to the Court of Protection. In such cases, the Court not only protects the affairs of the patient, but also indirectly safeguards the reputation of the relatives who are handling the patient's affairs.

There is sometimes doubt as to whether a patient is fit to make a will and fitness to do so is called *Testamentary Capacity*. The criteria are that the person is fully capable of understanding what a will is and what it implies. He must also know the extent of the property to be disposed of and the relative claims of those people it is proposed to benefit or exclude. The person must also be of 'sound disposing mind' which means that his judgment as to the relative merits and demerits of his family are unclouded by mental disorder.

The commonest situation occurring in practice is where the patient is demented, and the procedure then is to obtain a statement from a reliable informant as to the family structure and the patient's estate and to test the patient's knowledge of these subjects in private. In cases where there is doubt, it is always wise to obtain the general practitioner's views and quite often benefit is obtained from asking a consultant to advise. I have not uncommonly come across situations where a patient signs a will which has already been prepared and doubt has *subsequently* been thrown on the patient's ability to make the will. The passage of time makes it extraordinarily difficult to be clear about the precise circumstances.

SUMMARY

This chapter has outlined the administrative structure of the reorganised National Health Service and the proposed plans for psychiatric services, both within the health services and the personal social services.

A scheme in which there is close liaison between workers in the two fields is described, with illustrative examples.

Some legal aspects of psychiatric practice as they may affect social workers are discussed.

It is increasingly found possible to treat a patient at home by the careful use of the domiciliary services, such as visiting community psychiatric nurses and social workers, supported by general practitioners, psychiatrists and, if necessary, attendance for day care or treatment.

The provisions of the Mental Health Act 1959 are basically that a patient may be detained in hospital if two suitably qualified doctors and the next-of-kin sign the appropriate forms. In different circumstances the patient may be detained for either a month or up to a year. A policeman may admit a patient from a public place on his own signature. Patients may also be compulsorily admitted from the courts.

The Court of Protection has been established to guard the interests of patients no longer able to manage their own affairs.

Appendix I

Brief paired-associate test

(Isaacs and Walkey simplified version of Inglis Test)

Instructions (Adapted from Isaacs, 1962*):

1. Say to patient: 'I am going to read you a list of words, two at a time. Listen carefully because after I finish I shall expect you to remember the words that go together.'
2. Say to patient: 'When I say the word "knife", I want you to say "fork".' 'When I say the word "east", I want you to say "west".' 'When I say the word "hand", I want you to say "foot".' Allow an interval of about 5 seconds between the presentation of each pair.
3. Then say three stimulus words in random order, thus:

   ' "East":   what word did I ask you to say?'
   ' "Knife":   what word did I ask you to say?'
   ' "Hand":   what word did I ask you to say?'

4. If patient gives the correct answer, say 'Yes, that is right'. If the patient gives the wrong answer, say 'no' and give the correct answer. If patient does not answer within ten seconds, give the correct answer. Do this three times in random order.
5. Repeat with Set 2.

Set 1   Set 2

Word-Pairs	Order		
Knife–Fork	3	4	7
East–West	1	6	8
Hand–Foot	2	5	9

Word-Pairs	Order		
Cup–Plate	2	6	9
Cat–Milk	3	5	7
Gold–Lead	1	4	8

References:

Inglis, J. 'A paired-associate test for use with elderly psychiatric patients'. J. Ment. Sci. *105*, 440–443, 1959.

*Isaacs, B. 'A preliminary evaluation of a paired-associate verbal learning test in geriatric practice'. Geront. Clin. *4*, 43–55, 1962.

Isaacs, B. and Walkey, F. A. 'A simplified paired-associate test for elderly hospital patients'. Brit. J. Psychiat. 110, 80–83, 1964.

Isaacs, B. and Walkey, F. A. 'Measurement of mental impairment in geriatric practice'. Geront. Clin. *6*, 114–123, 1964.

Priest, R. G., Tarighati, Sh. and Shariatmadari, M. E. 'A brief test of organic brain disease: validation in a mental hospital population'. Acta Psychiat. Scand. *45*, 347–354, 1969.

Appendix II

Further reading

Articles and books that have been quoted earlier will be found in this list, with sufficient detailed information for them to be obtained by the interested reader. In addition, the details are given of other reading material and against all entries are the numbers of the chapters to which they refer.

For each book you will find the author (or editor), name of book, publisher, place and year of publication. For articles there are the name(s) of the author(s), title, journal, volume number (italicised), page numbers and year of publication.

For convenience, the reference to Dr. Steinert's chapter (13) are collected together at the end.

Reference	*Chapter*
Akindele, M. O., Evans, J. I. and Oswald, I. 'Mono-amine oxidase inhibitors, sleep and mood'. Electroenceph. Clin. Neurophysiol., *29*, 47–56, 1970.	2
Aldrich, C. K. *An Introduction to Dynamic Psychiatry.* McGraw Hill, London, 1966.	4, 12
American Pocket Medical Dictionary. Saunders, London, 1968.	1
The Amphetamines and Lysergic Acid Diethylamide (L.S.D.): Report by the Advisory Committee on Drug Dependence. H.M.S.O., London, 1970.	11

Arieti, S. (Ed.) *American Handbook of Psychiatry*, Vol. III.   4, 9
Basic Books Inc., London, 1966.

Balint, M. and Balint, E. *Psychotherapeutic Techniques in*   10, 12
Medicine. Tavistock Publications, London, 1961.

Berne, E. *Games People Play*. Penguin Books, Har-   10, 12
mondsworth, 1968.

Brain, R. *Brain's Clinical Neurology* (4th Ed.). Oxford   4, 5, 6, 11
University Press, London, 1973.

Brown, G. W., Carstairs, G. M. and Topping, G. 'Post-   9, 12
hospital adjustment of chronic mental patients'. Lancet,
2, 685–689, 1958.

Caffey, E.M. *et al.* 'Discontinuation or reduction of   9
chemotherapy in chronic schizophrenics'. J. Chron. Dis.,
17, 347–358, 1964.

Davidson, Sir Stanley and Macleod, J. *The Principles and*   5, 6
Practice of Medicine (11th Ed.). Churchill Livingstone,
Edinburgh, 1974.

Department of Health & Social Security. *Amphetamines,*   11
Barbiturates, L.S.D. and Cannabis. Reports on Public
Health and Medical Subjects, No. 124, H.M.S.O., Lon-
don, 1970.

Drever, J. *A Dictionary of Psychology*. Penguin Books,   1
Harmondsworth, 1973.

Dunham, H.W. *Community and Schizophrenia*. Wayne   9
State University Press, Detroit, 1965.

Eddy, N. B. *et al.* 'Drug Dependence: Its significance and   11
characteristics'. Bulletin of the World Health Organisation, *32*, 721–733, 1965.

Ewart, R. B. L. and Priest, R. G. 'Methaqualone Addiction   2
and Delirium Tremens'. Brit. Med. J., *3*, 92–93, 1967.

Fish, F. *An Outline of Psychiatry for Students and Prac-*   1, 8, 10
titioners (2nd Ed.). John Wright, London, 1968.

Foulds, G. A. *Personality and Personal Illness*. Tavistock   1, 8, 12
Publications, London, 1965.

Foulds, G. A. and Hope, K. *Manual of the Symptom–Sign*   3, 8, 12
Inventory. University of London Press, 1968.

Forrest, A. *Companion to Psychiatric Studies*, Vols. I and   1, 4, 5, 6,
II. Churchill Livingstone, Edinburgh, 1973.   7, 8, 10, 11

Goldberg, E. M. and Morrison, S. L. 'Schizophrenia and   9
Social Class'. Brit. J. Psychiat., *109*, 785–802, 1963.

Greer, S. 'Effect of Psychiatric intervention in attempted   10, 12
suicide: A controlled study'. Brit. Med. J., *1*, 310–312,
1971.

Gwee, A. L. 'Koro—its origin and nature as a disease   11
entity'. Singapore Medical Journal, *9*, 3–6, 1968.

Reference	Chapter
Harlow, H. F. *et al.*, *The Maternal Affectional System in Rhesus Monkeys*. In Osler and Cooke: *The biosocial basis of mental retardation*, Ch. 5. Wiley, New York, 1963.	12
Hill, O. W. (ed.) *Modern Trends in Psychosomatic Medicine 2*. Butterworth, London, 1970.	11
Hinton, J. *Dying* (2nd Ed.). Penguin Books, Harmondsworth, 1972.	4, 12
Hollingshead, A. B. and Redlich, F. C. *Social Class and Mental Illness: A Community Study*. Wiley, New York, 1964.	
Inglis, J. 'A paired-associate test for use with elderly psychiatric patients'. J. Ment. Sci., *105*, 440–443, 1959.	6
Isaacs, B. 'A preliminary evaluation of a paired-associate verbal learning test in geriatric practice'. Geront. Clin., *4*, 43–55, 1962.	6
Isaacs, B. and Walkey, F. A. 'A simplified paired-associate test for elderly hospital patients'. Brit. J. Psychiat., *110*, 80–83, 1964.	6
Isaacs, B. and Walkey, F. A. 'Measurement of mental impairment in geriatric practice'. Geront. Clin., *6*, 114–123, 1964.	6
Janowsky, D. S. *et al.* 'Playing the Manic Game'. Archives of General Psychiatry, *22*, 252–261, 1970.	10
Kales, A. *Sleep: Physiology and Pathology*. Lippincott, Philadelphia, 1969.	2
Kendell, R. E. *The Classification of Depressive Illnesses*. Maudsley Monograph No. 18, Oxford University Press, London, 1968.	7
Laing, R. D. and Esterson, A. *Sanity, Madness and the Family*. Pelican Books, Harmondsworth, 1970.	8
Leff, J. P. and Wing, J. K. 'Trial of maintenance therapy in schizophrenia'. Brit. Med. J., *3*, 599–604, 1971.	9
Lidz, T. *et al.* 'The intrafamilial environment of schizophrenic patients: II Marital schism and marital skew'. Amer. J. Psychiatry, *114*, 241–248, 1957.	9
Mayer-Gross, Slater and Roth. *Clinical Psychiatry* (3rd Ed.). Bailliere, Tindall and Cassell, London, 1974.	1, 4, 5, 6, 7, 8, 10, 11
Oswald, I. *Sleep*. Penguin Books, Harmondsworth, 1966.	2
Oswald, I. *Sleeping and Waking*. Elsevier, Amsterdam & New York, 1962.	2
Oswald, I. and Priest, R. G. 'Five weeks to escape the sleeping-pill habit.' Brit. Med. J., *2* 1093–1099, 1965.	
Post, F. *The Clinical Psychiatry of Late Life*. Pergamon Press, Oxford, 1965.	4, 6

Reference *Chapter*

Priest, R. G. 'Skid Row—U.K. and U.S.A.' Proc. Roy. Soc.   8
Med., *63*, (5), 441–445, 1970.

Priest, R. G. 'The Edinburgh Homeless: A Psychiatric   8
Survey'. Amer. J. Psychotherapy, *25*, (2), 194, 1971.

Priest, R. G. 'A new approach to sleep disorders'. Gazzetta   2
Sanitaria, *22*, (1), 3, 1973.

Priest, R. G. 'The homeless person and the psychiatric ser-   8
vices: an Edinburgh survey'. Brit. J. Psychiat., *128*,
128–136, 1976.

Priest, R. G., Tarighati, Sh. and Shariatmadari, M. E.   7, 8
'Affective states in schizophrenia'. Brit. J. Soc. Clin.
Psychol., *12*, 283, 1973.

Priest, R. G., Tarighati, Sh. and Shariatmadari, M. E. 'A
brief test of organic brain disease: validation in a mental
hospital population'. Acta Psychiat. Scand., *45*,
347–354, 1969.

Rose, F. C. 'Disorders of memory'. Brit. J. Hosp. Med., *9*,   3, 6
223–232, 1973.

Ross, E. K. *On Death and Dying.* Tavistock Publications,   4, 12
London, 1970.

Rycroft, C. *A Critical Dictionary of Psychoanalysis.*   1, 12
Nelson, London, 1968.

Sahakian, W. S. (Ed.) *Psychotherapy and Counselling:*   10, 12
Studies in Technique. Rand McNally, Chicago, 1969.

Sandler, J. *et al. The Patient and the Analyst. The Basis of*   10, 12
the Psychoanalytic Process. George Allen & Unwin,
London, 1973.

Sargent, W. and Slater, E. *An Introduction to Phy-*   10
sical Methods of Treatment in Psychiatry. Churchill
Livingstone, Edinburgh, 1963.

Stengel, E. *Suicide and Attempted Suicide.* Penguin Books,   10, 12
Harmondsworth, 1964.

Thompson, C. W. 'The presentation and recognition of
schizophrenia in a service setting'. J. R. Army Med. Cps.,
113, 75–81, 1967.

W.H.O. *Prevention of Suicide.* World Health Organisation,   10, 12
Geneva, 1968. (Public Health Papers No. 35.)

Withers, E. and Hinton, J. 'Three forms of the clinical tests   4, 6
of the sensorium and their reliability'. Brit. J. Psychiat.
119 (548), 1–8, 1971.

References—Chapter 13

Department of Health & Social Security. *Better Services for the Mentally
Ill* (Cmnd 6233). H.M.S.O., London, 1975.

Department of Health & Social Security. *Services for Mental Illness Related to Old Age*. H.M.S.O., London, 1972.

Department of Health & Social Security. *Hospital Services for the Mentally Ill*. H.M.S.O., London, 1971.

Department of Health & Social Security. *Local Authority Social Services—Ten-Year Development Plans 1973–1983*. H.M.S.O., London, 1972.

Mental After Care Association Annual Reports. Mental After Care Association, London, 1971.

The Mental Health Service After Unification—Report of the Tripartite Committee. British Medical Association, London, 1972.

The National Marriage Guidance Council Annual Reports. National Marriage Guidance Council Headquarters, Rugby, 1973.

Priest, R. G. 'The Edinburgh Homeless: A Psychiatric Survey'. Amer. J. Psychotherapy, *25*, (2), 194, 1971.

The Samaritans Annual Reports. The Samaritans, London.

Young Fabian Pamphlet No. 24, *Hostels for the Mentally Disordered*. Fabian Society, London, 1971.

Appendix III

Glossary

aetiology: the study of the *causes* of disease.

affect: (pronounced with the stress on the first syllable). The emotional state or mood of the patient.

acute: lasting only for a short time. (N.B. This does not *necessarily* mean *severe*—any more than 'chronic' does.)

antidepressant: a drug that does not produce stimulation in normal subjects but which relieves depression in the mentally ill.

autonomic nervous system: a system of nerves, originating in the brain or spinal cord, that serves the involuntary muscles and glands of the organs of the body (such as the heart, lungs, stomach, gut, blood vessels, etc.).

It is divided into the *sympathetic nervous system* which prepares the body for instant action (fight or flight reflex) and the *parasympathetic nervous system* which is to do with recovery, feeding and rest.

cathartic: releasing dammed-up feelings. (*Catharsis* is the release itself.)

central nervous system (C.N.S.): that part of the nervous system that makes up the brain and spinal cord. Contrasted with the *peripheral nervous system* which contains the nerves radiating from the C.N.S. to the remainder of the body, and the *autonomic nervous system* which supplies nerves to organs (*e.g.* heart, bronchi, gut, bladder) and their involuntary muscles and glands.

chronic: lasting for a long time (as opposed to *acute*).

cognitive: to do with the intellectual function rather than the emotions or drive.

cyst: a balloon-like lesion containing fluid.

delusion: a delusion is a false belief, held by the patient despite proof to the contrary, that is not held by others of the same cultural background as the patient.

dynamics: the complex interplay of psychological forces that 'make a person tick'. 'Dynamic (or psychodynamic) psychotherapy' is often used loosely to describe insight-oriented or psychoanalytic psychotherapy, in contrast to supportive psychotherapy. There is little justification for this usage.

hallucination: a hallucination is a perception experienced by the subject that has no basis in reality (in contrast to *illusions*).

Hallucinations may be auditory, visual, gustatory, olfactory or tactile (hearing, seeing, tasting, smelling, feeling).

hypnotic drug: a sedative that is prescribed for use as a sleeping tablet.

hypothalamus: a low-lying part of the brain in the mid-line, from which the pituitary gland hangs down.

illusion: an illusion is a perception that derives from a distortion of a real stimulus to the senses.

Examples are conjurors' tricks, or misidentifying the dressing-gown hanging behind the door as an intruder (*e.g.* in poor light).

It is contrasted with a hallucination, in which there is no external stimulus.

informal: psychiatric patients may be treated in hospital either on a *compulsory* basis, against their will, or as *informal* patients, when they are free to leave when they like. Relatively few are in fact detained compulsorily.

lesion: medical term for a localised area of disease process, *e.g.* a cut, a bruise, a tumour, an abscess.

lobe: one of the four main divisions of the surface of the brain.

milieu therapy: the therapeutic approach that looks at the whole environment (or milieu) of an in-patient (as in a *therapeutic community*) rather than concentrating on his individual treatment. (See *therapeutic community*.)

morbidity: a state of disease.

myelogram: a special X-ray of the spinal cord in which a fluid, opaque to X-rays, is injected to highlight any abnormality.

neurone: the whole nerve cell, including the body (containing the nucleus), the axon (long branch) and the dendrons (short branches).

Parts of the brain which contain large numbers of cell bodies are referred to as *grey matter*. Parts that contain mainly axons are called *white matter*.

neurosis: one of the milder forms of mental illness, akin to everyday states of anxiety, depression, etc.

neurotic: to do with neurosis.

personality: the long-enduring character make-up of a person (as opposed to symptoms and signs of mental illness which are usually more transient).

phenomenology: a study of the *phenomena* of disease, that is to say the *symptoms* and signs (*qq.v.*). This is contrasted with other approaches that concentrate on the dynamics or underlying psychopathology.

phenothiazine drugs: a group of drugs (within the tranquilliser division) that is used for treating major psychoses, such as hypomania, schizophrenia and organic brain syndromes.

primary tumour: a primary tumour is a growth that *starts* in the organ in which it is found. Its origin is demonstrated, as a rule, by the fact that microscopically it is shown to be composed of cells similar to those of that organ. Primary tumours are usually single.

psychodynamics: (see *dynamics*.)

psychosis: a general term for the severe forms of mental illness, akin to insanity or madness.

psychotic: to do with psychosis.

psychotomimetic drug: a drug that can produce symptoms of psychosis even in a previously normal individual (*e.g.* L.S.D.).

psychotropic drugs: drugs that produce an effect on the mind (usually referring to those used medically). They include antidepressants, major tranquillisers (anti-psychotic drugs), minor tranquillisers (anti-anxiety drugs), sedatives (drugs that relieve anxiety in small doses but produce unrousable sleep in large doses), stimulants (*e.g.* amphetamines) and the mood stabilising drug, lithium.

reference, ideas of: when a person believes that everyday events around him have a special meaning for *him*, these feelings are known as ideas of reference. For instance, a person may believe that the newspaper headlines, although appearing to be about someone else, really refer to him.

secondary tumour: a secondary tumour is a growth that is found currently in an organ of a patient but which had started elsewhere in the body. Cells from the distant primary may circulate in the blood-stream, settle in the new organ and continue their growth there. Secondary tumours are often multiple.

sedative: a drug that relieves anxiety in small doses and produces sleep in large doses (*c.f.* tranquilliser).

sign: a disease feature which is revealed only when the physician makes his examination, or when the patient is observed, in contrast to a *symptom* (*q.v.*).

stupor: a state of severe general immobility and lack of response, but where consciousness is not entirely lost.

sulcus: a groove on the surface of the brain.

symptom: a disease feature about which the patient *complains*, in contrast to a *sign* (*q.v.*).

syndrome: a collection of symptoms and signs in a recognisable, familiar pattern (as opposed to a *disease*). Thus the characteristic acute organic brain syndrome is the well-known clinical picture of delirium: this is not a disease in itself, since it can be caused by a number of different illnesses (infection, thrombosis, etc.).

therapeutic community: a hospital or unit that gets away from the traditional hierarchy, where patients are given more say in the running of the unit, and in helping other patients, group discussions are frequently held and uniforms discouraged. It tries to concentrate on making the whole atmosphere therapeutic rather than concentrating on the treatment of individual patients. (See also *milieu therapy*.)

tranquilliser: a drug that relieves anxiety without impairing consciousness (*c.f. sedative*).

transference: the unconscious feelings in a patient that affect the relationship with his therapist. They may be inappropriate and unjustified. His expectations may derive from experience of important figures earlier in his life, and be carried over unthinkingly into the current relationship.

Positive transference means favourable feelings, *negative* transference unfavourable feelings.

N.B. The definition of further terms may be found by looking up the relevant pages in the general index, or in some cases in the mini-index for Chapter 4 (p. 102).

Index

For details of other titles in the Psychiatric
Topics series and a full list of titles and prices
of books on related subjects, write for the
FREE Macdonald & Evans Social & Medical
Studies catalogue, available from:
Department P6, Macdonald & Evans Ltd.,
Estover Road, Plymouth PL6 7PZ